REMEMBERING MASS VIOLENCE

Oral History, New Media, and Performance

Edited by Steven High, Edward Little, and Thi Ry Duong

Remembering Mass Violence breaks new ground in oral history, new media, and performance studies by exploring what is at stake when we attempt to represent war, genocide, and other violations of human rights in a variety of creative works. A model of community-university collaboration, this collection includes contributions from scholars in a wide range of disciplines, survivors of mass violence, and performers and artists who have created pieces based on these events.

This anthology is global in focus, with essays on Africa, Asia, Europe, Latin America, and North America. At its core is a productive tension between public and private memory, as well as dialogues between autobiography and biography and between individual experience and societal transformation. *Remembering Mass Violence* will appeal to oral historians, digital practitioners, and performance-based artists around the world, as well as to researchers and activists involved in human rights research, migration studies, and genocide studies.

STEVEN HIGH is Canada Research Chair in Oral History, co-director of the Centre for Oral History and Digital Storytelling, and a professor in the Department of History at Concordia University.

EDWARD LITTLE is a professor in the Department of Theatre at Concordia University.

THI RY DUONG is the coordinator of the Cambodian Working Group with the Montreal Life Stories Project.

Remembering Mass Violence

Oral History, New Media,
and Performance

Edited by STEVEN HIGH,
EDWARD LITTLE, and THI RY DUONG

UNIVERSITY OF TORONTO PRESS
Toronto Buffalo London

© University of Toronto Press 2014
Toronto Buffalo London
www.utppublishing.com
Printed in Canada

ISBN 978-1-4426-4680-3 (cloth)
ISBN 978-1-4426-1465-9 (paper)

Library and Archives Canada Cataloguing in Publication

Remembering mass violence : oral history, new media, and performance /
edited by Steven High, Edward Little, Thi Ry Duong.

Includes bibliographical references and index.
ISBN 978-1-4426-4680-3 (bound)   ISBN 978-1-4426-1465-9 (pbk.)

1. Human rights in mass media. 2. Human rights in art. 3. Oral history – Social
aspects. 4. Crimes against humanity – Social aspects. 5. Violence – Social aspects.
I. Little, Edward J. (Edward James), 1952–, editor of compilation II. High, Steven
C., editor of compilation III. Duong, Thi Ry, 1982–, editor of compilation

P96.H85R44 2014   323.01'4   C2013-906012-X

University of Toronto Press acknowledges the financial assistance to its
publishing program of the Canada Council for the Arts and the Ontario Arts
Council.

Canada Council   Conseil des Arts
for the Arts   du Canada

ONTARIO ARTS COUNCIL
CONSEIL DES ARTS DE L'ONTARIO
50 YEARS OF ONTARIO GOVERNMENT SUPPORT OF THE ARTS
50 ANS DE SOUTIEN DU GOUVERNEMENT DE L'ONTARIO AUX ARTS

University of Toronto Press acknowledges the financial support of the
Government of Canada through the Canada Book Fund for its publishing
activities.

Contents

Part Five: Rwanda in the Aftermath of Genocide

Illustrations

REMEMBERING MASS VIOLENCE

Oral History, New Media, and Performance

Introduction

STEVEN HIGH AND EDWARD LITTLE

What could be simpler to understand than the act of people representing what they know best, their own lives? Yet this act is anything but simple.
— Sidonie Smith and Julia Watson, *Reading Autobiography*[1]

Stories are the tools we need not just to survive, but to overcome. They are a protection that allows us to save ourselves, but also active instruments for changing the world – because there is power in words. They are made of air but leave their mark.
— Alessandro Portelli, *The Battle of Valle Giulia*[2]

Anthropologist Julie Cruikshank writes that stories, like good scholarly monographs, "explore connections underlying surface diversity."[3] The same is true of edited collections. On the surface, the essays comprising this anthology are about disparate instances of war, genocide, and human rights abuses. They are remembered and interpreted within a variety of historical, geographic, and temporal contexts. The violations range from political repression to discrimination, dispossession, rape, torture, and mass murder. The locations encompass Northern Uganda, Argentina, Turkey, Morocco, Cambodia, New Orleans, Rwanda, Winnipeg, and Montreal. The events extend from European "contact" and the dispossession that continues today, to the bitter aftermath of Hurricane Katrina in 2005. Yet while the essays in this collection evoke the past, the potential for deeper connections occurs in the present act of remembering. As Walter Benjamin reminds us, if the experienced event is finite, the remembered one is infinite.[4]

After years of debate, most historians now value survivors of mass violence as "human witnesses to a dehumanizing situation."[5] Some have gone further, saying "we cannot understand war without knowing human suffering."[6] Outside of the academy, the "unprecedented rise" of personal testimony often proceeds from the belief that sharing life stories can lead to personal and social transformation.[7] The authenticity of the stories being told to us is essential to this process. The affective power of verbatim theatre, for example, depends in large part on this claim to truth.[8] There is a lot at stake in the face of persistent genocide denial. Large Holocaust testimony projects such as Steven Spielberg's Survivors of the Shoah Visual History Foundation have recorded the stories of tens of thousands of survivors. Thousands more have told their horrific stories to truth commissions and international tribunals in a growing list of countries, including Canada.[9]

Yet, while the collection of survivor testimonies has become a large-scale endeavour, remarkably little space is being dedicated to these oral accounts in historical writing and human rights reports.[10] Typically, recorded life stories are being used in one of two ways: as a highly affective "illustrative device" (strategically placed for maximum impact) or as aggregate data in a "wider accumulation" of (ideally emotionless) eyewitness evidence.[11] Either way, the stories are not permitted to breathe. In this regard, historians and human rights lawyers approach testimony in much the same way:

> The need to build a credible case renders the individual story less important than the accumulation of many stories of violation, told in a certain way, and told again and again. The high level of concern about the reliability and credibility of "oral-information" in fact-finding and documentation means that the affects attached to recollections of pain and suffering become particularly suspect, and are treated as potentially subversive to the project at hand.[12]

By comparison, oral historians and artists approach survivor accounts in a much more holistic way. Both attempt to understand the inner logic of not only *what* we are hearing, but what we are *not* hearing. A life story is best understood as a living thing, forever changing. As Alessandro Portelli asks, "What is our place in history, and what is the place of history in our lives?"[13] For both oral historians and artists "errors, inventions, and myths lead us through and beyond facts to their meanings."[14]

The relationship between the individual and the collective has proven to be particularly vexing in the study of memory.[15] By and large, for example, the field of memory studies has been anchored in those disciplines that study representation such as literature, film, and cultural studies.[16] Perhaps, because of this, oral history and memory studies have been kept separate. Historian Alon Confino has blamed this bifurcation on the agenda of memory studies, "which is often satisfied to recount how the past was publicly represented."[17] In this scholarship national publics and the state loom large. Oral history, by contrast, is "built around people."[18] Meaning is studied in practice, "in the small interactions of everyday life" of our interviewees and in the efforts of scholars and artists to grapple with interpretation.[19] As Raymond Williams has suggested, culture is "lodged inside social relations and forms of material practice."[20] Individual and collective memories are best understood as overlapping.[21]

Productive tensions between public and private remembering are at the core of this collection. When asked to make sense of their life's journey, interviewees naturally draw upon "pre-existing story-lines and ways of telling stories."[22] This is particularly true where testimony is most well established and public. "In general," writes Holocaust scholar Henry Greenspan, "first interviews tend to evoke versions of experience that are 'proven' – ones we already know are tell-able by us and hearable by our listeners."[23] This is no doubt true. But remembering is by its very nature a dialogical process. Everyday encounters are integral to the memory-making process, and the stories people tell are therefore "very much embedded in social relationship."[24] Events are thus woven into stories that are meaningful to the teller and to his or her listeners. As a result, oral history is "never the same twice, even when the same words are used, because the relationship – the dialogue – is always shifting."[25] In effect, oral history constitutes a dialogue between autobiography and biography, between individual experience and societal transformation.[26] Here life stories are windows into the subjective.[27]

Oral history is one of the few fields of historical study that is truly transnational. We tend to read globally, but act locally. The reason for this is twofold. First and foremost, oral historians belong to an interdisciplinary community of practice that comprises scholars from many disciplines as well as community-based researchers and projects. A shared methodology, rather than a shared geographic or historic context, brings us together. We are similarly connected by our shared interest in life stories. Individual subjectivities rather than national publics form the basis of our analysis. Though an interdisciplinary field, oral history nonetheless remains fixated on the interview. Interviews are recorded, transcribed, analysed, and stored in an archive. While new digital technologies are opening up a world of possibilities for multimedia authorship and collaboration, an archival mindset continues to predominate. This collection resists this mindset in both form and substance as our contributors explore the intersections between oral history, digital media, performing arts, and political activism.

These essays originate in the conference "Remembering War, Genocide and Other Human Rights Violations: Oral History, New Media and the Arts," held at Concordia University in Montreal in November 2009. It was an initiative of the Centre for Oral History and Digital Storytelling and the Montreal Life Stories project, a major collaborative research project examining the life stories of Montrealers displaced by mass violence.[28] Our call for papers emphasized both public engagement and our commitment to the life story as a whole. Too often oral history interviews with survivors begin and end with the violence. This may tell us a great deal about what happened but little about its long-term impact on the people interviewed. The longue durée of the life lived, with the requisite attention to the "before" and the "after," provides a different context in which to explore the far-reaching impact of mass violence. Here, both what is remembered and why become profoundly important. Researchers, artists, activists, and citizens come together to ask how life stories can be more effectively communicated in an ethical manner *and* contribute to deeper social and political engagement. Self-reflectivity and questions about the role and impact of the researcher, and the "intentions and values"[29] of the artist, are key. Collaborative projects involving various combinations of oral history, participatory media, and performance are born.

The Remembering War conference was remarkable in its contributions. The mix of academics, artists, activists, educators, and community-based researchers was lively and potent. Presentations ran a gamut of academic papers, poetic utterance, music, image, excerpts of live performance, and examples of new media – sometimes mixing or hybridizing these approaches. The venue and size of the conference facilitated meaningful exchange. Many of the presenters spoke of their experience working with projects that must balance the complexities of commemoration with factors such as "compassion fatigue," outsider intervention,

1.1 Poster for the Remembering War Conference organized by the Montreal Life Stories Project and the Centre for Oral History and Digital Storytelling. November 2009.

and the physical and psychological risks associated with premature promotion of reconciliation or forgiveness. Most of the presenters shared a belief that commemoration – if it is to avoid an inward-looking historical focus that risks perpetuating trauma – must be somehow linked to a forward-looking social or political engagement. As we had hoped, the conference was fuelled by a deeply shared commitment to public engagement within a range of imaginative, social, and political spaces. There was everywhere evident a genuine interest in each other's work.

The "Remembering War" conference was planned as a way to put the work we were doing in the Montreal Life Stories project into conversation with like-minded projects, scholars, activists, and artists. As a result, nine of the seventeen chapters in this edited volume originate in the project and all three co-editors sat on its coordinating committee.

From 2007 to 2012, Montreal Life Stories was a veritable incubator for innovative research and artistic practice. Hundreds of people were interviewed over several sessions, often in their home language. Everyone in the project assisted with interviewing. As a result, team members have interviewed their parents, grandparents, other community members, members from other cultural communities, and each other. Each one of these couplings led to a different kind of conversation. These life stories were then integrated into online digital stories, animated films, radio programming, live performances, an artist-in-residence program, art installations, historical exhibits, and pedagogical resources. Digital media and the arts were an integral part of our oral history practice, as they are in the essays that follow.

An ethic of learning with, rather than learning about or from, permeates the collection. Contributors have sought ways to continue the collaboration after the interview. Deepening the conversation through "sharing authority" was a guiding principle and value of the Montreal Life Stories project.[30] This participatory approach to research and research-creation is exemplified in our digital storytelling process. The results are short, three- to five-minute digital stories drawn from the interviews and uploaded onto the websites of our social media partners, CitizenShift and Parole Citoyenne. The process is collaborative. Instead of extracting short clips from the interview recordings that speak to us as interviewers, we ask our interviewees to choose a story that they would like to share with the world. Their choices are often surprising. Liselotte Ivry, a Holocaust survivor, chose the story of a British bombing of her work camp – an event that made her life and that of those she was with significantly harder. Many died. Why did she choose this particular story? Was it her way of showing the world's complicity in the Nazi atrocities? A high degree of reflexivity is built into our process.

If "location, location, location" is one of the oldest clichés in the business world, it retains its resonance in this collection. Our contributors locate themselves in a broad range of disciplines – as artists, writers, educators, activists, digital practitioners, academics, and even a high school student. Most of the contributors would likely not self-identify as being "oral historians," but rather as being in conversation with oral history. The entire chapter by Robin Jarvis Brownlie and Roewan Crowe, for example, is built around a single moment when they, as researchers, were challenged by a young Aboriginal woman who asked, "So you want to hear our ghetto stories?" Brownlie and Crowe, both

1.2 Keng Duong was interviewed by his daughter, Thi Ry Duong, as part of the Montreal Life Stories Project. Ry, one of the book's three editors, reflects on this experience in the Afterword.

non-Aboriginal, go on to say that the exchange was a "telling remind-er" of the power dynamics at work. Similar issues are identified in other chapters, as contributors grapple with the implications of author-ity granted their own social, economic, and political locations within the wider political logics of their research.

Discussions of subject position are perhaps at their most productive in multi-authored chapters where co-authors experiment with their au-thorial voice(s). In all, seven of the book's seventeen chapters are co-authored. In three of these cases, the co-authors adopt a conversational narrative structure that retains their individual voices, alternating be-tween one and the other. This degree of multi-vocality remains uncon-ventional in most scholarly writing, despite the fact that oral history is a "particular kind of collaborative conversation."[31]

In other chapters, a dialogical approach to writing allows co-authors to represent their collaborative practice and any differences in their individual political and disciplinary locations to readers. In "Co-Creating Our Story," for example, high school student Noelia Gravotta and teacher Megan Webster share perspectives on a classroom project on the Cambodian genocide. Similarly, in "Stories Scorched from the Desert Sun," Armenian autobiographer Hourig Attarian and drama-turge Rachael Van Fossen invite us into their act of translating life writing into verbatim theatre. In both instances, the dialogical structure allows the contributors to convey the nuance and complexity of their collaborative projects and explore their negotiations of the spaces in-between. Beyond the present anthology, the range of authorial voices will no doubt continue to expand as more and more work is produced collaboratively across disciplines and community–university divides. What is especially exciting to us, as co-editors of the present volume, is that the contributors have been able to modify the universalized authorial "we" without sacrificing the effectiveness and inclusiveness of the text.

The seventeen chapters that comprise *Remembering Mass Violence* have been selected and arranged to convey both the richness of the exchange engendered by the conference, as well as the collaborative and creative potential of oral history, new media, and live performance. The contributors bring experience from a variety of scholarly disciplines as well as arts and community-based organizations concerned with education, social justice, and human rights. The chapters reflect on the ethics, efficacy, challenges, and potential of placing oral history in conversation with fields as diverse as ethnography, archival science, psychology, transitional justice, drama therapy, music, theatrical performance, and new media practice. Several contributors are themselves survivors of mass violence. Most of the contributors are committed to participatory forms of research that transform communities from objects of study to what Henry Greenspan describes as "partners in conversation." This in turn depends on "shared authority" – a term oral historian Michael Frisch popularized in 1990 to describe the dual authority of the oral history interview – the expert authority of the interviewer and the experiential authority of the interviewee. This is, however, as Frisch notes, "a beginning and not an end."[32]

The collection is arranged in five thematic parts. The first of these, "Turning Private History into Public Knowledge," sets out a number of ideas that frame the discussion that follows: the drive behind the impetus to turn pain into story, the affective nature of such stories for those who tell and for those who listen, the limitations of celebratory and

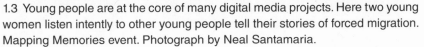

1.3 Young people are at the core of many digital media projects. Here two young women listen intently to other young people tell their stories of forced migration. Mapping Memories event. Photograph by Neal Santamaria.

psychiatric discourses, and the necessity to break down ritualized distinctions between tellers and listeners. Part 2, "Performing Human Rights," takes up themes of subject position, representation, and the potential role and implications of art and imagination within the context of the face-to-face interaction of live performance. "Oral History and Digital Media," part 3, extends the discussion to consider what may be gained and what lost in the larger-scale dissemination, access, and interactive engagement made possible through new media and participatory approaches such as digital storytelling. In part 4, "Life Stories," we consider the impact of the life stories approach through case studies of projects with Aboriginal youth in Winnipeg, black residents of New Orleans displaced by Hurricane Katrina, activist pensioners in Argentina, and Moroccan Jews in Montreal. Part 5, "Rwanda in the Aftermath of Genocide," returns us to considerations of testimony – here primarily within the context of work done by our Rwandan Working Group, one of the seven research clusters that made up the Montreal Life Stories project. This final part concludes with a consideration of testimony as advocacy for gay and lesbian human rights in post-genocide Rwanda.

Turning Private History into Public Knowledge

The first two essays in the collection are derived from the keynote addresses of Henry Greenspan and Lorne Shirinian that opened the Remembering War conference. Greenspan, a Michigan-based psychologist, suggests that we are far more likely to invoke survivor testimony than to actually listen to it. Greenspan pushes us to go beyond simple celebration of the idea of testimony and "bearing witness." He contends that psychiatric discourses centred on trauma stifle serious engagement with survivors and their memories. As a result, two "discrete and disconnected monologues" are created, as scholars and survivors speak past one another. He speaks of the essential need for direct engagement, challenging interviewers and interviewees to become partners in conversation.

Greenspan has spent thirty years in conversation with the same group of Holocaust survivors. Yet, as he reminds us, words don't come easily. Turning pain into a story is a complex task. There is of course a large scholarship on trauma and memory that speaks of how the horror of experience goes beyond the ability of everyday language to communicate.[33] As Leon, a Holocaust survivor interviewed by Greenspan, puts it, "It is not a story. It has to be made a story in order somehow to convey it. And with all the frustration that implies. Because, at best, you compromise. You compromise."[34] Greenspan, however, like Primo Levi, explicitly rejects framing the problem of communicability in psychological terms, including the psychology of trauma.[35] Rather, he advocates a more humanistic approach to research. The issue is what he calls "topographic": a problem of radically incompatible space. Where Greenspan raises questions about the limits of celebratory and psychiatric discourses pertaining to Holocaust testimony, the second essay, by Lorne Shirinian, affirms the important place of storytelling and testimony within survivor communities. Shirinian, a poet, playwright, activist, and scholar, is the son of one of the Georgetown Boys – orphaned male children sent to Canada to escape the 1915 Armenian genocide. Shirinian's life's work has focused on this legacy. In his contribution to this collection, he speaks of the crucial role of stories as a means of converting private history into public knowledge. He voices the conviction that "pain and grief can be tolerated somewhat if they can be turned into or related as a story." Yet the context for such stories must be forward-looking. For Shirinian, "our need to remember is a form of resistance to genocide denial and also is a refusal to be incorporated and engulfed by the genocide." He poignantly notes that traditional Armenian folk tales always began, "once there was and was not" – an enduring encapsulation of transiency, testimony, genocide denial, and hope.

These first two essays represent a spectrum of experience. For Henry Greenspan, an interviewer and psychologist by training, "listening to people remember, and reflect upon, particular historical circumstances is what we do." His attention is focused on the survivor–researcher relationship, and the conversation between these two locations. Lorne Shirinian is also a scholar, but he writes as a second-generation witness to the Armenian genocide. Near the outset, he lets us know that he "learned from an early age that being a diaspora Armenian since 1915 means having a connection to Western Armenian culture that developed over two millennia in its historical homeland that no longer exists. I had lost something I never really had." He grew up with family stories of violence and survival, and these became "part of my imaginary life from an early age." He explains how this inheritance has shaped his scholarly and artistic work: "I had become an interpreter of my parents' survival and a transmitter of the difficult knowledge they had passed on to me." Shirinian sees his role as that of the translator – Greenspan sees his as an interpreter and active partner in conversation.

One of the most powerful themes that have emerged from the thousands of interviews conducted with Holocaust survivors is the difficulty involved in "narrating, from the context of normality now, the nature of the abnormality then."[36] Taking our cue from Holocaust scholar Lawrence Langer, we consider it useful to think of survivor testimony as the ruins of memory. For Langer, memory "excavates from the ruins of the past fragile shapes to augment our understanding of those ruins."[37] The study of ruins, however, is fraught with problems. Andreas Huyssen, in his essay "Nostalgia for Ruins," points out that rubble is regularly transformed, even aestheticized, into ruin.[38] Is a similar process under way in regard to survivor testimony? Writing of the debris of imperialism, postcolonial scholar Ann Laura Stoler makes a sharp distinction between ruin and ruination. To ruin, she writes, is "to inflict or bring great and irretrievable disaster upon, to destroy agency, to reduce to a state of poverty, to demoralize completely."[39] By contrast, ruination "is an act perpetrated, a condition to which one is subject, and a cause of loss."[40] Stoler goes on to say that we need to understand how people live with and in ruination.

Clearly these insights into ruins and ruination apply not only to the physical destruction of the built environment, as the rubble of memory can also be aestheticized into ruin. For Lawrence Langer and others, the "pretense that from the wreckage of mass murder we can salvage a tribute to the victory of the human spirit is a version of Holocaust reality more necessary than true."[41] As a result, "words like survival and liberation, with their root meanings of life and freedom, entice us into a kind of verbal enchantment."[42] In different ways, and perhaps for different reasons, the two essays in this part seek to break the spell. Greenspan and Shirinian don't look upon the ruins from afar but engage directly with the people living in them.

Performing Human Rights

Oral history and performance enjoy a "unique synergy," according to Della Pollock.[43] In so far as oral history "is a process of making history in dialogue, it is performative. It is co-creative, co-embodied, specially framed, contextually and inter-subjectively contingent, sensuous, vital, artful."[44] In this part, the contributors reflect on the creation and reception of live performances that in various ways reference oral history. Perhaps not surprisingly, they also "play" with the received form and structure of the scholarly article. Several multi-authored essays, for example, reflect the "shared authority" of diverse collaborative approaches to creating live theatre. Others draw on conventions that break the mainstream theatre's traditional division between audience and performer. In "Soldiers' Tales Untold," Michael Kilburn explores the creative process of Shaw Pong Liu, a classical musician and composer who transformed Stravinsky's classic Faustian fable about a soldier's return from the battle front in the First World War into an invitation to reflect on the impact of war on US soldiers returning from Iraq and Afganistan. Focusing on the experience of post-traumatic stress disorder (PTSD), Liu uses elements of agitprop theatre, specifically the actor "planted" in the audience, to incorporate the verbatim testimony of contemporary veterans. The process of these apparent audience members gradually becoming recognizable as actors as they proceed to repeatedly "interrupt" the proceedings by speaking the perspective of the veterans, effectively performs a series of interventions to Stravinsky's text. Kilburn looks at how Liu manages to merge oral history and performance to create a space where the disjointed flashbacks and fractured narratives common to PTSD are represented in order that they

1.4 Contributor Elizabeth Miller listens to one of the life stories which were at the heart of the *Nous Sommes Ici/We Are Here* exhibition at the Centre d'histoire de Montréal. 2012–13. Photograph by Nick Kanhai.

may be reintegrated into a coherent narrative. Kilburn cites Jonathan Shay, who speaks of the "communalization" of trauma: "being able safely to tell the story to someone who is listening and who can be trusted to retell it truthfully to others in the community."

The other three chapters in this part originate in the Oral History and Performance group of Montreal Life Stories. The seven contributors are artists; some are also academics. None is a historian, yet all are deeply invested in the emerging field of oral history and performance. Their theatrical repertoire ranges from the universalism of Sandeep Bhagwati's "gestural theatre" to the intensely personal audience/performer interaction of Playback Theatre. Rachael Van Fossen and Hourig Attarian's collaboration, "Stories Scorched from the Desert Sun," falls somewhere between. For his piece, *Lamentations*, Bhagwati and his actors studied moments of social and cultural rupture and displacement in the gestures, facial expressions, and body language of videotaped Life Stories interviewees. These moments – embodied by actors working through a creative process of imitation, analysis, and synthesis – formed the basis of a performance text focusing on the visceral "essence of displacement: [where] a body, displaced in a new social and cultural environment, does not remain the same body. Its very gestures, its most embodied language is taken over by the will to survive, remodelled to conform, fit it, even basically communicate in this strange new world." In this highly reflexive chapter, Bhagwati presents an important critique of the confessional voice. Citing Richard Sennett's notion of the "tyranny of intimacy," he questions the assumption that an emotional truth makes a social and political point more valid and pertinent. Instead, he writes, it might produce "a cuddly and over-emotional de-emphasizing of the brute realities they had lived through." Bhagwati asserts that "art is an exercise in focus, not comprehensiveness." *Lamentations* asks us to consider what is lost when the personal comes to dominate the political. Bhagwati directed his actors to study the interviews with the audio turned off. In consequence, they knew very little about the person whose gestures they were adopting. This active suppression of voice raises questions of course, but productive ones.

Voice re-enters the conversation with the body in "Turning Together," a collaboratively written chapter by four members of the Living Histories Ensemble (LHE) – a Playback Theatre troupe based in the Performance Working Group. Playback invites audience members to share their stories in a workshop atmosphere. Once told, the actors, led by a conductor, "play back" the story through improvisational techniques involving repeated words and phrases, images, soundscapes, "bodystorming," and "fluid sculpture." Conductor Nisha Sajnani speaks of playback as a means of reintegrating fragmented stories: "Trauma creates gaps in the stories that we attempt to organize and tell about ourselves." LHE members bring expertise in theatre, group facilitation, community counselling, and drama therapy, and their chapter considers "performing process" as a mode of embodied inquiry. The ensemble is developing innovative approaches that combine collective interviewing/story-gathering with debriefing for interviewers and interviewees. LHE facilitated a playback session at the end of the conference, serving as a kind of debriefing session for participants.

The final chapter in this part represents a deeply reflexive dialogue between dramaturge Rachael Van Fossen and author Hourig Attarian on "testimony as process" within a performance research-creation project. "Stories Scorched from the Desert Sun" uses three voices to tell the stories of several girls who lived through the horrors of war and genocide in different places and at different times: Pergrouhi in 1915 Turkey – a child of barely six, who alone and unable to comprehend her loss, sleeps for several nights in a field beside the body of her murdered Armenian mother; Pergrouhi in her nineties recalling the event; Hourig herself and her friend Hermig in Beirut in 1975 – two children of the Armenian genocide on the cusp of puberty living on the same street as the religious and ethnic violence of the civil war erupts around them; and Hourig and Hermig as adults – recalling the deportation stories of grandparents and great-aunts and the trauma of their own experience of war. The Stories Scorched project focuses on ethical problems and dramaturgical solutions in the translation into performance of oral history that involves stories of graphic violence and trauma. To counteract the risk that the power and immediacy of theatre might create a counterproductive experience of sensationalized or eroticized violence, Attarian and Van Fossen adopted a Brechtian "reporting" style that supports a "more muted," less emotional approach to more graphic elements. This also facilitated the dramatic choice to foreground tensions between their own subject positions as Hourig wrestled with the personal impact of making her story public. As she explains, "What started as an exchange between the two of us, seeking to understand the perspectives we each brought to the performance, became a story in its own right as we delved deeper into our collaboration. What follows is the charting of that story: the 'storying' of the performance." The night of the performance Hourig witnessed her own story for the first time in public.

The politics of witness is of central concern to the contributors in this part and builds on the issues raised in the first two chapters. For Michael Kilburn, the structure of Shaw Pong Liu's A Soldier's Tale "implies a rejection of the framing of war as spectacle or pageant perpetuated by our media and politicians and a reminder of the veterans and casualties among us." Sandeep Bhagwati aims to do much the same thing in Lamentations, playing with idea of the bystander or witness. The challenge to familiar structures continues within the deeply reflexive, improvised approach taken by playback theatre. In her co-authored chapter, Rachael Van Fossen quotes Julie Salverson on the need to avoid the voyeuristic appeal and "almost erotic quality" in which actors sometimes perform pain.[45] These four chapters provide us with a great deal to think about in response to fundamental ethical questions about how we tell difficult stories in theatre. Similar questions are taken up in the context of digital media.

Oral History and Digital Media

In this third part, contributors engage with various ways in which digital technologies and the Web are reshaping the ways in which people remember and narrate their own lives; how digital media are transforming the way we understand, represent, and interpret the past; and the collaborative potential for exchange and action within these transformations.[46] In "Oral History in the Age of Social Media Networks," Reisa Levine, a producer with CitizenShift, reflects on her experience of partnership with Montreal Life Stories. She describes the experience as a meeting of two worlds, where negotiating the practical and ethical concerns of putting oral history online became a primary concern. In academic circles, some raised concerns about the ethics and responsibility of relinquishing control of oral history to digital media countercultures and the "participative Web." Could this be done responsibly and ethically? As Levine explains: "Regardless of our differing terms, the fundamental notion of 'sharing' and by extension, of 'respect,'" united us. As the project shifted from an archival to a digital storytelling mindset, Levine noted: "Something intriguing is emerging out of the collection of media about this project. The body of work is beginning to tell a story in and of itself."[47]

The next chapter reflects on the creation of one of the digital stories housed on the CitizenShift website. *Life in the Open Prison* is a thirty-three-minute documentary film produced by thirteen Montreal-area high school students. The project won the Oral History Association's teaching prize in 2009. Co-authors Noelia Gravotta, then a high school student, and teacher Megan Webster reflect on their nine-month journey beginning with training in oral history methods and ethics, moving on to learning about the Cambodian genocide, interviewing survivors, and ending with the production of the film. Like other contributors to this collection, the co-authors chose a conversational narrative where each speaks in turn. This alternating voice allows each author to individually reflect on what mattered most to them:

> **Megan:** "Ironically, it was hearing a sex educator talk about how to teach children about the origins of life that I learned how to talk to students about death. How do you know when kids are ready to learn about sex? They'll ask, she said. Until then, stick to the big picture: provide accurate facts, let the child set the pace. I exhaled." ...
>
> **Noelia:** "While Ms Webster privately struggled with how to deal with concepts of genocide, I began to consider my own family's history. My

1.5 Digital stories from genocide survivors could be accessed through QR-coded posters in Montreal's subway system in 2012. Four hundred Metro cars were equipped with posters like this one. Photograph by Nick Kanhai.

parents had been university students in Argentina during the bloody dictatorship of Jorge Rafael Videla, during which between 15,000 and 30,000 citizens suspected of 'leftist sympathizing' were murdered, while thousands more were imprisoned and tortured. While the mass atrocities in Argentina and Cambodia were vastly different, there were certain distressing parallels ... I began asking my mother about her experiences. At first, caught off guard, she only told me about the historical and political causes for the rise of Videla and the 'official' history of those five years of·dictatorship. It was a detached story like Mr A's. After a few of these conversations, she began inserting details, describing the fear of passing soldiers with machine guns to go to school. She could be jailed or tortured if she was caught without her identification papers. She told me, haltingly, of the disappearance of her cousin, of the murder of her friend's brother."

As a pedagogical exercise, one could not hope for more. "Before taking this course, genocide was just a concept," writes Gravotta. "By wrestling with the stories of Mr A. and Mr Pong," the project team learned much more. "One of our biggest concerns while storyboarding was that the narrative was not only Mr A's and Mr Pong's; it was our interpretation and manipulation of their accounts to convey our message." As the film took shape, their stories became "our story." The chapter constitutes an eloquent, and at times poetic, "dialogue about authority, pedagogy, and collaboration" that manifests "how engagement with oral history provides students and teacher with avenues for deep learning, identity formation, and relationship building."

The final two chapters in this part tell us more about how new and old media can be integrated into a participatory process. Jessica Anderson and Rachel Bergenfield write of their experience in Northern Uganda, where they encountered communities struggling with the aftermath of the Barlonyo massacre. They observed a profound disconnect between local communities and governmental and non-governmental agencies working on transitional justice, remembrance, and economic development. As Anderson and Bergenfield put it: "The 'dots' were not connected," the use of multimedia was "largely extractive and geared towards foreign audiences." In response, they worked with local partners to develop strategies of "community information integration ... a process of making knowledge about the conflict accessible and actionable in any way the community and individuals find meaningful for conflict transformation." In their chapter, they describe their "story-based approach" that emphasizes people's daily routines within what they describe as an "emerging space of locally owned, sensitive, and purposeful multimedia." This they found "unearthed far more illuminating information about the state of 'reconciliation' or 'remembrance' in a community." As for the book itself, it consisted of photographs, a map depicting the massacre, a historical timeline tied to personal narratives, and limited amount of explanatory text written in Langi, the local language. The simplicity of the book reminds us that the media we adopt should be based on what makes the most sense in furthering our objectives and not on what is flashy at the moment.

The last new media project discussed in this part, undertaken by Michele Luchs and Liz Miller, focuses on newly arrived male refugees to Montreal. These men are provided with a maximum of three weeks of shelter in government-subsidized Project Refuge hostels. Luchs and Miller, working in partnership with the residents and Project Refuge's coordinator, developed a series of participative photo-story media workshops aimed at encouraging connection between current short-term residents while providing something meaningful that the men could leave behind for those who would come after them. Luchs and Miller describe their own learning process: "What we realized was that while personal stories are often easier for outside audiences to connect to, the interactive element of the collaborative process offered an invaluable opportunity for the participants to engage together and connect." Luchs and Miller frame their chapter within the larger context of education and advocacy, migration and tolerance, globalization and "dialogue to sensitize the general public about the impacts of policy changes on the lives of individuals."[48]

Life Stories

In part 4 our contributors shift their attention to living testimony and recorded interviews within what is effectively a case study approach. In its own way, each chapter reflects on issues concerned with the power and location of the researcher-interviewer. In "So You Want to Hear Our Ghetto Stories?" Robin Jarvis Brownlie and Roewan Crowe write about their experience as two white scholars developing a pilot project with female Aboriginal youth at the Ndinawe Youth Resource Centre in inner-city Winnipeg. The title of their piece comes from an initial question posed as a challenge by one of the participants. As the authors explain: "Her query seemed to express a recognition of her vulnerability to exploitation, colonization, and exoticization through our research – and even through our presence in her community. It also suggested her awareness of the ways that 'ghetto stories' can lend authority – or 'street cred' – to those who can appropriate them despite their own social distance from such experiences." In response, rather than electing to interview these young women about their lives, Brownlie and Crowe effectively addressed the concerns of the youth by bringing in invited speakers – elders and mentors – who then shared their stories of aboriginal women's resistance. Through this approach Brownlie and Crowe effectively "interrogate the ways in which cross-cultural research and colonial practices intersect, and work to envision research initiatives that can contribute to decolonizing practices."

Race and power are also at the heart of D'Ann Penner's study of the social and political impact of Hurricane Katrina on African American residents of New Orleans. Her chapter, "Dishonour, Dispersion, and Dispossession," is a strongly worded condemnation of human rights violations. Penner makes the case that the United States government failed to adhere to its own "Guiding Principles on Internal Displacement." Citing Mindy Thompson Fullilove, Penner invokes the notion of "root shock" as "'the traumatic stress reaction to the destruction of all or part of one's emotional ecosystem.'" She writes: "For myself, I cannot rid my soul of the depression, trauma, and overwhelming loss I have imbibed during conversations with narrators who were hours or days travel away from New Orleans, their family members, and their community." Clearly place matters.

For her part, anthropologist Lindsay DuBois offers some important words of caution in her chapter "The Romance of Reminiscence." While fieldwork and deep listening are nothing new to anthropologists, and first-hand accounts can be enormously compelling, DuBois makes the case that we must critically interrogate the production of testimonies and, "more specifically, we need to examine how we, as researchers, are implicated in them." DuBois's contrasting study of immobilization and activism amid two separate groups in Argentina is essentially concerned with how politics, ideology, and research methodologies shape the stories we hear. DuBois contrasts the oral historian's deep listening to language and narrative with the ethnographer's attention to "both how people behave and what they say they are doing." She reminds us of Portelli's classic article "Research as an Experiment in Equality" that demonstrated "how attempts at political neutrality on the part of a researcher can produce more distortions than expressions of solidarity might."

The final chapter in this part examines the exodus of Jews from Morocco after the Second World War. Historian Yolande Cohen asks us to consider patterns of migration and the subsequent re-composition of individual and collective identity. Her study is longitudinal, drawing from life history interviews conducted in Montreal in the 1980s and 2000s. Why did those interviewed leave Morocco? How is their migration remembered today? Why did they choose to come to Montreal? While the primary focus is on departure, Cohen nonetheless shows us how the arrival of thousands of French-speaking Sephardic Jews in Montreal affected social relations in the city. Jewish Montreal, which was overwhelmingly English-speaking before their arrival, became a little more francophone, openly showing its diversity.

The chapters in this part remind us of the politics of public remembering and oral history collection. Public and scholarly fascination with first-hand accounts makes anthropologist Lindsay DuBois uneasy. She asks that we "critically interrogate the production" of testimonies because how people make sense of their pasts, and how we as researchers and artists interpret, and are implicated in this memory work, is "very much a political process." Other contributors clearly agree. Influenced by feminist scholarship, Brownlie and Crowe raise questions about the intersection of cross-cultural research and colonial practices. "How is it that we had access to these young people?" they ask. The contributors join the work of others exploring the ethical challenges of working with difficult stories or marginalized people.[49]

Rwanda in the Aftermath of Genocide

In part 5, survivors' voices once again take centre stage as our contributors shift our attention away from the research process and return us to testimony. We are reminded that there is a tremendous amount at stake in how atrocity crime is remembered. This can be seen clearly in the aftermath of the 1994 Rwanda genocide in which Hutu génocidaires murdered up to 800,000 Tutsi men, women, and children.[50] In Athanasie Mukarwego's "Témoignage" we read her first-person public testimony, delivered at Montreal's fifteenth commemoration of the Rwandan genocide in April 2009. It reads, in part:

> I didn't … I never saw him again. That's how it was but by the time the genocide ended I was really angry, I was, I lost the awareness that I knew more, there was no link between me and my children, because I could not communicate with them, although we were in the same house. And when I still had breath I shouted. And when I cried it made my children cry. They did not see me but it's like they lived the same problem as I lived because I was crying when they cried, I cried when they cried. It is thanks to the army of the Patriotic Front that I was able to leave the house again and face the day. (applause)

Her story is a particularly horrific one. Her husband was murdered in the early days of the genocide and she was raped, gang raped, and forced into sexual slavery. She was told that she would be raped to death. In the weeks that followed, she was raped so often and by so many men that she began to suffer serious gynaecological problems, nausea, and difficulty breathing. All she could smell was the sperm: "l'odeur de sperme, l'odeur de sperme, l'odeur de sperme." Some of these men were her neighbours, one was even a friend of her murdered husband. She longed to die.

At several points in the transcript, there are references to audience "applause." This may startle the reader, given the subject matter; however, this serves to remind us that the story we are reading was originally told in public as part of Montreal's fifteenth commemoration of the Rwandan genocide, an event organized by the Association des Parents et Amis des Victimes du Génocide des Tutsis au Rwanda, or Page-Rwanda. The day of reflection is organized annually by and for the city's Rwandan community. Madame Mukarwego's story – and the courage that it took to share it – resonated with everyone in the room. One of the listeners that day was Monica Lafon, a student intern with the Montreal Life Stories Project. She later reflected on the experience in her bi-weekly report: "I remember her [Mdm. Mukarwego's] expression when she said she was abused, again and again, again and again. It seemed as if she didn't have any emotions left to go with her words. Then she sat down ... and the woman next to her just patted her back." This testimony presents us with an important reminder of the devastating impact of war, genocide, and other human rights violations.

The gendered nature of crimes committed in Rwanda in 1994 is the subject of the following article, written by a four-person team based mainly in Montreal's Rwandan community: Emmanuel Habimana, Carole Vacher, Berthe Kayitesi and Callixte Kabayiza. Their paper examines the use of rape by Hutu militia during the genocide, contextualizing the sadistic violence described in the public testimony of Madame Mukarwego. According to various sources, including African Rights and Human Rights Watch, more than 300,000 Tutsi women and girls as young as ten were raped during the genocide. Men and young boys were also raped. The authors characterize rape as a "crime of envy." Tutsi women were targeted because, for some, they had become a powerful symbol of privilege and physical beauty. Mass rape became a weapon of extermination. Those women who survived this trauma have faced public hostility and serious health issues (e.g., HIV). Yet these rapes have been met mainly by silence. "In reality, the scale of the rapes during the genocide remains unknown," they write. Madame Mukarwego's testimony challenges both silence and cultural taboos.[51]

There are other untold stories in post-genocide Rwanda. The collection ends with the story of American-based archivist Valerie Love's encounter with Rwanda's lesbian, gay, bisexual, transgendered, and intersex community during the summer of 2009. Love's concern is with "archival documentation strategies and the use of oral history in order to represent communities and experiences which are not included in traditional archival documentation." This memory work is politically urgent, as the absence of a recognized history plays into the ongoing denial by the state of this community's existence. Collecting testimony for educational and political purposes, she cautions, must be empowering for the individuals involved. The chapter raises compelling questions about "the role of advocacy and activism within the archival profession" as well as the perception and provision of human rights in the aftermath of genocide: "We must see these testimonies as a call to action, a call for recognition of suffering and of perseverance, and work together as archivists and educators to share these stories, where appropriate, and advocate for those who have had their rights denied."

This section on Rwanda reminds us that the aims of community-based testimony projects are often political: to counter denial, to bring perpetrators to justice, to foster reconciliation and personal healing. Sharing stories also serves the important function of (re-)building community solidarity and providing a tool for community activism. It is not by coincidence that feminists were pioneers of oral history in North America and Europe. In recent years, survivors have been at the forefront of activism. Public testimony has been central to the April commemorations of the Rwandan genocide, a time when Rwandan Tutsi come together to remember lost loved ones. Perhaps the biggest legacy of the large Holocaust testimony projects, at least in the short term, was not the interview recordings but rather the effect that this had within the community. Interviewees quickly became interviewers, speakers, docents, and so on. In effect, oral history activated them. We see a similar pattern in North America's gay and lesbian community, where HIV/AIDS testimony has served to mobilize the community and bind people together by memory.[52]

Finally, this anthology approaches public and private acts of remembering mass violence from a great variety of perspectives, contexts, locations, and events. The encounters written about in these pages come in many forms: actual meetings, encounters with landscape, collaborative art projects, and the exchange of stories.[53] There is considerable strength in this diversity. We leave the final word to Thi Ry Duong, our co-editor of this collection. We have worked closely with Ry for the past five years as part of Montreal Life Stories; she was leader of the project's Cambodian working group and a member of the coordinating committee. Like many others in the project, Ry has a personal connection to the life stories being recorded. Her father was interviewed, as was she. In her afterword, Thi Ry Duong shares with us the story of her father, who lived through the Khmer Rouge regime. It is her story too. Rereading these pages from our own vantage points as a university-based scholar and an academic-artist practitioner, we are reminded of something public historian David Glassberg once wrote: the "distance between academic and popular history will not be bridged by historians reaching out to 'the public,' but rather by their reaching in to discover the humanity they share."[54] The same is true of other areas of research and research creation.

NOTES

1   Sidonie Smith and Julia Watson, *Reading Autobiography: A Guide for Interpreting Life Narratives* (Minneapolis: University of Minnesota Press, 2010), 1.
2   Alessandro Portelli, *The Battle of Valle Giulia: Oral History and the Art of Dialogue* (Madison: University of Wisconsin Press, 1997), 40.
3   Julie Cruikshank, *The Social Life of Stories: Narrative and Knowledge in the Yukon Territory* (Lincoln: University of Nebraska Press/Vancouver: UBC Press, 1998), 1.
4   Benjamin quoted in Alessandro Portelli, *The Death of Luigi Trastulli and Other Stories: Form and Meaning in Oral History* (Ithaca: State University of New York Press), 1.
5   Nanci Adler, Selma Leydesdorf, et al., eds., *Memories of Mass Repression: Narrating Life Stories in the Aftermath of Atrocity* (New Brunswick: Transaction Publishers, 2011), ix. Geoffrey H. Hartman, "Learning from Survivors: The Yale Testimony Project," *Holocaust and Genocide Studies* 9, no. 2 (Fall 1995): 194–5.
6   Selma Leydesdorff, "When Communities Fell Apart and Neighbors Became Enemies: Stories of Bewilderment in Srebrenica," in Nanci Adler, Selma Leydesdorf, et al., eds., *Memories of Mass Repression: Narrating Life Stories in the Aftermath of Atrocity* (New Brunswick: Transaction Publishers, 2011), 21–40.
7   Kay Schaffer and Sidonie Smith, "Conjunction: Life Narratives in the Field of Human Rights," *Biography* 27, no. 1 (Winter 2004): 1. For a discussion of audiovisual testimony and humanitarian video archives, see Bhaskar Sarkar and Janet Walker, eds., *Documentary Testimonies: Global Archives of Suffering* (New York: Routledge, 2010); and for the sharing of life stories online, Helga Lénart-Cheng and Darija Walker, "Recent Trends in Using Life Stories for Social and Political Activism," *Biography* 34, no. 1 (Winter 2011): 141–79.
8   Derek Paget, "Verbatim Theatre: Oral History and Documentary Techniques," *New Theatre Quarterly* 3, no. 12 (1987): 317–36; Alison Jeffers, "Refugee Perspectives: The Practice and Ethics of Verbatim Theatre

and Refugee Stories," *Platform* 1, no. 1 (Autumn 2006): 1–17; and Alison Forsyth, ed., *Get Real: Documentary Theatre Past and Present* (New York: Palgrave-Macmillan, 2009): especially relevant are the chapters by Alison Forsyth, "Performing Trauma: Race Riots and Beyond in the Work of Anna Deavere Smith," and Y. Hutchinson, "Verbatim Theatre in South Africa: Living History in a Person's Performance."

9   There is a growing scholarship on the Truth and Reconciliation Commission of Canada. One of the more interesting studies is Paulette Regan's *Unsettling the Settler Within: Indian Residential Schools, Truth Telling and Reconciliation in Canada* (Vancouver: UBC Press, 2010). There is an immense scholarship on South Africa's TRC. Important questions about the discourse of individual and national healing are raised in Sean Field, "Beyond 'Healing': Trauma, Oral History and Regeneration," *Oral History* 34, no. 1 (Spring 2006): 31–42.

10 Nor is there much focus on forced migrants as human agents. See David Palmer, "'Every Morning before You Open the Door You Have to Watch for that Brown Envelope': Complexities and Challenges of Undertaking Oral History with Ethiopian Forced Migrants in London, UK," *Oral History Review* 37, no. 1 (2010): 36.

11 Tony Kushner quoted in Michael Rothberg and Jared Stark, "After the Witness: A Report from the Twentieth Anniversary Conference of the Fortunoff Video Archive for Holocaust Testimonies at Yale," *History and Memory* 15, no. 1 (Spring-Summer 2003): 88. Survivor testimony is closely associated with the South African Truth and Reconciliation Commission, with 20,000 making statements (2,000 of them publicly), yet in the TRC's final report testimonies are illustrative. Mark Saunders, *Ambiguities of Witnessing: Law and Literature in the Time of a Truth Commission* (Stanford, CA: Stanford University Press, 2007), 151.

12 Kay Schaffer and Sidonie Smith, "Venues of Storytelling: The Circulation of Testimony in Human Rights Campaigns," *Life Writing* 1, no. 2 (2004): 6. Similar conclusions are drawn in Tony Kushner, "Oral History at the Extremes of Human Experience: Holocaust Testimony in a Museum Setting," *Oral History* (Autumn 2001): 83–94.

13 Alessandro Portelli, *The Battle of Valle Giulia: Oral History and the Art of Dialogue* (Madison: University of Wisconsin Press, 1997), ix. See also Alessandro Portelli, "'The Time of My Life': Function of Time in Oral History," *International Journal of Oral History* 2, no. 3 (1981): 162–80.

14 Alessandro Portelli, *The Death of Luigi Trastulli and Other Stories*, 2.

15 Mary Jo Maynes, et al., *Telling Stories: The Use of Personal Narratives in the Social Sciences and History* (Ithaca, NY: Cornell University Press, 2008), 1.

16 Paula Hamilton and Linda Shopes, eds., *Oral History and Public Memories* (Philadelphia: Temple University Press, 2008), introduction.

17 Alon Confino, "Telling about Germany: Narrative of Memory and Culture," *The Journal of Modern History* 76, no. 2 (June 2004): 409.

18 Paul Thompson, *The Voice of the Past: Oral History*, 3rd ed. (Oxford: Oxford University Press, 2000), 23.

19 Julie Cruikshank, *The Social Life of Stories*, 40.

20 Raymond Williams, quoted in Geoff Eley, *A Crooked Line: From Cultural History to the History of Society* (Ann Arbor: University of Michigan Press, 2005), 22.

21 Confino, "Telling about Germany," 410. See also Marianne Hirsch and Leo Spitzer, "The Witness in the Archive: Holocaust Studies/Memory Studies," *Memory Studies* 2 (2009): 151–70.

22 Luisa Passerini, *Fascism in Popular Memory: The Cultural Experience of the Turin Working-Class* (Cambridge: Cambridge University Press, 1987), 8.

23 Henry Greenspan, *On Listening to Holocaust Survivors: Beyond Testimony*, 2nd ed. (St Paul: Paragon House, 2010), 2.

24 Mary Jo Maynes, et al., *Telling Stories: The Use of Personal Narratives in the Social Sciences and History* (Ithaca: Cornell University Press, 2008), 3. See also Julie Cruikshank, *Do Glaciers Listen? Local Knowledge, Colonial Encounters and Social Imagination* (Vancouver: UBC Press, and Seattle: University of Washington Press, 2005), 9.

25 Julie Cruikshank, *The Social Life of Stories*, 40.

26 Alessandro Portelli, "Oral History as Genre," in Mary Chamberlain and Paul Thompson, eds., *Narrative and Genre* (New York: Routledge, 1997), 25.

27 Daniel James, *Dona Maria's Story: Life History, Memory and Political Identity* (Durham: Duke University Press, 2000), 186.

28 The Life Stories of Montrealers Displaced by War, Genocide, and other Human Right Violations project conducted 500 interviews with survivors of mass violence. These interviews can be consulted at the Centre for Oral History and Digital Storytelling. About a third of the interviews, where interviewees agreed to full public access, have been integrated into a searchable database using Stories Matter software (developed in-house). Visit Montreal Life Stories at www.histoiresdeviemontreal.ca/.

29 Tim Prentki and Jan Selman, *Popular Theatre in Political Culture: Britain and Canada in Focus* (Bristol: Intellect Press, 2000).

30 Collaborative approaches have been foundational to feminist oral history. See Sherna Berger Gluck and Daphne Patai, *Women's Words: The Feminist Practice of Oral History* (New York: Routledge, 1991). For a Canadian perspective, see Denyse Baillargeon, "Histoire orale et histoire des femmes:

Itinéraires et points de rencontre," *Recherches Féministes* 6, no. 1 (1993): 53–68. Resistance to oral history in the history discipline is explored in Steven High, "Sharing Authority in the Writing of Canadian History: The Case of Oral History," in Christopher Dummitt and Michael Dawson, eds., *Contesting Clio's Craft: New Directions and Debates in Canadian History* (London: Institute for the Study of the Americas, 2009), 21–46.

31 Henry Greenspan, *On Listening to Holocaust Survivors*, 217. For an example of historians experimenting with multivocality, see Joy Parr, Jessica Van Horssen, and Jon van der Veen, "The Practice of History Shared across Difference: Needs, Technologies, and Ways of Knowing in the 'Megaprojects New Media Project,'" *Journal of Canadian Studies* 43, no. 1 (Spring 2009): 35–58.

32 Michael Frisch, "Sharing Authority: Oral History and Collaborative Process," *Oral History Review* 30, no. 1 (2003), 112.

33 Some of the key works are Kim Lacy Rogers and Selma Leydesdorff, eds., *Trauma: Life Stories of Survivors* (New Brunswick: Transaction Publishers, 2004); Shoshana Felman and Dori Laub, eds., *Testimony: Crises of Witnessing in Literature, Psychoanalysis, and History* (New York: Routledge, 1992); Cathy Caruth, *Unclaimed Experience: Trauma, Narrative and History* (Baltimore: Johns Hopkins University Press, 1996); and Dominick La Capra, *Writing History: Writing Trauma* (Baltimore: Johns Hopkins University Press, 2000).

34 Greenspan, *On Listening to Holocaust Survivors*.

35 A similar point is made in Sean Field, "Beyond 'Healing': Trauma, Oral History and Regeneration," *Oral History* 34, no. 1 (Spring 2006): 31–42.

36 Lawrence Langer, *Holocaust Testimonies: The Ruins of Memory* (New Haven: Yale University Press, 1991), 22.

37 Ibid., 128.

38 Andreas Huyssen, "Nostalgia for Ruins," *Grey Room* 23 (Spring 2006): 8.

39 Ann Laura Stoler, "Imperial Debris: Reflections on Ruins and Ruination," *Cultural Anthropology* (Spring 2008): 8.

40 Ibid.

41 Langer, *Holocaust Testimonies*, 165.

42 Ibid., 171.

43 Della Pollock, *Remembering: Oral History Performance* (New York: Palgrave-Macmillan, 2005), 1.

44 Ibid., 2; and James Thompson, *Digging Up Stories: Applied Theatre, Performance and War* (Manchester: Manchester University Press, 2005). For collaborative approaches to oral history and performance, see Alicia J. Rouverol, "Collaborative Oral History in a Correctional Setting: Promise

and Pitfalls," *Oral History Review* 30, no. 1 (2003): 61–85; and Erica Nagel, "An Aesthetic of Neighborliness: Possibilities for Integrating Community-Based Practices into Documentary Theatre," *Theatre Topics* 17, no. 2 (September 2007): 153–68.

45 Julie Salverson, "Anxiety and Contact in Attending to a Play about Land Mines?" in *Critical Pespectives on Canadian Theatre in English* 17 (Toronto: Playwrights Canada Press, 2010), 77–8. See also Julie Salverson, "Change on Whose Terms? Testimony and an Erotics of Injury," *Theater* 31, no. 3 (2001): 119–25; Julie Salverson, "Performing Emergency: Witnessing, Popular Theatre, and the Lie of the Literal," *Theatre Topics* 6, no. 2 (1996): 181–91; and Roger I. Simon, "Afterword: The Turn to Pedagogy: A Needed Conversation on the Practice of Curating Difficult Knowledge," in Erica Lehrer, Cynthia Milton, and Monica Patterson, eds., *Curating Difficult Knowledge: Violent Pasts in Public Places* (New York: Palgrave Macmillan, 2011), 199–200.

46 Steven High, "Telling Stories: Oral History and New Media," *Oral History* (Spring 2010): 101–12.

47 See also Clemencia Rodríguez, *Fissures in the Mediascape. An International Study of Citizens' Media* (New York: Hampton Press, 2001). For more on the international digital storytelling movement, see Knut Lundby, ed., *Digital Storytelling: Mediatized Stories: Self-Representations in New Media* (New York: Peter Lang, 2008); Joe Lambert, *Digital Storytelling: Capturing Lives, Creating Community* (Berkeley, CA: Digital Diner Press, 2002).

48 For more on Elizabeth Miller's thoughts on participatory media, see *Mapping Memories: Participatory Media, Place-Based Stories and Refugee Youth* (Montreal: Marquis Publishing, 2011); Elizabeth Miller, "Building Participation in the Outreach for the Documentary *The Water Front*," *Journal of Canadian Studies/Revue d'études canadiennes* 43, no. 1 (Winter 2009): 59–86; Elizabeth Miller, "Queer in the Eye of the Newcomer: Mapping, Performance and Place Based Media," *InTensions Journal* 4 (Fall 2010), online publication.

49 For a wider discussion of the ethics of collaboration in the context of Aboriginal history and storytelling, see Sophie McCall, *First Person Plural: Aboriginal Storytelling and the Ethics of Collaborative Authorship* (Vancouver: UBC Press, 2011).

50 Scott Straus, *The Order of Genocide: Race, Power and War in Rwanda* (Ithaca: Cornell University Press, 2006); Josias Sumujanga, *Origins of the Rwandan Genocide* (Amherst: Humanity Books, 2003), and Christopher C. Taylor, "The Cultural Face of Terror in the Rwandan Genocide of 1994," in Alexander Labon Hinton, ed., *Annihilating Difference: The Anthropology of Genocide* (Berkeley: University of California Press, 2002): 137–78.

51 For more on the gendered nature of the violence in Rwanda, see Eddah
    Mutua Kombo, "Their Words, Actions and Meaning: A Researcher's
    Reflection on Rwandan Women's Experience of Genocide," *Qualitative
    Inquiry* 15, no. 2 (February 2009): 308–23; and Elssa Martinez, "Survivre
    à la violence organisée: parcours et témoignage de deux femmes rwan-
    daises" (MSc, École de Service Social, Université de Montréal, 2010).
52 Paula J. Draper has spoken of Holocaust survivors as a "closed group"
    largely "bound together by memory." Paul J. Draper, "Canadian Holocaust
    Survivors: From Liberation to Rebirth," *Canadian Jewish Studies* 4, no. 5
    (1996–7), 50.
53 Julie Cruikshank, *Do Glaciers Listen?* 9.
54 David Glassberg quoted in K.T. Corbett and H.S. Miller, "A Shared
    Inquiry into Shared Inquiry," *The Public Historian* 28, no. 1 (Winter 2006):
    32–3; D. Glassberg, *Sense of History: The Place of the Past in American Life*
    (Amherst: University of Massachusetts Press, 2001), 210.

PART ONE

Turning Private History into Public Knowledge

1 Voices, Places, and Spaces

HENRY GREENSPAN

Not only are we not the centre of the universe, but the universe is not made for human beings; it is hostile, violent, alien.

– Primo Levi, *The Search for Roots*

The experience of persecution was, at the very bottom, that of an extreme *loneliness*.

– Jean Amery, *At the Mind's Limits*

For oral historians, images of "voices" and "places" are familiar. Listening to people remember, and reflect upon, particular historical circumstances is what we do. For me, that has meant primarily listening to Holocaust survivors. And so that is my focus here.

The notion of space deserves further explanation. As I use it in this chapter, I intend it in a literal, topographic sense. I will be concerned with dimensions, with connections and fissures, with what is inside and what is outside. So while "place" indicates geographic location, "space" is a more abstract, essentially geometric concept in what follows. It is even a kind of physics.

This will take a little time to unfold. I will proceed through a series of voices and places, each one, I hope, informing the others. How they inform each other, though, will not be evident at the start. So I ask for your patience. Think of this chapter as one of those films that begins with a series of what seem like discrete subplots. Only eventually do their relationships within the wider story emerge. Only gradually do the various voices and places also begin to suggest something about a certain kind of space.

Kosice, Czechoslovakia, 1946

In April 1946, Agi Rubin awoke from an Auschwitz nightmare and wrote about it in her diary. Agi is a Holocaust survivor I've known for thirty years and with whom I've collaborated on many projects, including a co-authored book. In one of our early conversations, in 1980, she retrieved her diary and read – translating from the Hungarian as she went – some of what she wrote that night. She was seventeen years old at the time, and she titled the diary entry, "Auschwitz: The Endless Haunting." In 1946, "endless" meant one year.

> The sound on the radio tells me it's twelve o'clock. I'm sitting and I'm thinking back. The sound of the music tears at my heart because it always takes me back and makes me remember. Remember what? Don't ask. I shouldn't even write it. It's Auschwitz. Auschwitz and its flames and electrified barbed wire ...
>
> Can anyone comprehend what is happening? Broken-hearted Jewish prisoners are playing romantic music, the music of broken hearts ... The others, the killers, the ruthless German guards with their wine bottles, with their cigarettes, are enjoying themselves. They are having a party. If we are lucky, they will throw down a cigarette butt. One of us will pick it up.
>
> We are their prisoners, doomed to death. And I can only call us stupid, ignorant, crazy. Because to live like this – denied everyone and everything, kicked and shoved underfoot, degraded and humiliated – only people who would just as soon be dead could live through this. Having lived it, we are no longer among the living. The living could not survive it ...
>
> This cannot be true. That I am here, on this earth, all by myself. That there is fire. That there are people. That there are bones. That there are the suffocated innocents. This is impossible. That ours, that mine, are there ...
>
> My thoughts have started to wander again. They are wandering to Auschwitz. They are visiting the flames. And who knows where else they are wandering?
>
> My pen wants to go on and on, by itself. It is sliding from my hand. At times like this, my strength leaves me. It leaves me each time I see it all again. It leaves me when I see the truth once more.[1]

In 1946, seventeen-year-old Agi revisited a place that was impossible, and where she was alone.

Jerusalem, Israel, 1981

Other voices. The first World Gathering of Jewish Holocaust Survivors took place in Jerusalem over four days in 1981. Survivors came to Israel from every continent. I was not there, but the Public Broadcasting Service (PBS) in the US produced nightly half-hour reports summarizing the events of each day. I audiotaped the broadcasts, and I summarize a bit of them here.

After a brief lead-in of still photographs with which all the programs began – images that have become iconic of the Holocaust (the small boy in Warsaw with hands raised, *Arbeit Macht Frei*, wires and remains) – one of the commentators made the following introductory remarks to the first broadcast of the series:

> In the opening sequences we showed you a glimpse – even a glimpse is enough – of the savagery of the Holocaust. We didn't do this to shock you, although it is shocking. We did it so that you better understand the triumph of the human spirit. One cannot understand what it means to have been a survivor unless you know *what* they have survived.
>
> These heroic people who are gathered here today have not come to resurrect the nightmares of the past. They have not come to mourn. They have come to celebrate life. To bear witness. And to pass it on to their children and their children's children. This is more valuable than all of the material assets they could pass on. *This* is their true legacy.[2]

From the start, one must wonder how it is possible to "bear witness" *without* mourning and *without* resurrecting "the nightmares of the past"? (Think again of Agi.) And indeed, these remarks alone already suggest a celebration of the *idea* of testimony, the idea of "heroic people" bearing witness, rather than any serious engagement in what that witnessing concerns. Of that – represented by the opening photos – "even a glimpse is enough." And what we are really seeking to understand is something else: "the triumph of the human spirit."

Still, as notable as this celebration of survivors as heroic witnesses, themselves engaged in "celebrating life," was the appearance further on in the broadcasts of a quite different way of discussing survivors and their legacies. The shift was particularly apparent as the commentators turned to those whom they called "the bearers of the legacy," the children of survivors. For what had earlier been applauded as a sacred transmission (from children to children's children) was now portrayed as the passing on of psychiatric burdens and universal affliction. Indeed, within this rhetoric, the nightmarish past was not only resurrected but had gained full possession of the intergenerational future. Thus one reporter introduced her interviews with children of survivors: "Throughout the world there are tens of thousands of young people who have never met. And yet they dream the same nightmares, share the same fears, and deal with the same emotional problems. Although they live separated by continents, they shared an experience which has marked them for life."[3] If this change of discourse was not clear enough, the questions that the reporter then asked three children of survivors – an Israeli, an American, and an Australian – left no doubt about the transformation. They proceeded:

"Do you have any particular nightmares?"
"Do you think there is a problem between survivors and their children in an inability to communicate?"

And, finally, a question that seemed to finish off the previously invaluable legacy once and for all:

"Do you feel that you'll ever get rid of the legacy of the Holocaust?"

For their own part, the children of survivors had no difficulty coming up with exemplary nightmares, family tensions, and related problems. But they also were clearly uncomfortable with the questions and seemed to be pushing to speak about something else. For all, this had to do with more essential ways in which the Holocaust had entered into their awareness. Thus, the Israeli said that "the Holocaust is part of me, as everything is part of me. As my hands are part of me. As my eyes are part of me." Referring to the nightmare she had remembered, the American was quick to add, "More than that – those are only things that happened a few times – more than that, it's something that goes with me through my everyday life." Likewise, the Australian agreed that she would never "get rid of the legacy of the Holocaust." But she continued, "Nor do I want to. It's part of my history ... it goes back to the whole Jewish history."[4]

At least in the segments of the interviews that were broadcast, these comments were never followed up with further questions or discussion. They were left as simple assertions, perhaps as protests, which did little to modify the primary theme that nightmares, fears, and emotional problems were now what "the legacy" was about.

Even so, the matter was not left within psychiatric discourse either. Towards the end of the broadcasts, when discussing the fact that there would never be another such gathering of survivors (in fact, there have been a few), the commentators again raised the theme of redemptive rebirth through the passing of the legacy. They had this to say in final summary:

> It is true that this is, this was, a one-time event, a moment in history. But I do not think it will disappear. There was a legacy that was passed on, there were seeds that were sown, there will be flowers that will blossom forth from this, through the second generation, through the children of survivors, and through all of us who have observed this week.[5]

It was left up to us, the viewing audience, to determine what sort of flowers these might be and how to understand their rootedness in a legacy presented alternately as priceless and as pathogenic. Meanwhile, we might also wonder how much more, excluded by the scripts of both veneration and diagnosis, remains unheard – and, in response, unspoken.

Of course, survivors should be honoured and their testimony cherished. And whatever the struggles of survivors or their children in the aftermath, they ought to be understood in the most serious way. The problem with the celebratory and psychiatric discourses is that testimony and the realities of the lives of survivors and their children are *not* seriously engaged. Rather, as I have emphasized, in place of entering into actual recounting, celebratory discourse fixes on the *idea* of "bearing witness." As typically invoked, the psychiatric discourse functions similarly – charting "emotional problems" substitutes for entering into the impact of the destruction for anyone in particular. That is why, I think, the children of survivors who were interviewed protest. Their knowledge of the Holocaust is not a checklist of symptoms, they each insist, but something complexly lived: "Part of me," part of "my everyday life," "part of my history." And that is also why, I think, their protests were ignored. To pursue them would require the kind of developing dialogue that discourses like these preclude.

In the end, then, the split between celebratory and psychiatric discourse overlays a more profound division – a "division of labour" within the process of recounting itself. On their side, the survivors' "job" is to talk about the Holocaust: to *be* witnesses or testifiers or passers-on of legacies. Our "job," by contrast, is to talk about survivors – either as heroic people who have such a task to fulfil or as haunted victims of the destruction. Whichever rhetoric we invoke, two discrete and disconnected monologues are now created *between* survivors and ourselves. Survivors provide witnessing and testimony about the Holocaust; we provide observations – or testimonials – about survivors.

Defining the Question

It is usually at this point that I would emphasize the alternative to such ritualized ways both of speaking about and practically engaging survivors. I would quote survivor Ruth Kluger reflecting on her listeners, saying what many other survivors say but with her particular ironic verve: "If they did listen, it was in a certain pose, an attitude assumed for this special occasion; it was not as partners in a conversation."[6] And you would read (some of you, yet again) what I have often written about what it means to be "partners in conversation," about sustained and collaborative dialogue, about the differences between "knowing *with*" survivors and only knowing *from* them (the usual testimony model) or only knowing *about* them (the model of most interpretive projects, literary, psychological, or historical). I would emphasize that the collaborative relationship itself is as important a creation (or co-creation) as any other "product" it may yield. And I would note that most of what I've learned about all of this – dialogue, knowing with, the centrality of the relationship – I've learned from survivors themselves.[7]

But that is not the primary road I will follow here, at least not immediately. And what I will pursue may surprise readers who know how seriously I take, and have tried to practise, the principles just listed.

Nevertheless, what I want to emphasize most immediately is this: There is one thing that is not in any conversation with survivors, not in my own interviews and not in those undertaken by others. And, on this level, it doesn't matter if one is the most informed, engaged, sensitive, authority-sharing interviewer possible – that is, a paragon of interviewer virtue. You will still never hear – in *any* of the interviews done with survivors – the Holocaust, the destruction, itself.

Now, of course, I don't mean that in the simple-minded sense that no event is inside its retelling. Or that there are always multiple perspectives. Or point to the distinction between memory, personal or collective, and a presumably more objective history. I mean, rather, that this event and other events that inhabit the same dimension (one of those topographic terms to which I will return) are, at core, the *negation* of attempts to retell them, and especially to retell them in storied form. And if I were to summarize in one short sentence one of the things – just one – that I have heard from every survivor with whom I have spoken, even those with whom I have spoken over more than thirty years, it would be simply this: What I have told you is not it.

I recognize that this will not sound especially novel. The notion that the Holocaust is somehow unspeakable or unknowable has itself become iconic – part of a rhetoric as predictable, and sometimes vacuous, as the talk evoked earlier about lessons and legacies, witnesses and testimony. I also recognize there is a certain danger in pursing this thread. It may be dismissed – and, among academics, it usually *is* dismissed – as "mystification," as putting the Holocaust outside of history; indeed, as an attack on historical knowledge itself. Nothing could be further from the truth. But these assertions are common, and they have themselves developed their own predictable rhetoric.

So one must proceed with care. It is almost inevitable that we will reduce the issue to terms that are most familiar to us. And these do contain some truth. Thus, it is common to assume that the problem is language – we lack words or narrative forms that are big enough, bad enough, or horrific enough to convey the destruction. Or we may view the problem as psychological. Imagining the destruction – particularly for those who lived it, and secondarily for those of us who know it only through imagination – is just too terrifying or painful. Like Agi, we can only go so far.

So the issue may be partly one of language, partly one of psychology. But can we go further? How can it be that a humanly created event – absolutely part of history – escapes articulation? It is certainly *not* "beyond imagination," but precisely the opposite: *It is all too real.* Some survivors say "surreal." But precisely why?

Lodz Ghetto, Poland, 1941

Oskar Rosenfeld was deported from Prague to the Lodz ghetto in 1941. He was a playwright and a freelance writer who became a main contributor to the *Ghetto Chronicle*, the official and public (i.e., open to German eyes) record of ghetto life and ghetto death. He also kept an extraordinary private journal that was found after the war.

Rosenfeld himself was not a survivor. He was on one of the last transports from the ghetto to Auschwitz, where he was killed in 1944. And yet I use this reflection of his as the epigraph for my book, *On Listening to Holocaust Survivors*. While Rosenfeld did not survive, it seemed to me he touched the core of what I was trying to understand from so many who did.

In 1942, he wrote in his diary: "The pain does not touch upon something human, on another's heart …" Stop there for a moment. How can there be pain that does not touch upon a human heart? Where else can pain touch? Rosenfeld continues: "… but rather is something incomprehensible, linked with the cosmos, a natural phenomenon like the creation of the world."[8]

Whatever else, Rosenfeld suggests something about (again that word) dimensions. The locus of the pain he evokes is simply different from the confines of a human heart. As perceived by his own human heart, it was "out there" rather than "in here." Or, to say it differently, it was everywhere, *all* encompassing – "a natural phenomenon like the creation of the world."

Turin, Italy, 1986

Primo Levi, who has become the most revered of survivor-writers, said the same thing. Indeed, he went further. Not only was the pain not psychological in the usual sense, it was reflected in a different physiology as well. For Levi, it was also cosmic, but his analogy was not the creation of the world, but rather its *un*-creation; perhaps *de*-creation. In his last book, published posthumously, Levi wrote:

> In the Lager [the camp] colds and influenza were unknown, but one died, at times suddenly, from illnesses that doctors never had an opportunity to study. Gastric ulcers and mental illnesses were healed (or became asymptomatic), but everyone suffered from an unceasing discomfort that polluted sleep and was nameless.

To define that unceasing discomfort in any usual psychiatric way, Levi said, was "reductive and ridiculous." He continued:

> Perhaps it would be more accurate to see in it an atavistic anguish whose echo one hears in the second verse of Genesis … [the moment *before* Creation] a deserted and empty universe crushed under the spirit of God but from which the spirit of man is absent: not yet born or already extinguished.[9]

"The pain does not touch upon something human," said Rosenfeld. "A deserted and empty universe," said Levi, "from which the spirit of man is absent." Both Rosenfeld and Levi assume a perspective that is cosmic, not personal. They try to describe what is all-encompassing, what is "out there" – or, at core, what is *no longer* out there, which I would summarize as simply this: a universe in which it is still possible to imagine living. This is not a moral judgment: that is, "I would not live in a universe like that." It is meant literally. The habitable universe is gone – not simply desecrated, but de-created. And the result is a total rootlessness, an unqualified homelessness. [10] Using italics (which he very rarely did), Jean Amery called the result "an extreme *loneliness*."[11]

How does one retell a universe in which, in essence, nothing human happens – where, even if one personally remains alive, the universe has become "deserted and empty," a void? And so whatever one's individual experiences – including the most horrific – become, quite literally (and here again we must think spatially) *beside* the point.

Levi insisted that the hardest thing to convey was not trauma, not horror, but "the all-pervasive *lack* of events." He continues, "Because memory works in precisely the opposite way: the single, clamorous, terrifying episodes, or conversely the happy moments, prevail and invade the canvas, whereas as one lives them, they are part of a totally disintegrated reality."[12]

The Fate of Stories

The wonderful project that is based here at Concordia – Life Stories of Montrealers Displaced by War, Genocide, and Other Human Rights Violations – has developed a software program called Stories Matter. And stories do, indeed, matter. I will say more about why. But stories cannot retell a totally disintegrated reality devoid of human heart, human spirit, and even human speech.

Working hard to convey his memories of the Holocaust, and to explain why he could not convey them, Leon, another survivor whom I have known for many years, invoked "a landscape of death where, in effect, nobody beholds it":

It appears to be devoid of the human element, of the redeeming feature of a human emotion. Maybe a poet could evoke something approaching it, but even sound, even sound would be out of place. There's *no* sound actually. There is no sound. It would have to be a silent poem.[13]

In another conversation (one I have described many times), at the culmination of Leon and I wrestling together over the significance of a particular story of his, Leon exclaimed about his memory of the destruction in general: "It is *not* a story. It has to be *made* a story in order to convey it. And with all the frustration that implies. Because, at best, you compromise. You compromise."[14]

Stories do matter. But they are fragments that always point beyond themselves. They are "compromises," as Leon said, partial and provisional attempts. Often, they reveal the most precisely when they fail: when voice breaks, retelling dissolves or starts to wander. At such times, we see the destruction not *in* survivors' accounts, but indirectly, as an imprint *on* survivors' accounts – that is, as a wound; that is, as a story's mutilation.

The Moral of the Story

So why write of this here? It is certainly not to suggest that we can know nothing. On the contrary, every one of the excerpts cited in these pages from those who survived and one who did not exemplifies what we *can* learn. The lesson is not comforting, but it is genuine.

Having learned it also puts us in a different relationship with survivors – a more mutual, and potentially, collaborative one. Here, too, the issue is topographic. In the usual testimony model, or storytelling model for that matter, survivors are on one side of the table and we are on the other. The Holocaust is somehow "inside" survivors and our job, as interviewers, is to "get it out" – to "elicit the testimony," as almost all the manuals say.

But if the destruction, at core, "does not touch upon another's heart," if it is cosmic not personal, then it is also not "inside anyone." It is not the "survivors' problem," or possession, or legacy, but – if we allow it – the problem, possession, and legacy of all of us. And that, in turn, means that, notwithstanding the critical difference between knowing from experience and knowing only through imagination, survivors and we who speak with survivors are – relative to the destruction – on the *same* side of the table. Interviews become less about our asking questions and survivors providing answers than about us and survivors asking the *same* questions – trying, together, to go as far as we can go.[15]

Knowing this, I think we also value differently the stories, including the life stories, that we do have. They are themselves survivors. And, measured against the "not story" from which they are retrieved, we *should* value them differently. At the least, we should appreciate their fragility; their incompleteness; the continuing possibility that, in the very act of their retelling, they will be consumed again. That fragility and incompleteness are not altered because a story is recorded, archived, or otherwise used (e.g., in artistic or curricular projects). On this level, technology or publication makes no difference. There is no way to freeze such stories, or make use of them, that changes their partial, provisional, uncertain core.

And this leads to the final point, which is simply the other side. We live in an "age of testimony," as is often repeated, and we live no less in an age that celebrates stories and storytelling. And, indeed, celebrating survivors as "storytellers" is part of the rhetoric of witness and testimony and legacy and generation to generation that I cited earlier. Potentially, it is equally distracting. Writing during the Nazi period but before the genocide, Walter Benjamin reminded us that we celebrate stories and storytelling most when history provides fewer and fewer tellable tales.[16]

United States Holocaust Memorial Museum, Washington, DC, April 1993

One last story, not from the Holocaust but from its remembrance. As I began with Agi Rubin, so I return to her; specifically, to her memory of going through the United States Holocaust Memorial Museum in Washington when it first opened in 1993. Agi is herself one of the survivors who is represented in the video *Testimony*, which plays continuously at the end of the museum's permanent exhibit. She and her husband, Zoli, who is also a survivor, were invited to tour the exhibit before it opened to the public. I had the honour of being with both of them, and this is Agi's memory of one moment from that day going through the museum. Over the thirty years I have known her, this was the only time I saw Agi experience what we usually call a "flashback." Agi said:

> It was not the video that brought things back. It was midway through, turning a corner and seeing the railroad car, the "cattle car," that stands in the center of that section. For whatever reason, it was *this* that got to me. This object in the middle of the museum tore through the years, and tore through me, and brought me back …
>
> Everything and everyone else disappeared. I was entirely paralyzed. My knees started to give way. It was as though I could see vividly our little

group – my mother, my aunt, my little brother – in the far right corner of the car, just where we had been. They were still inside, and I could not move. I could not do anything.

At the same time, there appeared to be no way to go to the next section of the exhibit without walking through the car. Later, realizing other survivors had had difficulty here, the museum created another pathway. But, at the time, there seemed to be no choice.

I closed my eyes. I did not want to see them there. I did not want to go through, but I knew that I had to. Zoli and Hank were both with me, and they each took one of my arms and supported me. I kept my eyes closed, and together the three of us ran through the car, with me carried along between them. Once I was on the other side, it was as though it had all been a dream. I was safe. I was with the two of them. I had come back to life, to *this* life, and I had no more difficulties that afternoon in the museum.

Looking back, I am still not certain why it was this that got to me. Indeed, I ask myself why didn't I want to see my family again – those who were everything to me? Why didn't I reach out? …

I think it is simply this: I knew where the car was going. I knew the fate that awaited them. I knew there was no escape, no safety, no exit. As much as I missed them, as much as I still yearn for them, I could not bear to see their terror. I could not bear to see them disappear into nothingness again. I simply could not bear it.[17]

Three Cattle Cars

I end with my own voice and with an image: one which I intend as a small gift for all of us who spend our lives in the midst of horrific retelling. I call it "three cattle cars." And the key is to imagine that we are in these three cars simultaneously. Of course, I can only describe them serially. But the essential thing is to think of ourselves in all three cars at once.

The first is the car that Agi revisited. The one that went over the cliff, irreversibly. No escape, no safety, no exit. We know where it's going because we know where it went.

Those who have been to Yad Vashem, Israel's primary Holocaust memorial and museum, will know that such a car is represented. While walking on the museum grounds, one suddenly turns a corner and sees a railroad track that juts out over a ravine. Halfway across, it stops. And on the track there is a railroad car, heading inexorably towards the abyss.

Along with survivors, that is the first car that we are in.

We are also in a second car which is on a track that leads out and away from the ravine. In other words, this car is on the track that leads to our continuing lives, as it has led to survivors' continuing lives; that is, to their lives *as* survivors. Along with survivors, we are in that car as well.

And finally, and again at precisely the same moment, we are in a third car. This car is perched on the edge of the cliff *now*. And we know where it is headed. We know where other cars just like it have gone. But this car, the third one, is not simply one we remember. This car is moving. This car is present. And it is as though this car, the third car, is interviewing *us*.

And it is asking us ... asking us ... asking us ...

NOTES

1 Agi Rubin and Henry Greenspan, *Reflections: Auschwitz, Memory and a Life Recreated* (St Paul, MN: Paragon House, 2006), 100–3.

2 PBS, *Holocaust: The Survivors Gather* (15 June 1981). The fuller context of such rhetoric is discussed in Henry Greenspan, *On Listening to Holocaust Survivors: Recounting and Life History* (Westport, CT: Praeger, 1998), 29–56, and in the second edition of that book, *On Listening to Holocaust Survivors: Beyond Testimony* (St Paul, MN: Paragon House, 2010), 45–77.

3 PBS, *Holocaust: The Survivors Gather* (17 June 1981).

4 Ibid.

5 PBS, *Holocaust: The Survivors Gather* (18 June 1981).

6 Ruth Kluger, *Still Alive: A Holocaust Girlhood Remembered* (New York: Feminist Press, 2003), 94.

7 All of these issues are most fully elucidated in Greenspan, *On Listening to Holocaust Survivors: Beyond Testimony*.

8 Quoted in Alan Adelson and Robert Lapides, eds., *Lodz Ghetto: Inside a Community under Siege* (New York: Penguin, 1989), 276.

9 Primo Levi, *The Drowned and the Saved* (New York: Vintage, 1989), 85.

10 Jean Amery wrote of irremediable homelessness in a number of the essays in his *At the Mind's Limits: Contemplations by a Survivor of Auschwitz and Its Realities* (Bloomington: Indiana University Press, 1980). See also John Roth, "Returning Home: Reflections on Post-Holocaust Ethics," in John K. Roth, ed., *Ethics after the Holocaust* (St Paul, MN: Paragon House, 1999), 280–95, 324–32.

11 Amery, *At the Mind's Limits*, 70.
12 Quoted in Marco Belpotti and Robert Gordon, eds., *The Voice of Memory: Interviews, 1961–1987* (New York: New Press, 2002), 251.
13 Quoted in Greenspan, *On Listening to Holocaust Survivors: Recounting and Life History*, 17–18.
14 Ibid., xvi–xvii.
15 Such a collaborative approach to interviewing is explicated in Greenspan, *On Listening to Holocaust Survivors: Beyond Testimony*, especially 217–61.
16 Walter Benjamin, "The Storyteller in Artisan Cultures" (1936), in Paul Connerton, ed., *Critical Sociology* (New York: Penguin, 1976), 277–300.
17 Rubin and Greenspan, *Reflections*, 192–4.

2 So Far from Home

LORNE SHIRINIAN

Traditional Armenian tales begin, "Once there was and was not." This not-so-simple sentence encapsulates the legacy of the Armenian genocide and its denial. Once there was, and now there isn't. I learned from an early age that being a diaspora Armenian means having a connection to a Western Armenian culture that developed over two millennia in a historical homeland that, since 1915, no longer exists. I had lost something I never really had. Those of us of the second generation who live with the aftermath of the Armenian genocide and the Shoah understand our loss in a similar manner. Writer Henri Raczymow describes the legacy of the Shoah: "The world that was destroyed was not mine. I never knew it. But I am, so many of us are, the orphans of that world."[1]

I am a second-generation witness to the Armenian genocide. In 1915 my father lost all of his family except his mother. Although she survived, she never saw her son after 1919. On my mother's side, all perished except for my mother and one of her brothers. At the end of the First World War, Near East Relief gathered many of the survivors and put them into camps.[2]

Young orphans like my parents went through a series of orphanages in Turkey and the Middle East. The war for Turkish independence, started in 1919, eventually forced the relief agencies to move the orphans away from further persecution in 1922, out of their homeland forever. In my father's and uncle's cases, they were placed in the safety of the Lord Mayor of London's orphanage in Corfu, Greece.

In 1923, the Canadian government, through pressure from the Armenian Relief Society of Canada and church groups, reluctantly agreed to bring some of the orphan survivors to a farm home that had been set up for them in Georgetown, Ontario, about forty kilometres northwest of Toronto. There they would be trained to become farmers. The Lord Mayor's Fund of London, England, selected 109 boys from the orphanage in Corfu to come to Canada. My uncle was in the first group of 50 who arrived in 1923. My father arrived in the second group of boys in 1924. This core group of orphans became known as the Georgetown Boys. Others arrived later. This humanitarian gesture was considered Canada's "noble experiment" as allowing them to enter Canada went against the prevailing immigration policy. In addition to the boys, 39 girls were brought to the Georgetown orphanage. My mother was one of them. After a short stay at the home, the girls were sent out as mothers' helpers throughout southern Ontario. I am, then, intimately connected to the Georgetown boys and girls, orphan survivors exiled from their homeland, the first generation of the modern Armenian diaspora.

I grew up with their stories. Massacres, survival, and orphans were part of my imaginary life from an early age. In Toronto in the 1940s and 1950s, our home was an unofficial Armenian centre, where people gathered and picnicked.

In the evening, they would sit in the living room and talk. I would sit at the top of the stairs and listen to their stories. When I came down and approached them, they would change the topic, but I could see the tears in their eyes as they were retelling and reliving the horrors they had witnessed thirty-five years earlier. I realized there was something dark in our background that continued to haunt them. I wondered what it was and whether it would also haunt me.

I began writing at an early age, around fourteen or fifteen. I published my first stories and poems in community papers and journals and my first book of poems in 1971. I was driven to understand what had happened to my parents and their generation and how the aftermath of genocide affected my life. I carried this need over to my academic career. In my doctoral thesis, I created a theoretical framework for a critical analysis of Armenian North American literature and have spent all my life since as a creative writer, a professor, and a researcher writing about the consequences of the genocide.

All of this led me to consider what residue of the past has remained accessible and apt to be represented? Why are some memories known while others are forgotten? It became clear that some public memories are subjected to power struggles from both inside and outside communities. But who establishes authorized versions of memories? Why are some silenced?

I want to share with you how I remember genocide as a second-generation witness to this crime against humanity. Some of my writing is motivated by two well-known impulses: to give voice to the silenced and to preserve the victims' names – especially those of my family. By the silenced, I mean not only those who were killed, but also those survivors who did not have the words, the language to even begin to understand what had happened to them. The scope of the genocide was so overwhelming that it robbed them of speech to the point that a degree of mutism remained with many survivors all their lives. What they lived through could not be experienced because language did not provide them with the terms and positions with which to experience them; consequently, they remained traumatized.[3] Pain and grief can be tolerated somewhat if they can be turned into or related as a story. The survivors needed to believe in a world in which their sorrow had meaning. Many found that their religion offered an uncomfortable answer. Both my father's and mother's beliefs moved along a continuum: at times what they experienced was felt to be meaningful, while at other moments they fell to the other extreme, believing it was all devoid of meaning and without purpose – that is, absurd. The difficulty of speaking of the Armenian and other genocides is not found in the awful nature of the events themselves, but rather in the way they are represented in language and in other media.

One thing I learned very quickly as I began writing about the events of the Armenian genocide was that, although I never lived through them, they had greatly shaped my life. Growing up in the diaspora in Toronto as a Canadian Armenian or Armenian Canadian, I wondered what sustained and nourished my Armenian identity here. In those years from 1945 to the mid-1960s, before the arrival of numbers of Armenians from Cyprus and especially from Lebanon in the 1970s, sadly the defining factor of my Armenian identity was the genocide. This was reinforced as the parents of my Canadian school friends still remembered the campaigns to aid the "starving Armenians" and often reminded me of it. I had become an interpreter of my parents' survival and a transmitter of the difficult knowledge they had passed on to me. This is something one does not accept lightly. I know many who have refused to accept the genocide their parents survived as a relevant part of their lives.

As my poetry, fiction, and drama became known and I was asked to give readings, and later as an academic speaking at conferences in

North America and Europe, I came to understand that the cultural re-call that inhabited my writing was something that I was actually per-forming. Memories of trauma need to be narrated and integrated into society and be legitimized in order for the bearers of the trauma to be-gin to break loose of its grip. Traumatic events need to be made narrat-able, and this implies the necessity of an other or others, an audience to listen. Bearing witness to historical trauma solicits acknowledgment. Sharing stories of trauma calls on our basic human and ethical obliga-tion to listen to one another. My hope is that by representing my fa-ther's memories, they can move from the private domain to public memory and finally into history. One should not take this lightly, for Armenians know full well that genocide denial refutes and robs them of their history.

Trauma becomes the unconscious or naive re-enactment of an event that cannot be left behind.[4] My parents found themselves knowing and not knowing; there was the deep need for representation while at the same time there was the great difficulty of representation because of the enormity of the event. Once there was and was not. The unassimilated nature of the terrible events of the Armenian genocide – that is, what was not known – constantly returned to trouble my parents and, later, me. At the same time, the story of the wound, what they witnessed and suffered, what was known, constantly tried to communicate the truth that remained unavailable.

My father's attempt to tell me his story of survival, the traumatic events – those imperfectly understood – only succeeded in communi-cating its very incomprehensibility. "What returns to haunt the victim … is not only the reality of the violent event but also the reality of the way that its violence has not yet been fully known."[5] As Cathy Caruth states so well, the crisis at the core of so many narratives of trauma emerges as a question. "Is the trauma the encounter with death, or the ongoing experience of having survived it?"[6] This helped me understand my fa-ther's silence concerning his survival. All his life he must have moved between a crisis of death and the crisis of life – that is, his survival. He lived with the unbearable nature of the genocide and the story of the unbearable nature of his survival, which he was reluctant to tell be-cause so many of his family perished. He must have asked himself a thousand times why he survived, to which he had no answer. No doubt this induced guilt he bore all his life.

How do we create our own histories in relation to a past that is over-whelmed by extreme events? The Armenian genocide still continues to compel forms of re-enactment by those who did not experience the original events. One wonders what the point is of such reconfigurations of the genocide by second- and third-generation witnesses. Is it simply an endless identification with the victims? It shouldn't be. We cannot allow victimhood to organize and determine the future. We have become part of a community of memory in which we question old assumptions and try to come to a greater understanding of what occurred in 1915 and our relationship to it. In *The Ethics of Memory*, Avishai Margalit imagines a debate between his parents over the consequences of the Shoah. His mother says, "The only honorable role for the Jews that remains is to form communities of memory – to serve as 'soul candles' like the candles that are ritually kindled in memory of the dead." His father responds: "We, the remaining Jews, are people, not candles. It is a horrible prospect for anyone to live just for the sake of retaining the memory of the dead. That is what the Armenians opted to do. And they made a terrible mistake. We should avoid it at all cost. Better to create a community that thinks about the future and reacts to the present, not a community that is governed from mass graves."[7]

This is harsh and sobering criticism; however, unlike the Shoah, the Armenian genocide has never been generally recognized. In fact, all inheritor governments in the land of the perpetrators have denied the genocide despite the mass of official government records, histories, and eyewitness testimonies. Our need to remember is a form of resistance to genocide denial and also is a refusal to be incorporated and engulfed by the genocide. Roger Simon points to forms of remembrance that acknowledge that meaning is mutable over time. Implied is the acceptance of both continuity and discontinuity, not only through repetition and retelling of the story, but also through "the story of the telling of the story."[8] This somewhat self-conscious perspective I have adopted as a writer and filmmaker places the Armenian genocide in relation to the circumstances of how I represent them in the present. It accepts subjectivity and the difficulty of recovering knowledge from the past while using these events to produce new knowledge. I am conscious that what I write in some way substantiates what should be remembered and even how. In writing about the genocide, I realize that I am committing to a version of the past and that by sharing poetry, fiction, drama, and film about it, I am asking readers and viewers to commit to that version.

Part of my project is to turn history which has survived – that is, private history – into public knowledge. To accomplish this, I render my own mediated experiences of memory: that is, memory of the survivors' memories, a vicarious past assimilated through oral and written histories, photographs, films, memoirs, novels, poems, and plays, for example. Marianne Hirsch calls this vicariousness *postmemory*: "the relationship of children of survivors of collective trauma to the experiences of their parents, experiences they 'remember' only as the narratives and images with which they grew up, but that are so powerful, so monumental, as to constitute memories in their own right."[9]

One is not attached to these images through recall or remembrance. This takes place through a process of projection, investment, and creation.[10] To a large extent, I grew up dominated by the narratives of the Armenian genocide, which to a certain extent displaced my own and which ultimately became my own. Hirsch calls this identification with those who witnessed the trauma *retrospective witnessing by adoption*.[11] We can problematize the notion of postmemory because nothing can transform a person's "lived memories into another's."[12] Nevertheless, while I will never know what my parents witnessed and lived through, I, as their son and a second-generation witness, do know those of the first generation. I received and inherited their legacy, and that cannot be discounted.

Those of us who relive the stories of the Armenian genocide vicariously form a community of memory in which remembrance always places its members in an ethical relationship – not only to the past but to all forms of persecution – and motivates us to repair the damage. Remembrance is about the future. The nagging question in all of this is whether the working towards some semblance of healing necessitates forgetting. As an artist I often ask myself this. My most recent play, *Monumental*,[13] explores this very idea. There is no easy answer. Certainly time will force a readjustment of perspectives. Nevertheless, I feel it is imperative to continue to remember the genocide that destroyed half of the Armenian nation in 1915. How this will call future generations into action to reimagine and represent the events remains to be seen.

Three Poems by Lorne Shirinian

I Have No Memories of Ithaka[14]

Father, I imagined you like Ulysses gone those twenty years. But he returned to claim his home and family. You never returned. Orphan child, visible ethnic, moored offshore, quarantined for life, waiting for an onshore breeze, waiting for your ship to come in. You tried to hide the scar.

but I have no memories of Ithaka.
only tales of years of wandering as a child
from the fabled land
Ithaka to Canada————stretches like a scar
holding the departed to a return
the umbilical unfolding like nostalgia
memories of Ithaka.
choices and consequences not fashioned by will
but by circumstance
you taught me survival is the denial of the self
This is our journey from Ithaka
as long and deep as a mortal wound
But I have no memory of Ithaka
I find no solace in your past
rigid like a corpse awaiting resurrection
Forced then to face the future
and transformations
transplanted orphan of Armenia
you attempted to graft your sons
to an alien branch
no more weakness
no more inadequacies
the hope
and having done so
having given in to your hybrid life
you bandaged your bleeding pride
and waited
You are lived wisdom
history and memory
my journey's point of departure
so speak to me
in you the ancient voices of Ithaka
may stir what lies dormant in me
speak to me
so that the scar from Ithaka
to Canada
can join past and future time
But I have no memories of Ithaka
home port of departure
home port of arrival
harbour of desire and homecoming

you said once that a life of only memory
is a wasted life
and you embraced in your way your new land
fought the impulse to freeze time
If we are to worship, you said, let it be a living thing
no walls
no museum halls
your life was an acceptance
and you learned that in the voyage from Ithaka to here
to live here and the distance from Ithaka
you became a stranger to both
Once departed, you knew, Ithaka would never be the same
and neither would we
I have no memories of Ithaka
yet, silently like a slow, lingering desire,
an obsessive longing, and painful yearning
Ithaka beckons us to return

Evolution[15]

(On looking at a photograph taken in Western Armenia
in 1915 and one taken of me in 1997)
look how my skin colour has changed
the light of my flesh is somewhat duller now
but my hair is clean and neat
combed just so
and note the clothes
though last year's cut
still freshly pressed
the whole presents a sense of inattentive style
a portrait of studied carelessness
do you see the book in hand
held with serious intent before the massey library
and you
lost brother from the lost homeland
standing incredulous before the foreigner's lens
having just come from the morning's labour in the fields
you are dressed in soiled cloth
and stand proud before your home
a loose arrangement of earth and stone

but why is your hand raised in the air
do you call to your son only half seen beyond the frame
is it to signal
to warn of their certain arrival
do you point to the cloud of dust rising
like a threat over the western hills
is that fear in your eyes
when i place our pictures side by side
we stare at each other
and though 82 years have passed
since that day you stared apprehensively
at the camera
i understand your wonder
in my eyes i see what you felt that day
for i too look for signals beyond the city walls
i keep one bag packed
and on some dark moonless nights
i leave the car running
the map open
and bury a few gold coins under the flowers
by the front porch

identity papers[16]

first there are the unnamed dead
and their voiceless stories
that vex the restless mind
family history mute
into the new world
lives abridged, discounted and disbelieved
then life in the shadows
an economy of words carefully measured
a thin mask of normalcy worn with inhibited pride
that cannot cover the wound
so many slaughtered
hope murdered
the future driven into exile
there is a map of mythologies
of towns and villages named only in tales
once there was and there was not

haunts us
a curse drove the people from their homes
those who survived were scattered in the world
no one remained to mourn them
i've been here for 63 years
anchored by the dead weight of harsh history
and i'm still waiting for release

NOTES

1 Henri Raczymow, "Memory Shot Through with Holes," trans. Alan Astro, *Yale French Studies* 85 (1994): 103.
2 The inability of the Ottoman Empire to reform and modernize itself led to continued corruption and economic mismanagement. The repeated appeals of the 2 million Armenian citizens of the empire for autonomy and protection from predation and massacre went unanswered. As a way of settling the *Armenian Question*, as it became known, the leaders of the Ottoman Empire put into effect a plan to eliminate the Armenians. Beginning on 24 April 1915, soldiers entered towns and villages throughout the empire and forced Armenians into columns that were force marched towards the eastern desert. Through starvation, disease, and outright slaughter, by 1918, approximately one and a half million Armenians were killed. Many women and children were taken into Turkish households and thus suffered identicide. For more detailed information on the history of the Armenian genocide, see Taner Akcam, *A Shameful Act: The Armenian Genocide and the Question of Turkish Responsibility* (New York: Metropolitan Books, 2006); Raymond Kévorkian, *The Armenian Genocide: A Complete History* (London: I.B. Tauris, 2011); Vahakn Dadrian, *History of the Armenian Genocide* (Oxford: Berghahn, 1995); Lorne Shirinian, "Introduction," *The Georgetown Boys* (Toronto: Zoryan Institute, 2009), xiii–xlvi.
3 Ernst Van Alphen, "Symptoms of Discursivity: Experience, Memory and Trauma," in Mieke Bal, Jonathan Crewe, and Leo Spitzer, eds., *Acts of Memory: Cultural Recall in the Present* (Hanover: University Press of New England, 1999), 27.
4 Cathy Caruth, *Unclaimed Experience: Trauma, Narrative, and History* (Baltimore: Johns Hopkins University Press, 1996), 2.
5 Ibid., 3.
6 Ibid.

7   Avishai Margalit, *The Ethics of Memory* (Cambridge, MA: Harvard University Press, 2002), viii–ix.

8   Roger Simon, "Introduction: Between Hope and Despair – The Pedagogical Encounter of Historical Remembrance," in Roger Simon, Sharon Rosenberg, and Claudia Eppert, eds., *Between Hope and Despair: Pedagogy and the Remembrance of Historical Trauma* (New York: Rowman and Littlefield, 2000), 7.

9   Marianne Hirsch, "Surviving Images: Holocaust Photographs and the Work of Postmemory," in Barbie Zelizer, ed., *Visual Culture and the Holocaust* (New Brunswick, NJ: Rutgers University Press, 2001), 215–46.

10 Marianne Hirsch, "Projected Memory: Holocaust Photographs in Personal and Public Fantasy," in Mieke Bal, Jonathan Crewe, and Leo Spitzer, eds., *Acts of Memory: Cultural Recall in the Present* (Hanover: University Press of New England, 1999), 8.

11 Hirsch, "Surviving Images," 222.

12 Gary Weissman, *Fantasies of Witnessing: Postwar Efforts to Experience the Holocaust* (Ithaca, NY: Cornell University Press, 2004), 17.

13 Lorne Shirinian, *Monumental* (Kingston, ON: Blue Heron Press, 2010).

14 From Lorne Shirinian, "I Have No Memories of Ithaka," *History of Armenia and Other Fiction* (Kingston, ON: Blue Heron Press, 1999), 77–80.

15 From Lorne Shirinian, *Rough Landing* (Kingston, ON: Blue Heron Press, 2000), 59–60.

16 From Lorne Shirinian, "Rendering the Timeline," a work in progress.

PART TWO

Performing Human Rights

3 *Soldiers' Tales Untold*: Trauma, Narrative, and Remembering through Performance

MICHAEL KILBURN

Stravinsky's *The Soldier's Tale* (*L'histoire du soldat*, 1918) is a classic Faustian fable of temptation, loss, and irredeemable knowledge. A contemporary deconstruction of the piece by Boston-based composer Shaw Pong Liu (*Soldiers' Tales Untold*, 2008) uses the narrative and musical architecture of the original as staging to present the unincorporated testimony of combat veterans. Her strategy confronts both the rarefied abstraction of the classical art world and the blithe complacency of a civilian public insulated from the reality of war. It also suggests new formal possibilities for acknowledging, documenting, and processing the psychological and social trauma wrought by war through a collaboration of oral history, the arts, and community outreach.

Based on a Russian folk tale, Stravinsky's *The Soldier's Tale* tells of a soldier returning home from the front who is waylaid by the devil and tricked into surrendering his fiddle in exchange for a book of knowledge. After three days' apprenticeship in the ways of the book, the soldier returns to his home village only to find that his friends and family no longer recognize him. He realizes that instead of three days, three years have passed and the villagers now take him for a ghost. He eventually recovers his fiddle from the devil but has lost the ability to play. He wanders alone, following the classic morphology of the Russian folk tale, until he finally outwits the devil and saves the princess. But the tale does not end happily, as the soldier's desire to see his mother once more leads him to cross a forbidden boundary and costs him all he has regained. As the devil's triumphal march drowns out the soldier's plaintive violin, the narrator intones the moral of the fable:

You must not seek to add
To what you have, what you once had;

You have no right to share
What you are with what you were.
No one can have it all,
That is forbidden.
You must learn to choose between.

When Liu saw the Fellows of the Academy production of *The Soldier's Tale* at Carnegie Hall in 2007, she found the performance aesthetically compelling but disturbingly disconnected from the socio-political reality of the time. With two wars raging, revelations of torture and atrocity, multiple and involuntary "stop-loss" deployments of troops, and an administration and public in patriotic denial of the human costs of its military engagements, the obvious analogies, resonances, and lessons of the piece seemed lost in abstraction. She writes of the 2007 performance:

> The isolation of the concert hall magnified the societal ignorance of the ongoing wars in Iraq and Afghanistan. Nobody on stage or in the audience seemed to think it necessary to acknowledge that there were real soldiers with real stories fighting for our country at that moment, some fighting and dying, some fighting and coming home to an uncertain afterlife. In that moment, the idea of juxtaposing excerpts of Stravinsky's *The Soldier's Tale* with actual veterans' stories came to me as a way to challenge this casual disconnect between the art music world and the world outside. To bring social, political and individual realities into the sanctified concert space and transform both in the process. *Soldiers' Tales Untold* is the genesis of a struggle to be a conscious artist, to make socially relevant work, and to meld the constructive forces of art, education, community and dialogue.[1]

Months of research on the impact of combat stress on veterans and a careful restructuring of the composition culminated in a dramatic revisioning of Stravinsky's classic tale. Liu's *Soldiers' Tales Untold* remixes the original score with atonality and passages of improvised music. C.F. Ramuz's libretto is punctuated with verbatim excerpts of testimony culled from published oral histories of American and Russian veterans of the Second World War, Vietnam, Iraq, and Afghanistan. Building on the extant themes of the fable – the loss of innocence, betrayal, the difficulty of homecoming – Liu makes the analogy to contemporary veterans achingly clear. What began as an aesthetic attempt to deconstruct the abstraction of high art quickly acquired broader sociocultural implications. Her growing understanding of post-traumatic stress disorder (PTSD) and empathy towards veterans – whom she had initially regarded as complicit – was reinforced by her chance encounter and collaboration with several veterans who had auditioned for roles in the performance:

> At that time I still felt like soldiers had some responsibility, like they weren't very innocent in my mind. But it was through then doing the research that my perspective shifted a lot, to feel like a lot of people get funneled into the military – either they're misled or they just don't have other options – and that made them less culpable to me. It made them also victims of something that they weren't prepared for.[2]

It may seem disingenuous in the context of the general suffering wrought by war to focus on the victimization of soldiers, who may themselves be responsible for the suffering of others. But the original narrative context of *The Soldier's Tale* also effectively frames the broader critical consideration of war that Liu seeks, especially given that the average North American is much more likely to encounter a veteran suffering from PTSD than an Iraqi, Afghani, or other civilian victim.

The piece premiered in spring 2008 and has since played in a variety of public venues – schools, colleges, churches, and community centres in Boston and Montreal. The use of public space and the disconcerting structure of the work, including the use of embedded actors in the audience, underscores Liu's intent to disrupt both theatrical and historical narrative conventions in order to provoke engagement and dialogue about war and bring consideration and awareness to the stories that usually remain unspoken and unheard.

Each performance starts conventionally enough: the lights dim and the narrator announces over Stravinsky's jaunty opening theme: "Down a hot and dusty road, tramps a soldier with his load."[3] The soldier sits and tunes his fiddle by a stream. The violin and clarinet trade modernist riffs as the bass line walks and the trombone punctuates. The devil appears, disguised as an old man, and demands the instrument from the soldier, offering a mysterious book in trade. As the two negotiate, following script, the devil promises accommodations of luxury and abundance. Suddenly someone in the audience mutters, "I never saw so much food." A few eyes glance curiously – Is someone distracted? Thinking aloud? Talking to themselves? – but quickly return to the stage. The performance continues uninterrupted and the audience maintains composure and focus as onstage the soldier goes with the devil to tutor him in fiddle playing and learn the ways of the book. Then the voice from the audience mutters again, an afterthought: "Many times before I'd gone to bed hungry." People begin to look around, some shush disapprovingly. As the story unfolds on the stage, more mutters and whispers are heard throughout the audience: "... hungry ... adrenaline's going crazy ... take every fear, every emotion you've ever felt and pack it into five minutes."

Returned to the road by the devil's carriage, the soldier resumes his journey home and the music reasserts itself with the upbeat opening refrain, only this time slightly more self-consciously. The soldier arrives at last in his village, but cannot reintegrate. His friends and neighbours turn away in silence, hurriedly closing doors and windows. His mother screams and runs away at the sight of him. "When I came home, I just couldn't fit in," murmurs a new voice in the crowd. Then the soldier sees his fiancée married with two children and realizes the depth of his betrayal. "The dirty cheat!" he cries, "I know what's happened! I know you! It wasn't three days: three years have passed!" The bass line staggers in syncopation. "They all take me for a ghost ... I'm dead among the living." The trombone moans and clarinet chatters, growls and overtones from the bass, as another voice speaks bitterly from the audience, "The true hell of war doesn't start until you come home."

As the story continues, more and more disruptions are heard from actors in the audience reciting fragments of testimony. The narrator and musicians on stage gradually begin to lose their composure and the musical score breaks down, devolving into incoherence and improvisation, a bitter soundtrack to the mutterings and plaints coming from the audience. Then, one by one, the embedded actors stand and begin to address their comments directly to those on stage and the other audience members. The musicians strike up the theme, trying shrilly to reassert their control of the performance. But the voices insist, speaking now in sentences instead of fragments and beginning to approach the podium. Onstage, the performers gamely endeavour to move the narrative forward as the soldier tries to start life anew, seeking to rescue a princess in another land. Yet the voices still will not be silenced or distracted. Even as the soldier regains his fiddle and revives the princess, they permit no release: "To this day my experiences are with me; I still wake up in the middle of the night." Finally, the embedded veterans take the stage, commandeer the microphones, and speak directly to the audience.

The music plays on and the narrator tries to get the story back on track, but her fairy tale cannot compete with the horror stories of napalm, shrapnel, and a parade of the living dead. "Oh happy day!" she says, "A happy new life begins!" A witness retorts, "That day in My Lai, I was personally responsible for killing about twenty-five people … shooting them, cutting their throats … cutting out their tongues. I did it." The music shudders and collapses under the contradictions of the competing narratives. The narrator slumps in defeat, and one by one the musicians put down their instruments and join in the oral testimony of the veterans. Gradually a cacophony of horrific recall swells from the stage before subsiding into verbal and musical fragmentation. The narrator manages to conduct a few bars of harmony to pronounce the moral: "No one can have it all, that is forbidden," before the structure collapses again. Finally the narrator, musicians, and veterans all drift into the audience, speaking directly to audience members, moving from one to the next like panhandlers of grief: "My parents had no way of sending me to college … I'm unable to work; unable to sleep … patriotism, you know, patriotism … I hear the screams of the people who died … I didn't sign up to have feelings like that." One by one, they fall silent and sit quietly back among the audience until someone decides the piece is finished. The performance is always followed by a discussion, in which audience members can reflect on their experience, ask questions, and sometimes share their own untold tales of personal or family experience of war.

Soldiers' Tales Untold is a challenging piece, not only in its subversion of performative expectations and aesthetic framing, but also in its direct invocation of traumatic stories and inconvenient truths that are usually silenced in public discourse. Improvisational departures from the familiar musical score and interruptions from the audience disorient the audience's expectations and leave them vulnerable to the disturbing content of the real soldiers' tales. The violation of the fourth wall in both directions and the use of embedded actors in the audience challenge the audience's privilege, anonymity, and passivity. The structure implies a rejection of the framing of war as spectacle or pageant perpetuated by our media and politicians and a reminder of the veterans and casualties among us. It is an attempt, as Liu says, to "break the civilian bubble."[4]

While Liu's primary aim is to occasion and provoke community dialogue about the traumatic consequences of war, putting the audience in the uncomfortable position of experiencing narrative breakdown and forcing them to finally hear the soldiers' tales in direct address suggests an even more socially demanding and responsible aesthetic. Liu's formal strategy mimics the disruptive logic of traumatic memory itself, ultimately deconstructing the musical narrative to provide a space for the direct and unprocessed testimony of veterans. This has a jarring, Brechtian *verfremdungseffekt* on the audience. It forces them to recognize the constructedness of the theatrical experience and perhaps also of the historical and political representations of war, to consider the existential plight of veterans in their midst who may have experienced trauma, and maybe even begin to question the social injustice that underwrote their traumatization. And at the same time it forces – or enables – the audience to experience aesthetically, in a small way, the discordant, dissociative symptoms of PTSD themselves. Musical and textual fragments repeat compulsively and without resolution, the social and performative conventions are violated, the narrative dissociates, the devil wins. It demands a new type of listening, which Cathy Caruth suggests is essential for understanding the significance of trauma: "The traumatic reexperiencing of the event thus *carries with it* what Dori Laub calls the 'collapse of witnessing,' the impossibility of knowing what first constituted it. And by carrying that impossibility of knowing out of the empirical event itself, trauma opens us up and challenges us to a new kind of listening, the witnessing, precisely, *of impossibility*."[5]

Contradicting and interrupting the narrative framework of *The Soldier's Tale* demonstrates the limits of language to witness or contain traumatic history. In her classic study *The Body in Pain*, Elaine Scarry describes how torture "unmakes the world" by rendering semantics meaningless.[6] Pain defies rendition in language; violations of human rights and dignity are literally unspeakable. Learning how to speak them is the first step towards recovery and reintegration into the social world. The closest social analogy to torture, says Scarry, is war, which not only obliterates human and physical objects, but deconstructs the very premise of civilization. The social and psychological trauma of war not only affects individuals and communities, but disrupts the social contract and the allegedly self-evident truths that bind the body politic. Like torture on a social scale, it literally "unmakes the world." Despite the ideological meta-narratives and symbologies of nationalism, freedom, justice, homeland, and so forth, the function of war is inescapably to inflict pain and wreak destruction on the enemy, and inevitably, if collaterally, on one's own soldiers and civilians. In certain circumstances – such as the moral ambiguity of the mission, betrayal of command trust, lack of logistical and social support, or broader bankruptcy of ideology – combat can also corrupt the mind, character, and capacity for social reintegration of the combatants, leaving survivors carrying unexploded ordnance within their psyche. This obviously carries a huge social cost as well, from the ongoing expense of physical and behavioural health care for veterans to the collateral damage inflicted by depression, suicide, domestic and workplace violence, and other issues of reintegration.

Where *The Soldier's Tale* suggests, *Soldiers' Tales Untold* makes explicit the narrative breakdown that accompanies the trauma of war. The audience is forced to relinquish their privileged position as passive spectators of a coherent story and confront the impossibility of the protagonist's dilemma; the ineffability of trauma. They are left with only fragments of soldiers' tales: both of the original Stravinsky and of their interventionist neighbours. The salience of this dramatic device is suggested by the authors of *Parallels*, an oral history study of combat PTSD and an important resource in Liu's rewriting of Stravinsky's piece: "The fragment is by far the most basic characteristic of contemporary warfare ... if the reader is to get an authentic understanding of combat, the act of reading should parallel the experience. As the soldiers had to make sense of the fragments, so must the reader."[7]

Despite Chris Hedges's claim that "war is a force that gives us meaning," war is also – and more so – a force that tears meaning asunder.[8] War traumatizes: the inherent violence, depravity, and dehumanization of combat afflicts soldiers and civilians, individuals and societies. For those who suffer combat PTSD, the jagged edges of their unassimilated experience gnaw and scrape at coherence and integrity, undermining the potential for reintegration and challenging society to acknowledge their grief. In its narrative deconstruction, *Soldiers' Tales Untold* lays bare the Faustian bargain of war: the bitter cost of knowledge and irredeemable loss of innocence.

Though PTSD would not be officially categorized as a mental disorder until 1980, the symptoms of combat-related stress were already apparent in Stravinsky's time. Traumatized veterans were said to be suffering from "soldier's heart," "shell-shock," or "battle fatigue." It was apparent, however, that such "war neurosis" was distinct from other pathologies in that it was not the result of any distortion, repression, or unconscious projection but rather the unmitigated and overwhelming *structure of its experience*: "The event is not assimilated or experienced fully at the time, but only belatedly, in its repeated *possession* of the one who experiences it. To be traumatized is precisely to be possessed by an image or event."[9]

The relationship of trauma to narrative, and particularly its resistance to narrativization, has serious implications both for the consideration and treatment of those suffering symptoms of PTSD and for their host societies. Narrative structures our experience of the world and the memories and meaning we create from it. Narrative is essential not only in maintaining individual psychological health, but in fomenting human society. Both socially and psychologically, the stories we tell are, as cognitive linguist George Lakoff says, the "metaphors we live by."[10]

But trauma can interrupt the narrative process by which we make sense of the world and establish our place in it, severing the normal function of mind to integrate memory, knowledge, and emotion in a meaningful synthetic whole. Traumatic memories are not true memories, assimilated into a linear narrative, but are, rather, encoded as fixed vivid images and sensations. These traumatic events and visions remain unprocessed and unintegrated into our life story. This dissociation is made manifest in fragmentary, contradictory, and sometimes violent expressions, with symptoms of hyperarousal, intrusion, anomie, and difficulty reintegrating into civilian society. By replicating these symptoms in the structure of her piece, Liu forces the audience to at least concede a space for the hypertextual fragments of traumatic memory and experience – a margin of error in the master narrative.

The response to *Soldiers' Tales Untold* varies according to audience and context. While younger audiences sometimes giggle uncomfortably, not knowing the protocols of high art or the socio-political context, most adult audiences are moved by the experience to reflect on family members or friends who served in the military and wonder at their untold tales. A response following a performance at a small lounge in Cambridge, Massachusetts, is typical: "I was thinking about my family and I don't even know if they killed a person, and I don't feel like I can ask them to talk about these things."[11] A Second World War veteran at a college presentation noted the emotional power of the performance: "It brings one's emotions up to the point that you almost want to scream in response … He's a human being, just like me. He has a family. He loves … he can find peace."[12]

While the piece has proven effective at opening a space for discussion about issues of war and veterans affairs in civilian communities, veterans themselves are typically more reticent about sharing their own experiences. Even those self-selected by their interest in the arts or involvement in activist groups seem to be wary of commenting publicly on the issues raised. While *Soldiers' Tales Untold* has never been performed exclusively for veterans, the response to a special performance for members of a Boston veterans' shelter illustrates the complexity of raising such questions. During the discussion period, one audience member spoke at great length of a fellow veteran who was homeless and suffered symptoms of PTSD. As Liu later reflected, "Suddenly the room got very uncomfortable because he wasn't giving a comment that we could say 'hmm' and move on from ... There was no answer, there was no solution: it's like somebody's suffering was laid out for us. Usually civilian comments have a sense of roundness about them because you're reflecting on something, but it's not an ongoing personal trauma."[13]

The strategy of incorporating the live testimony of combat veterans succeeds in terms of Liu's initial goals of confronting the abstraction of high art and pricking the civic conscience of the audience, but it clearly also raises dense theoretical, practical, and ethical issues – issues that have left the development of the piece in limbo. Who speaks in this new artistic forum, and for whom? What are the responsibilities of the artist, the audience, and society, particularly when invoking traumatic memories and buried histories? Can the arts help reconstruct the shattered narratives of the victims of trauma and reintegrate them into the community?

While demonstrating the incapacity of the mythic narrative to contain the unprocessed traumatic experience of combat and opening a window for civic dialogue, Liu's is still a tightly structured and self-contained composition. In the end the soldiers' tales remain untold. The uncomfortable silence that ends the play functions as an invitation to dialogue but also highlights the irreconcilable tension between the need and the impossibility of speaking. In her feminist analysis of trauma and recovery, Judith Herman recognized the malignancy of traumatic stress precisely in this dilemma between the will to deny and the will to proclaim, which is manifest within both individuals and societies.[14] Such cognitive dissonance has been described in various contexts throughout history as "double-consciousness" (W.E.B. DuBois), "doublethink" (Orwell), "hysteria" (Freud), or, in clinical parlance, "dissociation."

Reconstructing these shattered narratives, processing and integrating the traumatic experience into a coherent life story, is central to the therapeutic treatment of dissociation. Whether called *exposure, narrative,* or *testimony* therapy, telling and retelling the story of one's trauma is well established in clinical practice, indicating a positive correlation between narrativity and the alleviation of PTSD symptoms. Under the guidance of a trained interlocutor, the repeated verbalization of the traumatic event, especially considering – as in the case of oral history and testimony therapy – the broader context of a life story, gradually reiterates a coherent narrative that can be psychically integrated. The object of the treatment, often in conjunction with psychotropic drugs to dull the horror, is to allow the subject to master the narrative, to make sense of the event and thereby gain some ownership and control over it. Even the diagnostic recognition of PTSD in the 1980 *Diagnostic and Statistical Manual of Mental Disorders (DSM) III* appeared to help to contextualize and legitimate the heretofore inchoate suffering of its victims.

But employing narrative to alleviate individual suffering is only half the story. The *public* forums of storytelling and listening provide crucial elements of acknowledgment, communal mourning, forgiveness, and healing. As Jonathan Shay argues in his classic account of combat PTSD, *Achilles in Vietnam*, "Healing from trauma depends on *communalization* of the trauma – being able safely to tell the story to someone who is listening and who can be trusted to retell it truthfully to others in the community."[15] Retelling stories of trauma is crucial not only to the recovery and social reintegration of the individual victims, but also to social responsibility and restorative justice. Acknowledging the trauma present in the community in its members and its practices can promote healing and solidarity and prevent revictimization.

While Dr Shay's work advocates community responsibility for the care and rehabilitation of veterans, its main insight is the correlation of literary tropes of classic Greek narrative to contextualize the phenomena of combat, repatriation, and its related stresses to a general audience. In both *Achilles in Vietnam* and *Odysseus in America*, Shay locates the disparate, chaotic, and shattered voices of his patients in Homerian literary archetypes. Grounding the dissociative symptoms both historically and aesthetically enables a civilian audience to begin to comprehend the traumatic experience of veterans, and a veteran audience to move beyond alienation and the repression of their return. Shay suggests that considering the psychology of contemporary combat veterans through the lens of Homer's classic texts might yield a greater understanding of PTSD among mental health care workers and also educate the general public about its prevalence and effects. He also suggests that a greater understanding of the combat experience of contemporary veterans might even benefit literary studies of the text itself.

Liu's *Soldiers' Tales Untold* also invokes a classic text to frame the experience of combat veterans and raise consciousness of their dilemma. But she goes further than Shay's descriptive analogy, invoking the testimony of actual veterans to speak back to the orchestral text itself, challenging, infiltrating, and ultimately decentring it. The incorporation of traumatic testimony directly into aesthetic form has the potential to validate the historical experience of veterans and other survivors of war – a recognition often officially denied – while sublimating its post-traumatic effects.

Telling these *Tales Untold* in an aesthetically mediated, public form has great potential for collective narrative reconstruction and reconciliation. If, as Shay, Freud, Žižek, Liu, and others suggest, trauma is embedded in art and culture, then archetypal narratives such as the *Iliad*, Stravinsky's *Soldier's Tale*, or Hitchcock's films might provide a ready-made cultural rubric or framework the afflicted can grasp onto, a focal point around which they may begin to organize and make sense of their own traumatic experience. Recognizing that others have also suffered similar wounds may provide reassurance, solidarity, and cultural legitimacy to those suffering in silence and isolation. In addition, the public nature of performance art provides a forum for the social acknowledgment, respectful attention, and cathartic empathy essential to both private and public memory and healing.

While beyond the scope of her current production, Liu's use of storytelling, archetype, and narrative to frame, contextualize, and ground the trauma and alienation suffered by combat veterans suggests the potential for a more interactive or dialogic art therapy. After all, it is only when the soldier regains the ability to play his fiddle – when he finds his voice – that he is able to overcome the devil, surmount his alienation, and rejoin human society. As traumatic experience can interrupt the normal process of semantic encoding and assimilation of both memory and history, the mindful structured listening of oral history and the reassuring archetypical structures of the arts can rebuild trust and solidarity and induce social recognition and reintegration. Liu herself recognizes the incompleteness of the project and envisions having veterans collaborate more directly in the creative process in its next phase, perhaps shifting it towards a therapeutic rather than a critical diagnostic function. She says, "The piece is incomplete until I have more veterans as collaborators. I'm someone on the outside trying to share what I see from a civilian perspective and an artist's perspective as well. I would like to have more sanction from people who actually know what I'm talking about."[16]

The collaboration and investment of veterans is key to the ongoing development of the production and the realization of its therapeutic potential, but, as Judith Herman has noted, recovery also depends on a social context in which such stories are possible to tell and to be heard.[17] Denial, secrecy, shame, and repression are both psychological and social functions of the aftermath of trauma, both a subconscious reflex and the eighth stage of genocide. This buried conflict can only be overcome by acknowledging, integrating, and communicating the trauma, and this is only possible in the context of a political movement that demands it, be it civil rights, women's liberation, the anti-war movement, truth and reconciliation, or victimology. As Herman says, "Survivors challenge us to reconstruct history, to make meaning of their present symptoms in the light of past events."[18] The central problem confronted in both the structure and function of Liu's production is how such dialogue can take place in the absence, if not criminal negligence, of political will. Without the support of public institutions, what should be the role of the arts and the responsibility of communities to acknowledge and address the needs of their most vulnerable members?

Finally, the therapeutic potential of performative art and other social media in the public recognition and memorialization of trauma also contains a critical and cruel irony. Victims of war, genocide, and other human rights violations – including soldiers – deserve empathy, support, and treatment, but we must not forget the moral of their story. Trauma happens for a reason, usually a political one, and addressing the symptoms of PTSD should not obscure or forgive the root cause of the affliction. As witnesses to what Caruth calls "an impossible history," the victims of trauma also bear a responsibility to carry and convey it:

> It is indeed this truth of the traumatic experience that forms the center of its pathology or symptoms; it is not a pathology, that is, a falsehood or displacement of meaning, but of history itself. If PTSD must be understood as a pathological symptom, then it is not so much a symptom of the unconscious, as it is a symptom of history. The traumatized, we might say, carry an impossible history within them, or they become themselves the symptom of a history that they cannot entirely possess.[19]

This may seem a cruel burden to place on the traumatized, but it is the cost of their true rehabilitation. They are witnesses to impossible histories that must be told. The wars in Vietnam, Iraq, Afghanistan, and elsewhere were and are perpetuated by the efforts of political elites and the complicity of the public in burying their true costs. Human rights violations continue with impunity because of the lack of political will to confront them and the structural contradictions of allegedly global institutions based on state sovereignty and self-interest. Witnesses, victims, and veterans of the atrocities of our "catastrophic age"[20] are ignored, silenced, prescribed into an antidepressant-fuelled half-life, forgotten in refugee camps, or otherwise consigned to irrelevance so that we may be spared an awkward cross-examination.

A society that refuses to acknowledge trauma – particularly the trauma it perpetuates through its own policies of privilege, repression, and ignorance – engenders the perpetual revictimization of survivors by forcing them to carry alone this burden of "impossible history." As Judith Herman said at the 1990 Harvard Trauma Conference, "Every instance of severe traumatic psychological injury is a standing challenge to the rightness of the social order."[21] Accepting the social responsibility of remembering, and of creating consensual meaning, may finally allow the witnesses to be dispossessed of the event; to finally forget. This gets at a central irony of the relation between trauma and memory: We must remember so they may forget. If we do not accept the responsibility of memory and history, if we choose to forget, then they are condemned to live in the ever-present horror of the event.

Shaw Pong Liu's *Soldiers' Tales Untold* demonstrates an ethical artistic response to this dilemma. In using a classical narrative archetype first to frame then to submit to these untold tales, she creates a forum that both respects the humanity of life stories and seeks a critical dialogic engagement with the social and cultural meta-narrative. This should be a model for oral history and the arts: to promote social and political engagement, bearing witness to the traumatic history of our informants and carrying their burden forward. Confronting the traumatic reality of war, shorn of its jingoism and euphemism, might give us pause in starting another. Narrative may provide some comfort and understanding, and the arts a cultural forum and legacy, but the only truly effective treatment for PTSD is prevention.

NOTES

1 Shaw Pong Liu, *Soldiers' Tales Untold: About*, n.d., retrieved from http://www
   .soldierstalesuntold.org/.
2 Shaw Pong Liu, interview with the author, 13 October 2010.
3 Quotes from *Soldiers' Tales Untold* are taken from an audio recording of the
   performance at Endicott College on 28 April 2009.

4 Ibid.
5 C. Caruth, ed., *Trauma: Explorations in Memory* (Baltimore: Johns Hopkins University Press, 1995), 10.
6 E. Scarry, *The Body in Pain: The Making and Unmaking of the World* (Oxford: Oxford University Press, 1987).
7 A.T. Hansen, A.S. Owen, and M.P. Madden, *Parallels: The Soldier's Knowledge and the Oral History of Contemporary Warfare* (New York: Walter de Gruyter, 1992), 10.
8 C. Hedges, *War Is a Force That Gives Us Meaning* (New York: Anchor Press, 2003).
9 Caruth, *Trauma*, 5.
10 G. Lakoff and M. Johnson, *Metaphors We Live By* (Chicago: University of Chicago Press, 1980).
11 Liu, *Soldiers' Tales Untold*.
12 Ibid.
13 Liu, interview.
14 J. Herman, *Trauma and Recovery: The Aftermath of Violence from Domestic Abuse to Political Terror* (New York: Basic Books, 1997), 1–2.
15 J. Shay, *Achilles in Vietnam: Combat Trauma and the Undoing of Character* (New York: Simon and Schuster, 1995), 4.
16 Liu, interview.
17 Herman, *Trauma and Recovery*, 3.
18 Ibid., 3.
19 Caruth, *Trauma*, 5.
20 Ibid., 11.
21 Cited in Shay, *Achilles in Vietnam*, 1.

4 *Lamentations*: A Gestural Theatre in the Realm of Shadows

SANDEEP BHAGWATI

I

We cannot keep our hands, eyes, shoulders, neck still when we tell the story of our life. We move them to underline statements, to visualize spaces and movements, to delineate people and actions – and, in comforting ourselves, to assure ourselves of our own reality.

Many of these movements are specific to our social environment, and our level of understanding the gestures of people around us will often determine whether we feel at home or at sea in any specific social situation.

In many non-Western performing arts (such as Bharata Natyam, Kuttiyattam, No, or the different types of Chinese opera) codified gestures are central to the expressivity and the semantics of a performance. Western theatre has largely turned away from intense use of gestural material sui generis, privileging spoken word, whole-body physicality, set design, music, and other theatrical parameters. Gestures are used mostly to underline these other parameters, not to establish their own layer of meaning.

In attempting to understand displacement, however, gestures are of overwhelming importance. Displaced persons are often slow to adapt to new languages and customs, but gestures, the most immediate expression of belonging and distance in any social situation, are more easily adopted. North American societies, via the model of Hollywood movies, have developed a very restrained set of largely unified and codified everyday gestures – displaced persons must adapt to this very quickly or be socially isolated. This means they soon learn a new set of context-dependent gestural material, in the process amalgamating the gestures from their own culture with the codified North American gestural repertoire.

In the research leading up to the performance of *Lamentations*, we studied dozens of life-story interviews from a major oral history project at Concordia University called Life Stories of Montrealers Displaced by War, Genocide, and Other Human Rights Violations, analysing the multiple ways in which different socially and culturally determined gestures overlap.

Hundreds of such gestures were decontextualized and studied as abstract movements (without sound) by a team of actors and dancers[1] who individually and in small ensembles aimed to first emulate the gestures faithfully, then reconstruct them into new gestures and reinvest these gestures with meaning.

This has generated an intercultural and hybrid repertoire of hand, eye, and shoulder movements which then was used to create an evocative stage performance, recontextualizing this gestural material together with text fragments.

Thus the stage becomes a realm of shadow gestures, where aspects of displaced life stories are embedded into a fabric of expressions that seemingly are common to us all – where the very alienness and incongruity of these gestures will create disturbances, displacements, and drama.

II

The theatre production *Lamentations*[2] has its origin in a simple observation I made about myself when I was very young. I was born in India and come from a large and boisterous Indian family; but my mother is German, and so I was also raised in German ways and customs. I have lived in Europe since I was six, but stayed in India for several months every year – and I could not help noticing that I not only was fluent in several spoken languages, but also had two different sets of body languages.

This, of course, is in no way special – in fact, we know that our body language changes with our social role. And as each of us has many different social roles, we all master different sets of body languages.

Most of the differences are subtle enough, but they serve a main social purpose: to signal the degree of congruity with a given social environment. We would be quite disturbed, for example, by a lover interacting with us with the body language expected at a corporate finance meeting. We tend to homogenize this inner gestural diversity, the essentially chameleonesque nature of our existence, in order to consolidate it into something we then call our "identity." We would so like to forget that identity is one of the most persistent illusions we know.

The discrepancies between my Indian and my German set of body languages, however, were and still are so significant that the very distance between my two "gestural mother tongues" forced me to confront an aspect of my being that others can elegantly gloss over.

III

Rewind to a few years ago: I was just about to write a research-creation grant around the concept of "ephemeral roots" in today's world when Steven High's offer to join the Life Stories of Montrealers Displaced by War, Genocide, and Other Human Rights Violations project led me to ask the question: How would displaced persons experience the gestural repertoire of a strange country and culture? Would they understand it, adapt to it, learn it?

I was interested in the question of "gestural accent." Does such a thing exist? Do people who were raised into one gestural language learn another gestural language with ease and fluency? Do they develop hybrid gestural repertoires? Again, from my entirely non-scientific everyday observations of people on the street, in cafés, and on public transport, I had a hunch that this was indeed the case.

As an artist, I then asked myself what this could mean for theatre. A recent immigrant to North America myself, I see people in the streets of Montreal use a gestural vocabulary that in my previous habitats – in Berlin, Paris, etc. – I had only encountered in mediocre North American TV series and Hollywood films. To my eyes, this particular way of gesturing was something bad actors did, not real people I knew. Suddenly, displaced to Montreal, I saw people gesturing and vocalizing in this Hollywood style everywhere. I saw young couples repeating the empty, actorly love gestures from mushy TV dramas ("hand on the heart" for "I truly mean it," or "finger pulling eye down" for "I do not believe this," etc.) and I could not shake off the feeling that they were all indeed some kind of ham actor troupe, out to mislead and manipulate me (and perhaps each other) with their gestures. There were moments when I felt I had stumbled onto the set of *The Truman Show*.

One of the first things I did after my arrival here was to sit in on auditions for a new collective creation theatre piece[3] that I had been asked to develop with students at Concordia University. In the course of the audition, I asked each auditioning student to tell and gesture a story about identity from their own lives. I expected a lot of oh, ah, hemming and hawing awkwardness. I still remember my utter confusion when almost all the actors not only pattered along quite happily about the most intimate aspects of their lives, but also without fail used the same Hollywood gestures to convey their stories to me – gestures that to me seemed hackneyed beyond belief.

IV

One of the intriguing surprises that led me to *Lamentations* was my initial encounter with the video interviews made by the Life Stories team.[4] Here, my assistant Florian Götz and I found a rich lore of non-standardized gestural languages, some of them hybrid, some of them tightly and consciously controlled.

I remember one interview with someone who had been implicated in a tyrannical regime as a member of the higher administration: he did not move so much as a finger throughout the entire interview. Only when asked point-blank about his personal judgment on the tyrant did he gesture in a solitary, short movement – he scratched the top of his head before answering in a very controlled way.

At the beginning of the interviews we could clearly, and somewhat unsettlingly, discern in the interviewees their knowledge of how to behave and move when on camera. But the further into the past they delved, the more other kinds of gestures emerged – movements would spill out of the TV screen, become things of their own, fearsome and, in many cases, awkward, as if reined in, or terminated abruptly.

V

I wondered how I would address all these insights as a theatre director when I met with the actors I had chosen for this piece. I did not have a plan, a script, or a set trajectory for our process. We had no performance in sight; nothing would force us to settle for things we did not want to do.

But what *did* we want to do? We looked at edited footage that Florian and I had prepared – "moments of truth," as we called them, essentially portraits of the gestural language of each particular interviewee. These "moments of truth" contained truth also in something I had surmised but had not been sure I would see: superpositions of familiar gestures with unfamiliar gestures, sometimes one breaking out of the other, or taking over the other. This, to me, became the essence of displacement: a body, displaced into a new social and cultural environment, does not remain the same body. Its very gestures, its most embodied language, are commandeered by the will to survive, remodelled to conform, fit in, even basically communicate in this strange new social environment.

As a first step we had each of the actors mimic exactly what was happening on the screen. Sometimes, we would make them turn away from the screen and compare their body memory of the gestures with the actual interview, cueing them if they lost the thread – until they were perfectly in sync. At this point it was not yet clear to me whether I would reconstitute a fictitious and hybrid gestural language from all the interviews or do something else. Suddenly, my work as a composer became relevant to this theatrical project.

VI

As a composer of chamber and orchestral music, I have developed a compositional strategy I call "comprovisation" – where composer and performers share authority in creating a performed instance of a new work. This approach to creation rests heavily on something I call "encapsulated traditions." Most musical improvisation is far from being as spontaneous as the word suggests. Indeed, all musical improvisers rely heavily on sets of stylistic criteria, structural rules, and support – and on their embodied memory of musical phrases, inscribed into their body through continuous practice and enriched by repeated performance. Each music improviser relies on a specific tradition of improvisation, often so heavily that musicians from different improvising traditions have the same problem of communication that speakers of different languages have.

In my comprovisations, I invent (compose) the stylistic criteria that make up such traditions. Each piece comprises several of these different encapsulations, for my intent is not to invent yet another tradition of improvisation, but to create a polyphony of improv approaches within the architecture of a larger work. Only when each musician has embodied all the encapsulated traditions of the work do we come together and create the superstructure, the communications between them that allow an orchestral composition to grow out of intertwined individual improvisations.

VII

I am sure you will have made the connection by now: each interviewee could be seen as one encapsulated tradition, one consistent body language that the actors could learn and then improvise upon. I asked each actor to choose one interviewee they felt close to, or comfortable with, or intrigued by. Interestingly, there was no fight – everyone chose a different person. In this process, we obviously had to let go of all the "wonderful material" present in all the other interviews. But art is an exercise in focus, not in comprehensiveness.

Once we had made our decision, the next step for the actors was to go from imitation to analysis and then to synthesis. The fragments we could see onscreen were extremely isolated moments of a person's life, and even of the interview. In some cases there were too few gestures for a gestural repertoire to be fully established. The actors had to use physical extrapolation, observing themselves while imitating the gestures: what kind of muscle sets were being activated, where the gestures went, what was common between them.

This process is akin to martial arts practice or to Asian forms of theatre, where the student learns to copy the exact movement from the master before studying the inherent emotionality. Yet there is a subtle but important difference. In the Asian forms, the movements are whole body movements that are already composed and optimized. In our process, as it developed, we had to find optimal recombinations of the disjointed gestures of sitting people. We never saw their legs. I remember a long rehearsal in which everyone tried to make an educated guess about how each of the interviewees were actually sitting, and then tried to imagine how they would walk.

But limitation always also affords a strength: it forced the actors to empathize and embody the other even more.

VIII

The first test for our work was a performance on 13 June 2009 at a study day of the Life Stories project. In a normal conference room, all four actors sat at and around a table and gestured, largely independently. We had agreed, in the manner of a jazz band, on an intro, four solos, and an outro, but otherwise the actors could do whatever they wanted, provided they faithfully reproduced "their" interviewee.

Two interesting insights emerged from this very sketchy and rough presentation. First, the gestures "worked." The audience, composed

4.1 Research volunteer Reuven Rothman.
Image by matralab.

4.2 Actor Stephanie Merulla. Image by matralab.

4.3 Actor Vicky Tansey. Image by matralab.

mainly of university and community participants in a Life Stories project working session, reacted very strongly to the emotionality and the
transparency of the mute gesture. One response likened the performance to the muteness that for many survivors and onlookers is the
only possible reaction to unspeakable horror: Where words fail gestures
still will speak. Second, I started to notice unexpected connections and
an emerging dialogue between these seemingly unrelated gestural languages. I should have been prepared for this to happen – musical com-
posers since John Cage have vividly and in great variety explored our
minds' ability to reconstruct meaning and dialogue, cohesiveness, and
intention out of structurally and contextually disparate material. What I
began to see was the possibility of a true polyphony of gestural streams,
a mutually reinforcing interplay of diverse gestural languages.

IX

At this point, the question of text began to re-enter the stage. After all,
the interviewees had been talking about something important to them
while they were gesturing. What should we do with these often very
emotional statements? Up to now I had decidedly disregarded them:

We had edited the "gestural moments of truth" from the interview videos without any regard to content, sometimes even cutting in midword. I then had asked the actors, while imitating the video clips, to turn off the sound so as to better concentrate on the movement. I thus clearly did not want to make any artistic use of the very testimonies that had been the raison d'être for the interviews in the first place. But why?

My palpable aversion to testimonials again stems from my experience of displacement in North America – and the audition experience with students I mentioned previously. The fact that young people can prattle on easily about matters of personal intimacy while being prudish with their bodies is strange for a European. There, bodies can be bared in public without any problem, but people do not easily bare their souls to strangers. In North America, however, I encountered what I privately label "Oprah porn": a pervasive and obligatory promiscuousness about the most intimate of emotional experiences that to me seems as unhealthy as the excessive bodily prudishness exemplified by the hullabaloo around Janet Jackson's "nipple-gate."

In his book *The Fall of Public Man*, Richard Sennett writes: "The term 'gemeinschaft' means, originally, the full disclosure of feeling to others ... a special social group in which open emotional relations are possible ... converting the immediate experience of sharing with others into a social principle."[5] As anyone who looks at texts critically will know, testimonials made under such social duress to confess are most likely fabrications or "snow jobs," intended to mislead the probing questioner and protect the speaker. They need not be consciously fabricated; indeed, they are most convincing if the speaker is convinced of their truth. They subvert the desire to be known into the desire to be acceptable.

As a theatre artist, my squabble with most of the "confessional" theatre striving to faithfully do justice to the real experience of victims of political and social breakdowns or oppression is that such an approach irresponsibly panders to a widespread fallacy: namely, that somehow an "emotional truth" makes a social and political point more valid and pertinent. When we believe in the superior social veracity of "authentic" feelings of "real" people (because we want to "engage the audience"), we all too often disenfranchise intellectual analysis, political awareness.

Especially in North American media, the private has become political to the point of distraction. On CBC's *The National*, supposedly an independent and fair public news broadcast, incidental homicides routinely receive more coverage than wide-sweeping changes in any area of government policy. It seems easier to talk about politicians' love lives than about their economic acumen, easier to worry about whether a penis entered a forbidden vagina than worry about the war in Afghanistan. Such a strong media bias reinforces political ignorance and thus creates an anti-democratic smokescreen for political machinations. Sadly, the aesthetic obsession with "human interest stories" thus becomes an accomplice in this ongoing effort to eclipse both the faceless agendas and vested interests and the cultural and sociological contexts that fundamentally fashion and sway our lives. Sennett writes:

> The refusal to deal with, absorb and exploit reality outside the parochial scale is … a universal human desire … Community feeling formed by the sharing of impulses [reinforces] the fear of the unknown, converting claustrophobia into an ethical principle … Unfortunately, large scale forces in society may psychologically be kept at a distance, but do not therefore go away.[6]

Scientists make simplified models to understand complex issues; artists use fictions for the same purpose – to make a complicated situation as clear as possible by eliminating the noise around it. The political theatre I am interested in makes a social quagmire emotionally and intellectually tractable – by fictionalizing it, by making it inauthentic, if you will. Adorno's phrase for this is *"zur Kenntlichkeit entstellen"*[7]: that is, to distort something until its hidden nature is revealed.

In other words, my discomfort with using the interview texts in this artistic production was that this would be an obscurantist approach to their reality – a cuddly and over-emotional de-emphasizing of the brute realities they had lived through.

X

But if not these texts, then which? None – and let the gestures speak for themselves? We discussed this option in the team, but felt that this much reticence would cloud the issues that interested us as much as too much extrovert "authenticity" would. The ultimate solution for this dilemma were two classical texts of Western civilization: "Flow My Tears," a song by Elizabethan composer John Dowland, and the biblical Lamentations of Jeremiah.[8] Both texts transform personal woes into stark and intransigent laments. And their classical nature would counter the "bias towards the living" inherent in working on interview testimonials. For listening to a collection of raw oral reports can easily evoke empathy, but it can also blind us to the fact that what has happened so recently is neither new nor unexpected. The Babylonian displacement of the Jewish nation portrayed in the Lamentations of Jeremiah, the repeated forced resettlements of millions throughout Chinese history, the ignominious displacement of Aboriginal North American populations, the displacement of the Acadians, the Black Atlantic slave trade etc. – in each of these, and in countless other maelstroms, human rights were crushed in the most abject manner. No people is immune to this seemingly inevitable and sinister shadow of civilization, as either victim or perpetrator. It is what humans do – because they are social animals. Any work of art about displacement and its horrors must thus make us aware of this realm of shadows that governs our world.

XI

This last thought underlines a final concern that surfaced in the course of the theatrical implementation of our gestural research. Again it was a problem with testimonies. People who go to see critical plays about sensitive issues tend to be empathic listeners. And people who tell their story of suffering tend to portray themselves as victims. I will never forget attending a concert in Salzburg in 1985 at which I inadvertently eavesdropped on a conversation in the aisle behind me. Two people who evidently had not met since the Second World War were telling each other their stories of escape and exile, how they had barely evaded their captors by crossing ice-cold rivers barefoot and hiding in the mountains. With shaky old voices they lamented their sorry fate and how their suffering had so long been ignored by the world at large. Only after some time had passed did a revealing exchange between them make me realize that they must have been officers in the Nazi SS. And by not speaking up after this realization, I became a condoning bystander to their crimes.

XII

Raul Hilberg's analysis of the perpetrator-victim-bystander triangle in his eponymous book[9] clearly shows that these three roles are far from being unequivocal, especially if a conflict drags on. It would be wrong to indicate which actor represented a legitimate victim and which actor could be cast as a perpetrator throughout. In *Lamentations*, identification

4.4 Scene from Sandeep Bhagwati's gestural theatre *Lamentations* (Callahan Connor, Bryan James, Vicky Tansey, Stephanie Merulla).

with the actors is always a risky thing, because the persona who has just suffered so intensely may well perpetrate quite horrible things in the next second. Also, in our full staging of this work, the spectators, usually comfortably ensconced in an observer's position, must stand in the same space used by the actors. Only centimetres separate them from the cruelty; they could stop it – and, of course, do not. And throughout the play, spectators are displaced and can never be sure whether or not the floor they stand on will suddenly become the stage of conflict. One spectator described his emotions to me after the first full theatrical performance of *Lamentations* on 8 November 2010[10] in the Hexagram Black Box at Concordia University:

> I felt lost and disoriented, forced to take in the collective state of the audience as a whole. I observed the different tactics people administered when unsure as to how to navigate or conduct themselves. Some chose to move to the perimeter of the room, hiding against the walls, or in shadows. Others chose to unify with other audience members, joining in more collective participatory positioning, where awareness was heightened and safety in numbers could be embraced. With this said, the way the piece was staged was staggering and ominous. I felt very vulnerable.[11]

Welcome to the realm of shadows, where an actor's mute gestures invoke the suffering of absent people, where the audience wants to avoid looking too closely for fear of becoming implicated, where all the words we hear are those of the dead, spoken by the living. And where the close observation of one person's gestures reveals how complex the inner oscillation must be between the strong desire to embrace the bland but safe banality of life in the aftermath and acknowledge the very real presence of the horrors we have all perpetrated, and seen, and survived.

NOTES

1 Florian Goetz (assistant director), Vicky Tansey (dancer), Stephanie Merulla (actress), Bryan James (actor), and Callahan Connor (actor).
2 *Lamentations* was part II of a long-term research-creation project (funded 2008–11 by the Fonds Québécois de Recherche en Société et Culture, as well as, in 2006–8, by the Sammlung Essl Foundation [Austria] and, since 2011, by my Canada Research Chair funds and the Montreal Life Stories Project) called *Racines Ephémères*, which looks at various sensory effects of displacement and migration (primarily gestural language, speech and music accent, as well as the effects of simultaneity and congruence in spatially and/or emotionally separated settings) through the creation of several interdisciplinary works of art. Part I is an installative concert work for eight musicians moving and gesturing through a huge space (first performed in Vienna as part of the Wien Modern Festival 2008). Part III will be a video installation combining music from part I and gestural videos from part II in a digitally interactive setting that will track audience reaction for a continual recreation of visual space and sonic environment (a preliminary maquette of this work was installed at the Bibliothèque Nationale de Québec in Montreal from 6 March to 2 April 2012). *Lamentations* was performed twice in November 2009, for different audiences: once for the participants of the conference that gave rise to this book, and once for the local professional theatre community, invited through a mailing list and Facebook. Both performances were presented as research-demos – free entry but without general publicity.
3 These auditions were not those for *Lamentations* but for another piece called *PerSonAlia* (2006–7), which looked at the intricacies of identity in modern societies. *PerSonAlia* was a two-term creative undergraduate

performance project straddling the Theatre and Music departments at Concordia University.

4 The Montreal Life Stories project conducted 450 interviews with survivors of mass violence. These interviews can be consulted at the Centre for Oral History and Digital Storytelling. About a third of the interviews, in which interviewees agreed to full public access, have been integrated into a searchable database using Stories Matter software (developed in-house).

5 Richard Sennett, *The Fall of Public Man* (New York: Knopff, 1977), 310–11.

6 Ibid.

7 A phrase from Adorno's *Aesthetic Theory* that has become a stand-alone idiom in German aesthetic discourse. Theodor W. Adorno, *Ästhetische Theorie*, ed. Gretel Adorno and Rolf Tiedemann (Frankfurt am Main: Suhrkamp Verlag, 1970).

8 These were used in a slightly modified form: I extracted key sentences from the Lamentations of Jeremiah and translated them anew from Latin into colloquial, contemporary North American English. The texts were used very sparsely, and often incongruously – spoken in the stage action often without any dramatic referent, as a further layer of meaning, as a semantic prop. The Dowland song was sung by the actors using the original text.

9 Raul Hilberg, *Perpetrators, Victims, Bystanders: The Jewish Catastrophe, 1933–1945* (New York: Harper Collins, 1992).

10 An unpublished, complete DVD documentation of this performance can be obtained on request from matralab@gmail.com. A short highlights reel and a few photos can be accessed at http://matralab.hexagram.ca/projects/?title=RacinesEphémères-Lamentations.

11 Ryan Hurl, email correspondence with the author, 9 November 2010.

5 Turning Together: Playback Theatre, Oral History, Trauma, and Arts-Based Research in the Montreal Life Stories Project

NISHA SAJNANI, WARREN LINDS, ALAN WONG, LISA
NDEJURU, AND MEMBERS OF THE LIVING HISTORIES
ENSEMBLE/ENSEMBLE D'HISTOIRES VIVANTES

Date: 29 May 2010, 10:45 a.m.
*Setting: 2010 Congress of the Social Sciences and Humanities of Canada,
Montreal, Quebec. The conductor, Nisha Sajnani, is standing and addresses
an audience of sixteen theatre artist-scholar-practitioners, educators, students,
and community organizers. Eight actors sit on chairs placed at the front of a
black box theatre space. They include Joliane Allaire, Warren Linds, Lucy Lu,
Laura Mora, Lisa Ndejuru, Mira Rozenberg, Deb Simon, and Alan Wong.
There are two chairs stage right, one for the conductor and an empty chair
for storytellers from the audience. On stage left is Paul Gareau, the musician,
behind a table laden with instruments.*

Nisha: This is a transcript of one performance interspersed with current reflections. We will be sharing with you the story of the Living Histories Ensemble (LHE)[1] and, in particular, the ways in which we have been thinking about our work as a form of arts-based research through performative inquiry. We have chosen this format because it reflects the performative nature of our praxis, and because we feel that the best way to bring the reader into our process is not to describe it, but to engage the audience within it. Sharing our learnings in the form of a script also reflects the conversational, collaborative ethic and aesthetic that have been an important part of our approach to performing oral histories.
Alan: Over the past three years, the LHE has been working within a multi-disciplinary community-based research initiative titled Life Stories of Montrealers Displaced by War, Genocide, and Other Human Rights Violations. This project has brought together seven working groups in an effort to record and archive 500 interviews with "survivors"[2] of mass atrocity. The oral history and performance working group has been exploring the project's goals of fostering collaboration and

partnership between diverse communities, "developing interdisciplinary pedagogical tools, and making a significant, original contribution to the preservation of historical memory in Canada by raising questions about the long-term repercussions of crimes against humanity."[3]

Warren: This has meant that our work has become a meditation on the relationship between the archive, which is the material that endures, and the repertoire, which "enacts embodied memory: performances, gestures, orality, movement, dance, singing – in short, all those acts usually thought of as ephemeral, non-reproducible knowledge."[4] We have examined how best to convey experiences of displacement through photography, mixed media installations, theatre performances, classroom teaching, online education, filmmaking, and radio documentaries. The LHE was originally conceived both as a form of embodied inquiry into the experiences of the interviewers associated with the project who were conducting the life story interviews, and as a performative approach to collective storytelling within and among communities that share a history of displacement.

Lisa: In the beginning, we wanted to develop a performance based methodology that could advance the project's goals. However, as the project progressed, many among our various working groups began to ask the question "Why?" – Why dig up stories if only to expose corpses? What purpose does it serve for those involved other than, as the description of the project states, "coming to an understanding of what these experiences mean to '*them*' and to help 'us' better understand the impact of violence and displacement"?

Warren: These questions were troubling to us. If the larger goal of the project was to raise questions about crimes against humanity, then were we trying to work towards recording a more complete picture of Canadian history, or did the project imply some other effort, such as to remember the repercussions of violence as a strategy to prevent such a history from repeating itself? Was the project a way of working towards an integration of lived experience in Montreal so that those who had experienced mass violence might more easily coexist with and among those who did not share such histories of betrayal, pain, and loss?

Alan: Initial articulations of the Life Stories project grappled with avoiding a facile and removed inquiry into the experience of collective trauma, wherein those labelled as "survivors" would do the telling and an unaffected and neutral "other" would do the listening for the purpose of privileging a record: the archive. Efforts at interrupting this dichotomy between the listener and the teller in the life story interview involved framing the encounter as an experience of what Michael

Frisch terms "a shared authority."[5] By this Frisch is referring "to what should be not only a distribution of knowledge from those who have it to those who do not, but a more profound sharing of knowledges, an implicit and sometimes explicit dialogue from very different vantages about the shape, meaning, and implications of history."[6] Consequently, researchers in the project began to make a conscious attempt to develop their approach to the interview and storytelling process as one involving an exchange of information – a conversation that would allow the teller and listener to become interlocutors working together to articulate and make sense of the historical narrative being offered. As such, "sharing authority" could be viewed as "sharing stories."

Nisha: We decided to draw on a form of interactive theatre that has its roots in oral history called Playback Theatre that I will describe in more detail a little further on. However, to invite you to "visualize" this form and to begin to consider it as an approach to inquiry, I will ask you think about your associations to and experiences of "shared authority." (Turning to the actors) Have any of you ever had a moment of sharing authority that you could tell us briefly about?

Lucy: I belonged to a project called Herstories, the participants of which attempted to work in a non-hierarchical way. It was a struggle, and it took us some time to find a way to meet each other in a collective way where we could share leadership. It was as if we were so used to working within a hierarchy that … well, it took a lot of time.

Nisha: Lucy's experience of sharing authority as a fluid sculpture. Let's watch!

The LHE represents Lucy's experience through an embodied collage of sound and movement relating to their interpretation of the words and feelings she used to describe her experience. This is called a "fluid sculpture."[7] Two actors step forward and mime pulling at opposite ends of an invisible thread, another actor reaches over this imaginary thread and makes an encouraging "come here" motion with her hands, while another actor squats centre stage, back to the audience, and attempts to reach out to hold her hands.

Nisha: (to the audience) Do others here have an experience of shared authority – where it worked, where it failed, or where it was attempted?

Audience member (theatre educator): I was working with a group of youth and was trying to empower them to take on leadership and to … share authority. So, I left the room while they were creating in the hope that they would not be influenced by my decisions. When I re-entered

the room later, they told me that they had wished I hadn't left the room … that they wanted the leadership … they wanted me there.
Nisha: (to the actors) As a fluid sculpture. Let's watch!

The LHE does another fluid sculpture. One actor steps forward and looks out into the audience, repeating, "What should we do, I don't know what to do, will this affect my grade?" Another crouches behind the first and appears distressed, slowly letting a sob emerge and amplifying it over the duration of the sculpture. Another steps out to stage left and observes the action with a crumpled forehead and a "wondering" look.

Nisha: (to audience member who shared experience) Did you see your experience reflected in what was played back? Is there anything else you would like to say about your experience of shared authority?
Audience member (laughing): It made me think about how shared authority does not always mean no hierarchy.
Nisha: (to the audience at large) Does anyone else have an experience of shared authority?
Audience member (graduate student): I feel like when I am asking my group for stories … when I am doing my research … that I am trying to make it shared, but it always feels like some sort of … gentle manipulation … like I am leading them and not like it is really shared.
Nisha: Let's watch!

The LHE does another fluid sculpture. This time, one actor leads an invisible being around the stage space by a leash. Another repeats, "This story will make my career!" Another appears to be pulling and collecting an unseen substance from the chest of another actor sitting on the floor. Another is squatting stage left and looking disgruntled. Another looks pleased.

Nisha: (to the audience member who shared experience) Is there anything else you would like to say about your experience of shared authority?
Audience member: 'That's it! Especially the look on her (pointing to one actor) face!
Nisha: Thank you for sharing your stories. So this is Playback Theatre. The conductor and teller are involved in a conversation, and this conversation is moved into an immediate, ephemeral repertoire. The teller, conductor, actors, and audience members are interlocuters working together to draw closer to the notion of "shared authority" and to create a shared meaning. How many of you have seen Playback Theatre before?

Three audience members put up their hands.

For those who have not seen it, it is a form of improvisational theatre developed by Jonathan Fox and his theatre company in 1974, wherein the experiences of audience members are played back through a variety of short and long dramatic forms. The roles associated with it include: a group of actors who may be drawn from a particular community or recruited for a particular purpose or theme and who are (more often than not) not formally trained in the art of acting; a musician; and an intermediary figure, common to much participatory theatre, who stands between the audience and the stage. In Playback Theatre, this figure is known as the Conductor. Of course, Playback Theatre could not take place without you (gesturing at audience), the storytellers and story listeners.

The utopian impulse of Playback Theatre lies in Fox's romantic attempt to counter isolation and oppression by providing a space where any story can be told and artistically represented towards generating insight and perspective on the human condition.[8] He writes about it as an "act of service" and as "artful citizenship," wherein different experiences can be shared and witnessed. As a form of community theatre, it has attracted several thousand practitioners working in over 200 Playback Theatre companies worldwide. It has also attracted critique. We are going to share things that we have heard – or experienced ourselves – about Playback as a form of cultural activism. We will do this as a Rhapsody, which is the name of a form that we have developed to convey intense feelings or ideas.

All of the actors take one step forward and turn their backs to the audience, and each one, in a clockwise rotational motion and in random order, turns towards the audience and delivers a reflection on the theme (in this case a critique of Playback) with a pressured urgency in their voices. When another actor turns, he or she effectively interrupts the other actor who was speaking, who once cut off immediately turns around to face the wall again. These rotating reflections continue until each actor has spoken at least twice. They freeze in an image of their emotion on their second turn, which brings the form to an end.

The Rhapsody: *It is way too literal! / Feelings? Talk about feelings!? What is this? Therapy?! / You want me to give you my story and you are going to do what? You are choosing what? Where are you going with that? / That was just ··· sloppy ... amateurish. You're not artists!/Just nod and agree ... you liked what you saw ... just nod and agree ... / What do you people really feel? You* *actors are not telling me anything about yourselves. You're not neutral!/Any story? I can tell any story? Well, what about how much I hate THOSE people – you know, THOSE people! Play that back!/Where is the analysis?/You're not anything like me. What makes you think you can play my story?*

Nisha: As you heard, Playback Theatre has drawn critique for its at times overly literal representation of lived experience, its unrefined aesthetic, and, most seriously, its potential recapitulation of hegemonic relations of power. The risk here is that complex human experiences become reduced, shaped, and enshrined in sacredness by a seemingly benign authority (the Conductor or Interviewer), then represented through means not of the teller's choosing by actors whose values remain hidden, and then delivered to a public who may feel some pressure to consent to the action and its signification. Also, the strong textured affectual terrain a theatre like this can create for the audience is not always comfortable and can result in an overly serious performance, especially when attending to themes such as genocide and mass atrocity. Others critique Playback for being too cathartic, in that it threatens to purge the audience's rightful indignation about injustice by focusing too much on general humanitarian values and by privileging the place of emotion in this work.

These are all challenges for us, so we ask: What can we come to know about the experience of displacement or about listening to experiences of displacement – or even about shared authority, for that matter – through this embodied inquiry? What does this form of art offer in the way of praxis and generative research?

Lisa: Shaun McNiff defines art-based research as the "systematic use of the artistic process … as a primary way of understanding and examining experience by both the researchers and the people they involve in their studies."[9] Lynn Fels, in her discussion of performative inquiry, suggests that such an investigative method seeks an interplaying of identification and interpretation through performance that involves risk and collaborative creativity that performs itself in "spiralling circles of realization and recognition."[10]

Alan: Our own "spiraling circles of realization and recognition" begin in workshop-style rehearsals that, rather than being a prelude to performance, are part of our research process.

Warren: For a few of us, the process of our work conjured up images of an encounter on a bridge – like the bridge that Peggy Phelan describes when referring to the necessity to accept that we will never understand that which is different from ourselves; but we need to see this inevitability as generative: "It is in the attempt to walk (and live) on the rackety bridge between self and other – and not the attempt to arrive at one side or the other – that we discover real hope."[11]

Nisha: While we do not normally stage our rehearsals as part of a typical Playback Theatre performance, we would like to share aspects of our rehearsal with you as a way of making our process of walking this bridge transparent – actively demonstrating this for you in the moment through what Ingrid Mündel calls "performing process" – to bring you closer to our experience of how we have approached our own relationship to "displacement" as a collective.[12]

Moving onto the Rackety Bridge:
The Rehearsal Process as Performative Inquiry

Nisha: During the research creation process, which has involved the ensemble probing the project's themes, we drew on various other forms of improvisational theatre, including the improvisational techniques of Viola Spolin[13] and David Read Johnson's *Developmental Transformations*, a form of applied theatre defined as "the continuous transformation of embodied encounters in a playspace."[14] Developmental transformations has been theorized in relation to, among other sources, the practice of improvisation developed by Viola Spolin; Jerzy Grotowski's concept of the "via negativa," wherein the art of acting is reliant on the elimination of the internal blocks between impulse and action; and Gilles Deleuze and Felix Guattari's ideas on the relationship between being, becoming, and control.

During the rehearsal, we come together in an unstructured gathering, greeting one another. We find our way into the circle and begin to stretch. *The troupe performs the ritual of stretching and freezes.* This would lead us into a form of unison sound and movement, which not only brings us towards a sense of cohesion, but also into an encounter with one another, all the while developing our capacities to notice differences in each other's gestural universe.

The troupe performs this sound and movement exercise and freezes. This exercise gives way to an exercise reminiscent of Spolin's "Join the Scene" and Johnson's "transformations," whereby one person begins a sound and movement or repeated defined action and enters the circle. He or she is joined by someone else in the circle, mirroring each other, allowing their expressions to become amplified, exaggerated, defined, diminished, differentiated, and transformed in an unpredictable pattern until someone else from the circle "taps out" someone in the middle and replaces him or her, spontaneously transforming the scene and repeating the emergent enactment. This process repeats until everyone has been in the centre at least once. LHE refers to this process as "bodys-torming," a kind of embodied, relational free association wherein emphasis is placed on spontaneity, risk, and our capacities to remain present with one another while attending to what is emerging in the "play." We warm up in accordance with the chosen inquiry – in this case, the experience of displacement – through our methods of thematic bodystorming. *The troupe demonstrates this exercise through three pairs coming into an encounter with each other.*

At some point in our rehearsal, this play gives rise to a formal invitation to shape one's personal experience as a narrative. Consequently, we resume our structured circle and, using a Playback Theatre form called "fluid sculpture," reflect on our experience in the "here and now."

The troupe demonstrates fluid sculptures for each member's story relating to the theme.

Emerging Learnings

The LHE performs its own learnings through a method we refer to as "Fire-works": one at a time each actor steps forward to a chosen spot on the stage and shares a brief poetic reflection about his or her learning, then freezes in a sculp-ture that, for that actor, reflects what he or she has just said. This repeats until all actors have spoken their thoughts and taken a position on the stage. The resulting image represents an embodied reflection of our collective learning.

Nisha: Our ensemble has become, in a way, a microcosm of the Life Stories project itself, in that we have come together with our different and distinct histories and coexist in the same place. In fact, as a team we exist in a Playback Theatre diaspora, having all worked with different companies in Montreal, with some after a time moving to different parts of Canada and the United States. Yet we continue to come back to this place together to meet, to bodystorm, to perform. Over the past three years, several learnings have emerged from our performative inquiry about our experience of displacement and our methodology.

Going Deeper

Lisa: Our process has been very much like tilling soil, digging up our individual and collective memories that call up moments, fragments of association and experience that we have attempted to come close to while remaining in relationship with one another. Over time, we have noticed that our initial expressions have remained very much at the surface level, such expressions consisting of repetitions of everyday predictable stereotypes. Our continuous play appears to have progressed from this surface play to increasingly profound and complex levels of engagement with the Other, allowing us to develop a greater sense of permeability, intimacy, risk, and proximity.[15] In the same way, we have noticed that repeated performances with the same group invites people to take more risks and to tell more nuanced stories.

Interrupted Stories

Warren: We have noticed that our experiences do not fold neatly into stories. This is especially true of the experiences we have shared with one another involving some form of loss or trauma. Trauma creates gaps in the stories that we attempt to organize and tell about ourselves.[16] The moments of our lives in which we have been overwhelmed by having to accommodate a forced intrusion or reality have revealed themselves more often as slippages, stutters, and spurts – a palpable yearning for coherence.[17] The combination of disparate, but coexisting, impulses has lent itself more easily to shorter forms in Playback Theatre where the actors have the freedom to reflect back.

Silence Does Not Mean Absence

Alan: While there is a certain imperative to tell, speak, and share experiences in Playback Theatre, we have found that the silences in the liminal spaces – those between words, sounds, and gesture – reveal much more than they conceal. Similarly, the urge to tell, the looks and gestures shared between audience members, the shifting in one's seat during Playback Theatre performance – these are just as important as the stories that are told. They reveal a different, yet equally valuable, kind of presence. It has become important to acknowledge and reflect both the seeming absences, hauntings, and traces of the unsaid as well as of what is said.

The Open Container

Nisha: One of the tensions in our work has been that which emerges between creating a space of safety and enabling risk to be taken. When an audience member tells a story in Playback Theatre, they permit it to move from the private to the public – from the individual to the collective imaginary – and this involves some risk.[18] We think about the performance space as a container that enables both actors and audience members to take these risks. Within it, they can tell stories of their lives in an atmosphere of relative mutuality.

Warren: The word for container comes from the Greek *tenemos*, "meaning a sacred space and time specially prepared and set apart in order to reconnect with ancient energies."[19] The ensemble, in its performance, creates such a container. It cannot be opened too wide or else it would hold, transmit, and allow nothing, thereby destroying the structure – so there would then be no connection between storytellers and listeners. Such a space would not allow the storytellers to risk releasing and revealing, through their stories, "what they know and what they are trying to discover."[20] But if the space is "too small or nonexistent, there is no room for the Other, no space across which the familiar and strange can exist upon each other"[21] – the ability to breathe, grow, and be inhabited is lost. Such a container must hold people within the tension that exists in both the pull of connection and the pushing back of difference between individuals.

Lisa: Martin Ringer links this aspect of connection to the need for adequate containment in groups within which participants have a "sense of being firmly held in the group and its task, yet not immobilized by the experience."[22] Julie Salverson points out that this firmness with flexibility means there must be a space or gap within the container: "This form is moulded as we work together holding the circle of knowing open and inviting a current that prevents steering a straight line through the story or arriving at a predetermined destination."[23] What we strive for are openings and not closings in every embodied reflection offered. No image or story is contained or closed fully; it is left hanging in the air, with no happy ending or easy solution, as a contribution to the collective imaginary.

Taking Risks/Risking Failure

Nisha: Over time, we have found that bodystorming has become a way for our ensemble to remain on the rackety bridge, to "tolerate the instability of being"[24] that threatens to keep us from being present with one another. Our embodied free association seems to follow the fault lines of our collective gestural memory, building momentum and transforming, giving rise to an emergent, spontaneous, and necessary capacity to notice one's own impulses in relation to others. It has involved risk – the risk to appear foolish, the playful failure, or in Salverson's words, the "foolish witness."[25]

Warren: During both our rehearsals and Playback performances we have noted that there is often a certain pressure to tell stories that make us look good, in which we are either the heroes or victims of the story. The same is true for much of recorded history. Meeting on the rackety bridge requires a risk on the part of the actor and the audience member (the teller) to reveal both preferred, and possibly unpreferred, aspects of themselves.

Alan: The images we create with and for audiences are a collaborative exploration requiring a risk to "leap" both into and out of embodiment. We take the risk to meet the teller, one by one, in a collaborative exploration, revealing a pastiche of possibilities with which audiences may converse. In response, we have seen audience members take the risk to meet us in the space between. As Salverson notes, "pleasure, joy and fun in this context are not spectacle or escape, but rather the deadly game of living with loss, living despite failure, living even despite the humiliation of trying endlessly."[26]

Shifting into the Non-verbal

Warren: Gadamer states that "any encounter with the language of art is an encounter with an unfinished event and is itself part of the event."[27] This idea has far-reaching implications for working with "Image." Every showing of the Image (e.g., the body as a sculpted frozen picture, or the "fluid sculpture" in Playback Theatre) becomes part of the Image, even if only in improvisation or rehearsal, because what is "essential to an experience is that it cannot be exhausted in what can be said or grasped as to its meaning"[28] As text, Image is a "cumulative, holistic process."[29] The Image is developing, and because it is silent, it allows other layers of the story to embed themselves into the actors and the participants–audience members in the workshop. Thus, the imag(e)inative work of art is always incomplete until it is presented to others who watch it, and even then it creates new openings.

Lisa: Using imagery to express something that cannot be represented in other ways allows us to explore paradoxes – coexisting and conflicting opposites. It is these visual contradictions in the embodied relations in the Image (e.g., someone smiling while doing something an observer would not think would result in a smile) that are complex prompts that open up questions, moving the exploration of the theme into deeper tissue, where there are more knots that need to be worked through. Image becomes part of a spiralling process that sparks our imaginations, enabling us to dream of alternative futures.

Alan: Playing with the image means that we play in a certain vocabulary and aesthetic (from the Greek word *aisthesis*, meaning perception or sensation – a breathing in or taking in of the world). This language includes our responses to the image presented. Thus, as expressive forms, images speak, showing the shapes they are in: "They announce themselves, bearing witness to their presence: 'Look, here we are.'"[30] We explore, fool around, muck about, hypothesize, juxtapose, and then retranslate the image back into a written or oral vocabulary by inviting verbal reflections from each teller after each embodied reflection, and by inviting other stories from other audience members. Objectivity then is freed from the literal. Each image becomes a subject "out there" performing in front of us. A story bears witness to itself in the image it offers, and its depth lies in the complexities of this image.

Nisha: Our challenge has become about how to extend these learnings and interweave them into our chosen public form, that of Playback Theatre. Thus far, we have found three ways to integrate some of these values into the Playback Theatre aesthetic: the introduction sequence, the conductor's questions, and a new form that we refer to as the "Bridge."

Welcoming Others onto the Rackety Bridge: Introductions in the Performance

Nisha: Usually, Playback Theatre companies begin a performance with an introduction that is intended to extend trust, invite a wide array of experiences, and demonstrate the playback form. The LHE attempts to facilitate resonance within the audience by intentionally providing a wide array of experiences relating to the theme. We have made efforts to ensure that the stories we choose do not all make us look like simple heroes or victims. We also are intent on ensuring that the bodies that make up our team are diverse and can visibly signify varied social locations and experiences. Here is an example of an introduction sequence, using three members of our team:

Three members of the LHE step forward one at a time and share a brief introduction. The other actors create a tight, multi-levelled chorus behind them.

Alan: I have dealt with otherness my entire life – as a gay man, a racial and ethnic "margin resistor," and a sufferer of mental illness. I am constantly seeking ways to tackle my outsider status, and so I try to relate my own otherness to that of different Others through different ways of storytelling. Through narrative performance that is interactive and participatory, I attempt to converse with those whose stories I am embodying. Every story I perform – or retell – has something of me inside it, and in this way, I am talking it out with the storyteller, trying to make sense of both his or her life and mine; our othernesses, and making every effort to understand each other, to come to terms with our histories, and to find common ground.

Lisa: I have a hard time staying anchored in the strong and able part of me and feel unsure, overwhelmed, or inadequate. I am afraid, for example, that I will not be able to bear a healthy child and raise it to be well and strong. Nothing says that this is caused by experiences of loss or displacement. My parents and my parents' parents went through prison, exile, refugee camps, murder. I have experienced none of the violence first-hand. Gathering the stories of my family through the Life Stories project and working with my own reality within our Playback group feels a lot like re-membering – in the sense of putting the pieces back together. Being in the group allows me to be present to both my own and all the other stories, to process rather than disconnect or be numb, to be present right here right now with the whole of me and with everyone: whole and enough.

Warren: As a Jewish man growing up in the 1950s and 1960s in a medium-sized city in Western Canada, I watched TV programs and films documenting the Holocaust, but it seemed far away to me. As far as I knew at the time, no close family relations were murdered, although I knew my father's family had escaped pogroms in Latvia and Lithuania to come first to England, then to Canada. Yet my parents lived through that tragedy throughout the Second World War, so their memories and emotions were passed onto me. I live as part of a historically displaced people. I am also a theatre facilitator and practitioner working with other marginalized groups.

Guiding Us into Safe Uncertainty: The Role of the Conductor

Nisha: We have also thought about how some of our learnings affect the ways in which we think about the role of the Conductor. Fox describes the Conductor as occupying a liminal space between the actors and the audience, not separate from either, but a conduit for feelings, words, and images. In addition to the Conductor being a fellow actor and emcee, Fox states that the "function of the Conductor is also shamanistic, leading actors and audience in the direction of … the '*illud tempus*,' that locus of meaning and rejuvenation which we often think of as a paradisiacal Eden but whose actual rediscovery is fraught with uncertainty."[31] It is the Conductor's questions, invitations, prompts, and framings that shape the conversations that unfold over the course of a rehearsal or performance. This role shapes what can be said and what critique is possible.

When we think of the metaphor of the rackety bridge, the Conductor is a guide who ensures that those on the bridge are in this process of "safe uncertainty," which is "always in a state of flow, and is consistent with the notion of a respectful, collaborative, evolving narrative, one which allows a context to emerge."[32] So the Conductor develops such a space – where stories shared can live beside, rather than replace, each other. In practice, the Conductor avoids attempts at too-strictly managing the flow of the conversation, allowing instead for loose associations between audience members. In a traditional Playback performance, the conductor might ask, "Did that fit with the spirit, if not all the details, of what happened?"[33] We have attempted to avoid premature closure or easy consent to what has been played back by asking audiences to consider the reflection offered, but not to remain bound by it.

Audience member (therapist/scholar): How do you tackle the ways we are complicit in each other's oppression and liberation? Where is that in what you do? I am really interested in this because of my own history and how I have chosen to focus more on the side of my family that has experienced more marginalization, as belonging to a First Nation's community, than the other side.

Nisha: This is a good segue to the new form we have developed that we refer to as "the Bridge," which we have in the past also called the "Overture."

The Bridge: Meeting the Teller in an Embodied Conversation

Warren: In the Bridge, we are trying to develop a method that performs this "third space"[34] as the stories of the actors and those of the audience bounce off and resonate with each other, not to resolve themselves, but to live in front of all of us. This is a space that is formed when two stories intersect with each other. Where the two meet is a space of flux. We don't know what is going to happen in this space. Willie Ermine, Raven Sinclair, and Bonnie Jefferey point out that the encounter of cultures that give rise to these stories creates an "ethical space" where people from "disparate cultures, worldviews, and knowledge systems can engage in an ethical/moral manner."[35] The knowledge of our practice of performing on the rackety bridge is not simply information; it is also performative, involving a "complex heterogeneous blend of knowledge, practice, trusted authority, spiritual values and local social and cultural organization: a knowledge space."[36] It is in this form that our attempt to play the foolish witness is perhaps most palpable. Here we attempt to disrupt the usual objective neutrality of the Playback actor and risk, instead, encountering the teller somewhere on the rackety bridge.

Nisha: (to audience member): We will play back your questioning about complicity through the Bridge. In this form, the actors will reflect on a moment from their own lives that resonates with the experience you have shared and will then return to offer you a reflection of your wonderings. Let's watch!

The actors have their backs to the audience, as in the beginning of the Rhapsody, and one by one turn to face the audience with a personal story that resonates with the audience member's story. It could be from a theme, an incident, an emotional connection the actor feels with the story; the important thing is that, unlike traditional Playback Theatre forms, where the actor is a neutral person "mirroring" back the recounted story to the audience, here the actors are recounting stories that happened to them in their own lives. One actor turns once and recounts his or her own story, and then, at an appropriate moment, another actor turns and does the same, while the first actor turns around with his or her back to the audience again until the time comes to turn again to continue telling his or her story. This continues so that after two or three "turns" every actor has been able to tell his or her own story. Each actor freezes on the third turn. Once all actors have positioned themselves in a still image, there is a pause. The musician offers five beats of a drum or other instrument, and the actors slowly step forward and move into a fluid sculpture that is now, again, a reflection of the audience member's story.

Alan: I grew up in a middle-class Chinese-Canadian family. I recently bought a condo in Villeray, a working-class neighbourhood in Montreal. I feel torn, as if I –

Warren: I have been researching my father's working-class history and ignoring my mother's middle-class history. I was raised middle class myself, but I never –

Deb: I am a white woman from a middle-class background, and I often feel like I have so much privilege –

Lucy: My parents were refugees from Vietnam, but even though they were refugees who fled a war zone, they still came from a place of privilege as Chinese –

Laura: I come from Mexico, and I am white, but even though I am white, I know that I have Aztec blood in me –

Lisa: My background is Rwandan, and because of this Life Stories project, I've been talking with my family about their experiences –

Joliane: Even though I'm a French Québécoise, I went to an English CEGEP[37] in Montreal. After the second referendum on sovereignty in Quebec –

Warren: So despite the fact I'm so interested in my father's history with respect to class, I have never bothered to look at how my own mother's family achieved its wealth, especially how they may have depended on people who worked for them to get that wealth.

Lisa: And when I talked to my grandmother about her experience of fleeing out of the country into refugee camps, she spoke of leaving her property and people behind. I wondered if she meant "owning people" literally.

Lucy: And because my family comes from a place of privilege, I have always felt uneasy about the fact that I have been able to live such a comfortable life while many other refugees and their families have not.

Alan: I mean, I have always been against gentrification, and now here I am engaging in the very thing against which I've spoken out – and I like my condo!

Laura: And I feel Aztec, I feel Indian inside me, but yet I also know I am white on the outside, and everyone treats me a certain way because I am white.

Joliane: Some of my classmates would mock me about the francophones losing this referendum, saying that we should have learned from the last one. And I got so mad because I thought they were right, why didn't we learn?

Deb: I just don't know how to reconcile myself with that, but I know I have to be aware of it.

Paul (Musician): (provides five beats of a drum)

The LHE then moves into a fluid sculpture of the audience member's experience.

Nisha (to audience member): Were we able to meet you in your story? Is there anything else you would like to say about your wonderings after seeing this reflection?

Audience member: I didn't see myself in all of it, but some parts really stretched what I was thinking about and clarified the ongoing struggle to keep going, even though I carry such mixed history and cannot escape my own complicity.

Turning Together on the Rackety Bridge

Nisha: Over the course of our presentation, we have drawn on the metaphor of the "rackety bridge" to explore how we might stay in conversation with each other about the experience of displacement. Our focus on conversation is informed, in part, by Russell and Ison's notion that living systems are closed to information:

> We take this to mean that human beings cannot be informed in any predetermined manner by another's communication. What we, as humans, could do and actually do is converse together. Over time, if the conversation is satisfying, change happens at a biological level; the person has learned to be in the world differently and this difference is expressed as an "improvement" ... The only, albeit critical, goal is a commitment to stay in the conversation as long as it is a satisfying experience.[38]

Lisa: To this end, we have experimented and explored how practices like *Developmental Transformations* and *Playback Theater* make it possible to experience "satisfaction" in conversation especially when the subject matter threatens to pull us away from feeling present with one another.
Warren: Interestingly, "the roots of 'conversation,' *conversare*, mean 'turn together.'"[39] Another metaphor for how we might stay in conversation, embodying the rackety bridge, is drawn from the biological – the "ecotone,"[40] where permeable spaces bump up against one another. Ecotone is a term used in botany and ecology to designate the transition zone between plant communities, such as marshland and, better, the drained ground. "Tone" is a Greek term that means "tension," as in maintaining muscle tone. Ecotones are borderland places where the interplay of resources and nutrients contain the characteristic species of each, generating rich possibilities for living. These overlapping places are places of complexity and dynamism. For this to happen in a human interaction requires conversation and dialogue. This social domain (the performance) involves conversations not just as methods of communication, but also as acts that create spaces where ethical dialogue takes place: "The purpose of being in a conversation is to keep it

going"[41] and to allow for a constant and ongoing commentary on what is being signified.

Alan: Our ensemble will continue to offer up performative approaches to inquiring into the experience of interviewers and interviewees associated with this project. We have begun to do so in partnership with the Maison d'Haiti, a Haitian community organization in Montreal, as well as the Montreal Holocaust Memorial Centre. While we will continue to refine our methodology, our attention is currently directed towards developing and maintaining the conditions necessary to ensuring a "safe uncertainty" in these performances. We have been thinking about the necessity of working with the same group over time and about the importance of working with and within an ongoing community organization. Part of the rationale behind this is that witnessing representations of the experience of displacement and listening to stories about fear and loss, while offering opportunities for expression and perspective, can also call up more distressing feelings. For this reason, we have found it important to work with organizations that can offer additional resources to participants, such as counsellors and available staff.

Nisha: As Peggy Howard points out, by going through similar experiences, we might listen better to the experiences of others.[42] Our performative inquiry continues to provide each member of the LHE with opportunities to encounter their own histories and present experiences of being (dis)placed as well as opportunities to extend the conversation to diverse audiences. In this way, we have attempted to come closer to a form of communication that can be a cooperative and communal activity that "is both individually satisfying to all participants (and at no one's expense) and leaves something recognizable behind"[43] – something that can be called up as long as we remember it. The rackety bridge is the journey *and* the final destination.

NOTES

1 For more information on the LHE, see www.creativealternatives.co.
2 We use this word provisionally as we recognize it is a contested term.
3 Histoires de vie Montreal/Montreal Life Stories Project, at www
   .lifestoriesmontreal.ca/.
4 Diana Taylor, *The Archive and the Repertoire: Performing Cultural Memory in the Americas* (London, Durham: Duke University Press, 2003), 20.
5 Michael Frisch, *A Shared Authority: Essays on the Craft and Meaning of Oral and Public History* (Albany: State University of New York Press, 1990).

6 Ibid., xxii.

7 Jo Salas, *Improvising Real Life: Personal Story in Playback Theatre* (New Paltz, NY: Tusitala, 1993).

8 Jonathan Fox, *Acts of Service. Spontaneity, Commitment, Tradition in the Nonscripted Theatre* (New Paltz, NY: Tusitala, 1994).

9 Shawn McNiff, "Arts-Based Research," in J. Gary Knowles and Ardra Cole, eds., *Handbook of the Arts in Qualitative Research* (Los Angeles: Sage, 2008), 29–40.

10 Fels cited in Warren Linds, "A Journey in Metaxis: Been, Being, Becoming, Imag(in)ing Drama Facilitation" (PhD diss., University of British Columbia, 2002), 147.

11 Peggy Phelan, *Unmarked: The Politics of Performance* (New York: Routledge, 1993), 174.

12 Ingrid Mündel, "Radical Storytelling: Performing Processes in Canadian Popular Theatre," *Theatre Research in Canada* 24, nos. 1–2 (2003): 147–70.

13 Viola Spolin, *Improvisation for the Theatre: A Handbook of Teaching and Directing Techniques* (Evanston, IL: Northwestern University Press, 1963).

14 David Read Johnson, "Developmental Transformations: Toward the Body as Presence," in David R. Johnson and Renee Emunah, eds., *Current Approaches in Drama Therapy*, 2nd ed. (Springfield, IL: Charles C. Thomas, 2009), 89.

15 Ibid.

16 David Read Johnson, "Performing Absence: The Limits of Testimony in the Recovery of a Combat Veteran," in Eva Leveton, ed., *Healing Collective Trauma Using Sociodrama and Drama Therapy* (New York: Springer, 2010), 55–78.

17 Ibid.

18 Nick Rowe, *Playing the Other: Dramatizing Personal Narratives in Playback Theatre* (London: Jessica Kingsley, 2007).

19 Julie Salverson, "Performing Emergency: Witnessing, Popular Theatre, and the Lie of the Literal," *Theatre Topics* 6, no. 2 (1996): 185.

20 Julie Salverson, "The Unimaginable Occurrence: Storytelling, Popular Theatre, and an Ethic of Risk" (Master's thesis, Ontario Institute for Studies in Education, University of Toronto, 1996), 47.

21 Ibid.

22 Martin Ringer, "The Facile-itation of Facilitation? Searching for Competencies in Group Work Leadership," *Scisco Conscientia* 2, no. 1 (1999): 5.

23 Ibid.

24 Johnson, "Developmental Transformations," 90.

25 Julie Salverson, "Taking Liberties: A Theatre Class of Foolish Witnesses," *Research in Drama Education* 13, no. 2 (2008): 253.

26 Julie Salverson, "Clown, Opera, the Atomic Bomb and the Classroom," in Tim Prentki and Sheila Preston, eds., *The Applied Theatre Reader* (New York: Routledge, 2009), 39.

27 Hans-Georg Gadamer, *Truth and Method*, 2nd rev. ed., trans. Joel Weinsheimer and Donald G. Marshall (New York: Continuum, 1989), 99.

28 Ibid., 66.

29 Paul Ricoeur, "The Model of the Text: Meaningful Action Considered as a Text," in Paul Ricoeur and John B. Thompson, eds., *Hermeneutics and the Human Sciences* (Cambridge: Cambridge University Press, 1981), 212.

30 James Hillman, "Anima Mundi: The Return of the Soul to the World," *Spring* (1982): 77.

31 Fox, *Acts of Service*, 134.

32 Brian Mason, "Towards Positions of Safe Uncertainty," *Human Systems: The Journal of Systemic Consultation and Management* 4 (1993): 195.

33 Fox, *Acts of Service*, 226.

34 Bhabha quoted in Jonathan Rutherford, "The Third Space: Interview with Homi K. Bhabha," in Jonathan Rutherford, ed., *Identity: Community, Culture, Difference* (London: Lawrence and Wishart, 1990), 211.

35 Willie Ermine, Raven Sinclair, and Bonnie Jefferey, *The Ethics of Research Involving Indigenous Peoples* (Saskatoon, SK: Indigenous Peoples' Health Research Centre, 2004), 20.

36 David Turnbull, "Reframing Science and Other Local Knowledge Traditions," *Futures* 29, no. 6 (1997): 560.

37 *Collège d'enseignement général et professionnel*. Students enter CEGEP after completing six years of elementary school and five years of secondary school.

38 David Russell and Ray Ison, "Maturana's Intellectual Contribution as a Choreography of Conversation and Action," *Cybernetics and Human Knowing* 11, no. 2 (2004): 134.

39 Lloyd Fell and David Russell, "The Dance of Understanding," in Lloyd Fell, David Russell, and Allan Stewart, eds., *Seized by Agreement, Swamped by Understanding*, http://www.pnc.com.au/~lfell/dance.pdf.

40 Phil Booth, email to Warren Linds, 23 January 1998.

41 Klaus Krippendorf, "Major Metaphors of Communication and Some Constructivist Reflections on Their Use," *Cybernetics and Human Knowing* 2, no. 1 (1993): 61.

42 Peggy Howard, "Interpreting the Evaluation Experience through Embodiment, Conversation and Anecdote," *Qualitative Studies in Education* 9, no. 2 (1996): 167–80.

43 Krippendorff, "Major Metaphors," 61.

6 *Stories Scorched from the Desert Sun*: Performing Testimony, Narrating Process

HOURIG ATTARIAN AND RACHAEL VAN FOSSEN

In January 2009 Hourig Attarian and Rachael Van Fossen came together to work on a performance creation for the oral history and performance group,[1] within the larger Community and University Research Alliance project Life Stories of Montrealers Displaced by War, Genocide, and Other Human Rights Violations at Concordia University. In the following months, the collaboration led to a complex dialogue on process between Rachael and Hourig, which resulted in a new collaborative text, presented at the "Remembering War, Genocide and Other Human Rights Violations" conference.

Beginnings

As part of the Untold Histories project of the Oral History and Performance Group, we collaborated (Rachael as dramaturge and staging director, Hourig as author of the text) to create a theatrical staged reading based on oral histories of the Armenian genocide and on narratives of lived experiences of war. An adapted source text,[2] originally written in the form of a "storytelling essay," was retitled *Stories Scorched from the Desert Sun* for its incarnation as a performance.

We faced a number of issues in our deeply reflective collaboration, including concerns raised by the tight time frame for both text adaptation and staging rehearsals. In looking at how testimonial storytelling lends itself to performance, we needed to be attentive to points of convergence and divergence among the multilayered perspectives of author, dramaturge, director, and cast. Exploring testimony as a process that hinges on the transformative aspects of telling and sharing these stories through performance, we became aware of an act of "multiple voicing." We found that both performing the stories and storying the performance create a cathartic, introspective, and proactive process as witness for all involved (including cast, writer, dramaturge, and audience). Most importantly, this approach creates a space of collective ownership for the events and experiences retold.

Arising from this collaboration, a dialogue ensued between dramaturge and author on the notion of "testimony as process," even when focusing on "product" such as a performative public presentation. We have since found that our initial engagement in the performance as a learning experience has opened up new possibilities for our evolving collaborative dialogue. What started as an exchange between the two of us, seeking to understand the perspectives we each brought to the performance, became a story in its own right as we delved deeper into our collaboration. What follows is the charting of that story – the "storying" of the performance. Intended as performative dialogue, our text intertwines with excerpts of the original script.[3]

Storying the Performance

CHORUS 1: My memory will retain what is worthwhile.
CHORUS 2: My memory knows more about me than I do;
CHORUS 3: it doesn't lose what deserves to be saved.
CHORUS 1: Eduardo Galeano.[4]
HOURIG: These are the stories of several girlhoods told in three voices. I am Hourig.
YOUNG PERGROUHI: My name is Pergrouhi. My mother's name was Hadji Mariam. My father's name was Boghos. I don't know my family name.
HERMIG: And I am Hermig. Our voices come together to tell the stories of many young women.
HOURIG: Young women who lived through the horrors of war and genocide in different places and at different times.

Rachael: In January 2009, my good friend and colleague Ted Little approached me to ask if I would be interested in acting as dramaturge for a performance creation piece being undertaken by Hourig Attarian, in her capacity as artist-in-residence for the oral history and performance group. I remember that my initial inner response was decidedly mixed. I am always most interested in working on performance creation that deals directly with the lives of real, usually living, people, and I am increasingly interested in pursuing the staging of verbatim texts.

On the other hand, I felt nervousness about working on a piece for which I had not been involved at the beginning of the development process; all the more so if dealing with genocide stories, and with a writer who feels very close to the material. Would what I had to offer interfere with expected "authenticity" of the stories? With the original intent of the writer in putting these stories forward? This invitation came at a time when my own creative preoccupations involved questioning the very notion of authenticity. These days I am especially intrigued by building on performance as artifice, an artifice that can reveal what a rigid notion of "authenticity of voice" may not be able to reveal, and I worried that my creative interests would be inappropriate to the material. I worried also that I am not an expert in testimony specific to trauma. I stewed about how to present such stories to a public without sensationalizing horror. Then as now, I was wary of testimonial performance in which an audience's "hyperemotionality … superficially looks like compassion and caring."[5] I wished to avoid what Ann Cvetkovich characterizes as "empty sentimentality and its not-so-distant relation, incapacitating awe."[6]

Hourig: My work with Rachael, the cast, and the musician in March 2009 became the latest episodes in what had already been several evolutions of the writing. When I look back at it, this is a set of multilayered stories that has been with me for the past eight years. With each new stage, a new layer is added to the stories and a new incarnation results.

Rachael: One phone conversation with Hourig and I discovered I needn't have worried. She seemed open to my tentative suggestions about how we might proceed on a tight timeline towards a scheduled March 2009 public reading of a work-in-progress. I felt much reassured that we would work well and creatively together. For one thing, we found things to laugh about. For another, we agreed to enter this collaboration understanding that every aspect of it, including the staged reading, would be a process of exploration, of experimentation in how we could stage these difficult stories as performance.

Hourig: When my friend and collaborator Hermig Yogurtian and I were preparing the original text for publication a few years ago, we envisioned a cascade of three voices each telling a different yet ultimately a similar story. Each of the stories had layers and substories in it as well, and we certainly saw it all very much intertwined. But how do you represent all that textually? All we could do was to contextualize it in the introduction and explain our vision. Looking at the published text now, it does of course have a cyclical aspect to it, yet it is also very

much bound by the linearity of a written text. Rachael not only immediately understood this, she also proposed a true intertwining of the
text onstage. Thus, what the audience heard and saw during the March
performance was actually stories flowing into one another seamlessly,
complementing each other. Because we let the different voices of the
characters talk to each other, the audience was led in and out of different episodes of the stories. For example, as the teenage characters of
Hourig and Hermig tell stories of their war memories, there are cuts
with a few lines from one and a few lines from the other, but the stories
fuse organically, reaffirming the recounted experiences.

HOURIG: Hermig and I grew up together on the same street in Beirut, amid the
   chaos of civil war, our blossoming friendship our lifeline to sanity, our defi-
   ance to the turmoil engulfing us.
HERMIG: We had hardly taken in the full impact, the immensity of our grandparents' stories when our war started.
HOURIG: The year was 1975. The day 14 April. Three days before I turned
   twelve.
HERMIG: It was April 1975, when the first incident occurred.
HOURIG: It was a bright spring day. The early morning ritual when our whole
   household was up always started with the aroma of coffee my father
   brewed for himself and my mother.
HERMIG: Not yet twelve and in the sweet twilight zone of childhood, that
   borderline space where realities and fantasies flow in and out of each other
   seamlessly, still trying to make sense of the deportation stories. Barely
   twelve, our first rush of hormones and our first infatuations landed upon
   us with full force. Grade six, awaiting that most important of all events in
   a young person's life, graduating from primary school, the celebration, the
   heady expectation of going on to high school and making our grand exit
   from the realm of childhood and being accepted into the world of grown-
   up people, so we would be able to go to the parties that previously only
   our elder sisters were allowed to attend, and perhaps be allowed to wear
   bell-bottom pants …
      Barely twelve, when our war started.
HOURIG: My father opens the green shutters of the verandah, to let the sunshine and the waking street noises in. This morning there is an eerie silence
   on the street and my father behaves in a strange way. Instead of finding him
   in the kitchen boiling the coffee, I see him peering out through the cracks of
   the green shutters. My mother is standing next to him. They are talking in
   low whispers.

MOTHER: "No school today, go back to bed,"

HOURIG: Is their response to my and my brother's bewildered looks.

FATHER: "It is not safe. There has been an incident."

HERMIG: It was a shooting on a bus carrying civilians. (TO HOURIG) Maybe the schools will be closed!

HOURIG: I couldn't understand why the shutters had to stay closed. I couldn't understand why the sunshine could not be let in. It was only three days before I turned twelve.

HERMIG: Little did we know then that this would be our long march in the desert that our grandparents had gone through in their time, our own baptism in blood and fire.

HOURIG: The summer I turned twelve, I had my first period. I walked through the threshold of womanhood as I bled out the pain I felt in my heart.

The summer I turn twelve is a very hot one. My bedroom window that overlooks the garage of a neighbouring building stays open at night, in the hopes of carrying a waft of a breeze inside. Instead, what invades my bedroom are the moans and cries of the blindfolded young boys I see hurled into the dark abyss of the garage during the day.

The year we turn twelve, Hermig and I meet daily to talk about the books we have read, the boys we have crushes on, the school we would go to if the roads were safe again, and the childhood that was robbed of us.

HERMIG: The bus incident was a story we only heard on the news, but soon the real fighting spreads all around Beirut. It usually starts with rounds of machine gun fire. Then we hear the militia yelling at people to empty out the streets, stay indoors, and stock some food ... This sends my parents into a flurry – making sure that everyone has returned home from wherever they were, and then closing all the shutters and ordering us not to go near the balconies. There isn't anything an eleven-year-old wants to do as much as disobey her parents, and of course this for me was a directive to go and watch what was happening on the streets through the slots of the shutters. And I did.

YOUNG HERMIG: A man is being tied from his feet to the back of a pickup truck and being dragged around in the streets. The gravel is tearing him apart, and he is all bloodied. It is only a very short glimpse, but enough to catapult me full force into a new world, where suddenly my grandparents' stories of death and hunger stop being "stories" and acquire the full force of reality. All the penance that an eleven-year-old is capable of – why was I jubilant at skipping school for a week? Oh dear god, I'll go to school Saturdays and Sundays too, study until the late hours of the evening, please let this not happen.

HERMIG: My pleas are in vain. Ours is not going to be an adolescence of bell-
   bottom pants and parties …

Hourig: Through the performance it was now possible to see on stage
what we had tried to envision textually a few years ago. The text takes
very tangible form in its new representational mode through the performative act. This act of translation from one mode to another was
joyful and rewarding. And seeing that incarnation of the text was absolutely fascinating for me.

Rachael: Given the emphasis we wished to place on an open-ended process, we quickly determined that both of us preferred not to have an all-
professional cast. Where for a certain kind of process it can be valuable
to have professional actors with experience in new play development, in
our case I felt discussions of characters' journeys in more or less "standard" terms might actually prevent us from the kind of discoveries we
hoped to make towards "new" ways to stage difficult testimony. It "felt"
to both Hourig and me that what was most important was to work with
people who do, yes, have training in theatre performance, but who are
perhaps first and foremost curious and relatively new to the process of
script development, in order for this script development process to be,
itself, a new one. Working with students would help us to continue to
consider the whole experience as a learning process for ourselves. We
ended up with a wonderful, talented, and brave cast of three – two acting students, Amena Ahmad and Suyi Liu, and Maya Dhawan, a young
but mature professional artist.

Hourig: I loved the fact that the cast was multiracial, because it emphasized in a very specific way the universality of the stories. However, seeing
the text on stage and going through the rehearsals, I must admit I went
through very conflicting feelings. On one hand, going through the process of rehearsals felt like going through sculpting sessions, shifting and
changing sometimes in minute details, until there was an end product on
performance night. At the same time, the process of rehearsals gave me the
opportunity to step out of my story, to become an observer, whereas before
I was very much part of the story. This had both its good and bad points,
since being the observer and the listener of my own stories took a toll on
me emotionally. This feeling was very pronounced, especially on the night
of the performance. On the other hand, it felt rewarding, because having
the stories reach out to a larger audience was really a dream come true.

Sitting through the rehearsals and later on in the theatre hall, the
roles of narrator and listener had definitely reversed for me. Listening

to how the voices we had written about became embodied in a very real sense, I found myself in the position of witnessing my own story; while Rachael and the cast, who were the original witnesses if you will, became the narrators. It has always been difficult for me to deal with my own war memories. Talking about survivors' memories and survivor stories has always been a first vehicle in that sense. It is a way of bridging into my own stories, trying to understand my life story or my life experiences through the telling of other life stories which have been indelibly, inevitably more harrowing, more difficult, more traumatic than mine could ever have been. Doing that has also proven to be a healing journey.

Rachael: I find it fascinating to listen to Hourig speak about how she shifted from considering that the performers and I were witnesses to the stories, to being herself an observer, or witness, to testimony by others. Her experience of our changed positionalities both illustrates and complicates the notion that "the listener to trauma comes to be a participant and a co-owner of the traumatic event." I find Hourig's perception of her transformed role all the more interesting when we also consider Dori Laub's further analysis that "the listener ... has to be at the same time a witness to the trauma witness and a witness to himself."[7]

Part of my ongoing discomfort in working with testimonial material stems from a concern that often, instead of paying attention to the important act of witnessing, I am paying attention largely to technical details: in this case, how to bring to theatrical life stories that are largely about death, and how to lift stories told about past events into the theatrical present moment. It can sometimes feel callous and unfeeling to be the person worrying about what is going to "work" theatrically. And, admittedly, I am sometimes thinking in terms of what will keep an audience engaged – some would say entertained.

Hourig: On the night of the performance I was engaged in an act of "multiple watching." I was watching the actors, I was watching parts of my life story, I was watching the audience, and a part of me internally was watching me watch the actors and my story ... I realized that it was much more difficult hearing my story out loud, than hearing Pergrouhi's stories, my great aunt Anoush's story, or Hermig's grandmother's and great grandmother's, Azadouhi's and Nouritza's, stories. I felt I had literally come face-to-face with my twelve-year-old self, seeing what she has been through in a new light. I thought about how I have felt compelled to share these stories, but also how healing is certainly a life-long journey. My hope in the end is that we learn to see where the transformative and empowering aspect of telling these stories lies, and that despite being very difficult journeys these stories also contain the seeds of healing.

Rachael: The first time we met, Hourig and I shared some good chuckles. I have a memory of Hourig looking to me, and saying, "Well, the stories are not really so graphic, so ..." I wasn't sure how to respond, feeling that perhaps Hourig was looking to me for reassurance that I could not in all honesty provide. I remember hesitating, and then responding tentatively, "Well, parts of it are pretty graphic ..." Hourig, and then I with some relief, fully belly laughed. Being able to laugh together is important to me, offering not only a release from difficult material, but also an increased sense of intimacy and shared experience between relative strangers. We talked also about the challenges of presenting such difficult material to an audience, feeling unable in our particular context, and within our limited time frame, to interject comic material.

ALL: (In unison) Pergrouhi.

PERGROUHI: When we went to Yaremja, they let us sleep in the barn.

YOUNG PERGROUHI: The animals return to the shed after having grazed the whole day, and we are allowed to sleep here, in a pit, almost. But the heat, the fleas, and the lice are unbearable.

My mother reminds me: "Listen, my child, your name is Pergrouhi, my name is Hadji Mariam and your father's name was Boghos. Don't you ever forget that."

During the day I go play with the Turkmen kids in the field. One day I noticed that my mother is lying on the ground. I go closer and see that her eyes are open. I speak to her, but she won't answer me back. I go back to play. I am only a child, barely six years old. I play during the day and go and sleep next to her at night.

PERGROUHI: For three days I slept like that in my dead mother's bosom.

YOUNG PERGROUHI: After three days, the old lady says to my cousin, "go tell her, her mother's dead." So she comes and tells me.

Four Turkmen bring a hemp sack, open it, put my mother's body in the sack and take it out. I am crying and running after them. They take her out in the fields and bury her there.

PERGROUHI: They just covered her with some earth and came back.

YOUNG PERGROUHI: I go every day to where her body lies and cry endlessly, "mother, mother, please come back, please get up, mother, please." But my mother doesn't answer back. They come and take me back in and tell me not to cry. They give me a rag doll to console me.

On the third day, I go to where she was buried again. Her arm is sticking out of the ground. Like a piece of wood. I am very frightened. The next day I go back. The dogs have pulled her body out of the ground and are ripping her apart. Those village dogs are very ferocious.

PERGROUHI: Those dogs were very ferocious. (pause) I have so many more things to tell, but I cannot go on anymore.

Hourig: Personally, one of the interesting aspects of the process of writing was seeing how it transformed from audiotaped and videotaped interview material, with an interview that had a specific purpose in terms of oral history, to a storied essay, and finally transitioning into a performative mode, making the personal public and political through an artful engagement. Going from the oral history interview into the performance is very much fusing life and art together in that moment and carrying the audience in its folds. It is a curious way of both suspension of disbelief because of the artistic engagement, yet at the same time total immersion in a life encounter, all within a temporal framework between the stage lights fading up and fading out.

In the transition to performance mode I felt particularly concerned about the graphic elements of violence and trauma that surfaced in the original stories. The transition from the written to the spoken word carries a lot of power, since you can reach an audience that is more or less captive in the theatre hall. The written word, despite all its graphic details, still has a certain mutedness that is very different from the experience of the spoken word. As a reader, when I reach a disturbing part in a text, I can choose to close the book, take a break, choose not to continue reading, decide when I'm going to come back to it, or not come back to it at all. With the spoken word, what is going through to the audience is powerful, immediate, and strong.

The important question and concern for me then is how and what to do as writer in order not to sensationalize the violence. Of course the importance of these stories is all about memory against forgetting, public truth-telling, knowing and understanding our past, doing justice to the stories and to the people involved, but at the same time, it is also crucially about healing and creating awareness. In that context what is essential for me is that the story does not get bogged down in the violence and the trauma, because that is not the message, that is not where I want the story to stagnate. I also do not want us, as an audience, as readers, listeners, to be caught in that voyeuristic and grotesque trapping.

Rachael: I have been highly influenced in my thinking on testimonial performance and voyeurism by Julie Salverson's writing about avoiding an "erotics of injury" and the eroticization of trauma in performance of difficult testimony.[8] Of course the power of live performance is largely that the words of the text are received by multiple senses among audience: seeing, hearing, even feeling the words as they sonically fill the room means it is a more immersive experience. And we are not alone as we may be when we read the same story. We are in a room with other people and, in that sense, witnessing the stories in a form of public communal experience that can also heighten emotional response. This potential power of live performance may need to be tempered by writing and performance techniques that allow distancing – certain forms of humour, for example, can allow distancing and release. In our case, without that particular tool, how might we make the most of both those potentials – offering simultaneously a distanced and a heightened emotional response?

Hourig: This is where the transformative aspects of the act of "storying" and of the performance itself become very important. And again the question arises, how do you do that? This issue became a crucial node in my collaboration with Rachael, because we very much saw eye to eye in this respect. I also remember that this was an issue I addressed during rehearsals with the cast. When we talked about intentions of the characters, where the characters were leading, how they were going back into their stories trying to understand themselves, I asked the actors for "less emotion, more mutedness." This was primarily because the experience of horror and dehumanization the characters had been through is an unfathomable and unspeakable experience, and I certainly do not want an audience to be captive in that experience. I want an audience to be able to go through and beyond it; to see what it does to us, but to also be aware of how to reach beyond that. Not as people who belong to this or that ethnic group, but as human beings, embracing the universality of the stories and learning to go beyond the trappings of victimhood. In that sense another vital connection I see between oral history and performance is in what kind of a vehicle the performance wants to and can be to achieve this. And therein lie both its power and its accountability.

Rachael: Hourig's note to the actors about being "more muted" provided me with a conundrum for rehearsals. It is challenging to the work of the actor to mute a performance that has not yet been fully explored and experimented with. While I thought I understood what Hourig meant, and what and why she was looking for this "muted" effect to underplay the sensationalistic aspects of the stories, my usual inclination is to ask young actors to "go big" in rehearsals, to take risks, from which experiences we may make discoveries, but can also pull back the performances as needed. As soon as Hourig spoke, I knew that this approach would not be useful, and that she would probably find such experimentation excruciating. Yet in actorly terms, "muted" is not an easily playable action. Asking for "muted," I worried, would increase rather than decrease the actors' tentativeness about dealing with personal and difficult material. We did make some conscious decisions about how to de-sensationalize the more graphic descriptions of violence.

What we settled on, for instance in the excerpt performed by Suyi Liu as young Pergrouhi, was almost literally a more Brechtian reporting style of performance.[9] I asked Suyi to play Young Pergrouhi as a curious young girl simply reporting the facts of the discovery of her mother's body. Her playable action became "I am trying to figure this out as I am speaking," with a near absence of sentiment. While avoiding a melodramatic sensationalizing, I believe that this choice also emphasized all the more the horror of subjecting an actual young girl – the real Pergrouhi whose words the character spoke – to the experience not only of loss, but of desecration.

Hourig: Reflecting on the interplay of oral history and performance, there is an element of performance in oral history to begin with. As a narrator, telling your story is an act of interpretation. At the time of the interview, you are making instantaneous decisions in your mind, deciding what to highlight, what to touch upon, what to go deeper into, what to leave out. And you are aware you are doing this for a certain audience. You are also probably going through a subtle act of self-censorship – there is very much that element of judging what is appropriate or not appropriate to be told, since you're aware that the interview is recorded for a purpose and will be available as public record or in archives. So you are already very much an editor of your story. You also become (some people in a rudimentary way, others through an innate storytelling gift) the performer of your life story as you retell it. For example, the survivor Pergrouhi was a master storyteller who held a listener captive with her recounting.

Rachael: The texts that ended up in the performance were performed, for the most part, verbatim from the original source material. There is one sense in which this was not true. In storytelling form, we may often hear the teller narrate the characters' adventures or misadventures using the past tense; in theatre, where the characters are not being narrated but instead performed by actors, of course these characters are ordinarily speaking in the present tense. Throughout most of the performance text, we changed the original from narrations of past events to show characters who were previously narrated about as if they were instead in the moment, and we as audience were watching events unfold as they were happening. One effect of this choice is to increase identification processes, and thus provide a means to emphasize the present relevance of stories from the Armenian genocide. The stories seem less Other to those of us without a direct relationship to the genocide.

Simultaneously we are disrupting identification by having young actors play several characters at many different ages, and having them move quickly back and forth between these characters. The effect of the intertwining of the three narratives therefore served, I hope, not only to achieve the cascade of related stories that Hourig has characterized, but also to keep audience members actively engaged – since they need to keep up with and sort out the various shifts.

HOURIG: (speaking to Hermig) The anatomy of our survival has deep, very deep roots. Resurrection is not a grace from heaven, but an imposed survival mechanism. This is what countless teachers have taught generations of Armenians. "You will avenge yourself by living/Living a thousand fold more stubbornly" wrote one poet. And so I have lived.

HERMIG: We met Pergrouhi when she was ninety-five years old. As we were recording, translating, and editing Pergrouhi's story, we started remembering and retelling the stories of our own grandmothers, great-grandmothers, and great-aunts. Trauma for us is not simply inherited memories of genocide stories. Soon it was our own memories of war and violence that we were writing about, something we had avoided doing for many years.

HOURIG: My last visit to Pergrouhi was on Sunday, 24 April 2005. There was a single red carnation in a vase, next to her bedside. Her voice was very tired. As I held her hand to say goodbye, she told me, "Thank you for coming, thank you for not forgetting me." It was to be my last visit to her, her last spoken words to me. Two mornings later she passed away.

What will always remain engraved in my memories of Pergrouhi is the image of her as a little girl.

On one of my visits, she is asleep when I enter her room. I sit next to her, holding her hand. She wakes, and tells me, "As soon as I closed my eyes I heard them coming, I heard them coming after me." I squeeze her hand softly and mumble a few comforting words to her. "The dogs are coming, they are barking loud, they are fierce. They're going to rip me apart just like they did my mother." She sounds so helpless. She is the little girl again who witnessed it all.

CHORUS 3: Ninety years had not been able to wipe away the fear.
CHORUS 1: Ninety years she had lived with this pain.
CHORUS 2: Ninety years and the wound is still raw.

Rachael: The term "staged reading" often conjures images of actors with music stands and very little if any actual staging. A usual audience for a staged reading of a work-in-progress is, in my experience, made up largely of theatre professionals, and the event considered part of the process of development for the script. Our audience would be quite a different one, and our goal was to explore and experiment not just with text, but with concrete ways to stage trauma and death, as I said before, in such a fashion that brings these to life. In other words, as much as we decided from the onset to consider adapting for a staged reading as a process, it was still important that the product – what we would put before the public – be theatrically engaging. We rehearsed quite a lot compared to usual standards for a staged reading, incorporating movement and live music with the interwoven stories, hence shifting from ideas of "authenticity" and "integrity" to notions of their being integral, integrated, and intertwined.

Hourig: Rachael and the cast and musician honoured and nurtured the stories they told on stage. They also became part of this journey on a personal and collective level. The stories of course have a life of their own beyond the actual persons who are involved in them. They are now a part of the lives of the audience who watched them just as they are a part of the creative, artistic, and personal journeys of the cast who were involved in them, who in turn brought their own stories into the retelling process as well.

Rachael: As Hourig and I continue to work together grappling with these issues, the piece itself is taking quite a different form than what anyone had imagined initially. We have discovered that the story of the script will no longer be constructed solely as stories of the Armenian genocide through multiple protagonist-survivors. The multiplicity of those interwoven stories remains important as a means to avoid essentializing of experiences of the genocide into a conventionally coherent narrative,[10] and so those oral histories will remain prominent in the piece. However a central storyline will explore – through characters of present-day Hourig and Rachael – our struggles and journeys around the "why's" and "how's" and "for whom's" behind the need to tell these stories in public forums. Our act of "storying the performance" for presentation at conferences has significantly influenced the form that a resulting script will take. We envision that elements of our own interwoven dialogue as

6.1 Three generations of women: Hourig's mother, great aunt, and grandmother. Image from Hourig Attarian family collection.

6.2 Hourig's father and uncle in the Beirut of the 1940s. Image from Hourig Attarian family collection.

6.3 Hourig's mother on the rocks by the Beirut seashore. Image from Hourig Attarian family collection.

6.4 Hourig's parents and grandmothers with her survivor great aunt Azniv, visiting from the United States. Image from Hourig Attarian family collection.

collaborators – a dialogue exposing challenges and opportunities in our process, and raising questions about how to proceed both ethically and theatrically in dealing with this testimonial material – will also be integral to a never-quite-final-but-maybe-final-ish script. A script that will be, probably always, in process. As Ann Cvetkovich writes, "[Trauma] demands an unusual archive, whose materials, in pointing to trauma's ephemerality, are themselves frequently ephemeral."[11]

Hourig: This will be a story with no ending. After all it is the nature of memory work that the portraits we create will always remain essentially unfinished.

NOTES

1 The Oral History and Performance Group is one of seven working groups of the Life Stories of Montrealers Displaced by War, Genocide, and Other Human Rights Violations Community University Research Alliance project, situated at the Centre for Oral History and Digital Storytelling, Concordia University. The project aimed to record life story interviews with 500 Montreal residents exploring their experiences of mass violence and displacement. For more on the project see www.lifestoriesmontreal.ca.

2 Refers to the essay Hourig co-authored with her friend Hermig on which the script of *Stories Scorched from the Desert Sun* is based. See Hourig Attarian and Hermig Yogurtian "Survivor Stories, Surviving Narratives: Autobiography, Memory and Trauma Across Generations," in Yasmin Jiwani, Candis Steenburgen, and Claudia Mitchell, eds., *Girlhood: Redefining the Limits* (Montreal: Black Rose, 2006), 13–34.

3 *Stories Scorched from the Desert Sun* was performed as a theatrical staged reading produced by Teesri Duniya Theatre on 28 March 2009 in Montreal, as part of the Untold Histories series of the Oral History and Performance Group. The cast members were Amena Ahmad, Maya Dhawan, and Suyi Liu, with Chimwemwe Miller as musician. Maya, Amena, and Suyi subsequently took part in our performative dialogue presented at the "Remembering War, Genocide, and Other Human Rights Violations" conference in November 2009, with excerpted versions of their original acting parts. In the original staged reading, the three actors played multiple characters at many different ages, in many instances shifting back and forth quickly between each character.

4 E. Galeano, *Days and Nights of Love and War* (New York: Monthly Review Press, 2000), 20.

5 Shoshana Felman and Dori Laub, *Testimony: Crises of Witnessing in Literature, Psychoanalysis, and History* (New York and London: Routledge, 1992), 73.

6 A. Cvetkovich, *An Archive of Feelings: Trauma, Sexuality, and Lesbian Public Cultures* (Durham, NC: Duke University Press, 2003), 21. Cvetkovich also writes of "sensational representations as a distanced response to social problems" (156). For an in-depth consideration of Cvetkovich's theorizing of "The Politics of Affect" and sensationalism, see the Introduction to *Mixed Feelings: Feminism, Mass Culture, and Victorian Sensationalism* (New Brunswick, NJ: Rutgers, 1992), 1–12.

7 D. Laub, "Bearing Witness or the Vicissitudes of Listening," in Felman and Laub, eds., *Testimony*, 57–8.

8 See Julie Salverson, "Change on Whose Terms? Testimony and an Erotics of Injury," *Theater* 31 no. 3 (2001): 119–25. See also more recent writing from Salverson such as "Witnessing Subjects: A Fool's Help," in Jan Cohen-Cruz and Mady Schutzman, eds., *A Boal Companion: Dialogues on Theatre and Cultural Politics* (New York and London: Routledge, 2006), 146–57; and "Clown, Opera, the Atomic Bomb and the Classroom" in Tim Prentki and Sheila Preston, eds., *The Applied Theatre Reader* (London and New York: Routledge, 2009), 33–40.

9 In his vision for a socially engaged and politically effective Epic Theatre, Bertold Brecht advocated a distancing effect (also known in English as the "alienation effect") in order that spectators avoid losing themselves in the emotions of a character. In this way Brecht and others influenced by his thinking hoped to encourage critical reflection in the audience. For more on the theory and theatre of Brecht, see John Willett's *Brecht on Theatre: The Development of an Aesthetic* (New York: Hill and Wang, 1964).

10 Ann Cvetkovich, in *An Archive of Feelings*, 2, writes "the story itself couldn't be articulated in a single coherent narrative – it was much more complicated than the events of what happened, connected to other histories that were not my own." See also Jim Mienczakowski and Stephen Morgan on "polyphonic narratives," in "Ethnodrama: Constructing Participatory, Experiential and Compelling Action Research through Performance," in Peter Reason and Hilary Bradbury, eds., *Handbook of Action Research: Participative Inquiry and Practice* (London and Los Angeles: Sage, 2006), 17, and Arlene Goldbard's "Complicating the Story" in her blog of 2 January 2009, at http://arlenegoldbard.com.

11 Cvetkovich, *An Archive of Feelings*, 7.

PART THREE

Oral History and Digital Media

7 Oral History in the Age of Social Media Networks: Life Stories on CitizenShift and Parole Citoyenne

REISA LEVINE

Back in 2007, when the project entitled Life Stories of Montrealers Displaced by War, Genocide, and other Human Rights Violations was still in its embryonic phases, a spark of an idea for collaboration was struck up between Dr Steven High, Canada Research Chair in Public History and Head of Concordia University's Centre for Oral History, and Dr Johannes Stroble, my thesis adviser in Concordia's Department of Educational Technology. The idea was to see if CitizenShift, the Citizen Media Web platform I was producing at the National Film Board of Canada (NFB), could become a partner on the Montreal Life Stories project.

Although at that point Life Stories was still at the proposal phase, it was nonetheless compelling enough to engage eighteen different academic and community partner groups to participate in the five-year initiative. In just one meeting with the fledgling Life Stories project team, we could sense that this was going to be a stimulating collaboration. What we could not have known at the time was how important our partnership would become in terms of making public the rich oral histories that were subsequently posted on the CitizenShift and Parole citoyenne websites and the impact they would have.

This essay came about from my participation in the conference "Remembering War, Genocide and Other Human Rights Violations: Oral History, New Media and the Arts," which was hosted by the Life Stories project. The reflections put forward here took root while I was preparing for the conference and continued to flourish throughout our five years as participants in the Life Stories project.

Through CitizenShift's collaboration with the Life Stories project, we have had some excellent opportunities to experience the benefits and challenges of creating and distributing digital stories, both over the Web and to live audiences. I have outlined our project's trajectory here as a narrative vehicle in which to expose some of the aesthetic, technical, and ethical considerations that our teams have been grappling with. These include the problems stemming from the balance of power between filmmaker, subject, and viewer and how technical quality and filmic language can influence the emotional impact of a digital story. I also reflect on notions of a "public" for these works and some of the problems and benefits of distributing them over the Web. I'll look at the predominance of database models and alternative ways of organizing content, such as curated playlists. And finally, I discuss the impact and potential for engagement that media of this nature can have on community-oriented sites (such as CitizenShift) as well as on the increasingly popular behemoth, YouTube.

The CitizenShift team comprises media artists and Internet practitioners and the issues raised here reflect this point of view.

CitizenShift and Parole Citoyenne – Media for Social Change

CitizenShift and its French-language sister site Parole citoyenne are two award-winning Web platforms that explore social issues through films, photos, articles, blogs, and podcasts. The sites were born out of the National Film Board of Canada (NFB) in 2004 at a time of a growing public awakening to the new tools of digital media production. Easy-to-use pocket cameras were becoming ever more accessible to "ordinary citizens" and the Web was abuzz with people who were making and sharing their own media.

The projects were initially inspired by the famous Challenge for Change program, which was developed by the NFB in the 1960s and 1970s, putting filmmaking tools directly into the hands of ordinary citizens. "The mandate of Challenge for Change was to provide the voiceless population of Canada with the means to communicate … it used film to promote social change and allowed the people themselves, not the experts, to express the social issues that concerned them."[1]

Today, over thirty years later, CitizenShift and Parole citoyenne have been referred to as the "digital offspring" of Challenge for Change[2] and have picked up on the spirit of community-driven media at the forefront of the Web 2.0 revolution.[3] They were among the World Wide Web's earliest pioneers in social media production and distribution, online before YouTube or Facebook and long before Twitter. That

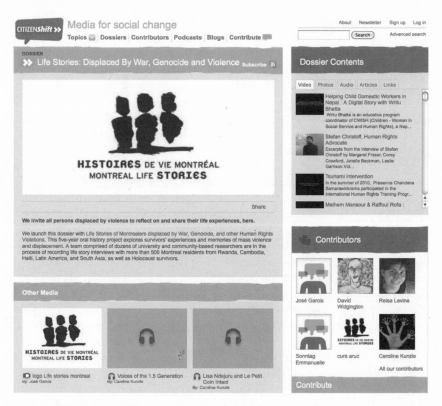

7.1 CitizenShift screenshot. Montreal Life Stories dossier.

moment, on the cusp of the read/write Web, was an exciting time to launch the two platforms, which quickly mobilized an active community of media makers and social issue advocates. As the sites progressed, we focused on building partnerships with organizations and individuals who were interested in creating and distributing media around specific social issues, and we were particularly keen on working with the Life Stories project.

Some Background to the "Video for Change" Movement Online

The zeitgeist of the early 2000s was embodied by a new wave of alternative media sites appearing on the Web, notably indymedia.org, one of the earliest of this genre. Sparked by political movements such as the

Zapatista Army of National Liberation (EZLN), the Seattle WTO protests of 1999, and the Genoa G8 summit in 2001, and stemming from a rich history of alternative print, film, and analogue media practices, the turn of the century brought on a new era of digital media countercultures.

Langlois and Dubois refer to these movements as "Autonomous Media."[4] John Downing's seminal research has revealed that they are also called "alternative media, citizens' media, community media, tactical media, independent media, counter-information media, participatory media, etc."[5] Regardless of what they are called, their essential role is to reveal the otherwise hidden stories generally not covered by the mainstream media, as well as to demystify the process of media creation in order to encourage greater participation.[6] Now in the digital era, independent media outlets facilitate interconnected networks, which subsequently allow for global connections.[7]

The new Internet ecology was the perfect garden in which to grow alternative media to new ambitions. For the first time in the history of media dissemination, the prospect of universal and unobstructed participation of the "masses" was a real possibility. Internet scholars and media pundits alike were calling the Web 2.0, or participative Web, phenomenon an unprecedented opportunity for digital empowerment. Although we have since come down from the high of those early days to face the limitations of this rhetoric (notably around access), at the time the hyperbole was almost euphoric.

A similar project to CitizenShift, which sprang up around the same time and is also still active today, is Engage Media,[8] a Melbourne, Australia–based activist Web portal focused on Southeast Asia. In addition to hosting citizen media reportage and political documentaries on their site, Engage Media also facilitates workshops to assist community groups with digital storytelling, media production, and Web distribution. Some other noteworthy examples include MoveOn, LinkTV, and Global Voices.[9] All of these started up at roughly the same time and with similar aims in hosting and promoting new Citizen Media content.

The Hub[10] is yet another example of a similarly focused site, but which appeared a bit later. Launched by Witness in 2007, the Hub was touted as being the "YouTube for human rights" and hosted a large array of video reports on human rights issues and abuses from around the world. In spite of the considerable resources that Witness spent on the Hub, it was decided in 2010 to close the site to new uploads, keeping it online only as an archive. Witness's strategy here is of particular interest, as it outlines the current challenges many independent media websites are facing. In a blog post by executive director Yvette Alberdingk Thijm explaining their decision,[11] she mentions YouTube as being a big detractor, as well as the costs of technical maintenance. Witness will now be collaborating directly with YouTube to enhance their growing numbers of human rights video content and to offer better security conditions for potentially sensitive materials.[12]

As with many of these online entities, CitizenShift has also had to deal with considerable changes since its inception. In the summer of 2009, after five years of existence at the NFB, the CitizenShift and Parole citoyenne projects were cut and passed on to the not-for-profit, Montreal-based organization, L'institut du Nouveau Monde (INM). Besides the usual budgetary constraints that the film board regularly faces, it was felt that the two sites were now mature enough to "make it on their own" and it was time for the projects to fledge. Now at the INM, the two sites continue to live and grow, albeit in a very different environment than at the NFB. Nonetheless, CitizenShift and Parole citoyenne have evolved into unique hybrid media, blending multiple media formats, genres, and techniques within one hosting platform. There are actually very few sites like these that still exist online today, and CitizenShift/Parole citoyenne are currently developing new business models in order to sustain the sites into the future.

In the Beginning: Life Stories on CitizenShift/Parole Citoyenne

It took a bit of time at the outset of the project before our intentions were understood by the Life Stories working groups. I can clearly remember attending our first meeting in the fall of 2008, where we excitedly spoke about putting *the best* oral histories collected by the interviewers up on CitizenShift and Parole citoyenne. Our idea was to create *special versions* of the stories for public viewing and then *promote* them to our communities. This language ruffled a few feathers in some of the working groups, who knew little about our collaborative approach to media production or about our *social outreach* practices and were critical of the potentially manipulative processes behind filmmaking and marketing. We were questioned about how we would make choices on what was *good* for public viewing? How would the ethics around making these sensitive works public be handled? How would decisions be made around editing down the full interviews, which can sometimes last ten to twelve hours?

This critical questioning over our process and intent surprised us. For us as filmmakers, making decisions in the editing room around technical and aesthetic evaluations is the very heart of filmmaking. In his essay "Oral History and the Digital Revolution," Michael Frisch describes the documentary process as "the indispensability of editorial intervention, selection, shaping, arrangement, and even manipulation."[13] Michael Ondaatje's conversations with film editor Walter Murch reveal the art of filmmaking as moving things around until they become sharp and clear in order to "discover the work's true voice and structure." Murch compares the editing process to writing poetry, how juxtaposing two shots works like rhyme and alliteration; a deeper implication is born from the composition. The essence is to "make that flow an organic part of the process."[14]

Nonetheless, some members of the Life Stories project teams, who were wary of the potential to manipulate meaning through constructed sequences, were concerned that oral historians might see the act of editing the raw interviews as a form of censorship that could potentially "destroy the credibility of the history."[15] From our perspective as media creators we felt we had to help move the project beyond some of these constraining methodologies, while still respecting the fundamental ethics underlying the project. We wanted to convey the powerful impact that short films could potentially have in educating and effectively communicating these oral histories. For us it was clear that creating short, edited versions of the interviews for a public audience was essential, especially for the younger "millennial generation" who are more inclined to turn to the Internet as a learning medium and are especially drawn to short films.[16]

Finding Common Ground

Although we were intuitively conscious of the notions of *shared authority* – which is one of the guiding principles of the Life Stories project – coming from a media practitioner's point of view, we didn't necessarily frame this in the same terms or even recognize the terminology for that matter. To oral historians, sharing authority strives for a mutual cultivation of trust, collaborative relationships, and shared decision making, especially around the interview process, but also with the communities involved.[17] The historians on the Life Stories project were highly specialized in collecting testimonies from people who have lived through unimaginable horrors. Maintaining high standards for the ethics and rigour of their work is critical to the integrity of the project.[18] On the other hand, the CitizenShift/Parole citoyenne teams were approaching it from a social media and documentary production stance; the important thing for us was getting the works into a format suitable for public viewing on the Web. Our teams would talk about *open conversations, participatory media*, and *collective intelligence.*[19] It became apparent in early meetings that we would have to modify our language so that all project participants would understand our intentions. Regardless of our differing terms, the fundamental notion of sharing – and, as an extension, of respect – is essential whether one comes to it as an oral historian, a documentary filmmaker, or a Web 2.0 practitioner. These shared aspirations were a good place for our teams to begin to explore a common ground and gave us a solid base on which to build our collaboration.

The documentary process entails complex power relationships between creator, subject, and audience and has many ethical concerns built in. Filmmakers and theorists have been grappling with this for decades and new online environments have no doubt exacerbated the complexities. We were aware that the presence of the camera during the interviews (which is never negligible) might potentially influence the "performance" of the storyteller or skew the balance of power, thus upsetting that delicate shared authority. However, in cases where all participants in the process "see the film as an opportunity to jointly communicate a shared perspective on an aspect of life,"[20] the inherent power structures can be balanced.

Indian filmmaker Rakesh Sharma discusses his interviewing process in his 2003 documentary film entitled *Final Solution* as spontaneous and responsive. The film, set in Gujarat province in 2002–3, examines the rise of the right-wing Hindu nationalist propaganda machine and the terrible violence that ensued. Sharma is able to get candid and deeply revealing interviews from all sides of the conflict not by dwelling on "victim-hood" or sensationalist accounts, but rather by patiently listening to "everyday kinds of conversations."[21] It is through the sharing of these individual narratives that Sharma creates a meta-narrative in complicity with his subjects.

We can also see overlaps in the disciplines of documentary filmmaking and the documenting of oral histories when it comes to problems around the representation of memory and trauma. Speaking the unspeakable is a complicated dilemma confounded by memory and language. "Narrative memory, like history, is constructed or configured by emphasizing some things and leaving others out."[22] However, traumatic events seem to demand their inclusion into a story because of their dramatic nature and yet are exceedingly difficult to represent on film. Filmmakers have taken widely varying approaches to the problem. In some films, like Alain Resnais's 1955 Holocaust film *Nuit et brouillard*, the depiction is as poetic as it is horrific. Resnais initially refused the offer to make the film, but finally agreed to do it in collaboration with poet Jean Cayrol, who had survived the camps himself. This was Resnais's gut instinct and his way of employing shared authority, the balancing of power between creator and subject. However in his subsequent film, *Hiroshima mon amour* (1959), Resnais takes an entirely different approach, having come to the conclusion through his experience in making *Nuit et brouillard* that "documentary knowledge is impossible" and that one cannot represent the past "as it really was."[23] In *Hiroshima* Resnais reminds us that forgetting is as much a part of storytelling as trying to recreate a truth and there are only hints and allusions to the trauma for which we no longer need to see the graphic newsreels to understand. No matter how the filmmaker approaches the problem, representation is a delicate balancing act that must be handled with care.

Perhaps one point of divergence that remains between documentary filmmakers and oral historians is around the fundamental goals that drive the documentation of these kinds of difficult stories. Historians are mainly concerned with a carefully preserved documentation of the past, whereas documentary filmmakers are actively striving to shape the future. As Sharma quotes at the outset of his film: "Those who cannot remember the past are condemned to repeat it"[24] Or perhaps these very goals are, in fact, the crossroads where these two disciplines meet and merge onto common ground.

The Production Process

As we moved forward with our work on the project, the Life Stories and CitizenShift / Parole citoyenne teams began to get to know and trust one another. It also became increasingly clear that a crucial part of the project's mandate was to inform, educate, and engage not just a select group of academics but also a broader interested public.

That being said, in the beginning we had great concerns about the potential impact of the project because the first films posted on the site were somewhat lacking in technical proficiency. All the interviewers were carefully trained to listen to the storytellers; unfortunately, the filmmaking process was almost an afterthought. Even though we conducted camera workshops, several of the early pieces were not captured with much care for production values: for example, seating subjects in front of windows so they became underexposed, not capturing sound effectively, or leaving a very wide and alienating frame. It appeared that the interviewers were almost intimidated by the equipment and, in wanting to give the storytellers their utmost attention, mostly ignored the technical side. This is an unfortunate mistake, as the desire to honour the subject necessitates assuring the highest possible production values to make them look and sound as good as they can. This balance can take time to learn, sometimes years before a documentary filmmaker masters the art of manipulating the equipment so that it serves the subject without letting it detract from the interview process.

There is a big difference between the first films created in the project and the short films that were produced later on. The later films, made with the help of emerging or professional filmmakers, are much stronger aesthetically and therefore speak more directly to audiences. Because they are more skilfully constructed as short films, they touch us emotionally; we feel their impact. Media scholar Belinda Smaill talks about how the role of emotion in film can "rally and sustain movements engaged in seeking social recognition for groups and individuals."[25] Of course, the Life Stories short films are not constructed in the sense of being "made up," as the stories are as they are told and there is no fiction being written here. This is important for the integrity of the research aspect to the project, but also to the audience, as there is little tolerance for purposeful misrepresentation or dishonesty in these types of historical documentaries and first-person narratives. Nonetheless, according to the pioneering Russian filmmaker Sergei Eisenstein, filmmaking is defined by montage and paying attention to the camera, sound, and particularly the editing process; we can *create* meaning and impact in conveying the story.[26] Frisch refers to these constructions as "cooked" in the sense that the raw footage can only become meaningful once it has "presumed this kind of culinary role."[27] Walter Murch speaks of the "dance between the words and images and the sounds." He goes on to involve the audience as "co-conspirators in the creation of the work,"[28] suggesting that we all bring our own experiences and interpretations to films, as we do to all stories that are imparted on us. The careful balance between "cinematic construction" on the one hand and "the integrity of the stories" on the other is crucial for the Life Stories films.

VIDÉO
Groupe de travail: Haïti

00:47 ━━━━━━━┃   03:30 ◂|·····|||| ⋝⋞

Une contribution de cura aruc   ❤ ♡   Partager

7.2 Parole citoyenne screenshot. Elizabeth Philibert film. Haitian working group.

Because of this, great care has been taken throughout the project to do the cooking in close consultation with the storytellers, which has resulted in some wonderfully rich moments of true collaboration.

The converse to Frisch's cooked documentary film is the notion of the database. The Life Stories project also built a database tool called Stories Matter. This interface allows historians to consult the entire body of work collected during the interviewing process.[29] Database models containing non-linear or "raw" information can liberate media from preconceived paths and lead to exciting possibilities for historians and the public alike to create their own meanings.[30] While this can be hugely powerful and "more responsive, contingent, and sharable,"[31] it is mainly researchers who truly benefit from database representations, in spite of its predominance for online media. Just because YouTube is perhaps the quintessential database used today does not mean that it is necessarily the best way to present works of this nature to broad-based audiences.[32] This model is inadequate in helping viewers find and make sense of specific content and does a poor job of offering any context.[33]

The Life Stories media works found on CitizenShift / Parole citoyenne are situated somewhere in between a documentary film and a comprehensive database. We might consider this a contextualized collection or a "curated playlist" and agree with Jon van der Veen's notion of the important middle ground that a playlist occupies between the constructed narrative of the documentary and the unwieldy database.[34] In this case the curators are the Life Stories and CitizenShift / Parole citoyenne production teams who upload the works to the sites and make choices as to the content, texts, and tags associated with each work. It is this contextualized environment that distinguishes these platforms from other video-sharing sites.

Currently on the Sites – A Growing Collection

At the time of this writing there are over sixty videos published by the Histoires de vie Montréal / Montreal Life Stories project on Parole citoyenne and CitizenShift, organized into two dossiers (sections dedicated to specific topics). These numbers continue to grow as new materials are uploaded. There is also a wide range of content in the Life Stories dossiers, from the recordings of speeches to theatrical performances to walking tours to interviews with notable historians – and, of course, the digital stories. Some of the videos are highly polished, professionally produced public service announcements, while others contain shaky footage shot with a cellphone. This diversity is part of the charm and allure of the Life Stories collection.

A few of the works on the sites have tens of thousands of views, but the current average is around 5,000 unique plays per piece. However, these numbers are continuously growing as the part of the Long Tail phenomenon,[35] a pattern of alternative distribution particular to the Web, which describes the growth of niche content over a long period of time.

Life in the Open Prison – A Spinoff Project

Early in 2009, Megan Webster, a teacher from St George's High School in Montreal, contacted us about helping her students create a feature documentary film for the Life Stories project. At first we tried to discourage

AUDIO
Jean-Marie Rurangwa à «La vie rêvée des gens», CIBL 101,5 FM Radio Montréal

Jean-Marie Rurangwa à «La vie rêvée des gens», CIBL 101,5 FM Radio Montréal

◀ ❯ ▶

Une contribution de cura aruc		❤ ♡	Partager

Auteur / Crédit : **Emmanuelle Sonntag** Durée : **26:02** Licence : © Tous droits réservés Année de production : **2008**	Ecrivain, essayiste, poète, dramaturge ...le parcours muliticolore de Jean Marie V. Rurangwa débute par une vie d'exil au Burundi dans un camp de réfugiés et débouche sur un homme aux multiples talents artistiques qui essaie de faire connaitre son pays, le Rwanda, à la sortie du génocide de 1994.

< Précédent   Suivant >

Mots clés : artiste engagé, arts, exil, génocide, poète, Rwanda
Thème : Culture
Dossier(s) multimédia(s) : Histoires de vie : Déplacés par la guerre et la violence

7.3 Parole citoyenne screenshot. Jean-Marie Rurangwa podcast.

the idea of a feature-length piece as this seemed a bit much for high school students to tackle, but Megan and her students were not to be deterred. We initially put Megan in touch with the Life Stories team so that her students could receive the essential training that all participants go through before conducting interviews. CitizenShift then came in to conduct specialized camera and sound workshops, but the rest of the production was done entirely by Megan and her students. The final result is a gem of a documentary entitled *Life in the Open Prison: Survival Stories from Two of the Millions. Cambodia 1975–1979.*[36]

This is an excellent example of the types of artistic works that have "spun off" from the Life Stories project. Through making a documentary film, these students learned not only about the filmmaking process, but more importantly, about Cambodian history, other genocides, and about how they themselves could make a difference by using media to inform others. By directly implicating themselves in a creative process as well as investigating stories lived by their fellow Montrealers, these students are engaging more deeply than possible within more traditional and pedantic classroom methods.[37] It was gratifying to see the young learners beaming with pride on their accomplishments at the public screenings of their film, and the audience was completely engaged. Through this spinoff project we have direct evidence of how media can be used for deeper learning, a fundamental goal of both Life Stories and CitizenShift/Parole citoyenne.

The Life Stories Media Collection –
Using the Internet as a Popular Distribution Medium

Something intriguing has emerged out of the collection of media from this project. The body of work also tells a story in and of itself. Yes, there is the overarching theme of survival and persistence, which comes through in all of the individual pieces; but through the body of work there is also the story about a project. The Life Stories project is a story about gathering stories. It is also about how these stories are being used to honour survivors, share with others, and teach a new generation.

As mentioned in the "Remembering War, Genocide, and Other Human Rights Violations" conference description, one of the goals of the Life Stories Project is "to promote deep engagement with life stories that contain or are defined by experiences of mass human rights violations … its guiding principle is a sincere commitment to public engagement."[38] This raises an important question for us: Is it possible to engage deeply with a video clip that is viewed over the Internet?

A few empirical studies have emerged showing that people do have real emotional engagement with some Internet videos.[39] We also have some comments on CitizenShift / Parole citoyenne indicating that people are touched by the stories they watch. More notoriously, there have been several cases over the past decade where contentious video footage "leaked" over the Internet has had profound effects, or at least has caused considerable public uproar. Cases like the 2004 Abu Ghraib cellphone footage of prisoner abuse in the Iraqi jail and the 2010 WikiLeaks videos of US bomb strikes on civilians in Iraq are just a couple of examples.

One of the most potent characteristics of digital media, and what makes them such an effective advocacy tool, is that the works are free to travel and be integrated into a wide variety of environments. We

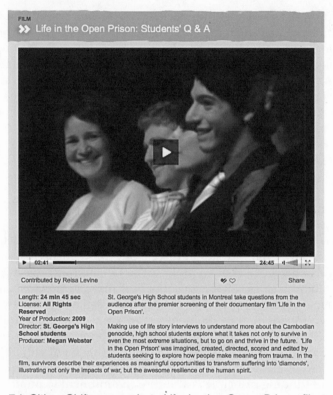

7.4 CitizenShift screenshot. *Life in the Open Prison* film, St George's High School.

have successfully used the technique of *embedding* throughout the Life Stories project so that the media works can reach greater audiences across multiple sites and sectors. But this loss of control can be unpredictable as we know that the location and context in which a person views media can affect their reception of it.[40] Because of these issues, many scholars are vehemently opposed to publishing oral histories online, and, as we saw at the conference, in some projects the media produced are maintained in a tightly controlled and restricted environment. This can be understandable when what is revealed might put people's lives in danger or otherwise revictimize them. In these cases, historians need to be highly sensitive to the ethics of releasing this media publicly.[41]

The counterpoint to this can easily be found on YouTube, where a simple search with the key term "genocide," (a significant term employed on YouTube to refer to stories of war, violence, and human rights abuses), turns up close to 100,000 videos, ranging from Armenia to the Ottoman Empire to Congo and Darfur to Kazakhstan to Canada's treatment of its First Nations peoples – just to name a few (and not to mention several references to heavy metal albums). As of 13 May 2012, YouTube was serving more than 4 billion videos per day,[42] and many of those "genocide" films have hundreds of thousands of views each. Individuals are now reclaiming control of their stories by filming themselves and publishing online. Clearly many people do feel an imperative need to share their stories, as part of a personal healing process, from a desire to tell the world what happened to them, or as a warning cry to prevent other atrocities. Digital storytelling has discovered the self-publishing power of Web 2.0, and the number of works of this nature on YouTube and many other sites is quickly growing.

Although we cannot yet predict the long-term impact of participatory media, there is nonetheless a definite shift in the way that media work on the Internet. Compared to traditional distribution models like TV, the Web offers real opportunities for exchange and action.[43] To take the notion of interaction further, Coleman and Ross in their recent investigation of the roles of "the public" look forward to a day where people will actually be able to intervene in what we witness. "If media interactivity can make teaching and learning more effective, commerce more convenient to conduct, public information more accessible, and friendships easier to maintain, surely it can also enable publics to make their presence felt in ways that can make a difference."[44]

Although Coleman and Ross and many others are optimistic, we are also seeing a growing number of websites that promote discrimination, racial stereotyping, and hate mongering. Unfortunately, material of that heinous nature can be found and shared online, and the Internet is also proving to be an opportune platform for racist violence.[45] Perhaps the Internet is only acting as a mirror (or magnifying glass) to reflect those notions that already exist within our societies, and online interactivity simply helps it spread more quickly and widely.

In addition to video-sharing sites, we now also have live-casting technologies coming up on the global mediascape. As Sam Gregory, program director at Witness predicts, live-casting, which allows anybody to stream live video directly from a cellphone, "will have powerful positive implications for sharing footage and engaging constituencies immediately."[46] However, Gregory also warns of potentially enormous security risks as well as escalating difficulties or even impossibilities of maintaining ethical standards.

The complex issues emerging from the rise of digital distribution stress the importance of organizations such as Witness and the work being done on CitizenShift and at Concordia University's Centre for Oral History and Digital Storytelling. Initiatives such as these are crucial for promoting a culture of empathy and ethical sharing. Strong stories will convey their message regardless of the screen they are viewed on. As media producers, curators, and disseminators, it is part of our job to encourage narrators to be mindful of their stories as we help to educate on the benefits of sharing (although storytellers often teach *us* about why sharing is so important for healing and teaching). We must remain vigilant and alert to the ethical and security issues around making personal stories public and monitor the progress of this new social paradigm. This is what we try to achieve with the Life Stories collection on CitizenShift/Parole citoyenne: offer enough contexts to frame the issues, but ultimately to allow the stories to speak for themselves.

Taking It Further

As mentioned, we now have over sixty videos online in the Life Stories dossiers. We know by the site's statistics that they are being seen, but we don't know enough about who is watching them and in what contexts (beyond some anecdotal evidence from educators and community leaders). This is certainly something that we need to research further. Subsequently, we would like to enhance the outreach process and improve the way we circulate these stories.

CitizenShift/Parole citoyenne have developed creative outreach strategies over the years involving a mix of traditional techniques as well as networked social media. In addition to the many ways one can use the Web for engaging communities, Liz Miller reiterates the importance of "tried and true approaches to on-the-ground engagement."[47] The CitizenShift/Parole citoyenne teams devote as much time and energy as possible connecting with people through community organizations, in educational settings, and through public screenings. As a

7.5 Parole citoyenne screenshot. *Childhood Disrupted* film. Montreal Life Stories.

community media platform, it's our goal to make these connections explicit, putting people in touch via the media works on the site. We know all too well that community does not just happen; you have to nurture it and "grow it" like a gardener.

Conclusion

We are proud of the work done to date on the Life Stories Montreal project; CitizenShift and Parole citoyenne are essential tools for the project's media dissemination. In addition to the growing collection of works on the sites, our collaboration has seen spinoff projects such as the *Life in the Open Prison* documentary; we have seen the videos used in schools, embedded in blogs, and presented at conferences and seminars. We have also held public screenings, and directly witnessed the healing power that personal stories and open discussions can have on communities in helping to make sense of complex histories.

However, beyond the important task of curating and contextualizing this content, the project has created a crucial intersection between the work of oral historians, human rights advocates, digital media producers, performance artists, and educators. In bringing multiple sectors together, we have helped to expose a common ground and mutual understanding and have proven the vitality of stepping outside of our disciplinary boundaries to work collaboratively. In addition to offering our platforms as a host and advocacy tool, we see our role as contributors to an online culture that aims to promote respect and tolerance. CitizenShift/Parole citoyenne and the Life Stories project are members of a new global media movement which is playing a direct role in shaping the new digital cultures. Through our work we are helping to guide norms and practices, influence tendencies, and promote effective solutions around the creation and dissemination of works of this nature. Ultimately, part of the engagement we are striving for through this project includes the question of how we, as individuals and communities, will react to future (and current) atrocities in light of what we have learned from past stories. It is by working together that we are able to honour the lives of these Montrealers and mobilize their stories in order to sensitize a greater public.

NOTES

1 NFB, "NFB Our History," http://nfb.ca/historique/1960-1969.
2 Thomas Waugh, Brendan Baker, and Ezra Winton, eds., *Challenge for Change: Activist Documentary at the National Film Board of Canada* (McGill-Queen's University Press, 2010), 4.
3 The term was coined in 2004 by Tim O'Reilly and then expanded in the 2005 article, "What Is Web 2.0?", http://www.oreillynet.com/pub/a/oreilly/tim/news/2005/09/30/what-is-web-20.html.
4 Andrea Langlois and Frédéric Dubois, *Autonomous Media: Activating Resistance and Dissent* (Montreal: Cumulus Press, 2005).
5 John Downing, "Uncommunicative Partners: Social Movement Media Analysis and Radical Educators," Media@McGill website, http://media.mcgill.ca/en/john_downing_keynote.
6 Stephan Coleman and Karen Ross, *The Media and the Public: "Them" and "Us" in Media Discourse* (Malden, MA: Wiley-Blackwell, 2010).
7 Joshua D Atkinson, *Alternative Media and Politics of Resistance: A Communication Perspective* (New York: Peter Lang, 2010), 56.

8 Engage Media, http://www.engagemedia.org/.
9 MoveOn, http://moveon.org/; LinkTV, http://www.linktv.org/; Global Voices, http://globalvoicesonline.org/.
10 The Hub, Witness, http://hub.witness.org/.
11 Yvette Alberdingk Thijm, http://blog.witness.org/2010/08/update-on -the-hub-and-witness-new-online-strategy/.
12 "New Collaboration with YouTube on the Power of Human Rights Video," Witness blog, http://blog.witness.org/2010/06/protecting-yourself-your -subjects-and-your-human-rights-videos-on-youtube/.
13 Michael Frisch, "Oral History and the Digital Revolution: Toward a Post-Documentary Sensibility," in Robert Perks and Alistair Thomson, eds., *The Oral History Reader*, 2nd ed. (London: Routledge. 2006), 102–14.
14 Michael Ondaatje, *The Conversations: Walter Murch and the Art of Editing Film* (Toronto: Vintage Canada, 2002), 21, 198.
15 Valerie Yow, "Ethics and Interpersonal Relationships in Oral History Research," *Oral History Review*, 22, no. 1 (Summer, 1995): 51–66.
16 Ezra Winton, "Beyond the Textbook," *Point-of-View Magazine* 77 (Spring 2010): 14–17.
17 Henry Greenspan, "Sharing Authority in Interpreting Survivor Testimony: A Worthy and Realistic Goal? Part 1" (CURA on CitizenShift, Life Stories Collection, 2009), http://citizenshift.org/henry-greenspan-sharing -authority-interpreting-survivor-testimony-worthy-and-realistic-goal; Steven High, "Sharing Authority: An Introduction and Sharing Authority: Building Community University Research Alliances Using Oral History, Digital Storytelling and Engaged Scholarship," *Journal of Canadian Studies* 43, no. 1 (2009): 12–34.
18 Histoires de vie Montréal – Montreal Life Stories, "Ethics Guide Summary: CURA Research Protocol," 2008, http://www.lifestoriesmontreal.ca/en/ ethics-guide-summary. For more background on the main tendencies within the oral history movement see Alistair Thomson, "Four Paradigm Transformations in Oral History," *Oral History Review* 34, no.1 (2007): 49–70.
19 O'Reilly, "What Is Web 2.0?" http://www.oreillynet.com/pub/a/oreilly/ tim/news/2005/09/30/what-is-web-20.html.
20 Jane L. Chapman, *Issues in Contemporary Documentary* (Cambridge: Polity, 2009), 163.
21 Rakesh Sharma: interview by Nicole Wolf in the 2004 Berlinale Film Festival, http://www.berlinale.de/external/de/filmarchiv/doku_pdf/20042196.pdf.
22 Michael S. Roth, *The Ironist's Cage: Memory, Trauma, and the Construction of History* (New York: Columbia University Press, 1995), 13, 205.

23 Ibid., 203.

24 George Santayana, 1863–1952.

25 Belinda Smaill, *The Documentary: Politics, Emotion, Culture* (New York: Palgrave Macmillan, 2010), 188.

26 Hart Cohen, Juan Francisco Salazar, Iqbal Barkat, *Screen Media Arts: An Introduction to Concepts and Practices* (Melbourne: Oxford University Press, 2009), 178.

27 Frisch, "Oral History and the Digital Revolution," 102–14, http://www.randforce.com/OHReader_Draft.pdf.

28 Ondaatje, *The Conversations*, 50, 90.

29 Steven High and David Sworn, "After the Interview: The Interpretive Challenges of Oral History Video Indexing," *Digital Studies/Le champ numérique* 1, no 2. (2009), http://www.digitalstudies.org/ojs/index.php/digital_studies/article/view/173/215.

30 Jon van der Veen, quoted in Joy Parr, Jessica Van Horssen, and Jon van der Veen, "The Practice of History Shared across Differences: Needs, Technologies and Ways of Knowing in the Megaprojects New Media Project," *Journal of Canadian Studies*, 43, no. 1 (2009): 48–56.

31 Frisch, "Oral History."

32 Geert Lovink, "The Art of Watching Databases: Introduction to the Video Vortex Reader," in Geert Lovink and Ned Rossiter, eds., *The Video Vortex Reader: Responses to YouTube* (Amsterdam: Institute of Network Cultures, 2008), 9–12.

33 Alexandra Juhasz, "Documentary on YouTube: The Failure of the Direct Cinema of the Slogan," in Thomas Austin and Wilma de Jong, eds., *Rethinking Documentary: New Perspectives, New Practices* (New York: McGraw-Hill/Open University Press, 2008), 299–311.

34 Van der Veen, quoted in Parr, Van Horssen, and van der Veen, "The Practice of History."

35 Chris Anderson, *The Long Tail: Why the Future of Business Is Selling Less of More* (New York: Hyperion, 2006).

36 *Life in the Open Prison: Survival Stories from Two of the Millions. Cambodia 1975–1979*, CitizenShift, http://citizenshift.org/life-open-prison-2.

37 Ruth Meyerowitz and Christine Zinni, "The Medium and the Message: Oral History, New Media, and a Grassroots History of Working Women," *Journal of Educational Technology Systems* 37, no. 3 (2009): 306–16. See also Michael Wesch, "Anti-Teaching: Confronting the Crisis of Significance," *Education Canada* 48, no. 2 (2008): 4–7.

38 Concordia University, "Remembering War, Genocide, and Other Human Rights Violations: Oral History, New Media and the Arts," 5–8 November

2009, http://storytelling.concordia.ca/memoire/, http://www
.lifestoriesmontreal.ca/en/ethics-guide-summary.

39 Jeffrey Bardzell, Shaowen Bardzell, and Tyler Pace, "Emotion, Engagement
    and Internet Video," *One to One Interactive, New Media Research*, 2008,
    http://www.onetooneglobal.com/wp-content/uploads/2009/03/affect-
    study-screen-view1.pdf. See also Sam Gregory, "Cameras Everywhere:
    Ubiquitous Video Documentation of Human Rights, New Forms of Video
    Advocacy, and Considerations of Safety, Security, Dignity and Consent,"
    Journal of Human Rights Practice 2, no. 2 (2010): 191–207.

40 Chapman, *Issues in Contemporary Documentary*, 134–5.

41 Dmitri Vitaliev, "Digital Security and Privacy for Human Rights
    Defenders," *Frontline International Foundation for the Protection of Human
    Rights Defenders*, http://www.frontlinedefenders.org/esecman.

42 Retrieved 13 May 2012. See also Henry Jenkins, "Nine Propositions
    towards a Cultural Theory of YouTube," in *Confessions of an Aca-Fan, the
    Official Weblog of Henry Jenkins* (28 May 2007), http://www.henryjenkins
    .org/2007/05/9_propositions_towards_a_cultu.html.

43 O'Reilly, "What Is Web 2.0?" See also Chapman, *Issues in Contemporary
    Documentary*, 111.

44 Coleman and Ross, *The Media and the Public*, 133.

45 Nelli Kambouri and Pavlos Hatzopoulos, "Making Violent Practices
    Public," in Lovink and Rossiter, eds., *The Video Vortex Reader*, 125–31.

46 Gregory, "Cameras Everywhere."

47 Elizabeth Miller, "Building Participation in the Outreach for the Documen-
    tary, *The Water Front*," *Journal of Canadian Studies* 43, no. 1 (2009): 83.

8 Co-Creating Our Story: Making a Documentary Film

BY TEACHER MEGAN WEBSTER
AND STUDENT NOELIA GRAVOTTA

"Happiness is the feeling that you have hope. Hope."

At the screening of the student-made documentary film about the Cambodian genocide, one student summarized our grade 11 humanities course: "It was about listening. More than hearing people talk about history, we learned to listen to stories of horrifying events, and why hope is essential to survival." This article documents the process of creating a documentary film based on oral history in a high school class. We, grade 11 student Noelia and teacher Megan, dialogue about authority, pedagogy, and collaboration. We show how engagement with oral history provides students and teachers with avenues for deep learning, identity formation, and relationship building.

MEGAN

Sharing Authority: Co-Authoring Curriculum

A year ago, I learned of an inter-university oral history project: The Life Stories of Montrealers Displaced by War, Genocide, and other Human Rights Violations. It explores experiences and memories of mass violence and displacement, aiming to connect university and community-based researchers.[1] In my seventh year of teaching at St George's High School of Montreal, I was searching for something to invigorate my practice. I applied to the Education subcommittee of the project to see if my Humanities students could be involved in interviewing survivors as a part of their course work.

When I discussed the possibility with my students, most of them were not aware that Montreal is home to one of the largest populations of Holocaust survivors, as well as significant numbers of survivors of mass atrocities in Cambodia, Haiti, and Rwanda. I shared my understanding of oral history: an approach that attends as much, or more, to the meanings of events as understood by the participants as it does to the events themselves.

When my students learned 500 survivors were recording their stories, a collective thrill ran through the group. We realized we could be a part of making history. Possibilities coalesced into a plan: students wanted to meet and interview survivors, and turn their conversations into a documentary film.

"So how do we actually do this?" I asked. One student suggested we apply to the Life Stories project as satellite researchers. I coached them on the appropriate format of letters of intent and, a week later, they were accepted by the Education subcommittee. Enthusiastic about the potential of the project, researchers agreed to provide training for my students on the process and ethics of interviewing.

We chose to explore the Cambodian genocide. "People need to know that the Holocaust wasn't the only genocide," my students argued. The project would require our singular attention for the rest of the year. Though it was difficult for me to abandon the lesson plans I spent the summer writing, the excitement of the new project overwhelmed my initial agenda.

Pedagogy

It was important that our exploration be grounded in clear pedagogical goals for student learning. Four central ideas shaped the course:

a) History is constructed and thus subjective.
b) Sharing authority creates potential for meaning making.
c) Attending to the life stories of others changes our own perspectives, identities, and opinions.
d) The way a story is told shapes its meaning. Therefore, in storytelling, one must attend to both form and content.

I structured the learning goals around the principles of differentiated instruction, an approach that ensures how a student learns coincides with their level of learning readiness and interest. The teacher's responsibility is to articulate learning targets while providing scaffolding for every student to reach the goal in their own manner.[2]

As an elective, we only met twice a week for seventy-five-minute periods – we would have to be efficient. Nothing in my education as a teacher prepared me to manage such a complex project. However, I was able to draw on my experience as a teenage camp counsellor at a progressive, leftist camp. There, I had learned how to make major decisions by consensus and how and when to empower individuals to make practical decisions. Building on those formative experiences, I gave my students a series of mini-lessons on leadership – from how to run a meeting to how to make decisions as a group while attending to outliers. We discussed strategies for negotiating, goal-setting, and time management.

To facilitate collaboration, we made a list of norms about how we intended to engage with each other. I wanted the students to feel that I was not determining the nature of our group dynamics, but that we were working together to create the kind of community we wanted to inhabit, both in the classroom and in the world. We articulated both concrete and abstract intentions, from committing to checking our email every day to "working hard not to take things personally and to keep moving in the direction of our goals." We ratified our norms by consensus, building a sense of shared ownership of our process and product.

It was important that students learn how to think and act like professional oral historians. Stacey Zembrzycki, an oral historian at Concordia, walked us through Alessandro Portelli's "What Makes Oral History Different." We discussed how the written word cannot objectively capture the non-verbal cues such as gestures, silences, and eye contact that are so significant to communication. After these workshops, students were convinced that film was the most appropriate medium for sharing life stories, while also noting that the lens of the camera represents a kind of gaze which, like writing, can never be completely objective.

Frank conversations about how much work students were willing to do were essential for our planning. Nine of the eleven students were willing to go "above and beyond" to see the project to fruition. The other two, honest about their readiness to commit, were given less "intense" roles that still felt fair to the group. Students ready to take greater responsibility claimed roles requiring more planning and organization.

We defined the five central teams required to complete the project. Every period, students would gather to work in small groups of two to six members. We chose a facilitator for each group by consensus who was responsible for communication with the other teams and for management of timelines and to-do lists. Most students participated in multiple teams, as different work was required at different times. Between September and October, the Research Team taught their peers about Cambodia. In January, the Interview Team met with survivors. From February to April the Storyboard Team transformed the collected data into a narrative. Throughout the school year, the Messaging Team created publicity documents and managed fundraising activities. Finally, the Production Team turned the storyboard into the final film in April and May.

Getting Along

When we outlined the steps required to go from total ignorance of Cambodia to the production of an educational documentary film based on interviews with survivors, we felt overwhelmed. The students' prior experience of history was "learning the dates when stuff happened." The idea that they were also going to learn what it meant to people who lived through the genocide was motivating – and intimidating.

As the vision for our film became clearer, the enthusiasm for the project intensified. Students bounded into class. At moments, I could almost hear the swelling soundtrack of the Inspiring Teacher Movie Hollywood would make about this project, my fantasy culminating with a scene at the Oscars. Yet the immensity of our ambition also made me anxious. When one colleague said, "You know, professional documentary filmmakers could not do this job in seven months. Why do you think you can? You don't have to make a professional film. It's just a school project," I was surprised by how relieved I was to feel that no one else had high expectations.

But when I shared my colleague's sentiments the next day, the students surprised me with their anger. Rather than relieving them of the burden of expectations, they seemed even more determined to challenge the ideas adults had about them. Not only were they going to make a documentary film in seven months, they were going to make a *good* one. They were so articulate and eager, I thought they really would make excellent characters in a movie.

That same week, they proved their intentions: the research group had planned a session to teach the class about the history of Cambodia. By sorting, synthesizing, and analysing information, they gained a deeper perspective on the events than those of us sitting in the audience. Knowing that they were going to meet Cambodians face to face to discuss the genocide had created an immediate and authentic need to research. If they didn't "do their homework," students weren't going to fail a test – they were going to look like ignorant and indifferent teenagers. It was a perfect example of how easily learning comes when it is required for a genuine social purpose and it made me wonder why, if teachers want students to learn, we learn material ourselves and feed it to students. Students should do the difficult cognitive work and teach us. For the rest of the term, I depended on the research team to check facts and explain things to the class when we were confused, and I was frequently corrected for my own historical errors.

I felt an even greater shift towards sharing authority when students stopped seeking my permission to speak by raising their hands. I was no longer the only one asking the leading questions and organizing the class. We were talking together, naturally.

NOELIA

Foundations for an Interview

It seemed like everything I was learning in my other classes was really about Cambodia. In World History, I read about Second World War journalist Martha Gellhorn's indignation: "We were blind and unbelieving and slow, and that we can never be again … And if ever again we tolerate such cruelty we have no right to peace."[3] Her accusations triggered mine: how could the international community ignore a *genocide* in a post-Holocaust world? My work on the research team was feverish as I pushed my group to explain, explain, explain. I read Haing Ngor's memoir, *Survival in the Killing Fields,* to better understand the events in Cambodia. In retrospect, I realize I was preparing myself for what I might hear in the interviews.

In addition to conducting research, we spent several classes practising deep listening in order to become better interviewers.[4] Ms Webster led three exercises to help us understand the importance of silence. In the first, one person told a story while the listener used only body language to demonstrate empathy. Being able to listen without the automatic "ohhh" or "that sucks" was crucial; we didn't want to remind the survivor that we were generations and worlds away from their experience by interjecting teenagers' North American-isms. In the second exercise, one person "told" their story only using their eyes while the other "listened." Finally, partners simultaneously tried to tell each other a non-verbal story. I was so occupied with fighting to understand that I forgot to communicate. Reflecting on the exercise, I realized that I didn't need to fully understand in order to listen with compassion. Our deep listening sessions taught me to create space for a story without allowing vast differences in age, culture, and experience to block the transmission of a message.

MEGAN

Making Connections

At the time that my students and I were exploring deep listening, I met a Canadian-Cambodian university student at a Life Stories meeting who would come to be known as "our angel." Vanaka volunteered immediately when I mentioned our project. He didn't know what he was getting into at that fortuitous coffee break. Our Angel introduced us to Mr A[5] and Mr Pong, the two survivors we would interview, who agreed to meet us only because Vanaka encouraged them to do so. He drove students to interviews, answered a million questions about Cambodian culture, and provided spontaneous translation when necessary. As one student articulated, "he was so, like, *in*."

By late fall, students had been trained in oral history interviewing strategies, ethics, and deep listening. We had a pivotal connection in the Cambodian community and plans to meet two survivors. During a class discussion about the complex relationship between the United States, Thailand, and Cambodia during the Vietnam War, I realized how much these students had learned about Cambodian history in just a few months. We were moving forward, but our May deadline was fast approaching.

NOELIA

A Worrisome Start

When we came back from December break, many of us were disheartened. I didn't believe we could finish the documentary, and some of us were desperately hoping Ms Webster would let the project silently drop so we could go back to the original structured, safe curriculum. Luckily, there were always one or two people who managed to convince us that "we are totally okay, we can finish."

Our optimism returned when we finally confirmed a date with Mr A. I seized the chance to conduct the interview, relishing the challenge. However, I grew apprehensive while preparing my questions. I was an outsider to the Cambodian community and a stranger to Mr A, and yet I was going to ask him deeply personal questions. I worried about the details. For instance, I learned from Stacey that certain emotionally charged words can limit a storyteller and block a story. After consulting with Vanaka, I decided to use phrases like "the events between 1975 and 1979," rather than "the genocide."

Interviewing Mr A

As I watched the highway overpasses tangle and roll by from the back-seat of Vanaka's car, more anxieties surfaced. I needed to capture, on some level, Mr A's experience of the genocide, yet my only assets were my interest in his story and what I had learned in class. Even the confidence I had gained from the workshops was shaken. Could I really capture his message given the generational and cultural gap? I wanted Mr A to think I was interesting and mature enough to receive his story. How could I? I was a sixteen-year-old who spent three days deciding whether to layer my hair or get a bob.

With these insecurities in tow, the two directors, the videographer, and I, the interviewer, awkwardly entered Mr A's house to inform him more thoroughly about the project and gain his permission to record the interview and share it with others. Gracious Mr A agreed to be interviewed, though he requested we maintain his anonymity by making only an audio recording of the interview. As we spoke, my eyes wandered around his museum-like home. Cambodian figurines and paintings of the countryside decorated his living room. I wondered how he could fill his house with objects that might remind him of the events of the 70s. The paintings depicted farmers working in rice paddies and children playing in villages. Miniature versions of the temples at Angkor Wat recalled idyllic scenes of monks and villagers following the daily cycle of life. Perhaps he was reminding himself of a time before the horror, of a long-gone peaceful Cambodia.

The interview took place a week later. As I sat down with Mr A, my hands were shaking. His smile looked tightly drawn; I wondered if he was as nervous as I was. "Are you ready?" I asked. "Yeah, I'm ready. I mean, I didn't prepare anything," he replied sheepishly. My heart was racing but I stayed casual: "Oh no … I mean, it's your life." I already felt inadequate. "I just wanted to start, uh, a little chronologically, so could you tell me about your childhood?" A little chronologically? How eloquent.

Eventually we relaxed, and the questions came naturally. He shared his experiences, from his life in the pre–Khmer Rouge period, through the terrible years, to his immigration to France and later Montreal. I was particularly fascinated by his recollection of the constant lies required to survive. He had to pretend he was eager to work, he was happy, he wasn't hungry. The Khmer people had to change how they spoke and acted, and all personal relationships were forbidden. Imagining Mr A as a teenager who, like me, must also have been struggling to grasp a hazy idea of "self," I was shocked by the complete suppression of individuality people suffered during the Khmer Rouge regime. By vividly describing the scene of his family dyeing their clothes black in order to conform, Mr A depicted an unimaginable reality. I wondered how one could grow while trying to erase personal identity and integrity. Of this feigned existence, Mr A poignantly claimed, "It's not a life."

Mr A also reflected on the gap that existed between genocide survivors and everyone else. He cannot understand the importance that others attach to the colour of their bedroom walls or the gravity of missing the bus. As he commented on the privilege we have to complain about trivial matters, I was aware of the extent his suffering had stayed with him, always colouring his perceptions. Simultaneously, I felt admiration for this person who could survive such physical and emotional hardship to become the gentle, smiling figure sitting in front of me.

This clear distance between us made it all the more surprising that Mr A later told Vanaka he had benefited from talking about his experience with us. He said it had helped him work through his memories. I, on the other hand, felt something was missing. Instead of an emotional account of a difficult period in his life, I felt I had received a general and detached retelling of main events. In my journal that evening, I wrote, "The weird thing is that even though I left this interview with fascinating stories and a unique perspective on the Khmer Rouge period, I don't feel like I got any closer to understanding the meaning of the event." In retrospect, I understand that it was only through actively working with the interview to transform it into a film that I was able to comprehend Mr A's message.

MEGAN

Nightmares of Murder

I became aware of a conspicuous absence of detail about violence in our discussions of Cambodia. Students spoke in vague generalizations: "the terrible things that happened when two million people died." There were several slides in the research group's presentation about war crimes under the Khmer Rouge, which included the killing fields and shocking death counts at the interrogation centres, but we never lingered on these points.

Nevertheless, as the students shared interview footage with the class, the emotional intensity of our work amplified. I found myself becoming obsessed with stories of mass violence. At home, I wasn't just reading about Cambodia, but also about Sudan, the Ukrainian famine, the Holocaust. One winter evening, in bed reading *First They Killed My Father*, a memoir recommended to me by a student who also seemed privately obsessed, I put the book down and wept. The author, Loung Ung, came of age in Cambodia at the same time as Mr A and their stories bore striking similarities: a confusing march out of Phnom Penh, the labour camps, starvation, and the family members "called away" never to return. Yet unlike the oral history of Mr A, which seemed stripped of gruesome details, Ung's story was laden with vivid smells, sounds, and tastes.

Then my nightmares began. They were a pastiche of every genocide story I had encountered. Once I was a child, trapped in a closet, hearing the murder of my family. How long did I have to wait until I could emerge? In another, I had to choose between dressing up as a soldier, executing my people and saving myself, or taking my own life. I would wake up with damp sheets from fearful tossing, my face wet and stained.

I didn't share these anxieties with my students. Intuitively, I followed what I perceived to be their lead: they didn't seem to want to know gruesome details. I didn't ask them to read memoirs like Ung's, though many did. I wrestled with this all year. Was I being too superficial? Was I avoiding difficult subjects?

Vanaka came to our class once and showed us pictures of a pretty Cambodia. We saw images of bustling markets, magical temples, water-buffalo pulling carts. Conspicuously absent from our conversation was any talk of genocide. Instead, he focused on the beauty of the land-scape, the idiosyncratic features of Cambodian culture, and culinary delights. Later, Vanaka told me he didn't just want to focus on the horrors of the past. He thought we had already studied the genocide, and he wanted to round out our perspective. But we hadn't, not really. I was too embarrassed to tell him that I just didn't know how to talk to the students about it.

Ironically, it was hearing a sex educator talk about how to teach children about the origins of life that I learned how to talk to students about death. How do you know when kids are ready to learn about sex? They'll ask, she said. Until then, stick to the big picture: provide accurate facts, let the child set the pace. I exhaled. My students all knew the big facts, and those who wanted details sought them out themselves. I was concerned that becoming too intimate with the latent potential for violence in others would raise fear, a sentiment I think is at the root of most violence. How could I nurture their most luminous virtues while simultaneously exposing them to the darkest possibilities within others? I want my students to trust each other, their neighbours, and their world.

I sometimes found the intensity exhausting and frustrating. While I only spent two and a half hours with my students in class every week, I was sleeping, eating, and breathing the project. Because of my emotional engagement with them, I began to withdraw energy from other classes, and I occasionally felt resentful about the amount of time the project consumed. Was it worth it? Was I over-invested? The project required a delicate balance of leadership and surrender that I never felt I achieved perfectly.

NOELIA

Oral History at Home

While Ms Webster privately struggled with how to deal with concepts of genocide, I began to consider my own family's history. My parents had been university students in Argentina during the bloody dictatorship of Jorge Rafael Videla, during which between 15,000 and 30,000 citizens suspected of "leftist sympathizing" were murdered, while thousands more were imprisoned and tortured. While the mass atrocities in Argentina and Cambodia were vastly different, there were certain distressing parallels. First, the United States supported fascist regimes from South America to Southeast Asia to prevent communism, creating instability which dictators like Videla and Pol Pot took advantage of. In Argentina, Videla waged a "war against subversion" in which anyone suspected of leftist sympathies (which ranged from outright protest to having a long beard) could "disappear"; in Cambodia, anyone suspected of right-wing sympathizing could be brutally slain.

I began asking my mother about her experiences. At first, caught off guard, she only told me about the historical and political causes for the rise of Videla and the "official" history of those five years of dictatorship. It was a detached story like Mr A's. After a few of these conversations, she began inserting details. She described, for instance, the fear of passing soldiers with machine guns to go to school – she could be jailed or tortured if they caught her without her identification papers. She told me, haltingly, of the disappearance of her cousin, of the murder of her friend's brother. Smiling, she told me of the adrenalin rush of reading *Las Venas Abiertas de America Latina* ("The Open Veins of Latin America"), a book banned, under threat of disappearance, for exposing the political crimes and corruption in Latin America from the time of colonization until the 1970s.

Through my mother, I heard the personal aspect of stories I felt were missing in Mr A's interview. I was then able to imagine the fear, uncertainty, and anxiety which must have shaped his experience. I visualized how, with a racing heart, he feigned ignorance in order to hide his education when a soldier showed him a watch and asked for the time. I pictured how he would forage for food at night with trembling hands. He didn't tell me what it felt like to do what was necessary to survive, but through my mother I gained a tenuous idea of it.

I became fascinated with life stories in general, curious about all the family stories I had never heard. During a trip to Argentina that December, I borrowed a video camera and interviewed my paternal grandparents using a life story approach. My grandfather was taken aback. He, like Mr A, was used to talking about events rather than emotions. He grew up in an extremely poor village in Italy and worked in the mines during his adolescence. For him, that was the end of it. But I was enthralled; I asked him what it felt like to work so hard every day at such a young age. He shrugged his shoulders and simply said "*No se*, I don't know. I just did it."

A Second Interview

In February, another student conducted a second interview for our film. Watching the footage of the interview with Mr Pong, I noticed the points where the interviewer asked a question I never would have considered, or allowed him to continue speaking when I would have interrupted. I became aware of the crucial role the interviewer plays in the narrative and I worried about the extent to which my questions and omissions had shaped Mr A's story. Was there a message he wanted to communicate that I hadn't facilitated? I also realized how important it had been for me to conduct an interview. In Mr A's presence, I felt the silences without a recording hiss. His words shaped my questions; my reactions shaped his responses. I had implicated myself in what became *our* narrative.

Yet because we were working with faceless audio due to Mr A's request for anonymity, I eventually began to feel detached from the story. We began to only call him by his pseudonym, Mr A, rendering him almost fictional. In contrast, working with Mr Pong's story while seeing his face on the screen created a growing intimacy with someone I had not even met.

Creating a Story

With the interviews completed, we struggled to determine the next step to transform the stories into a movie. In class, we discussed what was important in both interviews, but everyone had a different priority. Some believed the story should be organized chronologically; others, thematically. When one student said, "Don't include the stuff about France, it's not relevant," another countered with, "What are you talking about? It's absolutely relevant." We couldn't decide how to remove details from a life story without removing its essence.

Ms Webster suggested that the creation of a five-minute documentary would be achievable in the four months remaining. We decided to pare both interviews down to five minutes of audio, comprised of quotations that stuck out to us. When listening to the result, we realized our system was flawed. A story is not just a collection of amazing one-liners.

After heated day-long discussions and a laborious consensus process, we decided to organize our film around the theme of survival. While obvious on the surface, we wanted to expand the definition beyond physical survival. Mr A and Mr Pong's stories touched us because they managed not only to stay alive, but also to flourish psychologically, emotionally, and spiritually. When experiencing horrors beyond our most terrifying nightmares, they remained defiant and resilient. Mr Pong stated, "Happiness is not measured by your riches or money; happiness is the feeling you have hope ... hope." We began to understand that hope was another aspect of survival; it is what preserves and enriches life. Perhaps, we pondered, this was why the interviewees had not dwelled on the atrocities, instead offering more detail on their post–Khmer Rouge experience. This new theme focused our documentary.

We needed a mix of historical context, reflections on the experiences of Cambodians in general, as well as glimpses into the personal sphere of the participants. It was difficult to get the latter element, especially in the case of Mr A, because he repeatedly emphasized that his story was unimportant in the face of the great event. At one point, when I asked him how he felt during his escape from Cambodia in the post–Khmer Rouge period, he fell into an uncomfortable, heavy quiet. When he resumed, he described the trip objectively: "We went here, the Vietnamese army was stationed here, they took us into custody, we had to bribe them." Only silences, changes in volume, and nervous laughter indicated the emotions he never expressed in words. However, when we attempted to include these cues in the film, they were awkward. We struggled with the choice – we worried that we were cutting the heart out of the story.

Looking for a natural structure for the film, we had one storyboard member recount the participant's stories chronologically from memory, which allowed us to pinpoint the most essential moments. We then interviewed Dr Frank Chalk, a genocide historian, who provided context. With our skeleton in place, we transcribed the audio clips onto index cards and printed stills of our stock footage. We rearranged our cards on huge pieces of paper and taped them to the walls of the classroom to create our storyboard, literally surrounding ourselves with our story.

One of our biggest concerns while storyboarding was that the narrative was not only Mr A's and Mr Pong's, it was our interpretation and manipulation of their accounts to convey our message.[6] "It was a huge concern," the head of storyboard stated, "but I realized I couldn't tell their story exactly the way they had told it. That was why finding the theme had been so important, to be able to focus on one aspect of their story."

With one month to go, we were grateful that our two-person editing team already knew how to use Final Cut Pro and were able to get right to work. The editors worked side by side with the storyboard team, as we could not let go of the narrative in which we were inextricably involved. Throughout the process, the storyboard was constantly rearranged and we added more stock footage and still images. Production was the most time-intensive aspect of our project, as it required cutting up audio, finding and matching images, tweaking transitions, and generating the subtitles. Many of us spent all our free time in the computer room, working on the film early in the morning, during breaks, and after school until the janitor kicked us out at 10 p.m.

When we began adding visual images to accompany the audio clips, we became more aware of the possibility of having misinterpreted the survivors' stories. We had originally looked for shocking visuals: pictures of killing fields, skeletons, and torture. But because we had become personally attached to the stories and the survivors, we could hardly bring ourselves to put such terrifying images into the film. One student worried: "I was afraid the images would communicate a message I hadn't intended that would somehow offend the interviewees, especially images of dead people. I felt I was using them in a way that didn't have enough meaning, that I was somehow mocking the dead."

This fear was especially present during the screening of the documentary, with Mr A in the audience. While watching the opening sequence of the film, a jarring montage of skulls and images of torture, one student gravely whispered to his neighbour, "Oh my God, we might be giving him nightmares." Or we could be giving ourselves nightmares, I thought.

MEGAN

Their Story to Our Story

Life in the Open Prison finished rendering six minutes before the house lights dimmed in front of one hundred of our friends, collaborators, and peers. We wanted the evening to be not only a screening of our film, but a tribute to our participants, whom we were terrified of disappointing. The event opened with several speeches in which the students explained the mission of the project, their collaborative working culture, and their connection to the broader Life Stories project. When the lights dimmed and the film rolled, a collective breathlessness caught the crowd. I had seen the film, thirty-three minutes long, thousands of times, sitting on the computer room floor, in our classroom, in the cafeteria. The production team had been working on it around the clock for a month before the screening: adding music, smoothing transitions, adding intertitles and subtitles. But when I saw it all come together on that final night, the message of the film came through with such clarity and force that I felt I was hearing it for the first time: finding joy, forgiveness, and peace is always possible, no matter how terrible our conditions.

The film's screening was also an assessment situation designed for students to explain their learning to a real audience. The students' mastery of the Big Ideas of the course was revealed at the Q and A session held after the screening. In order for students to freely express the depth of their understanding, it was important for them to learn how to minimize interfering anxiety. Students practised rephrasing questions to buy a three-second "think" before responding, numbering their points to structure their responses, and turning a simple question into a thoughtful reply. The Q and A session, like a traditional exam, obliged students to explain what they had learned over the course of the semester. However, because the "exam" required students to mobilize their learning for an authentic purpose and explain themselves to a real audience, it became a meaningful learning situation in and of itself.

I, too, reflected on the factors contributing to the success of the project. First, because it was an elective, I had complete autonomy over the curriculum. I was able to define the learning goals and evaluation schemes. This project is an indication of how essential interest-driven curriculum is, and how important it is for teachers to continually adapt education to the individual, rather than requiring students to adapt themselves to the curriculum. Differentiating pedagogy and sharing authority convinced me that giving as high a degree of autonomy as possible to students produces exciting, authentic, and enduring learning. Second, I had the emotional and pedagogical support of my administration and peers, who had encouraged the positive publicity brought to the school.

I think the most important factor, however, for the success of the class project was the nature of the relationships between the students and me. The unique constellation of personalities in the class were perfectly aligned; we all seemed committed to drawing out the very best in each other. Because students felt their work was purposeful, they were unstoppable. In return, I worked harder and dedicated more. Nourished by the shine of their affection, I felt I was living my purpose.

Beyond pedagogy, engaging with these stories has reminded me that there is no suffering too dark to extinguish all possibility of hope.

NOELIA

Comprehension and Compassion

Before I took this course, genocide was just a concept to me. The traditional – and thoroughly inadequate – approach to studying history in high school is a focus on numbers and facts in textbooks. Of the genocide in Cambodia, the encyclopedias state: "1.3 to 1.8 million deaths." I couldn't even imagine that many people, let alone imagine that many people being slaughtered. The transformative power of genocide education emerged when we actively engaged with life stories, particularly in our work synthesizing and analysing information, intertwining both the facts and the emotions in the stories so as to create a narrative. The emphasis on dialogue in the life stories approach also facilitated a sense of connection to the individuals, of deeper understanding, and of meaningful education. We had to go beyond passively receiving information; we had to implicate ourselves in complex ideas and difficult emotions. I learned I had the authority to wrestle with the stories of Mr A and Mr Pong because it was only through this wrestling that I learned. I understood that events in history could become relevant once I came to understand their psychological costs rather than just their material costs. In turn, I have a more nuanced understanding of real-world, present-day problems.

Our project also facilitated my personal growth. I learned to recognize my habit of suppressing emotions when confronted with difficult information in the participants' stories. During the research phase, when I was reading about the Cambodian genocide, I felt *objective* terror. Later, this emotion became more complex as I engaged with the stories of real people. I worked through outrage and arrived at empathy. Yet I still didn't feel overwhelmed by what was overwhelming information.

That changed at the class dinner following our screening, when we discussed the course, the presentation, and the things people said to us afterwards. We confessed our not-so-secret frustrations at different points in the project ("Ethics took too long!"), our semi-secret anxieties ("I didn't think it was possible"), our shared favourite moments

("I LOVED meeting Mr A"). A student's father, who had been listening to our conversation, spoke towards the end of the night for a few brief, powerful minutes. He commented on how evident our admiration and respect were for each other. He spoke about what it felt like to watch the miraculous possibilities that emerge when skills, resources, interests, and passions come together for a common purpose.

While he shared what it meant to him, the son of a Holocaust survivor, to hear his daughter and her friends grappling with these issues, his voice broke, and I was suddenly aware how hard it had been for us to hear the survivors' stories. My throat tightened when I imagined that Mr Pong watched a murder, and that Mr A probably saw someone in their last moments before they died of starvation. I couldn't breathe when I thought about the grace with which Mr A could forgive Khmer Rouge members for their actions and the joy with which Mr Pong recounted his experiences in Montreal after all he had suffered. I wanted to leave. I wanted to be alone, but everyone would notice if I got up as he was talking. So I sat and let tears fall down my face.

I felt surrounded by the ghosts of the people who had starved, who had been beaten to death, who had been marched to exhaustion. I didn't imagine 2 million people as a concept; I considered them in terms of people whom I might have had the privilege of meeting. All of a sudden, "between 1.3 and 1.8 million deaths" became tangible. That was too many people to fit in that living room, too many people to squeeze into that house, too many people to fit into my school. It was too much. And that's when I learned about genocide.

NOELIA AND MEGAN

Our Story

Through our dialogue with our community, with others, and with ourselves, we now better understand how implicated we all are in narratives of injustice, suffering, and grief. By engaging with stories of horror, we grasped the amazing resilience of the soul to withstand horrific circumstances. Mr A's and Mr Pong's accounts of injustice motivated us to seek integrity in our everyday life, their narratives of suffering reinforced our impulse to relieve the grief of others, and their experiences of survival intensified our hope in life.

FURTHER RESOURCES:

Read the blog we wrote throughout the process, here:
  http://www.lifestoriesmontreal.ca/en/blogs/megan-webster
Watch two students discuss the meaning of the project: http://www
  .lifestoriesmontreal.ca/en/life-stories-in-education
Watch the trailer to our film on the Montreal Life Stories website: (http://
  www.lifestoriesmontreal.ca/en/cambodia-working-group)
And the complete film, here, on the CitizenShift website: http://citizenshift
  .org/node/27732&dossier_nid=22423/

NOTES

1 The project is funded by Concordia University and the Social Sciences and
   Humanities Research Council of Canada under its Community-University
   Research Alliance (CURA) Program. Some 40 academics and researchers as
   well as 20 Montreal community organizations are collaborating in the Life
   Stories project.
2 Tomlinson, Carol Ann, *The Differentiated Classroom: Responding to the Needs
   of all Learners*, (New York: Prentice Hall, 1999).
3 Martha Gellhorn, "Disbelief of Atrocities," *PBS* (2003), http://www.pbs
   .org/perilousfight/psychology/disbelief_of_atrocities/letters/.
4 "Deep listening" is a key principle of the methodological approach of
   the Montreal Life Stories group. Sheftel and Zembrzycki define deep
   listening as "listening for meanings, not just facts, and listening in such
   a way that prompts more profound reflection from the interviewee"
   (199). For a more extensive discussion of this approach, see Anna Sheftel
   and Stacey Zembrzycki, "Only Human: A Reflection on the Ethical and
   Methodological Challenges of Working with 'Difficult' Stories," *Oral
   History Review* 37, no. 2 (2010): 191–214, and Alessandro Portelli, *The Death
   of Luigi Trastulli* (Albany: State University of New York Press, 1991).
5 Our first participant requested to remain anonymous.
6 At the time I thought our anxieties stemmed from our youth and inexperience. It was much later, while writing this chapter, that I read Michael
   Frisch's (1990) collection of essays on oral history, *A Shared Authority*,
   and realized our concerns reflected some of the most pressing challenges
   facing oral historians. Frisch also identifies other difficulties we faced:
   how should we "frame" events so that experiences and memories can be

understood as big "H" History? And who is the author of oral histories? Is the author the one providing the content, or the one framing it into narrative? Or is it both, since interviewing is a collaboration, not just a transmission of "fact"? Frisch's work also implicitly poses a further problem: he discusses these central difficulties in the context of scholars and of those individuals telling their stories. But we students were neither scholars nor survivors. What authority did we have to manipulate a message or to interpret it? Michael Frisch, *A Shared Authority: Essays on the Craft and Meaning of Oral and Public History* (Albany: State University of New York Press, 1990).

9 Connecting the Dots: Memory and Multimedia in Northern Uganda

JESSICA ANDERSON AND RACHEL BERGENFIELD

We sat under the scorching sun and interviewed Mr Olanyo[1] for nearly an hour. We were researching the relationship between "transitional justice" and "economic development" in war-affected northern Uganda. As a traditional leader, he was accustomed to Western researchers and these kinds of questions. When we finished, he leaned back into the plastic chair, smiled, and asked us why we were not conducting the research his community actually needed. He then told us the story of Barlonyo.

Barlonyo is located near Lira Town in northern Uganda. As danger and insecurity increased in the community during the more than two-decade civil war between the Lord's Resistance Army (LRA) and the government of Uganda, residents came together to form an internally displaced persons (IDP) camp in 2002. In a span of three hours on 21 February 2004, the LRA massacred over 300 people in Barlonyo.[2] Misinformation about the massacre is rampant, including which party to the conflict perpetrated it and why the camp was not better protected by the military. During our meeting in early 2008, Mr Olanyo suggested that this has contributed to an uneven and disjointed process of remembering.

A government memorial marks the massacre site. Beside it is a large cement slab that covers the mass grave. Today, kids play soccer on the open grass around it, and youth sit and chat on the cement. The memorial plaque reads that only 121 people were killed. Mr Olanyo and, later, Barlonyo community members went on to suggest that the memorial neither holds symbolic power nor serves as a tool of government acknowledgment. Many community members believe this shows that those killed were not valued enough to be properly counted.[3]

Mr Olanyo underscored the need for a clear documentation of the facts and people's stories. He invited us to conduct this documentation. We were surprised because we knew of several different research efforts to document the massacre. Why didn't Mr Olanyo and other elders know about this? And would these efforts address community needs for remembering? The disconnects between local peacebuilders, like Mr Olanyo, the researchers, and the community members were tremendous. In Barlonyo, all three groups had related goals that could reinforce each other, but for some reason the "dots" were not connected.

We felt like bad researchers. We collaborated with local partners. We worked with the only public university in the war-affected area with a team of young Ugandan researchers. We presented our research to local audiences and distributed reports throughout the war-affected region. However, we knew our work never reached most of the people who had shared their stories and memories with us. Our research didn't get to most local peacebuilders. Both Western and Ugandan researchers who had worked in the region far longer than us communicated the same challenge.

We thus began a journey to "connect the dots," which began by listening to survivors. We found that many researchers and aid organizations[4] did not prioritize the integration of community stories and information into their local interventions. First, research and documentation of the events of the war and stories of survivors are not usually communicated to local peacebuilders. Rather, they are often delivered to a somewhat higher local authority or group, such as to the local government – but not, for instance, to the de facto but legitimate peacebuilder, such as a farmer's cooperative. Second, the current peacebuilding toolkit does not consider in depth the mechanisms through which local stories and experiences relate with remembering. Ultimately, some of the key "tools" that could support communities in their remembering, such as information and stories of the war in an accessible format, are often unavailable. In short, both accurate information and collective stories are not well *integrated* into peacebuilding interventions.

In this chapter, we first describe the Ugandan context and our journey in implementing the Barlonyo Remembrance Project. We then reflect on our lessons learned and broader gaps in peacebuilding activities. These gaps, which mainly stem from aid funding and research priorities, led us to use basic multimedia tools in the Barlonyo community. We also discuss how our project, and the overall process of integrating stories into peacebuilding work, can help to address these gaps. We hope that our small story can draw broader attention to the power and potential of integrating stories and information into peacebuilding by using multimedia.

Northern Uganda: War, Peacebuilding, and Multimedia

Since 1986 a civil war in northern Uganda between the Lord's Resistance Army (LRA) and the Ugandan government has displaced over 1.8 million civilians and killed tens of thousands more.[5] Both the LRA and the Ugandan Army committed widespread murder, rape, and abuse of displaced civilians, and the LRA recruited the bulk of its fighting force by abducting an estimated 60,000 to 80,000 people into its ranks.[6] The war currently remains unresolved, as peace talks between the LRA and the government of Uganda collapsed in 2008. The LRA moved its base of operations to the Democratic Republic of Congo, and activity continues in the Congo, Central African Republic, and South Sudan. Northern Uganda is now in a stage of post-conflict recovery.

Most civilians have left northern Uganda's IDP camps and are re-establishing their communities after decades of violence, insecurity, and deprivation. Relative to the tremendous amount of research conducted on the conflict, survivors know few facts about the events of the war. With limited access to information about the war, community members cannot use it in owning and designing their own peacebuilding[7] tools and processes, from memorials and educational curricula to community narratives and cultural activities. Ultimately, efforts to build peace are less effective and sustainable when survivors do not have the tools to promote their agency in this process.

Westerners and elites in Uganda have used multimedia to explain the conflict to foreign audiences and to advocate for resources and policy change. While multimedia may be useful for these purposes, it has not always been a connecting force within conflict-affected communities. Most notably, the *Invisible Children* documentary became part of Western pop culture, depicting the plight of children "night commuters" who travelled to town centres each evening to avoid LRA raids and abduction. Their documentaries were not intended for a Ugandan audience and were used widely as an advocacy tool in the US, even after the LRA left Uganda and Ugandan children stopped their "night commutes." Several other more sensitive and informed films, such as *War Dance* and *Uganda Rising*, have brought awareness of the conflict to Western audiences but have rarely been shared with the war-affected themselves due to understandable barriers in language, literacy, and technology. *War Dance* and *Uganda Rising* succeeded in their aims of broader aware-ness, but a disconnect remains between these projects and war-affected communities. Non-profit organizations also create short films and mul-timedia presentations about their programs and the conflict in general, but these projects are usually intended for donors. Foreign journalists and photographers regularly visited northern Uganda during the last several years of the war to collect information for foreign newspapers, journals, exhibits, and university projects. In sum, the history of multi-media in northern Uganda has ranged from Western-oriented to purely extractive. Perhaps no multimedia work better represents this than the Kony 2012 advocacy video, which was released three years after we wrote this piece. This work presents the northern Uganda story without history, time, or even many northern Ugandan people.

However, northern Ugandans do have experience in multimedia. There are some exceptional examples of multimedia's use as a tool of community peacebuilding and connection. The Refugee Law Project's Kitgum War Museum and Archives will showcase digital versions of archives, with a library and documentation centre. Located in Kitgum, the museum is in war-affected northern Uganda with reasonably con-venient access for many survivors. The Refugee Law Project similarly creates and screens documentaries on the war and postwar transi-tion that have been screened in northern Uganda. The Justice and Reconciliation Project created *Voices* magazine, a platform for survivors to discuss the postwar transition. They also regularly conduct commu-nity dialogues and radio shows related to peacebuilding and transi-tional justice. Some researchers studying livelihoods are experimenting by showing photographs of neighbouring regions to stimulate commu-nity dialogue on variations in human development between districts. Some limited projects draw on photography and film as a tool youth can use to tell their own stories. Other local groups have commissioned documentaries for resource advocacy. Thus, while multimedia has not largely been used with and by survivors, some limited efforts and trends are promising. Our project seeks to contribute within this emerg-ing space of locally owned, sensitive, and purposeful multimedia.

The Barlonyo Remembrance Project

Our organization, Collaborative Transitions Africa (CTA), initiated the Barlonyo Remembrance Project in partnership with the network of

Langi traditional leaders, a key group of local peacebuilders. Youth leaders who grew up in Barlonyo also informally advised and guided us during the project. At first, we simply wanted to bridge the information gap for which we, as Western researchers, felt partially responsible. After conducting focus groups in the community and strategizing and researching creative multimedia methodologies with our local partners, we identified a simple approach: we created a photo-based memory book to honour the lives of those affected by the massacre through interviews and focus groups with survivors. The book also relied on the Justice and Reconciliation Project's rigorous study of the massacre, which they documented shortly after we first met Mr Olanyo. The book mainly comprises photographs and limited text in Langi, due to the high rate of illiteracy in the Barlonyo community. It also includes a map depicting the massacre, a detailed timeline intertwined with personal narratives, photographs showing how the community has developed since the massacre, and the current needs of Barlonyo's survivors.

We expected the traditional leaders in Barlonyo to distribute the books at reconciliation and cleansing ceremonies.[8] We hypothesized that if they distributed the memory books at these events, the community could more effectively integrate facts and stories into their personal and familial remembrance processes. What happened was far from what we expected. A Ugandan community-based organization that trains community members in psychosocial counselling contacted us. They had acquired several of the books and were using them as counselling tools by asking questions of patients based on the stories and photos in the book. They also gave the books to patients who were interested, and patients reported back that showing the book to family members stimulated useful familial conversation and new engagements with the past. Some teachers in the community also started using the books in their classrooms. At the outset of this project we had simply intended to fill a community need and respond to gaps in research access. However, the ways our remembrance book was integrated into existing community efforts revealed the power of research and information – when harnessed appropriately through multimedia – to promote community peacebuilding and remembering. *Integration* is the key, not simply access to or provision of information; and multimedia is an ideal tool.

We realized that the disconnected dots we had discovered when we began the Barlonyo Remembrance Project were actually part of a much more significant gap in peacebuilding work; the integration of research and information into community efforts for peacebuilding is rare in northern Uganda. The Western-based peacebuilding toolkit commonly addresses the need for documentation and truth-telling interventions. However, these concepts have yet to be linked with community-based approaches: What happens when documentation is finished? How will it support the survivors who work tirelessly to support their own community's remembrance process?

As the project concluded, the concept and approach of *community information integration* emerged. We define it as "a process of making knowledge about the conflict accessible and actionable in a way that communities and individuals find meaningful for building peace." Community information integration intends to empower local peacebuilders and to respond to the gaps we located in northern Uganda that allowed information on the Barlonyo massacre to remain outside the community's access. It is this spirit of remembrance alongside the need to move forward that characterizes Barlonyo in the aftermath of the massacre today.

Situating Community Information Integration

We reviewed the peacebuilding literature for more insight into similar remembrance and information integration approaches. Peacebuilding, in our definition, focuses on the quality of relationships between different actors and institutions in order to end conflict and promote positive, sustainable peace.[9] In our experience, the linkages between donors, researchers, and local peacebuilders are somewhat weak in northern Uganda. The power of local peacebuilders has not been leveraged in remembrance processes, even though the peacebuilding literature recognizes that memory is an essential part of each of these relationships. Miall argues that within the peacebuilding field "memories are part of each party's socially constructed understanding of the situation, shaped by culture and learning, and discourse and belief. The way groups remember and construct their past is often central to the mobilization for conflict, and thus a crucial matter to address in reconciliation and cultural traditions work."[10] Not only do memories inform how people understand the conflict, but the ways in which memories are constructed can have positive or negative implications for building peace. The peacebuilding community has long acknowledged the centrality of truth and memory to its work. This field is most likely to involve the local peacebuilders, aid organizations, and researchers described in our discussion of the Barlonyo community's remembrance process.

However, the field does not relate Western sources of information with local peacebuilding efforts to address truth and memory.

Existing efforts to address truth and memory, such as storytelling and documentation, often target elites and national-level approaches. Establishing truth following war is a dominant theme in peacebuilding, and survivor storytelling, through radio shows or other media, is widely acknowledged as an important part of post-conflict healing.[11] Documentation processes are also common, and human rights and transitional justice organizations argue that documentation will help survivors remember their history and promote reconciliation.[12] However, current Western approaches for addressing truth often consider information as a form of justice in and of itself: storytelling and documentation are the end goal. Such efforts reflect the research dilemma seen in northern Uganda: information and stories are collected, but they ultimately are not integrated into the community.

Other remembrance activities, such as truth commissions, museums, and memorials, similarly might not address decentralized and community-based needs for remembrance. For instance, truth commissions by nature are state-sanctioned, and the state narrative of truth might not resonate with community needs for remembrance.[13] Similarly, museums often take a particular narrative of the events of the conflict, and they often do not have widespread community access. Truth commissions are similarly often in central, urban spaces. Ultimately, common approaches to "operationalize" truth and memories are top-down and do not promote more decentralized, community-based forms of remembrance.

Survivors need dynamic and interactive tools for remembrance, and this is the gap our approach of community information integration seeks to fill. However, practical barriers also exist to link local peacebuilders with the resources and information they need for these processes. In order to understand how a project like ours could be more sustainable and widely adopted in the peacebuilding field, we sought to understand why these gaps in integrating community stories exist, and which actors are in a position to collaborate with local peacebuilders in the future.

Disconnected Dots: Identifying Root Causes

As our work deepened, we identified several root causes for the disconnects in northern Uganda's international aid and research landscape. First, while a great deal of research that emphasizes survivors' stories and experiences has been conducted in northern Uganda, this research was rarely linked to actors at the community level. While some exceptional researchers and institutes make significant efforts to share and distribute research, they still face limitations given the size of northern Uganda and high levels of illiteracy. In this context, it is unclear what meaning a thick report can have for survivors. Ultimately, researchers en masse have not found ways to hand over their research to local peacebuilders so that it can be meaningfully integrated into the ways in which a community remembers, and moves on from, war.

Second, the incentives created by aid funding and priorities have dramatically affected remembrance, utilization of stories, and local peacebuilders. While funders have emphasized media and access to communication,[14] there has been little support for local groups in *integrating* and thus effectively using the information. Instead, most funding earmarked for information-related activities targets radio programs and educational materials.[15] Other information-related efforts, such as the documentation, memorials, truth commissions, and museums described above, focus on the national or regional level. While this is crucially important, it does not provide survivors with tangible tools they can use as they see fit in their own community remembrance processes, which can vary widely among individuals, families, and communities. In northern Uganda, aid for local peacebuilding has instead prioritized cultural and religious cleansing and reconciliation processes and large-scale social and political events. Some Lira residents expressed frustration about this to us. They noted that they could find funding for reburying the remains of killed family members or support for traditional reconciliation processes, yet they still did not know basic facts about the Barlonyo massacre. This approach does not prioritize community access and integration of information.

Our partners in Barlonyo also noted that funding is not available to build on approaches that are currently effective in their communities. Instead, they are forced to conform to certain issues and approaches prioritized by Western donors, or go without funding. New institutions have also emerged to capitalize on aid funding, and existing ones have altered their language and approach to donor priorities, sometimes called "NGOizing." For example, a local cultural institution now has program officers, and it regularly serves as an implementing partner of foreign government-funded programs. The nature of funding streams in this context restricts community innovation. Aid spending emphasizes Western-style organizations and structures instead of informal remembrance processes and local peacebuilders. For example, during independent research conducted by Rachel in 2008, she originally asked about "reconciliation" in her interviews. People commonly noted that they had not seen it, but they were "getting it on the radio," meaning that they heard sensitizations and the common pleas from their leaders for forgiveness and reconciliation over the radio. Rachel soon stopped asking these questions in semi-structured interviews, because they revealed nothing other than the capture of remembrance and healing language by elite actors. A story-based approach emphasizing people's daily routines unearthed far more illuminating information about the state of "reconciliation" or "remembrance" in a community.

In our analysis of these "disconnected dots," we found that while researchers are not largely linking their work into communities, aid funding also does not emphasize this information. Instead, it mainly emphasizes access to information, national structures for remembrance, or the formalization of local institutions for peacebuilding. We hope that community information integration, with its emphasis on informal, community-driven processes and life stories, can fill an important gap in this landscape.

Next Steps: Testing the Community Information Integration Approach

While these gaps in research and aid priorities and practice seem self-evident now, the nature of the research and aid landscape in northern Uganda has only become clear to us over the past six years working in the region. In the Barlonyo Remembrance Project we responded to community needs and the specific circumstances of the massacre without a clear picture of what the project would eventually look like. We learned that a decentralized and community-based response was important for survivors due to the nature of Uganda's civil war. With a range of affected ethnic groups and north–south divisions, the idea of a shared narrative was not necessarily important for survivors of the massacre. Instead, they were focused on remembering and acknowledging their individual and community experience with the conflict. In light of the Barlonyo memorial's painful misrepresentation of the community's experience, an alternative, more personal form of remembrance was similarly important. In light of these realities, we intended to create a responsive and community-embedded project to integrate memories and information about the community into local peacebuilding initiatives.

Now, we have a better understanding of why our project was necessary in the first place. We believe attention must be drawn to the deficits in aid and research priorities, and to think about the role of multimedia in more effectively linking local peacebuilders with the products of research and aid. In our project, multimedia was a powerful tool in bridging more elite access to and integration of information. Multimedia's peacebuilding potential has not been realized. Multimedia tools can resonate with illiterate, war-affected communities in a way that elite policy and academic reports never will. These tools can also serve as the basis for interactive and dynamic forms of remembrance that can be integrated into community initiatives over time and adapted as needed.

However, while the idea of a remembrance book was very useful in the Barlonyo community, community information integration can take on a range of forms. In the future, research could be integrated into existing activities such as culturally based reconciliation practices, memorial development, local advocacy, psychosocial counselling, or youth group–facilitated dialogues. CTA hopes to provide assistance for the development of multimedia tools, but activities will otherwise be entirely directed by community partners. The "remembrance book" model could be relevant in other communities, but local peacebuilders will determine the project's final shape.

Conclusion

Numerous disconnected dots exist in the northern Uganda aid, research, and multimedia landscape from the perspective of local peacebuilding. First, much research conducted in the region is very valuable to local peacebuilders. The facts and stories of this research can be integrated into existing community efforts, but language, literacy, and other practical barriers often prevent this from happening. Second, aid tends to focus on more top-down approaches to peacebuilding and memory. While it's exciting that the aid community in northern Uganda has listened to local leaders and emphasized traditionally based approaches to reconciliation and justice, current efforts tend to support local elites or institutionalize local peacebuilders. Third, while multimedia bears promise as an effective tool in "connecting these dots," it has largely been leveraged for foreign audiences.

In examining these disconnects, our project in Barlonyo yielded many lessons that most aid workers, researchers, and community-based leaders have already considered but similarly struggle to address. Many researchers are asking the "wrong" questions from the perspective of local peacebuilding. Their questions seek to contribute to foreign policy or academic literature that is removed from the daily lives of most survivors. Of those who are asking the "right" questions and working hand in hand with local institutions, many barriers still exist in getting research and information in an effective, meaningful way to those who need it. Our experience in Barlonyo suggests that listening to survivors' stories, identifying local assets and needs, and drawing on multimedia and community partnerships to build on these assets and address needs is an effective approach. Our experience also suggests that information is most useful when it is creatively *integrated* into ongoing local peacebuilding efforts. This differs from an "access to information" approach or the simple provision of research. It is also highly context-specific and differs from a "toolkit" approach to peacebuilding that prescribes out-of-the-box interventions.

Integration is the key. Research on life stories and basic facts of conflict events are tremendously useful to survivors and communities. Documentaries, reports, and other typical formats, however, are not useful alone. Even the best work will have a limited impact if it is not integrated into activities in the community. Multimedia is a critical tool in this process of information integration because it can bridge access issues, illiteracy, and other barriers between local peacebuilders and research. Because of their versatility, multimedia can also be adapted to the particular assets and needs of a community. For example, the Barlonyo remembrance books were used in far more wide-ranging ways than we had ever expected. While traditional leaders distributed them as expected, psychosocial counsellors in the communities also used them as tools in their sessions. Teachers used them to facilitate lessons about the community's experience during the war in some limited cases. These examples highlight other important differences in multimedia remembrance tools; unlike a predetermined program or an immobile memorial, survivors can use and draw on multimedia tools as they see fit. This dynamic tool can support and emphasize survivor agency over their own remembering and peacebuilding process in a way that current, "static" tools do not.

Our story is small. In writing this paper, we simply seek to share our reflections and those of the northern Ugandans with whom we collaborated. We will continue to test the community information integration approach, which is emerging and can be operationalized in many ways. At its core, it is about listening to community stories and then collaborating with local peacebuilders to integrate these stories into their efforts. We are confident it bears tremendous potential to support meaningful and authentic local peacebuilding.

NOTES

1 Pseudonym.
2 Justice and Reconciliation Project, *Kill Every Living Thing: The Barlonyo Massacre*, Field Note IX, February 2009, 2.
3 Ibid., 14.
4 Conflict transformation recognizes conflict as a natural phenomenon and seeks to transform conflict dynamics into positive, peaceful outcomes. According to this approach, conflicts are embedded in interpersonal, community, organizational, and international relationships, and building sustainable relationships is a critical part of the conflict transformation process.
5 Internal Displacement Monitoring Centre (IDMC), "Uganda: At a Glance" (2010), http://www.internal-displacement.org/8025708F004CE90B/ (httpCountries)/04678346A648C087802570A7004B9719?opendocument.
6 Jeannie Annan, Christopher Blattman, and Roger Horton, *The State of Youth and Youth Protection in Northern Uganda: Findings from the Survey of War Affected Youth* (Kampala: UNICEF, 2006).
7 Our organization, Collaborative Transitions Africa (CTA), uses a conflict transformation lens in its programming. CTA is dedicated to building lasting peace after violent conflict in Africa by aiding innovative, local initiatives and encouraging the ideas of survivors to help their own communities cope and recover. Founded in early 2008, CTA implemented two projects with local partners in northern Uganda through 2009. Following CTA's experience with the remembrance book, we are currently implementing the Northern Uganda Remembrance Program in Lira, Uganda, in partnership with the African Youth Initiative Network.
8 Cleansing ceremonies are often used in the region to welcome back community members who have been away for a long time. In the recent past, these ceremonies have been used to integrate former combatants into their communities.
9 Cordula Reimann, "Assessing the State of the Art in Conflict Transformation," in *Berghof Handbook for Conflict Transformation* (Berghof Center for Constructive Conflict Management, 2004); John Paul Lederach, "Conflict Transformation," *Beyond Intractability* (2010), http://www

.beyondintractability.org/bi-essay/transformation. www.berghof-handbook
.net/documents/publications/reimann_handbook.pdf (2003).

10 Hugh Miall, "Conflict Transformation: A Multi-Dimensional Task,"
in *Berghof Handbook for Conflict Transformation*, 8.

11 See Richard Mollica, *Healing Invisible Wounds: Paths to Hope and Recovery
in a Violent World* (Orlando: Houghton Mifflin Harcourt, 2006); Priscilla
Hayner, *Unspeakable Truths: Confronting State Terror and Atrocity* (New
York: Routledge, 2001); Martha Minow, "Truth Commissions," in *Between
Vengeance and Forgiveness: Facing History after Genocide and Mass Violence*
(Boston: Beacon Press, 1998).

12 International Center for Transitional Justice (ICTJ), "Memory, Memorials,
and Museums: MMM Program" (2010). http://www.ictj.org/en/tj/785.html
(retrieved in 2009).

13 Hayner, *Unspeakable Truths*.

14 For example, the first objective of the USAID Office of Transition
Initiatives' (OTI) large program in northern Uganda is to increase access to
information in key areas such as peace and recovery.

15 USAID OTI has a $6 million program that works directly with radio sta-
tions and partners to rebuild schools. Numerous other foreign NGOs with
private and foreign government funding also rebuild and support schools.

10 Arrival Stories: Using Media to Create Connections in a Refugee Residence

MICHELE LUCHS AND LIZ MILLER

Introduction

There are thirty-five men seated around fold-up tables in the Maison Haidar basement, a room that alternatively serves as a makeshift bedroom, a workshop space, or whatever the room is needed for. Today we – Michele Luchs and Liz Miller, documentary makers and educators – are using the room for our digital story/photography workshop and have just explained the first exercise to the group currently residing at Maison Haidar, while they apply for asylum. They look quizzically at us, each other, the coloured pens on the table, and the blank piece of paper in front of them. We have asked participants to draw a picture of the first place they would call home. Before long the room falls silent and the participants engage purposely in their colourful sketches of home. The blank pages transform into rooms, family portraits, and even maps of entire communities. This is now the sixth time we are leading this workshop, and each time we face an almost entirely new group of individuals with stories as diverse as the languages that fill the room. This digital story/photography workshop is one of a series that the residence coordinator, Sylvain Thibault, organizes for both newcomers and former residents of Maison Haidar.

The residence, Maison Haidar, is part of Projet Refuge, a program that provides a secure residence and emotional support to men who have fled traumatic situations in their home countries. Projet Refuge has been in operation for twenty years and is one of many programs coordinated by the Montreal City Mission.[1] Before the residence was in existence, refugees ended up in homeless shelters or on the couches of refugee advocates or family members. Advocates realized that inadequate housing contributed to the extremely stressful circumstances for individuals applying for asylum. Projet Refuge was developed to respond to this problem, and for years the project has provided three weeks of temporary shelter, acting as the first step in creating a new community for its residents. Sylvain created his workshop series to help newcomers get oriented, develop peer networks, and identify resources as they established themselves in Montreal.

The workshops cover subjects ranging from the history of social movements in Montreal, to confronting and combating racial profiling, to finding employment, and they are just part of the many activities Sylvain coordinates to help individuals establish themselves in a new place, Montreal. Recognizing that three weeks is an exceptionally short time to establish community, Sylvain also hosts a spaghetti dinner once a month where former residents reconvene, meet new residents, and as a group share updates, frustrations, and recent accomplishments with each other. Another innovative way Sylvain has helped newcomers integrate is via a community radio project, Radio Refuge,[2] an initiative he and three former residents began together that provides a regular forum for individuals with refugee experience to address their concerns to the larger public. The program fosters community not only among refugee claimants but between organizations serving refugees. The program is hosted by a different refugee advocacy group each month, and this collaborative initiative brings the groups together. Projet Refuge has been the anchor organizer of the innovative radio initiative, which offers a community beyond the temporary residence, hands-on training in radio, and an essential space for personal and political expression.

Projet Refuge is an example of some of the more progressive services offered to asylum seekers in Canada. While Canada receives only 0.2 per cent of the refugees in the world, until recently the country has enjoyed an impressive international reputation for both its interpretation of the refugee convention as well as the treatment of refugees.[3] For example, Canada recognizes women fleeing domestic abuse and individuals persecuted for their sexual preference or identity as eligible to apply for refugee status. But projects like Maison Haidar are only relevant if refugees can indeed enter the country.[4] For example, in 2008 Canada accepted almost 22,000 refugees. The Canadian government estimated that for 2010 it would accept half of this number. More recent policy changes have made it increasingly difficult to enter the country, and refugee advocates consider these policies a rollback to refugee rights. At the time of writing the government had issued Bill C-31, which makes it more difficult for asylum seekers and makes it possible for the government to revoke the status of refugees who are permanent residents.

Participatory Media

When Sylvain first approached us to be a part of his workshop series we were eager to collaborate. We had recently initiated Mapping Memories: Experiences of Refugee Youth, a research-creation initiative to explore how a participatory media project, using tools such as digital cartography, video, and photography, could help newcomer youth articulate their concerns and find commonalities and peer support in a period of transition.[5] Mapping Memories was the youth working group of the Life Stories of Montrealers Displaced by War, Genocide, and Other Human Rights Violations, a collaborative oral history project exploring Montrealers' experiences and memories of mass violence and displacement. Life Stories of Montrealers involved a team of university and community-based researchers who recorded life story interviews with Montreal residents and then brought them to the community through theatre, critical pedagogy, videos, and other innovative approaches. While the Mapping Memories projects had been directed primarily towards youth programs, Projet Refuge served newcomers of all ages and offered us a chance to work in an intergenerational context without the rigours of recruiting, since Sylvain had a ready-made group.

Furthermore, since one of our principles in collaborative research-creation was that research be initiated in response to a community need, we were further motivated by the fact that Sylvain felt the workshop would be useful for the residents at Projet Refuge.[6] We were inspired by Sylvain's use of the collaborative radio project to help newcomers adapt through self-expression and hoped that we might build on that model. Together we wanted to offer opportunities for these men to share stories and by doing so to strengthen their relationships with each other. We also wanted to see if the work produced might eventually reach a larger public to raise awareness of the challenges newcomers face – from learning a subway system to adapting to a new language and a new set of cultural norms. We hoped to reinforce Sylvain's commitment to counter negative stereotypes about refugees and to draw attention to systemic problems in the immigration system. Sylvain had expressed frustration that the public was insensitive to changes around immigration policy and that, too often, news stories framed individuals as victims instead of focusing on how they were adapting to a new place.

We were enthusiastic about collaborating on a participatory media project to address the gap between mass media representations and lived experiences. While participatory media has become a catch-all phrase for text, videos, and audio that circulate on the Internet and that challenge clear-cut divisions between audience and creators, we were using the term to describe a process that involves individuals in the creation of their own personal stories. Regardless of the technology used, a collaborative creative process can help individuals to reflect on the relationship of their personal experiences to larger social concerns.[7] Clemencia Rodriguez in her vision of citizens' media articulates how collaborative media projects can influence both identity construction as well as positions of power or personal agency: "Alternative media spin transformative processes that alter people's sense of self, their subjective positionings, and therefore their access to power."[8] We had followed the success of youth media projects such as The Documentary Project for Refugee Youth in New York, a group that used media art practices to build relationships with youth from Sierra Leone, Bosnia, Burundi, and Serbia over a period of several years. Other projects such as The Digital Media Project: Youth Making Place, based in Saskatoon, brought Aboriginal and immigrant youth together over time to make work about local sustainability issues.

Our unique challenge was that the individuals we were meeting had just arrived and we wondered if they were ready to be involved in a project like this. Was it too soon, given that most of them had only been in Montreal for a few weeks? We began the workshops with these concerns and throughout the process continued to ask ourselves a set of questions: What circumstances should we be taking into account when doing media workshops with recent newcomers? People tell stories for different reasons – what would be the motivating factor to share an arrival story? Would the workshops benefit the individuals? How? Would anything we produced be appropriate to share with a secondary audience? How would we balance a meaningful process and a finished media project that might benefit a larger public?

Key Factors for a Successful Workshop

Over the years we have discovered a number of key factors that must be in place for a participatory media workshop to be successful. One is to use the technology that works best within a given context. In this case, we wanted to ensure the greatest participation possible within a limited time frame. Given these constraints, cameras, pens, and paper were the most appropriate tools to lead these workshops. Another key principle we have discovered is the importance of developing media projects over time. When we first began planning with Sylvain, our hope was to work with a small group over four or five sessions. We intended to move from initial activities like photography to digital mapping, peer video interviews, and more. We quickly realized that this would not be possible due to the transitional nature of the shelter. Because residents couldn't stay at the centre for more than three weeks, Sylvain simply could not guarantee ongoing participation of individuals from one workshop to the next.

Instead of a series, our workshop became a one-time session with its own unique challenges. On a practical, pedagogical level, for example, it was difficult to plan a workshop without knowing the language and literacy needs of a group, or even the number of individuals who might show up each week. An additional concern was how to ensure "shared ownership" of a product created in the workshop if we might never meet these individuals again.[9] Mutual respect and shared ownership served as our guiding principles in the larger Mapping Memories project. We wanted to emphasize that a participatory media project is a joint venture between the participants and the facilitator. These frameworks are particularly important when working with newcomers who have struggled with past traumas. With refugees, having control over one's personal narrative is not simply a critical issue of self-representation but is often connected to personal security. And despite the best of our intentions and principles we were challenged by these particular circumstances. The photo essays would stay at the residence for others to appreciate, but was that enough? With full acknowledgment that participatory media projects *are* most effective when they evolve over time, we came to view the workshops as a first but incomplete step in our collaboration with Sylvain.

In addition to providing the space and recruiting past and present residents for the workshops, Sylvain organized social work student volunteers to help out during the sessions, along with our partner Colleen French of the Canadian Council for Refugees. Sylvain and the co-facilitators participated enthusiastically in the activities and helped lead the workshops. Most importantly, Sylvain was a visible support person for every individual in the room, providing what we called the "trust factor" in the equation. The presence of a key individual whom participants trust is pivotal to the success of a participatory media project. In fact, of all the factors needed for a successful workshop, the trust factor is the most essential.

Mapping a Memory Exercise

We organized the one-day workshops into two main exercises: mapping and photo stories. In the first part, participants individually drew maps about a place they called home or about their journey to Montreal, and then shared their stories with the rest of the group. We chose to integrate a drawing exercise to help individuals warm up to a creative exercise and share something intimate at the same time. The drawings worked well as a first step in dealing with sensitive stories because, unlike a photograph, they could remain anonymous. Participants could choose to write their name and country on the map, but this was not required. The mapping exercise was an effective means of jump-starting a collective conversation and building community. Before beginning the activity, we shared models of maps from past sessions, an essential step in clarifying the exercise. We explained that after drawing their map, they should write details that would help others imagine this place: recurrent sounds (birds, the sounds of children playing), colours that stood out, smells they remembered, and so forth. The maps were a useful way to communicate across cultural and language barriers, which was essential given the number of languages we were negotiating in one small room. While we provided simultaneous translation as participants described their drawings and recounted stories, the maps, like other forms of visual art or pedagogy, were effective communication tools on their own.[10] Even more important, they served as a means of collectively legitimizing a recent and difficult experience of departure.

Although the men seemed initially uncomfortable, once they began sharing their stories the room warmed up. The first participants often spoke tentatively and quickly, unsure of why their stories would matter to the others. But, as more participants around the table(s) spoke, the stories grew more intricate, spurred on by questions from other participants, nodding heads, and attentive eyes. The confirmation and careful listening they offered each other was timely and the stories and maps had many common elements. Some participants drew a place where they felt a sense of peace. In some of the maps, nature played a strong role – paths through the woods on the way to school, fishing and swimming in the sea, and pastoral scenes were drawn with wild bursts of colour. Some drew rooms in houses that represented "home." One participant, Alberto, drew his mother's kitchen in intricate detail, including brightly coloured flowerpots. This was the place where his family shared stories and secrets, a place he felt safe. Another participant,

Alfredo, described his family's house by the sea in Angola, bringing in fish from the boats with his father and swimming at the day's end. When he finished sharing his story, a participant from Haiti remarked, "I have nothing to say! His story is my story too."

But of course not all of the maps were pastoral. What the participants also had in common was a lived experience of dislocation caused by persecution or the threat of violence. One young man from Rwanda drew a village scene split into three parts: his family's home, a community event with dancers in traditional costumes, and in the corner, his four dead brothers lying side by side. In maps of their journeys to Canada, criss-crossed lines revealed hiding places and arduous paths over land and water before their arrival in Montreal. It had taken some participants years to get to Montreal, and in many cases we were meeting them only days after their arrival.

On one occasion during the sharing of the maps the group made the connection that every man at the table was also a father. Tears welled up in the eyes of many of the group and one man even excused himself, struck by a wave of emotion. What every man at the table also shared was a profound sense of longing for home and for the family members and children they had to leave behind. The group dealt with the situation well, acknowledging the pain and letting the moment pass. Shortly thereafter we were able to redirect the conversation to strategies of dealing with loneliness. Experiences like these helped us reflect on how to facilitate the intensity of the conversations that followed the mapping exercise. We wanted to embrace the difficult challenges they were facing and address emotions that surfaced, but we were also aware that our time together was limited.

There is a fragile balance between respecting someone's privacy and providing a collective space for participants to share a part of themselves. To strike this balance in our workshops we found it helpful to focus discussions on the tools and resources participants had discovered in their first few days or weeks in the city to help them adjust. Instead of emphasizing the pain of the recent past, we facilitated spaces to share strategies of coping in a new environment. We also had a list of psychological resources available that had been developed by the Life Stories of Montreal oral history project to which we could direct participants should overwhelming emotional issues surface within the workshop. And while the list was important to have on hand, what was most important was to have Sylvain in the room, as someone they knew and trusted and who would be around after the workshops. On one occasion, a participant who had recently emerged from a war-torn environment explained how faint the line between sanity and mental illness had been for him as he wrestled with his new environment. His message to the group was that having someone like Sylvain listen to him and help sort out decisions had helped him stay sane. He related: "Politics, religion, forced marriage, racial discrimination … we have different types of problems. You didn't know my problem but today I explained and you understood and you gave me advice. If I did not tell you my problem I would be dying silent with my problem. That is why you see some people go into the streets and kill themselves."[11]

A Photo Story in Four Frames

During the second part of the day-long workshop, participants worked in groups to create photo stories in four frames. The idea was to find a collective story about their departure from home or their arrival in Montreal. This method of telling a story with photos is often referred to as photo novella or PhotoVoice.[12] The technique is frequently used with youth groups and in participatory action projects as a first step towards critical dialogue about individual and collective needs and concerns. For example, in "I Was Here," a PhotoVoice project with young mothers with experience living on the streets, the photographs were used as catalysts to engage in conversation with decision makers. They were accompanied by a set of recommendations on how to improve services provided to these young women and their children. Projects like this often begin as mechanisms for personal expression and over time translate into advocacy opportunities. With the constraint of a one-day workshop we had to be realistic about our advocacy objectives. As a first step we identified *future* newcomers as the "target audience" and described the photo exercise as a means to communicate to future residents that they are not alone.

Before beginning the activity, we gave a short PowerPoint presentation about basic photo composition and showed models of photo stories created in past workshops. With each model, we asked participants to think about the story being told and how the individual photos added to that story. A key part of the production process was to provide time for the small groups to brainstorm ideas together. This part of the workshop helped participants realize how much they had in common as they shared and discussed story ideas. By creating a new story based on their shared experiences or by emphasizing one of the stories told in the small groups, the collective aspect took some of the burden away from those who were hesitant to take their story public.

After deciding on one story idea the group created storyboards. Storyboarding has long been used as a planning technique in film, video, and Web pages and by writers to work out ideas for key sequences in narrative texts. Storyboarding was especially helpful in this collaborative context, as it helped the group to physically build and negotiate a collective vision. When taking the photos, each group was accompanied by one of the facilitators who helped with photo composition techniques and offered creative consultations. When group members shared their projects and the story behind the photos, the projects become powerful. We were all surprised at how effective the finished pieces were in communicating a mood and how the photos seemed to move the group to a new place of intimacy. Humour was a part of many stories as participants recounted experiences of getting lost in the Metro system or feeling uncomfortable in huge winter jackets. Other stories recounted the pain and anger of being in detention or worrying about being accepted by Canadian Immigration. Smiling faces, hands shaking, hands on shoulders, and photos of groups eating meals around tables are common endings to these stories. The stories were yet another catalyst for discovering commonalities as men shared the pain of having left people behind (especially children and grandparents) and acknowledged their anxieties dealing with upcoming challenges, such as finding housing and employment, as well as facing the pressures and expectations they felt from extended family members.

Valuable Lessons

With each workshop we gained clarity on the elements that led to the best workshops. For example, taking the time to fully explain the production process and to share and discuss photos was key to the creation of strong photo projects. We learned this the hard way during one workshop when we were short on time. We hadn't shown enough examples of past projects or properly shown the participants how to use the cameras. And, instead of having participants work collaboratively, we asked them to work individually and take photos to add to their map drawings. We asked them to take a variety of shots and suggested that their photos could include such things as scars that had interesting stories or special objects they had brought with them from their country of origin.

As each man returned, we noticed that the photos were a series of vague, out-of-focus shots of scars and other items that were impossible to identify. Because of our rushed explanations, participants had not been clear on what they needed to do. We had introduced the solo portrait/object exercise because we hoped that connecting the map to an individual portrait would strengthen the potential for an outside audience to connect to that drawing. Yet we realized that we had inadvertently cut out the key component: the collaborative process. Through collaboration, participants became more forthcoming and the participants inspired each other to take creative risks. Our dual agenda to structure activities that both reinforced peer networks while also communicating the profound insights and stories that emerged in the room to an outside audience continued to be an ongoing challenge.

Sustained Participation

Despite the structural constraint of only being able to offer one-off workshops, some participants returned and did so for different reasons. Alfredo, for example, who also volunteered part-time at the centre, found the technique of using photos to tell stories useful for a resource he wanted to develop for residents who didn't read English or French. Using his new photo skills, he created a large visual map of different government offices around the city and a series of photo images to help residents find their way to those offices. The photos included images of street signs, Alfredo pointing at the bus number as he stepped onto the bus, and the signs outside the government building. Before each workshop began, he'd take us over to see the progress in his project, which over time covered most of a wall in the centre's basement. He had found a way to translate his new skills into a resource for others.

Another participant from the Congo returned to several sessions to present his group's photo story of being forced to leave his home. Each time he retold the story to a rapt audience it became more detailed and went far beyond the four photo frames on paper. By the third visit, his fleshed-out story included details about having worked for the government and how his political ties had put his life at risk and how he had to flee his country and his family to stay alive. Having an empathetic and engaged audience was important, and with each visit more of his story emerged. Henry Greenspan, in *On Listening to Holocaust Survivors: Beyond Testimony*, discusses the value of sustained acquaintance with the Holocaust survivors he works with, explaining how new discoveries and understandings surface over time.[13] While Greenspan is referencing one-on-one interviews, the same was true in a group context. Another participant from the Congo returned because he hoped to turn his story into a short documentary and wanted the help of workshop facilitators to begin the process. We encouraged returning participants to keep coming back and integrated them as co-facilitators of the workshops. They were helping others gain confidence to share their stories.

Safety and Consent

For most of the participants, however, their participation was indeed a one-day experience, and ensuring both safety and consent was of utmost concern. For example, we encouraged participants who did not want to appear in photographs to become their group's photographer. If we were working with individuals such as unaccompanied minors, we had them work together with a more experienced facilitator so that their stories could be handled more carefully. Explaining our objectives and securing consent across languages was an ongoing challenge, but we did slowly improve our methods over time. Previous experience had taught us that the most valuable ingredient when seeking consent was time, which we were short on. Especially when we are dealing with individuals in circumstances of transition or risk, consent is largely about trust and also comprehension. It takes time for participants to fully understand the purpose, audience, and intended use of a project. While we had hammered out our guidelines for ethics, privacy, and consent for the Mapping Memories project, we realized that if we were working with a different group each workshop, we needed to adapt both the content and the form for how we would seek consent.

For example, to help participants grasp where the maps and photo essays might be shared, we added very specific categories on the written consent form: "I agree to allow my map/photo story to be: 1) shown on the walls of the shelter to let future newcomers know they are not alone; 2) shared with educators, policymakers, and academics working to improve the circumstances of individuals impacted by a refugee experience; and/or 3) included on the Mapping Memories website to create greater understanding for individuals who could benefit from either the method or the results of the work." For each category we also attached a *why* statement or goal: for example, "to let future participants know they are not alone." At the beginning of the workshop we shared a PowerPoint presentation to complement the written consent form and to lay out our categories in a visual manner. At the end of the workshop, we revisited the written consent forms again to confirm where participants wanted to share their work. The process went more smoothly once we had mounted several photo essays on the walls of the residence so that participants could immediately understand how the resulting work would be displayed. Most participants were also interested in sharing their work with educators and advocates.

For many of the participants, the most complex decision was whether to have their images included on the website. Even presenting that option compromised some participants' willingness to take part in the workshop. The Internet is a complex venue because of its potential risks around ensuring safety, especially for individuals fleeing repression who have left family and friends behind. Because we did not have the time to fully engage with participants about these risks during our one-day workshop, we had to eliminate the Internet as a possible venue for sharing their work. It was too much of an unknown and too overwhelming for them to make such a decision so quickly.

Exploring Advocacy

While we were initially unsure how media workshops were helping this group of individuals in their early integration process, we did come to understand how a creative process linked to self-expression was facilitating peer connection within the group. Still we wondered how we might share the results with a larger audience. We knew that the personal maps and the photos were powerful, but they could not stand on their own; the audience would need more context. Sylvain was also interested in how the work might reach a larger public because, in addition to his work coordinating services for newcomers, he was advocating for refugee rights within the ever-changing framework of immigration and refugee policies. While he understood the need to build understanding with the general public, he was often frustrated with journalists who, in their need to meet a deadline, diminished the complexity of a situation and often overlooked the needs of the individual. While journalists need to find individuals who would "translate well" to a general public, Sylvain was concerned about how to convey the breadth and complexity of the refugee experience for advocacy and educational purposes. Packaged media stories had also inadvertently reinforced stereotypes he was working hard to dispel, when they framed individuals as victims or chose to represent the sensation of someone's past narrative over how services and policies impact a person's ability to adapt to a new place.

When working with any kind of media representation there is always a tension between the subject's right to privacy and fair representation, the media producer's desire to bring an issue to light through a compelling story, and the potential for audiences to misconstrue the intended message. In his essay "Ultimately We Are All Outsiders," Calvin Pryluck points out that "with the best intentions in the world, filmmakers can only guess how the scenes they use will impact the lives of the people they have photographed."[14] Participatory media attempt to restore the balance between the potential for a media maker to exploit a subject, and the opportunity for individuals to frame their own story. In working with newcomers, we discovered that their need to make their story public changed over time. When they first arrived, the newcomers in our workshops were eager to unpack what they had experienced in their home countries or in the process of coming to Canada. But as one former resident explained, this need changed over time. "Sometimes people want to know why you had to leave, what happened to you and you don't want to share – at first I didn't mind but now I want to share less – my story has become very intimate to me."[15] The complexity of media representation is that it captures and freezes a moment in time and people's lives and stories are constantly changing. The works created in the workshop were "snapshots" of individuals in transition. We had worked to restore the balance of who is telling the story, but were not able to permit the audience to see reflective and time-based personal expressions to communicate how these participants continued to adapt to their new surroundings.

As mentioned previously, we wanted to explore how to connect these projects to education and advocacy efforts. Experience has taught us that partners' and participants' understanding of advocacy becomes more concrete when there is a product, no matter how incomplete that product might be. So, in addition to mounting the photo essays in the residence, midway through our workshops we created a book of the maps, photo essays, and images of the production process to share with participants, future partners, and educators. The book was especially useful when the project was shared with teachers who were seeking examples of participatory projects that solicited "self-expression." While many educators are not working directly with individuals impacted by a refugee experience, they are looking for models of how to build collaborative experiences that will create community among their students, as well as products that grapple with themes connected to tolerance, migration, and globalization. The photos and maps provided a human face that helped bring statistics to life, even if they did not provide the full context that would help an outside audience to better understand their significance.

When we shared the book with teachers from around Quebec at a series of media literacy workshops offered by Quebec's Ministry of Education, their questions often focused on the stories behind the photo essays. They also wanted more information about how we had set up the production process so that they could try out this method with their classes. On another occasion we used the book as an opening exercise at the international conference "Remembering War, Genocide and Other Human Rights Violations: Oral History, New Media and the Arts" at Concordia University, where we invited small groups to discuss the themes being communicated through different photo essays. We used the "lack of context" to our advantage as a technique to get the groups thinking about the intentions behind each story. Following the exercise, we invited Colleen French of the Canadian Council for Refugees and Sylvain Thibault of Montreal Mission to "fill in the gaps" by discussing the larger context of immigration and refugee policies in Canada. The maps were also included in the twelve-month We Are Here exhibit at the History Centre of Montreal as part of the final exhibition of the Life Stories of Montreal project.[16] Twenty of the drawings were selected and beautifully presented with a range of inspiring and diverse projects that came out of the Life Stories of Montreal project. This was an especially important site to share the work because the exhibit offered context regarding the diversity of refugee experiences in Montreal. We included additional context regarding our workshop process. At the opening, Sylvain shared with us his plan to integrate a museum visit into his workshop series.

Because we had hoped to use the results of the workshops as catalysts for dialogue in sensitizing the general public to the impacts of policy changes on the lives of individuals, we started to ask ourselves what additional information would help the work stand on its own and make it useful in the areas of education, policy, and service. Spending so much time in the shelters had helped us understand how vital the residence was to a healthy integration for individuals who needed a safe space during a difficult transition. Government policies were continuing to impact the numbers of refugees applying for asylum and this affected the residence system dramatically. When we first began the workshops, Project Refuge managed three residences and our workshops were packed. By our last workshop, one year later, only eight residents remained in a residence with beds for over forty. With so few residents, Sylvain was forced to close two of the three shelters. Sylvain expressed his concerns that without residences specifically serving this vulnerable group, refugees would end up in homeless shelters as they did twenty years earlier – without support and without a chance to establish peer networks.

Given this volatile context, we realized that the story of the shelter itself was an important part of the context. Because of its precarious status, and because Projet Refuge was approaching its twenty-year anniversary, Sylvain invited us to create a short documentary and to invite past residents and some of the more engaged workshop participants to be involved in the production. One of the goals in making the documentary was to address common stereotypes about refugees as well as to offer an intimate portrait that would demonstrate how past residents had not only adapted but were making a contribution in Quebec. The finished film, *The First Door*, profiles three individuals who benefited from the Haidar residence. It also profiles the specific strategies Sylvain implements to "help newcomers help themselves." We have shared the documentary with a network of shelter coordinators from around Canada and with general audiences in Montreal. At Projet Refuge's twenty-year anniversary event, people began to discuss how this film could help the general public better understand how difficult it is to go through the refugee process and the patience and tenacity it takes to integrate into the fabric of Montreal. Representatives from the United Nations High Commissioner for Refugees (UNHCR) who attended the screening confirmed the importance of continuing to create this type of resource.

Conclusion

What became increasingly clear working with individuals with sensitive stories about the refugee experience is that telling a personal story either can be empowering or can reinforce isolation, depending on the context in which that story is told. One individual explained, "People often ask you where you are from but they are less interested in the story behind the answer. And because we are asked this so often you come to understand the questions as 'what are you doing here ... essentially do you belong?'"[17] To ensure respect for an individual sharing a sensitive story, Sylvain advises all volunteers working at the residence, "Before asking a question, ask yourself 'is this about personal curiosity or for the person's well being?'"

It was important to follow Sylvain's advice in our storytelling workshop, especially given how many individuals were involved. Over time, we learned how to structure activities and frame the discussion questions in a way that reinforced a sense of belonging among the group, instead of allowing our inherent curiosity or inadvertent *in*sensitivity to reopen fresh wounds. For example, a seemingly innocent activity of asking participants to share three things left behind raised emotions that were difficult to address in the context of a collective storytelling workshop. By shifting the question to share three things they brought with them (abstract or physical), participants were instead able to acknowledge each other's areas of strength and tenacity in the face of difficult times.

The privilege of doing the workshop again and again allowed us to reflect, refine activities, and bring a greater sensitivity to workshop facilitation. However, the results fell short in that the products from the workshop were limited to evocative snapshots rather than in-depth, reflective stories. An additional shortcoming was the participants' involvement in the important step of sharing their pieces with a wider audience. One of our principles in participatory projects is to ensure that participants are included at every step of the process, including distribution. The transitory nature of the residence and the brevity of the workshop simply did not make this possible. While we are thrilled that we have already had the chance to share the book with hundreds of teachers, we know that had we been able to include the storytellers in the presentation, it would have been meaningful for the audience and the participants would have had the chance to see how their stories make a difference. We had a lot of things in place for this workshop: a safe space, strong facilitation that improved over time, technology that didn't get in the way, activities that were adapted to the needs of the participants, and, importantly, a conviction that the workshops were taking place because of a need expressed by our partner, Sylvain Thibault. But, if we were to do it again, we would certainly want to find a way to bring more continuity into the equation.

NOTES

1 Montreal City Mission is an interfaith organization that works against poverty and social exclusion, and offers a wide range of services for asylum seekers.

2 Radio Refuge is broadcast through Radio Centre Ville. http://www
   .iciradiorefuge.org.
3 Canadian Council for Refugees, http://ccrweb.ca, World Refugee Survey,
   2009, www.refugees.org.
4 Canadian Council for Refugees, http://ccrweb.ca.
5 www.mappingmemories.ca.
6 For a full discussion of the principles leading the project, visit http://www
   .mappingmemories.ca/guiding-principles.
7 York University (Toronto, Canada), *InTensions Journal* 4 (Fall 2010): 3.
8 Clemencia Rodríguez, *Fissures in the Mediascape: An International Study of
   Citizens' Media* (New York: Hampton Press, 2001), 18.
9 For a full discussion of the principles guiding the project, visit http://
   www.mappingmemories.ca/guiding-principles.
10 Drawing has been increasingly used in diverse pedagogical environments
   as a way to share a story idea with others, as a technique to create a "first
   draft" of a story, or even as a tool for responding to literature. Graphic
   novels are also becoming increasingly popular and are able to present
   complex ideas clearly through images and text. The use of drawing is
   especially successful with students who are visual learners and with
   second-language learners to communicate abstract ideas they might not
   have the words for. It also allows educators to quickly see what students
   understand about difficult concepts.
11 Excerpt taken from *The First Door*, a twenty-three-minute documentary by
   Liz Miller.
12 PhotoVoice is based in London but has initiated projects and resources
   around the world. Their mission is to build skills within marginalized
   communities using photography and digital storytelling methods for
   individuals to express themselves. www.photovoice.org.
13 Henry Greenspan, *On Listening to Holocaust Survivors: Beyond Testimony*
   (St Paul, MN: Paragon House, 2010), 2.
14 Calvin Pryluck, "Ultimately We Are All Outsiders: The Ethics of
   Documentary Filming," in Alan Rosenthal and John Corner, eds., *New
   Challenges for Documentary*, 2nd ed. (Manchester: Manchester University
   Press, 2005).
15 Liz Miller, interview with Alberto, former resident of Maison Haider, for
   the Mapping Memories Project.
16 We Are Here was a twelve-month exhibit that showcased the range of
   projects coming out of the Life Stories project.
17 Liz Miller, excerpt from interview conducted for *The First Door* film, March
   2010.

PART FOUR

Life Stories

11 "So You Want to Hear Our Ghetto Stories?" Oral History at Ndinawe Youth Resource Centre[1]

ROBIN JARVIS BROWNLIE AND ROEWAN CROWE

The Project: Warrior Women

"So you want to hear our ghetto stories?" The question came from a young Aboriginal woman who was being asked to participate in our oral history project. Her query seemed to express a recognition of her vulnerability to exploitation, colonization, and exoticization through our research – and even through our presence in her community. It also suggested her awareness of the ways in which "ghetto stories" can lend authority – or "street cred" – to those who can appropriate them despite their own social distance from such experiences. It was a telling reminder of our positionality and the power dynamics that were at work when we conducted an oral history project with Aboriginal youth in Winnipeg's North End. We replied that we were not there to collect their ghetto stories; that those stories would not be part of our research. Rather, the project was about *their* gaining access to stories of Indigenous women's resistance through the women speakers we invited to participate. Her insightful comment remained relevant to us throughout the project.

In this chapter we discuss our oral history pilot project at Ndinawe[2] Youth Resource Centre and address some important questions it raised about research ethics and politics, and about how we, as white scholars, work with Aboriginal youth and communities. We interrogate the ways in which cross-cultural research and colonial practices intersect, and work to envision research initiatives that can contribute to decolonizing practices. By doing so we hope to make visible the eruption of colonialism into research processes. The project met some of our expectations but also raised many new questions and compelled us to examine the meanings and effects of research in Winnipeg's North End.

Over the winter of 2008–9, we conducted a small-scale oral history project with young Indigenous women in Winnipeg's North End. The project was run in collaboration with, and located at, Ndinawe Youth Resource Centre, an Aboriginal resource and drop-in centre.[3] The project involved two sessions of six weeks each with two groups of young Indigenous women, one group aged 16–24, the other 12–15. For each six-week session, we brought in two Indigenous women who related oral history to the youth, particularly addressing the theme of resistance. The youth took turns interviewing the women, and the week after each storytelling session some of them made art in response to the stories they heard. We framed the project around what it can mean to be a woman warrior in your community, an idea we adopted from Métis filmmaker Christine Welsh. Welsh's powerful video *Keepers of the Fire* explores the idea of the woman warrior, meaning women who have been actively involved in Indigenous struggles such as the Haida campaign to protect Gwaii Haanas from clear-cutting, the Mohawk standoff at Kanehsatake, and the fight to eliminate the patriarchal status provisions of the Indian Act.[4] We showed this video at the beginning of each session.

The three women who came to speak at Ndinawe were extraordinarily generous in their participation, in their sharing of stories, insights, and experience. The three women were: Anishinabekwe activist and mother Jo Redsky (who attended both sessions); Ojibway / Cree mother, filmmaker, and painter Jackie Traverse; and Anishinabe / Dakota artist and educator Lita Fontaine. The speakers were asked to share their own experiences of survival and resistance. Jo Redsky and Jackie Traverse grew up in the North End themselves and shared stories of personal struggle and surmounting challenges that resonated deeply with their listeners. They expressed pride in their origins and attachment to the North End as a community that had offered them a sense of belonging and identity. They conveyed powerful stories of overcoming racism, colonization, and the impact of the residential schools and the child welfare system. In situating their own stories within an understanding of colonial systems and power structures, they gave the youth a framework within which they could understand their own circumstances and experiences.

The speakers narrated a path through obstacles set in front of them as Indigenous women. Jo Redsky spoke about her political activism and community involvement, about taking leadership roles in her communities and claiming Anishinabe traditions, such as playing the drum, singing, and playing the flute. Jackie Traverse talked about her personal experiences with the child welfare system, which separated her family, about the impact of gangs, and about her journey as a visual artist. She shared her artwork relating to these experiences. Lita Fontaine worked with the young people by sharing her photographs of powwow dancing and regalia, drawing out their skills in creative interpretation and art making. The youth embraced all the speakers and made it clear that meeting the women had been encouraging and empowering. All these stories of strength and determination were important to them, as most are faced daily with the significant challenges of poverty and violence resulting from colonization and racism.

Our approach was to develop a feminist, community-based research project that contributed in a meaningful way to the community organization's programming. It was important to us to bring something of value to the community, rather than just extract research from it. We hoped to create a context for the sharing of stories of resistance, where Indigenous women spoke directly to the youth about their experiences with colonization – and also for a response to these stories through art making. In the pilot project, the young people met strong Indigenous women who had successfully met some of the same challenges the young women currently face, and they learned about some of the strategies that had allowed Jo Redsky, Lita Fontaine, and Jackie Traverse not only to prevail in the face of difficulties, but also to become leaders in their communities.

The original idea came from Jarvis's exposure to Telling Lives, an oral history project conducted in New York's Chinatown by the Oral History Research Office that used oral history to teach a wide range of skills to groups of predominantly immigrant children. That project was conducted within public schools and run on a large scale with full-time staff. We did not have the resources to replicate its scope but felt that some of the core ideas could provide a foundation for undertaking oral history with urban Indigenous youth. Those ideas included the building of skills and confidence through interactions with powerful storytellers who spoke about dealing with significant, often difficult, life experiences. Another important feature of the Telling Lives project was its participatory character, as the young people had a role in directing the project, choosing speakers, and determining their own activities. A number of them took part in producing an exhibit that showed some of the stories related during the project, which was displayed at a local venue.

Oral History and Stories

Telling stories is a powerful way to share experience and knowledge. Our project was intended to investigate what oral history and stories can offer in our attempts to address genocide and colonization as ongoing processes in Canada. Indigenous thinkers have increasingly emphasized the importance of stories in Indigenous intellectual and pedagogical traditions.[5] Cherokee author Thomas King's Massey lectures, published as *The Truth about Stories*, brilliantly demonstrate the power of Indigenous storytelling to shape understanding, and thus reality. As he writes, "The truth about stories is that that's all we are."[6] Quoting Anishinabe author Gerald Vizenor, he continues, "You cannot understand the world without telling a story. There isn't any center to the world but a story."

As Julie Cruikshank and others have illuminated in their work, storytelling is a richly nuanced communicative form.[7] A people's stories contain all the vital elements of world view and self-understanding that are not always articulated as clearly or fully in other forms of communication. They also express and embody the rootedness in geographic place that has been particularly characteristic of Indigenous peoples. The words of a Gitksan elder, confronted with Canadian officials claiming to own his land, powerfully convey the central symbolic role of stories and their connection to land: "If this is your land," he queried, "where are your stories?"[8] Cruikshank has also written about the ways in which oral narratives can facilitate social and political critique. Referencing the insights of Harold Innis and Mikhail Bakhtin, she suggests that "[oral] narrative challenges hegemonic institutions."[9] Innis and Bakhtin both identified "the open-ended possibilities inherent in oral dialogue" and Bakhtin discussed the "'dialogic,' relational possibilities of conversational storytelling as a model intrinsically opposing authoritarian speech."[10]

In our project, we witnessed the impact of creating a context for the sharing of critical and oppositional narratives, stories of experience that identified colonization as one of the most important problems Indigenous people face. By telling these kinds of stories, the speakers who came to Ndinawe gave the youth access to anti-colonial critiques and to knowledge of talk and action directed at dismantling colonialism. The young people had an opportunity to learn about decolonizing work such as political lobbying and organizing, public outreach campaigns, struggles to hold police accountable for shootings of Indigenous people, and the use of artwork such as painting, photography, and video to address the impact of colonization on Indigenous people and families.

The speakers offered their reflections on Indigenous culture and identity and on dealing with colonization in their everyday lives. Jackie Traverse told about her experience of being taken from her family at a young age by child welfare services. She recounted how she had been determined to stay with her younger siblings and prevent their separation, and how a social worker tricked her into leaving the room so that the siblings could be separated. She also showed her short film, *Two Scoops*, which relates the story of this experience.[11] Jo Redsky spoke about her own childhood experiences of surviving the colonial context of the North End and about being involved in political activism as an adult. She discussed the 1997 shooting death of Connie Jacobs and her nine-year-old son Ty at the hands of the RCMP, which occurred on the Tsuu T'ina Nation reserve. Jo has been involved in political organizing to call attention to the problems many Indigenous activists believe led to these deaths. She addressed the ways in which she has reconnected to Anishinabe beliefs and practices and forged a strong identity as an Anishinabekwe.

Both these speakers' contributions and their interactions with the youth exemplified Stó:lo educator Jo-ann Archibald's observations about the sharing of experience: "Sharing what one has learned is an important Indigenous tradition. This type of sharing can take the form of a story of personal life experience and is done with a compassionate mind and love for others."[12] In listening to the speakers, the youth showed clear interest and engagement, particularly when the stories resonated with their own struggles. With their stories, the speakers modelled ingenuity, resilience, and determination, the kinds of strengths that often appear in stories designed for young people. Yet these stories came directly from speakers who were present, who were relating their own experiences, and who shared with the youth Indigenous identity, direct experience of the Canadian colonial context, and childhoods lived in their own neighbourhood.

Danger from Euro-Canadian institutions was one of the common themes that emerged in the stories. In speaking of these issues, the speakers took on the hegemony of institutions such as the police and child welfare agencies. While Euro-Canadian society as a whole tends to depict these institutions as benign and protective, the speakers addressed how Indigenous people have often experienced them as harmful and violent. Child welfare agencies appeared as a source of family trauma, separating children painfully and sometimes permanently from their parents and each other. Police, too, appeared as agents of racism and anti-Indigenous sentiment, officials of an institution that served mainly to oppress members of the Indigenous community. In the case of Connie and Ty Jacobs, for example, the RCMP constable shot the two when he was attempting to assist child welfare workers in removing Connie's children from her home. By placing these powerful institutions within the colonial context, the speakers provided tools for the young people to connect common but apparently personal, "private" experiences with larger social processes and practices aimed at maintaining the subordination of Indigenous people as a group.

We had originally intended to have the youth offer their own stories in the context of the project, if they chose to do so. It was only when we met the youth face to face that we understood, on an experiential level, the power dynamics of the research situation and the multiple vulnerabilities they faced as young people living with the devastating effects of colonization, racialization, extreme poverty, and marginalization. We felt powerfully that it would have been unethical to involve their stories in this short-term pilot project, that under these circumstances we would end up feeling that we had simply "taken" their stories. The sessions were short – six weekly two-hour meetings – and we were not sure whether the project would continue, so it was not clear that we would have a long-term relationship with any of the participants. This was an important consideration, given the need we immediately recognized for the youth to form long-term relationships before sharing intimate knowledge of their lives. Under the circumstances, recording their stories would have been an exploitation of their poverty, inexperience, and disenfranchisement. It is not that the youth did not share stories about their lives with us, but that we chose to focus our research on the stories of resistance offered by Jo Redsky, Jackie Traverse, and Lita Fontaine.

The young women participants seemed to find the project meaningful and engaging. In the assessment forms completed at the end of each session of the pilot project, they expressed their appreciation for the speakers. It was clear that many had made a significant connection with the women and their stories. Ndinawe staff considered the project so valuable that they engaged one of the speakers to come back for further sessions to speak to the youth. The storytelling component of the project was highly successful, thanks in large part to the skill and generosity of the visiting speakers.

Decolonizing Research

In designing the project, we were interested in decolonizing research – in both senses in which the term can be understood. We wanted to work towards decolonizing the research process itself, and also to engage in research that contributed to undoing colonization. We were influenced by Indigenist and feminist methodologies.[13] Both these approaches highlight the analysis of colonization, race, and power relations. Indigenist methodologies work towards emancipation, decolonization, and the restoration of Indigenous thought, questioning research itself as a form of colonial knowledge production. As Maori scholar Linda Smith writes, "the term 'research' is inextricably linked to European imperialism and colonialism."[14] It is out of this reality that Indigenous scholars have developed alternative methodologies that "construct, rediscover, and / or reaffirm their knowledges and cultures … represent the aspirations of Indigenous [peoples] and carry within them the potential to strengthen the struggle for emancipation and liberation from oppression."[15]

As Indigenous scholars have pointed out, too often researchers have contributed nothing to Indigenous communities in which they have worked, as they simply visited briefly, acquired knowledge or information, and disappeared. Though community members gave their time and knowledge, they received little or nothing in return. Smith has expressed the feelings about such research that she has heard repeatedly in Indigenous communities: "At a common sense level research was talked about both in terms of its absolute worthlessness to us, the indigenous world, and its absolute usefulness to those who wielded it as an instrument. It told us things already known, suggested things that would not work, and made careers for people who already had jobs."[16] She further noted that research "is not an innocent or distant academic exercise but an activity that has something at stake and that occurs in a set of political and social conditions."[17] Accordingly, Indigenous scholars have encouraged anyone wishing to conduct research with Indigenous people to ask themselves what the community will gain from the project; who owns, designs, and directs the research; and who holds ownership of the project.[18] We had these questions at heart in designing and carrying out the oral history project at Ndinawe.

Understanding Our Positionality and Context

As researchers, we entered the project with a critical feminist stance, both locating ourselves and understanding the meaning of our location in the context of this inner-city social service agency. These locations included Jarvis as a queer/trans, feminist academic and white settler from a middle-class upbringing; Roewan as a queer, feminist artist / academic and white settler from a working-class background. The context we entered was one of a centre for Indigenous youth that confronts the serious social problems resulting from racism and the ongoing colonial process in Canada. These problems include severe impoverishment, hunger, and societal neglect; the long-term, intergenerational trauma resulting from residential schools; lack of employment; high suicide and murder rates; inadequate education systems; and the pressure on young people to join gangs. We had previous connections with some of the staff and quickly developed a good working relationship with other staff members. The centre itself offers vitally important services but the staff faces the neighbourhood's deep-rooted social problems with a minimum of resources – a discouraging and difficult situation.

In locating our project in this Winnipeg North End community, often cited as Canada's poorest inner-city neighbourhood, we entered a space that is framed in public discourse as a place to be feared, ignored, demonized, and pathologized, often in a sensationalist manner. It is racialized as Aboriginal space and simultaneously associated with a string of linked negative characteristics, including poverty, prostitution, gangs, car theft, gun violence, and murders. To those who do not live there, it is a space where violence is normalized; in the formulation of critical race theorist Sherene Razack, it is seen by mainstream white culture as an area "'outside' civilized society," though necessary to the latter for its own self-definition. The restriction of Aboriginal communities to certain areas of the city is facilitated by colonial discourses and practices that simultaneously enforce such segregation and naturalize it as a phenomenon that occurs by itself. The North End (actually located in the centre of the city) is constantly represented as a danger to non-Aboriginal people, even though Aboriginal people living in the area are usually the victims of any violence that occurs. Indeed, violence in the North End takes many forms, including not only street and domestic violence, but also the other colonial violences: poverty, state regulation and punishment, economic and sexual exploitation, police brutality.

The significance of racialized constructions of space is effectively explored in Sherene Razack's path-breaking anthology *Race, Space, and the*

Law. The volume aims to "unmap" the racialization of space under colonialism and to analyse how these processes function. Her own article in the collection examines a particularly relevant series of events that surrounded the 1995 murder of Pamela George, an Ojibway mother of two young children, by two young, middle-class white men. The article demonstrates the racialization of space in Regina and the constituting of the inner city as Aboriginal space to which whites have privileged access for adventure and conquest.[19] Similar processes are at work in the North End, where commercial sexual exploitation is one of the ways marginalized people, especially transgender and biological women, attempt to earn money, in the process facing extraordinary risks of violence. In recent years many street-involved women in Winnipeg have disappeared or been murdered. Some of them were known to some of the young women who participated in our oral history project. Thus, these colonial realities were very real to project participants.

We took this understanding of the colonial construction of space and race – especially relevant in prairie cities – into the project with us. In particular, we wondered how we, as privileged white scholars and authority figures, were crossing the line into these racialized spaces to come back with stories of survival – how our own discourses about doing research in the North End could be received and validated in these racialized terms. What is the relationship of non-Indigenous researchers to these oral histories of resistance and to the processes of colonization and decolonization? We understand decolonization to be a process of undoing colonial ways of thinking and acting, which for us required thinking about whiteness and its privileges, as well as the authority attached to universities and academic researchers. We also thought about matters such as language and research methods. Adopting this decolonizing stance led to the kinds of radical questioning that both Indigenist and feminist thought require. We often wondered, for instance, about the implications of two white professors assuming leadership roles in an Indigenous community organization: Was this just an updated form of colonialism? How is it different from, say, missionization or social services as historical agents of colonization?

Power

Race and whiteness shaped the power relationships and structures we operated within at Ndinawe. We entered this community with pre-existing connections with some of the staff and a power-sharing, collaborative model for the project. The youth and staff at Ndinawe were all Indigenous, as were all the speakers. We were aware of the ways in which whiteness and professional status are equated with authority and that the people we met at Ndinawe had undoubtedly often experienced whiteness as a source of privilege and power that could be used to their disadvantage. In addition, the fact that we arrived with a plan for a project, with money to pay for participation, and working in conjunction with the staff, provided us with power. These factors were all the more profound because they remained hidden, and, given the circumstances, we did not name them.

Though we arrived with the basic idea for the project, we intended to undertake a collaborative process with both staff and youth to design and implement it. This process was successful with regard to the staff but did not take place with the youth. Relations between the researchers and Ndinawe staff constituted a full partnership in which the staff's knowledge of the youth's needs and circumstances played a key role. In meetings held before the oral history sessions began, we determined many of the project's parameters: its timing, the creation of separate sessions divided by age category, the days and times of sessions, the speakers, and the basic activities that would be undertaken.

The pilot project showed us that a collaborative, power-sharing process with the youth would have required substantial time at the outset to build relationships with the youth, discuss possibilities, and create the program from the ground up. As it was, we did not budget sufficient time for such a process, and the result was that the project remained very much the model that we developed in collaboration with the staff and brought to the youth, who had little impact on its basic structure and approach.

Another consequence of the existing power dynamics was the risk of assimilative effects. There were several instances in which this was at play. For example, in introducing the youth to university-style group discussion, we were modelling to the youth a certain way of being in relation to knowledge. Similarly, in attempting to videotape the oral histories, we replicated a Western model for working with oral history, capturing a single storytelling experience through the use of technology and seeking to ensure its future availability as a recording. Although this model has also been taken up and adapted by Indigenous communities and scholars, our intent to maintain these recordings for posterity did lend itself to a Western approach that documents stories so that they can be accessed by anyone at any time, without the ethic of developing a relationship with the speakers. We do not mean to say that this model does not have value, but only that in using this approach, we did not model to the youth Indigenous knowledge practices which are often grounded in long-term relationships and learning stories "by heart." Finally, our use of language undoubtedly had an impact, which was highlighted for us when speaker Jo Redsky introduced herself as an Anishinabekwe and noted that she did not like the term "Aboriginal women." We had to ask ourselves what else we were communicating to the young women and what other assumptions were built into our speech and practices. These were some of the decolonizing moments that we experienced in carrying out the project and in our subsequent reflections on it.

Working with Youth

We are left questioning the politics of working with youth, especially marginalized youth. How is it that we had access to these young people? We did not have to obtain the consent of their parents and guardians, since Ndinawe has blanket consent forms for participation in its programs. We also had money to pay the youth and they needed money. We had connections to Ndinawe staff. These issues and other elements of the project brought disquieting moments of historical recognition. Paying the youth for their participation in sessions, for example, was one of the most profound experiences of colonial recognition, when we felt that the past was being replicated in the present. As the youth lined up to sign receipts and receive their envelopes of cash, we were reminded of other colonial processes like treaty signings and payments, and the many other kinds of colonial payments to Indigenous people, always accompanied by signatures on forms.

The exchange of money for participation raised more than one challenging issue. The payments to the youth – $20 per meeting attended – allowed some of the participants to purchase needed items, gifts for themselves, and Christmas presents, especially those in the first session, which ended in early December. For some, the money helped contribute to living expenses for their families. At the same time, Ndinawe staff had concerns about how the money would be spent, particularly with regard to the younger participants (those of the second session, aged twelve to fifteen). Given the profound poverty in the neighbourhood, there were many possibilities for competition over these resources and for pressure on the youth to part with them. Among other things, staff felt the young people might experience peer pressure and possibly even threats of violence if they did not use the money to purchase street drugs. Working within these realities, we faced questions about how to take responsibility for paying cash to these young people for their participation. This was a difficult negotiation with ourselves, with staff, and with the youth.

The issue came to a head immediately after the first meeting of the second session, when staff members told us that they believed a few of the youth had purchased drugs, and that they had done so with the cash from our project. It was under these difficult circumstances that consensus-based decision making was not upheld. The staff felt compelled, in keeping with the drop-in centre's policies, to take immediate steps in response to the problem, which included expelling one of the youths from our project. We were not involved in this decision. In consultation with the staff after these events, we felt we had no choice but to change the payment practice. For the first session, we had paid all the participants in cash at the end of the six weeks. But for the second session, after staff expressed their concerns to us, we determined that cash would not be given out. Instead, the youth were given a choice between a shopping trip with Ndinawe staff or a cheque delivered to a parent or guardian. We felt conflicted about this change, but we understood that the staff's goal was to ensure that money from the program did not place the youth at risk. For us, several issues coincided here. First, we were now in a position of controlling how the youth could use the money they earned. Second, we were aware of the historical relationship among colonialism, capitalism, and the drug trade, in which intoxicants imported into colonized communities serve in a variety of ways to justify colonization, repression, and intervention. Third, the change in the payment practice caused a rupture in our relationship with the young women. While we had open conversations with them about some of this in our sessions, it became a lasting source of fracture between us. It also apparently reduced the number of participants, which itself seemed to be a form of resistance to program changes they disagreed with.

The fact that we worked only with young women had important ramifications. The boys and young men understandably resented being excluded from one of the centre's programs, and particularly one that offered a rare opportunity to earn money and enjoy pizza dinners. Staff mentioned more than once that they would have liked to see a similar program for young men, to equalize opportunities and access to resources. Moreover, in the second session questions arose about who might be included, particularly with reference to a young person of apparently "male" self-presentation who socialized primarily with the young women. We wondered if this young person might have identified as transgender or two-spirit under the right circumstances, though no one at Ndinawe made reference to this possibility. We resolved the question by having the young women present vote on whether or not he could join the group, which resulted in a unanimous "yes" vote. Later, however, we wondered if this outcome had placed him at risk with the other young men, as his inclusion may have seemed even more arbitrary than a strict "women only" rule. It certainly had the potential to worsen his position at the centre as a young person who did not conform to standard patriarchal, heterosexual gender norms. As outsiders who made only short visits to Ndinawe over a period of several months, receiving weekly updates from staff, we never learned the complete story about possible unforeseen consequences for our participants.

One important benefit we felt the project provided to the youth and the community was discussions about research ethics and the importance of consent. The young people learned that if researchers wanted to work with them, they had the right to decide their own level of participation. The youth developed their skills in formulating interview questions as well as in posing questions and listening actively in interview situations. Though they were often shy at first and some chose not to undertake the interviewer role, all participants experienced exposure to comfortable, informal interview situations and a relatively structured interview process. The pilot project also gave us the opportunity to understand these kinds of dynamics more deeply if we chose in future to continue to work with young people and their own stories.

Despite our questions, in many ways it appeared that the staff, youth, and speakers were less troubled than we were by the tendency for our research to enact or mimic colonial practices. In post-program consultations, we found that this was a deeply meaningful project to the women who were involved, including the staff, the speakers, and the youth. The youth valued having access to stories of strength and resistance that they do not hear often enough, and they and the speakers immensely enjoyed interacting with each other. The young people were inspired to meet people who were standing up for their communities and this led to productive dialogues about the issues they were facing. They appreciated being paid for their participation and having another interesting evening activity; and they especially enjoyed the pizza dinners that were part of the experience. Indeed, we were struck by the centrality of the pizza dinners in the youth's evaluations at the end of the program. One participant said it was the thing she needed most at that moment in her life because of difficulties at home, a comment that suggests her appreciation of the nourishment and sense of community provided by these dinners. Others commented that they made new friends and some gained pride from the artwork they created and from attending regularly. The staff were inspired both by the idea of the community activist as woman warrior and by the decision to provide programming specifically for young women, who tended to participate less than the young men in many of the other programs and who had less group coherence.

Concluding Thoughts

A pilot project provides the opportunity to try ideas and approaches on a small scale and then critically reflect on the processes and outcomes. In working with disenfranchised, urban Aboriginal youth, we confronted the colonial links and patterns that are not always carefully explored in academic research. We sought to remain aware of our positionality and our impact on the youth and their community; of the assumptions that shaped our practices; and of the colonial power relations in which our project was necessarily embedded. In keeping with some of the insights offered by the speakers in our pilot project, we remain conscious of the often-hidden, sometimes-subtle dangers of Euro-Canadian institutions and their role within the colonial power apparatus. These institutions, often unwittingly, perpetuate the harms of colonization within Indigenous communities. One of the powerful roles that academic research can play is to disrupt the colonial discourses of benevolence that facilitate continuing repression by institutions such as the police and social welfare agencies. Universities, as well, can too easily participate in this institutional enforcement of long-standing colonial practices such as assimilation, segregation, demonization, and marginalization. When white settlers work with Indigenous youth, academic ethics requirements such as consent forms and signed receipts for honoraria can appear similar to treaty signings and other bureaucratic procedures that have historically underpinned the dispossession of Indigenous peoples' land, resources, and knowledge.

Decolonizing research requires practitioners to engage in radical reflexivity, collaboration, and power sharing, and to pay close attention to the replication of colonial practices. As Sherene Razack has written, such research allows us to "contest ... practices of domination through a resurrection of historical memory of colonization and its continuing effects." In the process, we "inhabit histories of domination and subordination for which we are accountable."[20] Our hope is that our research narrative will work to destabilize dominant discourses and challenge hegemonic institutions, calling into question the relationship between colonial practices and cross-cultural oral history research.

NOTES

1 The authors would like to thank Jim Silver for supporting this project and providing funding from the Social Sciences and Humanities Research Council of Canada (Community-University Research Alliance program), which funded this project through the Manitoba Research Alliance. We also thank the anonymous reviewers for their thoughtful engagement and productive questions.

2 "Ndinawe" is pronounced "Na-din-ah-weh." The centre's full name, Ndinawemaaganag Endaawaad, means "Our Relatives' Home" in Anishinabe.

3 We would like to thank the staff at Ndinawe, especially Cheyenne Henry, Rob Marriott, Kale Bonham, Heather McKenzie, Michael Champagne, Daryl Nepinak, and student intern Lea Neufeld, along with research assistant Stacey Abramson.

4 Christine Welsh, *Keepers of the Fire* (National Film Board of Canada, 1994).

5 E.g., Jo-ann Archibald/Q'um Q'um Xiiem, *Indigenous Storywork: Educating the Heart, Mind, Body, and Spirit* (Vancouver: UBC Press, 2008).

6 Thomas King, *The Truth about Stories: A Native Narrative* (Toronto: Anansi Press, 2003), 32.

7 Julie Cruikshank, with A. Sidney, K. Smith and A. Ned, *Life Lived Like a Story: Life Stories of Three Yukon Native Elders* (Vancouver: UBC Press, 1990); Julie Cruikshank, *The Social Life of Stories: Narrative and Knowledge in the Yukon Territory* (Lincoln: University of Nebraska Press, 1998); King, *Truth about Stories*; J. Edward Chamberlin, *If This Is Your Land, Where Are Your Stories?* (Toronto: Knopf Canada, 2003).

8 Cited in Chamberlin, *If This Is Your Land*, 1.

9 Cruikshank, *Social Life of Stories*, 72.

10 Ibid.

11 Jackie Traverse, *Two Scoops* (2008). This is an animated short film, produced, written, animated, and directed by Traverse.

12 Archibald, *Indigenous Storywork*, 2.

13 We would like to thank Dr Kiera Ladner for sharing her intellectual labour and insights concerning Indigenous and Indigenist research methodologies.

14 Linda Tuhiwai Smith, *Decolonizing Methodologies: Research and Indigenous Peoples* (London and New York: Zed Books, 1999), 1.

15 Lester-Irabinna Rigney, "Internalization of an Indigenous Anticolonial Cultural Critique of Research Methodologies: A Guide to Indigenist Research Methodology and Its Principles," *Wicazo Sa Review* (Fall 1999): 114.

16 Smith, *Decolonizing Methodologies*, 3.

17 Ibid., 5.

18 See, for instance, Archibald, *Indigenous Storywork*, 36; Smith, *Decolonizing Methodologies*, 10.

19 Sherene Razack, "Gendered Racial Violence and Spatialized Justice: The Murder of Pamela George," in Sherene Razack, ed., *Race, Space, and the Law* (Toronto: Between the Lines, 2002), 121–56.

20 Ibid., 128.

12 Dishonour, Dispersion, and Dispossession: Race and Rights in Twenty-First-Century North America – A View from the Lower Ninth Ward[1]

D'ANN R. PENNER

Hurricane Katrina's immediate aftermath in New Orleans shed an internationally televised spotlight on the rudimentary human rights for African Americans in the United States.[2] Domestically, the issue was whether state resources, ranging from rescue equipment and medical supplies to food and water, could be used in a racially disparate manner to privilege the lives and property of whites over African Americans in the Greater New Orleans Region, without accountability.[3] The United States government, the Army Corps of Engineers, and agents of the State of Louisiana have defended themselves against indirect class action lawsuits, not by justifying their agents' actions but by claiming sovereign immunity. Because of the Supreme Court's interpretation of the 11th Amendment in *Hans v. Louisiana*, decided during Jim Crow, state governments cannot be sued directly, even by their own citizens.

However, despite a flurry of initial government research grants to study poverty and resilience in relation to Hurricane Katrina, a dwindling of interest within academia mirrors the indifference of the larger world. The 2010 "anniversary" coverage that dominated the American news media assured viewers that New Orleans is "flourishing" like never before.[4] In the words of Roy Weiner, associate director of clinical research at Tulane Cancer Center, "I totally believe that New Orleans is and will be a better place in virtually every aspect because of how we have recovered from Katrina."[5]

In August 2010, I sat with Reverend Mildred Alcorn in a small rental unit in the Lower Ninth Ward, only blocks from her former home. Before the storm, the now fifty-eight-year-old woman combined ministry with her work as the director of a program of last resort for unemployed, homeless women. "Failure was not an option," she recalled. As Alcorn reflected on the fates of the significant people in her pre-storm social network – the sisters, nephews, godchildren, friends, and church members, mainly homeowners, who all lived within a six-block radius – she paused to admit that she still tears up every two to three days as she worries about how they are coping, alone, in distant cities. "Some losses can't be overcome," she gently chided me as co-editor of the book *Overcoming Katrina*.[6]

Roy Weiner may accurately capture the jubilation of the "new" New Orleans in the predominantly white neighbourhoods of Uptown, the French Quarter, and even Lakeview. But he cannot speak for Reverend Alcorn, and does not speak to the deleterious impact of Katrina's aftermath on (especially) Lower Ninth Warders who commanded the world's attention from 29 August through 4 September 2005.

I interviewed Alcorn as part of an oral history documentation project of human rights violations, entitled The Saddest Days Oral History Project.[7] From September 2005 through September 2010, I conducted at least one (and as many as seven follow-up) interview(s) with a total of 290 Katrina survivors, overwhelmingly African Americans originally from New Orleans, from a wide variety of educational, socio-economic, religious, and family backgrounds.

I am a "witness by adoption," the term Geoffrey H. Hartman, an expert on Holocaust narratives, used to describe Gentiles who document the Holocaust.[8] My emotional investment in these issues began as the child of German American tenant farmers in an Illinois village, where we were outsiders. I was drawn to books about slave narratives, African American firsts, and Black Power manifestos I found in the local libraries that spoke to my feelings of rootlessness while teaching me how to fight injustice. These authors and their subjects modelled endurance and resistance, lessons that were instrumental in my own struggle to overcome a personal history of trauma and moral injury.

During the interviews, I attempted to decentre power to avoid reinforcing "the survivors' humiliated feelings, instilled by their aggressors, that they are worthless and their stories meaningless," an inevitable byproduct of emotionless listening, according to Richard Mollica, director of the Harvard Program in Refugee Trauma.[9] "It may well be only through testimony that we can really write the history of such a cataclysm," Yale psychiatrist Dori Laub concluded after decades of work.[10]

The harms of the militarized seven-day aftermath of Katrina are best understood both by looking back to the deep history of race relations in the United States and by looking forward to how the use of federal resources furthers a revanchist local agenda in changing the racial demographics of New Orleans.[11] This chapter will examine African American narrators' experiences of human rights violations during Katrina's highly visible immediate aftermath (Phase I) and the more invisible-phase of permanent displacement and / or dispossession that began on 4 September 2005 (Phase II). Because decontextualized survivors' evidence has been used to create policies of which they have disapproved,[12] I end with recommendations from the results of my open-ended, semi-structured research. These recommendations take the form of present-tense strategies to address narrators' concerns for accountability and restitution keeping within a framework of constitutional rights.

Phase I: Dishonour and Dispersion

Despite the class diversity of the survivors I interviewed, most testified about human rights violations against themselves, their kin, or their community. To facilitate categorization, I follow "The Guiding Principles on Internal Displacement" (Guiding Principles) a non-binding treaty developed by the United Nations, and "The International Convention on the Elimination of All Forms of Race Discrimination" (CERD), a binding treaty signed by a United States president and ratified by the Senate.[13]

The first internationally recognized human rights principle violated against African Americans in New Orleans during the initial displacement from their homes was the right to life and security, Principle 10 of the Guiding Principles.[14] The narrators left little doubt that the people steered into the Superdome and the convention centre felt that their lives were in danger. "The scariest part of my ordeal," said Kevin Owens, a maintenance man for the B.W. Cooper Housing Development, "was being in the Superdome ... It was us against the military."[15] Deacon Harold Toussaint, a short, slender, fifty-five-year-old sommelier living in the Upper Ninth Ward, stayed in New Orleans for Hurricane Katrina because he felt God's call to take care of the elderly after the storm. On 1 September 2005, he attempted to ask a patrolling military unit for help evacuating The Esplanade at City Park:

I have to preface this by saying I had on a short-sleeved shirt and my pants were wet – I had no place to hide a weapon. So as I approached [the federal police], I just waved my hand out and said, "Oh, the 'guardsman' over there, he needs to talk to you." [They] pointed their M-16s, their

AK-47s, or whatever it was at me and said, "Get back! Get back! Get back!"
... I felt they were ready to shoot me! All they saw was that I was black,
and blacks are criminals.[16]

Assault rifles were pointed routinely at survivors "as if [they] were in
a concentration camp," to borrow the analogy of Shriff Hasan, a high
school teacher and playwright from the Gentilly neighbourhood.[17]
"There were police cars en masse. Every night that happened around
two or three a.m.," he amplified. "No, they didn't stop to see how we
were doing ... Hell no, it wasn't about protecting nobody! It was about
protecting their wealth ... Guns pointed at people out of car windows
like [they're] ready to shoot, I'm talking about if you breathed the
wrong way." This long-time resident of New Orleans characterized the
targets of the scare tactics – people he saw on the I-10 bridge, around
the Superdome, and inside and outside of the convention centre – as
"taxpaying citizens" and "decent human beings."

Failure to provide timely food and water after Katrina violated
Guiding Principle 7.[18] Elementary rescue equipment (life jackets, boats,
medical supplies) seemed to have been forgotten, and standard rescue
supplies (food and water) were in critically short supply.[19] It was not
until the evening of Thursday, 1 September 2005, the fifth day of the
disaster, that Michael D. Brown, director of FEMA (Federal Emergency
Management Agency) acknowledged that thousands were stranded
without resources in and around the ten-and-one-half-block convention centre. In response, a military helicopter dropped the first batch of
food and water: enough MREs (meal, ready to eat) for approximately
twenty-five people.

The lack of sanitary conditions also contravened Guiding Principle 7.[20]
Every convention centre or Superdome narrator I interviewed mentioned with repugnance the inadequacy of bathroom facilities, indoors
and outside.[21] Cynthia Banks, founder of a non-profit daycare, relayed
the story of her "second mother," a ninety-four-year-old West Indian
woman she called Mother Baker. Mother Baker was first separated
from her grandchildren and then deposited, alone, on a landing field
with a growing crowd of strangers by the National Guard. Two months
later, Mother Baker confided to Banks by phone, "Child, it's but God
that kept me on that hot, black tar three days. I had nowhere to go to
the bathroom."[22] Demetrius White, a computer technician who rescued over thirty people after Katrina, was among the 5,000 African
Americans who were corralled at gunpoint for two days at the outdoor

I-10 / 610 cloverleaf in Metairie. "You had five thousand people with nine port-a-lets," he reported.[23]

The withholding of medical treatment violated Guiding Principle 3.[24] The slowness of the government's response to hospitals – indeed, the failure to provide back-up generators alone – caused the deaths of many people at University Hospital, according to Dr Denise Roubion-Johnson, medical director of a public breast cancer centre.[25] On Saturday, 3 September 2010, a pregnant Anika Pugh, a purveyor of homemade sweets, was finally evacuated along with her three children to Baton Rouge, Louisiana, where she was housed along with thousands in a gymnasium at Louisiana State University. By the time she got there, she remembered, "I couldn't even walk up straight ... because the pain had just suddenly came down on me." She pleaded for medical attention. The rescue worker to whom Anika Pugh appealed for medical treatment had the power to validate Pugh's medical concerns as serious enough for hospitalization. Instead, she was given vitamins and iron pills, and told to lie down on a cot. Pugh miscarried a week later in Birmingham. She declined the Birmingham hospital's offer of a fetal autopsy because, as she explained, "I kind of have a feeling why my baby's gone, because it's like I was stressing from the start of everything, wondering ... how are we going to survive?"[26] She carries the loss of her unborn baby as another man-made, Katrina-related loss.

After the storm, Kenneth Anderson, a house painter, walked nine blocks through water, at times up to his chin, to get to his ill older brother. Because he found his brother out of food, he walked through more water to his sister's apartment, to which he had a key. "On my way back, that's when the helicopter stopped me," Anderson explained, "and told me I had to go with them. I say, 'I'm going to bring my brother something to eat.' He said, 'No, you have to evacuate.'" As a result, Anderson's brother was not evacuated until five days after the storm and went without food for several days.[27] Anderson's experience illustrates another routine practice of state agents that violated human rights standards: keeping families together, according to Principle 7 of the Guiding Principles.[28]

Almost all of the narrators who were eventually evacuated from the Superdome, the convention centre, or the I-10/610-cloverleaf staging ground blamed the extremely chaotic departures of buses as the leading reason why so many children ended up separated from their families.[29] Not only were thousands of separated parents and children still looking for one another as late as the spring of 2006, but nuclear and extended families that had lived in close proximity for decades were scattered across multiple states and, as of 2007, were in more than 5,500 cities.[30]

CERD was also violated during Katrina's immediate aftermath.[31] For the narrators who endured the aftermath of Hurricane Katrina in New Orleans, the event was made traumatic less by the winds or the flood waters, and more by the city's descent into a militarized zone in which they were singled out for race-based persecution.[32] According to some estimates, 20 per cent of the residents remaining in New Orleans after Katrina's landfall were non-blacks.[33] The death toll among whites in the immediate aftermath is proportionately high enough when compared to the deaths of African Americans to indicate that significant numbers of whites in Lakeview and the racially mixed neighbourhoods of Gentilly and Mid-City must have attempted to ride out the storm in their homes.[34] The Jefferson Parish Sheriff's Office reported that on the single day of 30 August 2005, approximately 500 people from Lakeview were rescued by helicopter.[35] Although the same sheriff's office reported rescuing people from their rooftops and attics in Mid-City and Gentilly, CNN reported on 3 September 2005, that "as more and more eyewitness accounts of conditions in the convention center and Superdome surface, it becomes plain that most if not all of those who survived unspeakable days and nights under inhuman conditions were black."[36] At every turn, the Saddest Days narrators saw examples of white privilege in action. They watched whites directed to refuge in Jefferson Parish by the same police officer who directed them to the convention centre.[37] The thousands of African Americans trapped at the I-10 / 610 cloverleaf watched as whites were dropped off, fed, and flown out within a few hours.[38]

On 31 August 2005, government officials, including governor Kathleen Blanco and Mayor Ray Nagin, made a decision to safeguard white property (that has not been proven to have been at risk) by calling off the rescue, bringing in the National Guard for "order," and withholding food, water, and medical supplies until after white-owned property was allegedly "secure."[39] In the weeks after the storm, Lance Hill interviewed approximately 200 National Guardsmen and law officials who explained that the operative policy had been not to allow food, water, or medical aid for the people who remained in the city in order to force people to leave the city.[40] These uses of federal and state resources to favour the dignified rescue and evacuation of one race of people – and security of their property and possessions – meant that more black lives were lost in Orleans Parish not only during the week after Katrina, but also during the last four months of 2005. Narrator after narrator has long lists of relatives, mainly elders, who died in the fall of 2005.[41] Not for the first time in American history, black people's lives were sacrificed to "protect" white private property.[42]

Phase II: Dispossession

One of the most passionate currents running through my 290 interviews was the intensity of the love African Americans had for their city.[43] Former residents of the Lower Ninth Ward were among those most proud of their neighbourhood. And yet today, 100,000 former New Orleanians have still not returned.[44] A local expert believes that up to 90 per cent of the Lower Ninth Ward is still vacant.[45] Many Lower Ninth Warders returned home in the winter of 2005–6 to discover everything they had worked for bulldozed without actual notice.[46] Formerly energetic, independent elders are dying prematurely as renters or occupants of a relative's spare bedroom.[47] According to the testimonies of several of the Lower Ninth Ward narrators, many of their neighbours were persuaded by insurance adjustors or Road Home Program bureaucrats to give up their land – upon which stood the splintered vestiges of their family home, which they'd owned outright before the storm – for as little as $5,000.[48]

The Army Corps of Engineers' negligent maintenance of the levees protecting New Orleans led to a massive synchronous displacement of African Americans, without the usual warning that accompanies eminent domain seizures, evictions, and bulldozing property.[49] The armed might of the National Guard was used by the city of New Orleans to deprive Lower Ninth Ward homeowners of sustained access to their properties in order to rebuild for more than eight months.[50] Federal resources for mitigating the damages caused by the Corps' negligent maintenance of the levees before Katrina have been diverted disproportionately to white neighbourhoods, especially Lakeview.[51] In *Greater New Orleans Fair Housing Action Center, et al. v. U.S. Department of Housing and Urban Development, et al.*, the Federal District Court of the District of Columbia ruled that the formula devised by the state of Louisiana for the distribution of federal funds for the rebuilding of areas most devastated by Hurricanes Katrina and Rita had a discriminatory impact on African American homeowners.[52] The court granted an injunction requiring the State of Louisiana to use a non-discriminatory formula for the few remaining candidates waiting for the processing of their Road Home applications.[53] Failure to safeguard the property of displaced individuals violates Guiding Principle 21.[54]

The Phase I human rights violations against Lower Ninth Warders stranded in New Orleans after Hurricane Katrina facilitated their transformation from homeowners to renters in several ways. Particularly in the fall of 2005, there was an unshakeable belief among many of the people I interviewed that there had been, at worst, an intentional attempt to kill African Americans. Answers to my question of whether narrators wanted to go home were intertwined with uncertainty about whether it was safe for them to rebuild in a predominantly black area of town in light of what was believed to be a pattern of dynamiting (or purposefully under-maintaining) their levees to protect Uptown and the French Quarter.[55] Irvin Porter, a Navy veteran, a retired school teacher with a master's degree from Southern University and a pioneering homeowner in Pontchartrain Park, explained his reluctance to rebuild in New Orleans: "Whether [the rebuilding of the levees] will be redone right or whether it will be designed to relieve one part of the city at the expense of another – all those things are still up in the air." In the end, he concluded that "the idea of losing the property that has been in the family forever, the product of so much hard work, scrimping, and faith" was too painful. Therefore, he gave up his American dream house in Pontchartrain Park and is still attempting restoration of a dilapidated house in Sunshine, Louisiana, better known as "Cancer Alley" – a safer choice, he hoped.[56]

These beliefs that influential whites tried to kill African Americans before, during, or after the storm were reinforced by the obvious racial discrimination that led to 20,000 whites being allowed to escape Orleans Parish across Jefferson Parish borders, while 80,000 blacks were contained at gunpoint. One result of the way the buses were finally loaded was that some of the black male narrators felt like their deaths had been hoped or planned for. According to Lance Hill, some African Americans believed they were being loaded on to buses to be taken away and executed.[57] Kevin Owens, a B.W. Cooper mechanic, described the way he was separated from his wife and extended family as a direct result of following military orders. After thousands of people were "packed in like sardines" to the area leading from the Superdome to the buses, Owens recalls a military commander's announcement: "We don't want nothing but women and children." This, according to Owens, caused panic. "Now you got children, little kids, and women holding on to their husbands and their boyfriends and their fathers, and, they're saying, 'No! You're not going to separate us from each other, because this is all I have left in the world.' The military commander responded, 'Don't do what we ask, nobody leaves. Come across this barricade and you will be shot!'" After much prayer, Owens concluded, "If we had been the animals that they were portraying us to be [on television] and acted like that, then they would have opened fire on us."[58]

Second, countless elderly homeowners from the Lower Ninth Ward gave up their struggles with insurance companies for reimbursement because of a handful of missing succession papers,[59] a deficit any second-year civil law student could have helped cure. In Atlanta, Dr Keith C. Ferdinand, the Lower Ninth Ward cardiologist who co-founded Heartbeats Life Center, witnessed heavily armed National Guardsmen stationed at FEMA processing centres ordering elders to go "home" and process their requests online. When Ferdinand's insurance company tried to give him a fraction of what his medical equipment at Heartbeats was worth, he hired a lawyer and demonstrated that he would not be intimidated out of his contractual rights because of his Ninth Ward zip code.[60]

On average, Lower Ninth Warders ended up 349 miles away from home, without their kinship networks to depend upon.[61] Had the community not been artificially torn asunder and scattered in many states, these elders could have been assisted by literate and computer-savvy pastors, public interest lawyers, children, nephews, nieces, and grandchildren.[62] Church and neighbourhood communities had long traditions of pooling resources and sharing information to overcome obstacles. These strengths would have allowed the elderly a chance to meet or resist otherwise impossible demands.[63]

Third, severe depression undercut many displaced people's will to fight for their property rights. This depression, triggered by the simultaneous loss of almost every constant in their lives, was deepened by the unique ordeal of the military occupation, and the vicarious pain of hearing how one's loved ones, especially the elderly, had been dropped off "essentially to die, without food or water."[64] Dr Ferdinand freely described the intense depression under which he was still labouring when his first interview was conducted in his makeshift Atlanta office in January 2006.[65] Three years later, this no-nonsense son of a military sergeant and a third-grade teacher he described as a female Joe Pesci still teared up when he alluded to his Ninth Ward community being taken from him in less than twenty-four hours.[66] In New Orleans, it is palpable in the intensity of the hugs and the unbidden tears when someone loved by an entire congregation makes it home for a rare visit.

For myself, I cannot rid my soul of the depression, trauma, and over-whelming loss I have imbibed during conversations with narrators who were hours' or days' travel away from New Orleans, their family members, and their community. Collectively, they are enduring what Mindy Thompson Fullilove, professor of psychiatry at Columbia University, calls "root shock," or "the traumatic stress reaction to the destruction of all or part of one's emotional ecosystem."[67]

The depression wrought by the dishonourable treatment of them-selves and their elders, compounded by the deportation of African Americans at gunpoint to distant cities not of their own choosing, made it exceptionally difficult for ordinarily determined people to fight for what they were legally entitled to from their insurance companies, FEMA, and the Road Home.[68] Narrator after narrator spoke of the need to submit the same required documents not once but multiple times, often without a final resolution and no independent review process.[69]

Fourth, the militarized dispersal of African Americans hundreds of miles from home has necessitated that displaced homeowners work a full-time job and raise a family, while commuting back to New Orleans to wrangle with insurance adjusters, Road Home bureaucrats, and con-tractors. Cynthia Banks, the founder of Free to Be Kids, has been over-coming adversity since she was five years old and her family's house burned down. When her husband died during open heart surgery and left her with four children under the age of fourteen, she moved back to New Orleans, made a down payment on a house in the Lake Carmel subdivision, and kept the note paid by working two full-time profes-sional jobs. After Katrina, Banks fixed up a run-down house near Dallas, Texas, and began working and commuting sixty hours a week as an un-insured, home health nurse. On weekends, she returned to New Orleans to oversee the rebuilding of her house.[70] Stress and chronic exhaustion led to a heart attack and strokes in the fall of 2008. This story illustrates the unique obstacles displaced people, even with decades of proven resilience, are facing.

By contrast, in 1965 Lower Ninth Warders commuted from Uptown. They were marked by frugality and a tireless will to work. This ethic is exemplified by Vallery Ferdinand, II, who saw active duty in the Second World War and the Korean War. He worked by day as a technician at the VA Hospital, and by evening and on weekends as a mortician's assistant. In his free time, he led his three sons in heavy manual la-bour details: gardening, clearing neighbours' lots for construction, and keeping the St Augustine grass neatly trimmed for the entire block.

With such a familial work force combined with local black handymen, rebuilding his family home from scratch after Hurricane Betsy took less than one year.[71]

The markedly disparate ways African Americans and their neighbourhoods were treated by state agents after Hurricane Katrina and by the use of federal resources for levee repairs, neighbourhood redevelopment, and grants to homeowners constitute not only human rights violations, but also constitutional violations of the 14th Amendment that guaranteed Equal Protection to emancipated slaves and their descendants. The combination of Phase I and Phase II racial discrimination has presented major disadvantages to African American homeowners, especially from the Lower Ninth Ward. The desolation of the Lower Ninth Ward, a pre-storm haven of working-class homeowners, has multiplied the post-1968 tendency to uproot and disperse entire black neighbourhoods, most recently housing developments.[72]

Accountability and Restitution

In late August 2010, Mayor Mitch Landrieu signalled that expropriating "blighted" properties was one of his highest priorities.[73] At the very least, an injunction should be issued to stay expropriations of the property of Lower Ninth Warders and others on any grounds before the pending appeal against the Army Corps of Engineers is resolved.

One reason the discrimination against Lower Ninth Ward homeowners has been tolerated by society at large is because of the relentlessly negative treatment of the Lower Ninth Ward in the media pre-dating Katrina. All around the country I have encountered virtual travellers to the Lower Ninth Ward who believe that its citizens were universally poor and violent. Every murder was covered in agonizing detail. John McCusker, a photojournalist for the *Times Picayune*, recalled how often he went into the Lower Ninth Ward to cover murders before the storm.[74] Meanwhile, even stories of extraordinary heroism, however, were omitted. Just as there is a cost nationally to a generation of young black men who are "marked" as criminals because of the high numbers of incarcerated young men and the lack of counterbalancing media coverage,[75] so too does an unchallenged negative stigma attached to an entire territory make it easier for a state to dismantle and relocate whole communities.[76] The post-Katrina dismantling of the Lower Ninth Ward has led to the dispossession and dishonouring of homeowning, tax-paying, church-going people – many of them military veterans[77] – on a scale that begs the question of how far Louisiana has journeyed from the days when its slavery regime was renowned as the cruellest and most deadly in the nation.[78]

It is not enough to turn only to alternative media outlets with feature stories about the best that our endangered communities have to offer, because the alternative media do not influence most voters or politicians. We must press more creatively and aggressively to have corrective stories told more accurately in mainstream venues. These efforts should be complemented with a publicized, targeted economic boycott of the sponsors of biased media representations.

Plans to reoccupy New Orleans with those in the diaspora who are willing and able to rebuild the city should be drawn up immediately. Rather than being violent, poor, and unskilled, many uprooted New Orleanians have abilities urgently needed to complete the restoration of New Orleans. A Works Progress Administration–style public works program aimed at an equitable restoration of the 51,000 vacant or "blighted" properties that either returns displaced homeowners to New Orleans or allows them to donate their property to the church or school of their choosing would help rebuild collapsed infrastructure, improve housing conditions, and offer meaningful employment to a generation of young African Americans.[79]

Finally, we must continue to give an independent accounting, unfinanced by political and government interests, of the ongoing consequences of the unique human rights violations and invisible genocides that targeted African Americans in Katrina's immediate and long-term aftermath. The necessary documents are readily accessible in the public records of the courthouse and the deceased's surviving relatives have a wealth of information surrounding the stresses and strains of their ascendants' last days. Should legal accountability be impossible to achieve, then at the very least the perpetrators will be tried in the courtroom of history, unfettered by statutes of limitations and a Supreme Court's privileging of a state's "dignity," no matter how racist, at the expense of constitutionally protected individual rights to liberty, property, and the pursuit of happiness.

NOTES

1 An unabridged version of this essay is available at http://jcia.aciajj.org/files/2012/02/Penner-3.pdf. For research support, I thank the Association of Black Cardiologists, the Benjamin Hooks Institute for Social Change, the

Institute for the Study of Human Rights at Columbia University, the Dart Society, Loyola University New Orleans College of Law, and the Southern Institute for Education and Research at Tulane University. Intellectually, I am indebted to Andrea Armstrong, Amy Cahn, Beverly Cross, Mitchell Crusto, Olúgbémiga Ekúndayò, Lance Hill, Johanna Kalb, Linda Shopes, and Abe Louise Young.

2 Adrien Katherine Wing, "From Wrongs to Rights," in David Dante Troutt, ed., *After the Storm* (New York: New Press, 2006), 130–40.

3 In addition to Orleans Parish, this area includes the predominantly white parishes of Jefferson, Plaquemines, and St Bernard.

4 See Brian Williams's NBC nightly news coverage from Trudi Green's rooftop in the Lower Ninth Ward on 28 August 2010.

5 Quoted in Jason Harris and Rob Volansky, "Five Years after Hurricane Katrina Work Still to Be Done," Health Policy, Patient and Practice Issues, *Infectious Disease News*, 1 August 2010.

6 Mildred Alcorn, interview with the author, New Orleans, Louisiana, August 2010. The book to which she alludes is D'Ann Penner and Keith Ferdinand, eds., *Overcoming Katrina: African American Voices from the Crescent City and Beyond* (New York: Palgrave Macmillan, 2009).

7 On my methodology, see D'Ann Penner, "Assault Rifles, Separated Families, and Murder in Their Eyes: Unasked Questions after Hurricane Katrina," *Journal of American Studies* 44, no. 3 (2010): 580–3.

8 Geoffrey Hartman, *The Longest Shadow* (New York: Palgrave Macmillan, 1996), 9.

9 Richard Mollica, *Healing Invisible Wounds* (Boston: Harcourt, 2006), 111.

10 Dori Laub, "From Speechlessness to Narrative," *Literature and Medicine* 24, no. 2 (2005): 265.

11 See Katherine Cecil, "Race, Representation, and Recovery" (MA thesis, University of New Orleans, 2009).

12 Penner, "Assault Rifles," 576–9, 597.

13 Wing, "From Wrongs," 133–4.

14 Ibid., 137.

15 Penner and Ferdinand, *Overcoming*, 144–7. On military violence, see Shana Agid, "Locked and Loaded," in Kristin A. Bates and Richelle S. Swan, eds., *Through the Eye of Katrina* (Durham: Carolina Academic, 2007), 55–69; Penner and Ferdinand, *Overcoming*, 32, 52–4, 57–8, 64–7, 74, 113, 124–6, 135–7, 144–8, 150–1, 156, 162, 165, 208–9, 225; and Rebecca Solnit, *A Paradise Built in Hell* (New York: Viking, 2009), 234–5, 245–66.

16 Harold Toussaint's interview is included in condensed form in Penner and Ferdinand, *Overcoming*, 49–59, here at 53. See also www.bbc.co.uk/programmes/p0099v7z.

17 Shriff Hasan, interview with the author, Houston, October 2005.
18 Wing, "From Wrongs," 136–7.
19 *Select Bipartisan Committee to Investigate the Preparation for and Response to Hurricane Katrina, A Failure of Initiative*, H.R. Rep. No. 109-377, at 7 (2006). On the blockading of Red Cross from New Orleans, see Lance Hill's commentary: www.southerninstitute.info/commentaries/?m=200608& paged=2. Hill was an active eyewitness in and around the convention centre the entire week.
20 Wing, "From Wrongs," 136–7.
21 Penner and Ferdinand, *Overcoming*, 72, 146, 163.
22 Ibid., 225. For Banks's story, see ibid., 60–9.
23 Ibid., 164. On White, see ibid., 159–67.
24 Wing, "From Wrongs," 136–7.
25 Denise Roubion-Johnson, "Spotlight on *Overcoming Katrina* Panel," Oral History Conference, Atlanta, October 2010. See also Penner and Ferdinand, *Overcoming*, 70–9.
26 Anika Pugh, interview with the author, Birmingham, December 2005.
27 Kenneth Anderson, interview with the author, Birmingham, December 2005.
28 Wing, "From Wrongs," 137.
29 Penner and Ferdinand, *Overcoming*, 7, 22, 33, 38, 46, 55, 67, 73, 76–8, 127, 135, 138, 145, 147–8, 165, 172, 195–6, 202, and 224.
30 Dana Alfred, Louisiana Disaster Recovery Corps (2007).
31 Wing, "From Wrongs," 133.
32 Sherrie Tomlinson, "No New Orleanians Left Behind," *Connecticut Law Review* 38 (2005–6): 1153–88; Rebecca Eaton, "Escape Denied," *Texas Wesleyan Law Review* 13 (2006–7): 136–9.
33 Russell McCulley, "Healing Katrina's Racial Wounds," *Time*, 27 August 2007.
34 Laura Maggi, "Official List of Disaster Victims Still Untabulated" (28 August 2008) at blog.nola.com.
35 Penner and Ferdinand, *Overcoming*, 224.
36 *CNN Reports: Katrina—State of Emergency* (Andrews McMeel, 2005), 100.
37 For examples of white privilege, see Penner and Ferdinand, *Overcoming*, 53–4, 58, 70, 74–5, 103, 123–7, 137, 144–5, 164–5, 221–2, and 224.
38 Ibid., 164–5.
39 Lance Hill, email correspondence with the author, June 2010.
40 Tomlinson, "No New Orleanians Left Behind," 1161; First Supplemental and Amending Class Action Complaint at 2–3, 5, *Dickerson v. City of Gretna*, No. 05-0667 (E.D. La. Filed 11 April 2006); Kevin Stephens et al., "Excess Mortality in the Aftermath of Hurricane Katrina," *Disaster Medicine and Public Health Preparedness* 1 (2007): 15–20.

41 Charles Duplessis, conversation with the author, March 2008.

42 Elizabeth Fussell, "Constructing New Orleans, Constructing Race," *Journal of American History* 94 (2007): 846–55; Ned Sublette, *The World that Made New Orleans* (Chicago: Lawrence Hill, 2008), 135–6 and 225; and Pete Daniel, *Deep'n As It Come* (New York: Oxford University, 1977).

43 Penner and Ferdinand, *Overcoming*, 8, 20, 30, 44, 47, 51, 58, 61, 70, 110, 133, 141, 152–5, 157, 160, 194, 199, 213, and 228–9.

44 Jonathan Tilove, "Five Years after Hurricane Katrina, 100,000 New Orleanians Have Yet to Return," *Times-Picayune*, 24 August 2010.

45 Keith Ferdinand, email correspondence with the author, 12 November 2010.

46 Keith Calhoun, interview with the author, New Orleans, Louisiana, February 2008. On bulldozing, see William P. Quigley, "Thirteen Ways of Looking at Katrina," *Tulane Law Review* 81, no. 4 (2007): 955–1017, here at 993.

47 Bernadette Capehart, interview with the author, New Orleans, Louisiana, August 2010.

48 Charles Duplessis, interview with the author, Marrero, Louisiana, February 2008; Trudi Green, interview with the author, New Orleans, Louisiana, July 2010; Calhoun interview. The Road Home Program ("Road Home") was an $11 billion federal housing recovery program intended to help homeowners rebuild after Hurricanes Katrina and Rita. It was overseen by the Disaster Recovery Unit of the Office of Community Development of Louisiana.

49 Peter Grier, "The Great Katrina Migration," *Christian Science Monitor*, 12 September 2005; R.B. Seed et al., University of California at Berkeley and American Society of Civil Engineers, *Report on the Performance of the New Orleans Levee System in Hurricane Katrina on August 29, 2005*, Report No. UCB/CITRIS-05/01, 31 July 2006, at 1–4.

50 Gwen Filosa, "City Opens a Section of Lower Ninth Ward," *Times-Picayune*, 9 May 2006.

51 Amy Laura Cahn, "Our Rights Are Not Cast in Stone," *Journal of Law and Social Change* 12 (2008–9): 37–71.

52 On the decision, see Jarvis DeBerry, "For Black Road Homers, a Hollow Victory," *Times-Picayune*, 20 August 2010. On Road Home practices, see Davida Finger, "Stranded and Squandered," *Seattle Journal for Social Justice* 7 (2008): 59–100.

53 DeBerry, "For Black Road Homers."

54 Wing, "From Wrongs," 140.

55 Penner and Ferdinand, *Overcoming*, 8, 27, 37–8, 48, 98, 140–1, 160, and 223–4.

56 Ibid., 27–8.
57 Hill, email correspondence with the author, January 2010.
58 Penner and Ferdinand, *Overcoming*, 142–51.
59 The rules of successions are clearly laid out in the Louisiana Civil Code to codify the values of dominant society in the disposal of a deceased's assets when he dies without a "valid" will. See Charles Henry Rowell, "An Interview with Judge Michael G. Bagneris," *Callaloo* 31, no. 2 (2008): 506–20.
60 Keith Ferdinand, "Community Consequences of Displacement and Recovery," Critical Incidents Analysis Conference, New Orleans, Louisiana, July 2010.
61 D'Ann Penner, "*Overcoming*: The Hidden Fury of Hurricane Katrina's Aftermath and Implications for the Future of New Orleans," *The Hooks Institute Working Paper Series* (University of Memphis, 2010).
62 By contrast, only 193 miles separated the average white Chalmette resident from St Bernard Parish. Quigley, "Thirteen Ways," 959–60.
63 Penner and Ferdinand, *Overcoming*, 10–14, 16–18, 80–1, 84, 96, 102, and 122.
64 Ibid., 173.
65 Ibid., 99.
66 "Tom Dent Authors' Showcase," New Orleans Public Library, October 2009.
67 Mindy Thompson Fullilove, *Root Shock* (New York: One World/Ballantine, 2005).
68 Penner and Ferdinand, *Overcoming*, 105. See also *Ridgely v. Fed. Emergency Mgmt. Agency*, 512 F.3d 727 (5th Cir. 2008).
69 Penner and Ferdinand, *Overcoming*, 27, 56–7, 103, 105, 127–8, 138–40, 166, 172–3; and Doris Smith, interview with the author, St Joseph, Louisiana, November 2005.
70 Penner and Ferdinand, *Overcoming*, 60–9; and Cynthia Banks, telephone conversations with the author, October 2007, February 2008, and November 2008.
71 On Vallery Ferdinand, II, see Penner and Ferdinand, *Overcoming*, 81–4, 89–96, and 230; Kalamu ya Salaam, *What Is Life?* (Chicago: Third World, 1994), 79–89; and Kalamu ya Salaam, "Pa Ferdinand," *Catalyst* (1989): 112.
72 Jeff Crump, "Deconcentration by Demolition," *Environment and Planning: Society and Space* 20, no. 5 (2002): 581–96. On the multiple damages such community uprooting does, see Fullilove, *Root Shock*.
73 Tilove, "Five Years After."
74 John McCusker, conversation with the author, Baton Rouge, September 2010.

75 On an entire generation being branded and the link to unemployment, see Devah Pager, *Marked* (Chicago: University of Chicago Press, 2007). On the paucity of media coverage of working- and middle-class African Americans, see Mitchell Duneier, *Slim's Table* (Chicago: University of Chicago Press, 1992), 121–3, 128, 142, and 164.

76 Loïc Wacquant, "Urban Desolation and Symbolic Denigration in the Hyperghetto," *Social Psychology Quarterly* 73, no. 3 (2009/2010): 1–5.

77 Penner and Ferdinand, *Overcoming*, 23, 24, 29, 30, 34, 43, 81, 90, 101–2, 115, 117, 137, 142, 151, 153, 168, 190, 193, and 220–1.

78 Rebecca J. Scott, *Degrees of Freedom: Louisiana and Cuba after Slavery* (Boston: Belknap Press of Harvard University Press, 2007), 12, 24–5; and Jordan Flaherty, *Floodlines* (Chicago: Haymarket Books, 2010).

79 Greater New Orleans Community Data Center, "Benchmarks for Blight," 7 May 2010.

13 The Romance of Reminiscence: Problems Posed in Life Histories with Activist Pensioners in Argentina[1]

LINDSAY DUBOIS

As an anthropologist, one of the most important things I do in field research is listen. I hope to hear stories that will help me understand how a given group of people experience, understand, and interpret the world. There is something enormously compelling about first-hand accounts, and I often animate my writing with these stories, hoping to communicate local perspectives and to populate descriptions of social processes which might otherwise seem too abstract. Even tales of horror can be fascinating – witness the enormous Holocaust literature. Yet this fascination makes me uneasy as well.

I write in sympathy with the framing of this collection and the conference out of which it emerged: testimonies are crucial avenues to understanding the traumatic past. All the same, we need to critically interrogate the production of these testimonies, and, more specifically, we need to examine how we, as researchers, are implicated in them. Oral history interviews (like all research methodologies, perhaps) do not just collect information, they produce it. A story is told to a particular audience under specific circumstances, shaping the narrative. Stories are also told in particular historical moments, calling into play what the Popular Memory Group called "the past-present relation."[2] People's view of the past is shaped by their prior history and their present circumstances. They understand and speak of the past in the context of other time periods.

As a researcher, I am particularly interested in the ways in which the past makes itself felt in the present. There are at least two important aspects of this process, both of which are common sense, but worth recalling all the same. First, the present is one moment in a complex web of social, political, and cultural processes. We are who we are because of these processes. Yet, and second, the meanings we attribute to these histories are diverse, as are the lessons we draw from them. It was this diversity that attracted me to history in the first place, because understandings of the past represent one of the most evidently political aspects of culture: the sense we make out of our pasts has to do with our ideas of the possible. By the possible I mean our sense of what is likely, reasonable, practicable, or out of the question. In any given time and place, certain courses of action are more thinkable (and therefore more doable) than others.[3] Our notions about what is possible thus represent a key site in which history and culture come together to shape our political ideas and actions.

In order to examine these matters, I reflect in this chapter on my own experience conducting research on Argentina's recent past. Thinking about the ways in which activist pensioners talked about a history which included political repression and economic immiseration, I was struck by how their narratives differed from earlier work I had done on the same period. Where my earlier work had revealed political demobilization and a cultural shift towards individualism, the pensioners use substantially the same events as resources for political engagement in the present. Although I foreground the pensioners' stories here, I read them against my earlier research because the contrast between these two research projects is instructive. Each produced silences, and each speaks to two sets of linked processes: remembering and forgetting, on one hand, speaking and listening, on the other.

Conducting Research in the Wake of the Argentine Dictatorship

In the early 1990s, I conducted extended ethnographic fieldwork in a working-class housing project in the suburbs of Buenos Aires. The research relied principally on participant observation, history workshops, and interviews. The neighbourhood called José Ingenieros had been populated in a squatter occupation beginning in 1972, becoming the site of intensive political organizing until the coup of 1976, when it was subject to surveillance, control, and violence at the hands of the military. While the dictatorship ended in 1983, economic subjugation continued through the end of the century. After eighteen months living in the neighbourhood, I came to see the state of disorganization in which the community found itself as a product of the recent history of political repression and economic decline. Observing and participating in everyday life there, as well as learning about the community's past, helped me understand a process which Argentine commentators refer to as the "disarticulation of social ties."[4] I came to see how and why fear, distrust, and cynicism supplanted cooperation and collective engagement, making the rebuilding of community very difficult. Although I knew people who resisted this larger shift, the challenges they confronted brought me to disheartening conclusions.

About a decade later I undertook a life history project with a group of activist pensioners in Buenos Aires. Although the project employed a range of methods, life history interviews lie at its heart.[5] The activist pensioners seemed to represent an óutpost of resistance to the neoliberal forces dominant in the country at the time. Before the crash of the Argentine economy in late 2001 and the consequent political mobilizations, they stood out for their remarkable persistence in a climate of quiescence in Argentine politics. Their unusual political engagement was attractive and seemed to promise insight into the conditions that foster political activism in difficult times.

Part of what drew me to the activist pensioners was my initial sense of how different they were from many of those with whom I had worked. In the earlier writing, I argued that the demobilization of residents of José Ingenieros was rooted in their collective experience. For example, their neighbourhood – like other highly organized working-class communities – was singled out by the military regime. Most dramatically, on several occasions the neighbourhood was surrounded as soldiers searched each apartment, conducting a "census." The activist pensioners are survivors of a similar history, however. Many of them were members of leftist political parties that were suspect. They too weathered the deep chill, and sometimes the direct violence, of dictatorship (1976 to 1983), not to mention the structural violence of the neoliberal policies that followed. If objective historical experiences could not fully account for the differences in the political responses of people in the two studies, this fact raised some new questions. To what extent does a political persona shape the story you have to tell, or, for that matter, the one you want to hear? As researchers, how do our methods shape the stories we hear? How do different methods require different forms of listening and different strategies of interpretation?

Listening to the Pensioners

If I was hoping for a more uplifting research project, the pensioners did not disappoint. For more than one thousand consecutive Wednesdays, they have protested in front of the National Congress in Buenos Aires. At times numbering thousands and confronting police in riot gear, at other times much smaller and less dramatic, these marches constitute the public face of the pensioners' movement. The Mesa Coordinadora de Jubilados y Pensionados de le República Argentina (the Mesa as they are known locally) leads the weekly protests.[6] The Mesa dates its origin as a political movement to some early demonstrations focusing on health care in 1968. The weekly protests began in 1990, moving around a bit until taking up their regular place Wednesday afternoons in front of the National Congress. In those days, the dire situation of the pensioners became a public issue, with a wave of suicides on the part of those who despaired of trying to survive on pensions that covered about 12 per cent of the cost of living. They could not eat, much less afford rent or medication.[7]

Some activist pensioners argue that media attention was not the main cause of their success; there were more concrete and specific reasons for the popular support in the days of the massive mobilizations. For example Luís Cortadi, long one of the central figures in the Mesa, explained why people started to show up for the weekly marches: "We [the Mesa] were the first ones to sue the pension funds. We put out flyers, people came. We had a lawyer, and the lawyer brought law suits. We were the ones who lobbied for the exemption from the housing tax – for those of us receiving minimum pensions and with only one home. The people recognized this, and the [free] subway rides, we also got that."[8] When the government made a move to privatize the pensions in 1994, the Mesa mobilized 40,000 protesters and collected one million signatures in opposition.[9] By the time most of the interviews were conducted in 2001 and 2002, the Argentine economy was in a state of profound economic crisis, which included the largest national default to date.[10] In addition to pensions, the second main concern of the Mesa was PAMI,[11] responsible for delivering health care to pensioners and administered by the state.

Because the state of pensions and of PAMI are obvious functions of the national social welfare state, the pensioners' situation is emblematic of larger processes of neoliberalism. The activist pensioners contend that they have historically and unfairly been "a variable in structural adjustment" equations (*un variable del ajuste*)[12] since both their pension plan and their state-administered health-care plan are large funds that the state can dip into for other purposes. Since 2003, the state has considerably expanded its welfare functions, paying pensions to large segments of the population. They also re-statized pension funds privatized in the preceding decade. However, although the activist pensioners are pleased with these gains, they eschew "*asistancialismo*" (welfare-type social assistance), which they believe undermines their rights as workers. Instead, the Mesa has insisted that the original terms and conditions of their pension plans be honoured and that they receive real control of the health-care system. These days, the protests are modest, with as few as forty participants. Many of those who persist do not particularly expect victory, but they carry on, every Wednesday, with, as their flyers proclaim, "*la fuerza de los que no se resignan*" (the strength of those who won't give up).

One striking characteristic of the activist pensioners is that a disproportionate number of them have some kind of history in "the old left"[13] – as communists, socialists, and anarchists. This political experience is quite diverse, ranging from current members of the Communist Party or one of the various socialist parties, to those who had broken with their parties, to others who spoke of an identification or sympathy with the old left. This identification was often described as emerging from concrete experiences in some of the institutions they sponsored, especially before the advent of Peronism. One must recall that Argentina is a country in which the intervention of Peronism from 1943 onward challenged, to a degree incorporated, and eventually all but eliminated "old" leftist traditions from working-class life.[14] Most working-class people in the interim have been Peronist. The non-Peronism of these activist pensioners is therefore striking, in part attributable to their age (most of those interviewed were born by 1930) but by no means reducible to it.

A History of Defeat?

In life history interviews these elder activists placed their current situation in a larger historical context. A few words on Argentina's recent history are thus in order here. After Perón's removal in a 1955 coup, Argentines lived through of succession of dictatorships and curtailed elections, ending with the bloodiest dictatorship between 1976 and 1983. During this last dictatorship, something on the order of 30,000 people were disappeared: they were kidnapped, held in clandestine detention centres, tortured, sometimes for months, and killed, their bodies anonymously disposed of. Disappearance in conjunction with exile, blacklisting, surveillance, and other more mundane strategies was used by the Argentine regime to exercise the kind of sweeping social control that is reminiscent of accounts one hears of the Soviet period.[15] Certainly the junta set out to reorganize national society. I am among those analysts who have argued that these twin processes largely succeeded in rending the social fabric (a process described by Hector, below).

Although some credit Argentina with the dubious distinction of coining the noun form "the disappeared," the Argentine case is less horrific than some of those we are considering in this collection. It strikes me that the less total and totalizing violence of the Argentine dictatorship highlights some of the terrible ambiguities produced by carrying on under a guise of normalcy. One of the most insidious of these is the way it forced people to live in bad faith – that is, having to behave in ways that are contrary to one's beliefs and values.[16]

Occaisionally activist pensioners spoke about this social and cultural transformation produced by the recent past. Hector Anzorena, a retired (unionized) waiter, son of an anarchist baker and born in 1930, laments:

> Understanding the difference between what we experienced and what is happening in the country … has been very difficult for me. I saw it, but had a hard time understanding it. I saw a process of disintegration, from the workers. Since the decade of the 80s, after the dictatorship of '76, that's where I began to see a change; people were more individualistic. I recall a phrase: "Oh! I'll do my own thing" [hago lo mio]. "What's that?" I wondered. But there were more and more people doing their thing. I thought it was just an expression of some small group; I didn't realize it was becoming the culture of the country. The "don't get involved [no te metas]. Look what happened, we didn't gain anything. One has to look after one's job, there's no point in struggle … it's not worth it." A culture based on individualism was being created … The media also showed you a reality as if it were the only one, and the other was an impossible utopia. And it cost me terribly. My worst years of struggle were when I had to come to accept a state of affairs with which I didn't agree at all. And to recognize that they had defeated us, ideologically, politically. And they broke all the ties of solidarity that there had been in the society … to believe more in the individual than the collective. Dating from the military, and the interference of global economic power.

Hector sees this cultural transformation towards individualism as the consequence of political repression (in the form of violence, the intervention and / or cooptation of unions, and so on) and economic restructuring fortified by a clear ideological message in the media. Although Hector sees this set of processes, he does not fall victim to it. He and his fellows make a different kind of sense of the history they share with other Argentines. Like many activist pensioners, Hector attributes his ability to survive the cultural transformation he observes to his upbringing in a different milieu.

When I asked why they participated in the pensioners' movement, many of those I spoke to described growing up in working-class communities shaped by anarchist and socialist politics and the values of solidarity and community they knew there. Hector also said:

> My influence ... although I wasn't an activist there, was the anarchism of my father and my family. They read a lot. They were semi-illiterate and they learned to read with the FORA newspaper – influenced by anarchism like the whole bakers' union. I remember the honesty; they were against crime and theft. They fought for a just society. It came out through our solidarity, the people, the neighbourhood ... anarchists and socialists were the majority until '46, Peron. This influenced the behaviours of the workers: humanism, personal growth, not the accumulation of money. It came from ideas which came from anarchism and socialism. All my brothers and my two sisters were marked by this commitment with the humble and dispossessed. We fought for justice. It was essential that no one ran over us. This marked my childhood and adolescence ... Despite our poverty, we weren't influenced to move toward delinquency. And our values were different, more tied to the human being, not to accept oppression, not to be a slave. This marked me and my brothers and sisters strongly.

Rather than leading to quiescence, these activist pensioners' histories are recalled in such a way as to underwrite their commitments in the present. They know that they are in the minority, however, often commenting that there are masses of pensioners who might join them in their protests but elect not to. Some of those who stay home draw different lessons from the same history.

Hopeful Stories

Like many of those who work with oral history, I find the first-hand accounts of those I work with moving, hopeful, sometimes heroic. For example, when I asked Ruebens Capellino what he thought of people who said the pensioners were not getting anywhere, he responded with a commentary which connected their protests to the massive social movements that erupted with the 2001 economic crisis in Argentina. He told me:

> Those who say this don't know that if the people don't get together and fight for their rights, nobody is going to come and deliver them. Until now, what we've accomplished is that everyone has come out to the street; now it's not just the pensioners in the street, but the *piquesteros* [unemployed], the pot-bangers [middle-class protesters] ... That's something we've accomplished! The fight has gone into the street. The pensioners started all this. They broke with the idea of "asking" – demanding the rights that we deserve. Politicians don't give you the time of day, they look the other way. They're going to have to listen.

It is difficult to know if Reubens and other activist pensioners are correct that there is a connection between their long-standing protests and the street protests that emerged with the 2001 crisis, but certainly many activist pensioners see one.

Describing the kinds of daily activities typical of the activist pensioners, Hector provides another example of the kind of narrative that draws one to this kind of research:

> I found just the place for me ... even though one doesn't accomplish great things. But we are convinced. We chose this ... We aren't going to give in to power, staying home. It's good for us to be out in the street, doing something, awakening the recognition of folks. It's tied to the solidarity of others with you ... It comes from my father and sharing a plate of food, and the neighbours ... You are shouting for all that you've lived, all that. It's not disconnected from that. Others say that we don't accomplish anything ... It's about feeling good doing something. I'm proud to be President of a senior centre where today, when it was three degrees, there were seven *compañeros* collecting signatures ... And it's more than the cold numbers. That's 450 people expressing solidarity. It's a commitment to solidarity, despite this trashy society we are living in. Solidarity is the only thing that is going to save us ... This morning we were cold, we were standing there ... but it's comforting. We aren't too humble to recognize that we have done excellent work. It's still possible to rebuild solidarity. That's what we're hoping. We know we are fighting for human dignity.

Hector's political message comes through clearly in this account, which contrasts sharply with the non-participation that was so marked in José Ingenieros. The political message in these excerpts expresses the speakers' points of view, but I suspect the listener's receptivity to them also had a part to play.

As may already be apparent, there are several reasons why the activist pensioners' stories are more positive than those I encountered in my previous work. Having written an account of the forces that conspired to defeat a once feisty, inventive, vibrant working-class community, I was principally interested in the reasons behind the unusual persistence of the activist pensioners. This question about how they maintained their engagement, not surprisingly, produced answers that were upbeat. The interviews consequently tended to produce silences about some of the less happy stories – about the compromises people were forced to make, for example, or about decisions one had come to regret. It is easier and probably more obviously useful to use the valiant past as a model for the present than to dwell on its injuries.[17]

All narratives produce silences. On the most basic level, to say some things is to refrain from saying others. People narrate their lives with a point. These politically engaged pensioners have political points to make. They draw selectively from their lives and experiences to communicate that point. They also often build on shared notions of how the story is supposed to go. Historian Daniel James has fruitfully examined the role of such scripts in his life history of Doña Maria.[18] He shows how, even though there are moments where it is an uncomfortable fit, Doña Maria strives to align her life story with the celebrated model of Mother and Peronist Woman. Likewise, the tales of a few of the lifelong political militants I interviewed seemed to be strongly shaped by official Communist Party narratives and political positions, raising questions about whose point of view was being expressed.

Finally, I wonder about the oral history methodology itself. Emily Martin makes an important methodological point in her review of Veena Das's work on communal violence in India.[19] Following Das,[20] she notes how much of the work of dealing with the traumatic past takes place in the realm of the everyday and the ordinary, partly because one of the most terrible effects of such experiences of collective trauma is that they undermine people's common-sense understandings of the nature of social life. The women Das works with have often been betrayed by their own kin, those whose love and protection they took for granted. Das is especially interested in the failure of language in these contexts. Thus, long-term ethnography is perhaps a stronger tool than the interview for understanding both the everyday struggle to make a life in the wake of the unspeakable and the way in which people make sense of such experiences. Das is not saying that the women she worked with could not or would not speak of violence; rather she writes, "my thought was that perhaps they had speech but not voice. Sometimes there words were imbued with a spectral quality … [or] I felt they were animated by some other voice."[21]

Her point, which strikes me as an important one for this collection, suggests another reason for the differences between the kinds of under-standings of recent Argentine history in my two research projects. The first was more traditional ethnography, while my work with the pen-sioners relied principally on life history interviews. The life histories, of course, tend to produce coherent (if always changing and dynamic) ac-counts. My year and half living in the housing project gave me more access to the ambiguities and contradictions. To provide just one ex-ample, living in a community stigmatized for its purported dangerous-ness and decay, I could see how the dictatorship's discourse about moral and social order could be persuasive – even for people who told chilling tales of encounters with security forces. Watching interactions with outsiders, one could observe how painful this negative reputation was to people, and how much it mattered. Yet this was rarely men-tioned and never discussed in a formal interview.

Lessons Learned?

I find this a somewhat depressing conclusion because it is difficult to do the kind of extended fieldwork required to flesh out such ambiguities and contradictions. It also does not seem quite right to me. Thinking about the difference between ethnographic and oral historical approach-es, I see both affinities and divergences. We have a shared preoccupation with what the world looks like from some other place or time. We take seriously, aim to understand, and hope to communicate the points of view of the people with whom we work.

Oral history, by its nature, privileges language and narrative and, perhaps as a result, the business of how people struggle to *make* sense (or meaning) out of their pasts. Certainly the pensioners who spoke to me clearly communicated their views of the world and how it should be – very much a political process. Ethnographers, on the other hand, have long argued that one needs to attend to both how people behave and what they say they are doing, recognizing that the two can be quite divergent. Perhaps as a result, we quite often find ourselves working with field notes recording messy and contradictory, sometimes apparently incoherent or nonsensical, human behaviour. This perhaps leads to a less clear (and maybe also less politically useful?) rendering of the perspectives of those with whom we work. However, as this book demonstrates, the lines between disciplines cannot be so clearly drawn, as increasingly researchers make use of methods and concepts from outside their home fields. As an anthropologist, I feel as if my understanding of how to read through and past difficult stories, and even silence, is very much informed by the work of oral historians like Luisa Passerini and Alessandro Portelli.

Further, I wonder whether the kind of romance I have been alluding to is a bad thing. Ought we to repress our political aspirations when talking to people about their lives? Portelli's classic article "Research as an Experiment in Equality" shows how attempts at political neutrality on the part of a researcher can produce more distortions than expressions of solidarity might.[22] Unsure of where Portelli stood, communists withheld information that might have revealed their political leanings. I do not think I heard or spoke to anyone at the conference out of which this volume emerged whose work was not shot through with political commitments. And how could it be otherwise? But it seems worth recalling and thinking about the stories we might not hear as a result.

NOTES

1 Earlier versions of this paper were presented at "The Politics of Forgetting" conference held at King's University in May 2008 and at "Remembering War, Geneocide and Other Human Rights Violations: Oral History, New Media, and the Arts" hosted by Concordia University in Montreal. Thanks to organizers and participants at two of the most stimulating conferences I have attended. Donna Young, Jennifer Lund, and several anonymous reviewers made incisive comments on drafts of this chapter. I also owe thanks to Mary Gaudet for her work on the activist pensioners project, as well as the Social Sciences and Humanities Research Council of Canada for funding it. Finally, and most importantly, thanks to the pensioners, who were so generous with their time, their wisdom, and their patience.
2 Popular Memory Group, "Popular Memory: Theory, Politics and Practice," in Richard Johnson, G. McClennan, Bill Schwartz, and David Sutton,

eds., *Making Histories: Studies in History Writing and Politics* (Minneapolis: University of Minnesota Press, 1982), 205–52.

3 My view here is informed by a Gramscian perspective, which takes seriously the interplay between political-economic formations and cultural practices. See, for example, William Roseberry, *Anthropologies and Histories: Essays in Culture, History and Political Economy* (New Brunswick, NJ: Rutgers University Press, 1991).

4 Lindsay DuBois, *The Politics of the Past in an Argentine Working Class Neighborhood* (Toronto: University of Toronto Press, 2005), 4.

5 My student Mary Gaudet and I conducted a total of thirty-one life history interviews, the majority with pensioners who were activists. See Mary Gaudet, "'We Are Going to Fight as Long as We Have Life': Histories and Politics of Argentine Activist Pensioners" (MA thesis, Dalhousie University, 2003). Other methods employed included interviews, casual conversations, a history workshop, the examination of leaflets and flyers, and participant observation at weekly protests and rallies.

6 "Mesa Coordinadory de Jubiladoes y Pensionados de la République Argentina" translates literally as Coordinating Panel on Retirees and Pensioners of the Argentine Republic, employing the Argentine Communist Party's idiom of "coordinating panels." On the relationship between *jubilados* and *pensionados*, see note 11, below.

7 See Peter Lloyd-Sherlock, *Old Age and Urban Poverty in the Developing World: The Shanty Towns of Buenos Aires* (New York: Macmillan Press, 1997), 65. The most famous individual from this period was Norma Plá, not a member of the Mesa. Plá eventually died of cancer. She is particularly famous for having made then–economy minister Domingo Cavallo, the prime author of Argentina's structural adjustment policies, cry when she confronted him about the plight of the country's pensioners. See Laura Zommer, "Falleció Norma Plá una mujer combativa," *La Nación*, 19 June 1996, http://www.lanacion.com.ar/167814-fallecio-norma-pla-una-mujer-combativa.

8 All quotes from activist pensioners come from interviews conducted by myself or Mary Gaudet, who also worked on the project (see note 5).

9 Antonio Fortes interview. See also Pablo Calvo, "La privatización no mejoró el sistema de jubilaciones," *Clarín*, 27 June 2004, http://edant.clarin.com/suplementos/zona/2004/06/27/z-02815.htm. In the end, privatization was an option strongly encouraged by the Menem government, but not obligatory.

10 The deepening economic crisis hit boiling point in December 2001 when currency devaluations, defaults on major international loans, and the

freezing of bank accounts led to a "social explosion" (according to the Argentine press) that included massive street demonstrations, waves of looting, and the removal of four presidents. For an excellent treatment of the economic, political, and social processes see Carlos Vilas, "Neoliberal Meltdown and Social Protest: Argentina 2001–2002," *Critical Sociology* 32, no. 1 (2006): 1.

11 Although everyone refers to the organization as PAMI, its official name is INSSJP, for "Instituto Nacional de Servicios Sociales para Jubilados y Pensionados." The health plan covers both *jubilados* and *pensionados*, a distinction we do not make so clearly in English. *Pensionados* include groups who receive government support, such as physically challenged children and war veterans. The organization delivers other services, but health care is its most important.

12 See Hugo de la Sota,"Carta de Lector: ¿A quién le importan los jubilados?" *La Nación*, 3 September 2008, http://www.lanacion.com.ar/1046207-a -quien-le-importan-los-jubilados.

13 For a similar distinction between the old and new left in Argentina, see María Cristina Tortti, *El "viejo" partido socialista y los orígenes de las "nueva" izquierda (1955–1965)* (Buenos Aires: Prometeo, 2009).

14 General Juan Domingo Peron was minister of labour as part of a military regime in 1943, when he began expanding workers' rights. He was democratically elected in 1946, 1951, and by proxy in 1973 after returning from exile. He died in 1974. See Luís Alberto Romero, *A History of Argentina in the Twentieth Century*, trans. James P. Brennan (University Park: State University of Pennsylvania Press, 2002). There is, of course, a leftist tradition within Peronism.

15 See Andrei Siniavskii, *Soviet Civilization: A Cultural History*, trans. Joanne Turnbull (New York: Arcade, 1990); Bruce Grant, *In the Soviet House of Culture: A Century of Peristroikas* (Princeton: Princeton University Press, 1995).

16 Derek Sayer, "Everyday Forms of State Formation: Some Dissident Remarks on 'Hegemony,'" in Gilbert M. Joseph and Daniel Nugent, eds., *Everyday Forms of State Formation: Revolution and Negotiation of Rule in Modern Mexico* (Durham, NC: Duke University Press, 1994).

17 There is a rich literature on the political shaping of oral-historical narratives. Particularly helpful are the work of Italians Alessandro Portelli and Luisa Passerini. For Portelli see *The Death of Luigi Trastulli, and Other Stories: Form and Meaning in Oral History* (Albany: State University of New York Press, 1991), and *The Order Has Been Carried Out: History, Memory and Meaning of a Nazi Massacre in Rome* (New York: Palgrave Macmillan, 2003). For Luisa

Passerini: *Fascism in Popular Memory: The Cultural Experience of the Turin Working Class* (New York: Cambridge University Press, 1987), and Luisa Passerini, ed., *Memory and Totalitarianism* (Oxford: Oxford University Press, 1992).

18 Daniel James, *Doña María's Story: Life History, Memory, and Political Identity* (Durham, NC: Duke University Press, 2000).

19 Emily Martin, "Review Essay: Violence, Language and Everyday Life," *American Ethnologist* 34, no. 4 (2007): 741–5.

20 Veena Das, *Life and Words: Violence and the Descent into the Ordinary* (Berkeley: University of California Press, 2007).

21 Ibid., 9.

22 Alessandro Portelli, "Research as an Experiment in Equality," *The Death of Luigi Trastulli* (Albany: State University of New York Press, 1991).

14 Mémoires des Migrations de juifs marocains à Montréal[1]

YOLANDE COHEN

Les migrations post-coloniales permettent d'appréhender les reconstructions communautaires et nationales à partir du positionnement singulier des migrants à leur arrivée dans leur nouveau pays d'accueil. C'est le cas des migrations maghrébines qui conduisent chrétiens (rapatriés et pieds-noirs d'Algérie surtout mais pas seulement), musulmans et juifs à quitter les espaces coloniaux et nationaux pour se retrouver dans des villes de la France métropolitaine, un peu plus tardivement au Canada et ailleurs dans le monde occidental. Parce que ces migrants transnationaux conservent dans un premier temps les caractères propres à leur pays d'origine, il convient d'étudier le phénomène dans une perspective longitudinale, de leur départ à leur arrivée. Il devient ainsi possible d'identifier les processus à l'œuvre et d'analyser au plus près les reconfigurations auxquelles ces migrations ont pu donner lieu.

Parmi ces masses de populations migrantes qui ont été poussées à quitter leurs pays dans le contexte de la décolonisation européenne, les juifs maghrébins occupent une place particulière.[2] Les conditions qui entourent les migrations de ces populations ont fait l'objet de nombreux travaux.[3] Toutefois, les historiens ne s'entendent pas sur les raisons qui ont motivé les départs des juifs d'Afrique du Nord (du Maroc en particulier), et qui ont conduit à la disparition presque totale de ces communautés juives deux fois millénaires en terre d'Islam. Pour les uns (Sami Chétrit), il s'agit d'un véritable déplacement de populations réalisé par les organisations sionistes israéliennes qui avaient besoin de main d'œuvre pour peupler le nouveau pays.[4] Pour d'autres (Trigano, Bin-Nun) il s'agit d'un exode, certes encouragé par les organisations sionistes internationales, mais qui prenait racine dans la volonté de ces

Juifs d'échapper aux humiliations et exactions commises à leur encontre au nom de la Dhimma.[5] Enfin d'autres encore considèrent ces migrations comme s'inscrivant dans une période de migrations massives, post-coloniales et post-Shoah, qui transforment radicalement les rapports, complexes, entre les différentes ethnies et communautés' religieuses dans ces pays. En fait, ce que ces débats historiographiques récents révèlent c'est l'enjeu politique et mémoriel que cette histoire représente pour les différents protagonistes parce que les paramètres de cette histoire sont encore largement mouvants.[6]

C'est pourquoi nous avons eu recours à l'enquête d'histoire orale pour enregistrer et évaluer les perceptions que les acteurs et actrices de cette histoire en ont gardées et transmises.[7] Nous présenterons ici les résultats d'une enquête d'histoire orale (N=6 en 2008–10) menée dans le cadre du projet *Histoires de vie des Montréalais déplacés par la guerre, le génocide et autres violations aux droits de la personne*.[8] Pour quelles raisons les juifs marocains ont-ils quitté le Maroc après la Seconde Guerre mondiale? Dans quelles conditions ces migrations se sont-elles effectuées? Quelle mémoire en ont-ils aujourd'hui et comment peut-on la transcrire et la transmettre? La reconstruction du passé de nos informateurs et informatrices en aval et leur projection dans un devenir incertain en amont nous ont semblé des éléments essentiels à décrypter, car ces deux pôles définissent leur positionnement particulier face à leur histoire et à la société dans laquelle ils ont été accueillis. Nous nous concentrerons ici sur la question des départs du Maroc.[9]

Nous faisons l'hypothèse qu'au travers leur récit ces personnes se livrent à un travail de reconstitution identitaire qui consiste à donner sens à leur départ du Maroc (dislocation), autour d'un patrimoine commun (sépharade) dont la communauté (relocation) reste le principal vecteur. Si leur origine ethnique et religieuse fournit la base traditionnelle de cette identité, la langue française, pourtant langue de la colonisation mais aussi de la modernité envisagée, va être pour eux un puissant levier d'intégration à la sphère publique montréalaise. La mémoire qu'ils ont de leurs migrations et les recompositions identitaires auxquelles elle a donné lieu sont au centre de l'analyse présentée dans ce texte. Ces va et vient constant entre leur passé (nostalgique) et leur présent (indicible), entre là-bas (le vieux monde) et ici (le nouveau monde), entre eux et nous etc. sont difficiles à rendre dans un texte de cette nature. Tout au plus, allons-nous tenter de montrer comment ces récits construisent un ailleurs mythique et nostalgique du passé et de leurs migrations, et qu'ils reconstruisent un présent idéalisé pour faire face à la souffrance et à la difficulté de donner un sens à ce qui ne semble pas en avoir encore pour eux ...

Les départs du Maroc: Une histoire d'émigration post-coloniale?

L'émigration des juifs marocains au Québec s'inscrit dans ce grand mouvement d'émigration qui en l'espace de moins de trente ans (principalement entre 1950 et 1980) a vu le départ de près de la totalité de cette communauté qui comptait quelque 250 000 personnes en 1950.[10] Le délitement des liens traditionnels qui existaient entre juifs et musulmans du Maroc va se traduire par une distance plus grande et l'accélération de leurs migrations, d'abord internes, des villages et bourgs vers les villes, puis externes, des villes vers d'autres pays, comme la France, Israël, le Canada.

Ces premières migrations des juifs ruraux vers les grandes villes de Casablanca, Meknès ou Rabat témoignent des transformations profondes que connaissent ces communautés depuis la fin du XIXe siècle et de l'impact économique et social de la colonisation française. Elles rendent également possibles des migrations plus lointaines car le déracinement a déjà eu lieu. Les directions sont diverses et touchent plusieurs régions du monde, en Israël, en Europe, en Amérique latine et en Amérique du Nord. Israël, terre promise, va être la destination prise par la grande majorité d'entre eux. La France, qui aurait été l'autre destination privilégiée, leur est à toutes fins pratiques fermée. La naturalisation française se fera au cas par cas, sur demande individuelle et pour services rendus à la nation, ce qui détournera la plupart des juifs marocains d'une immigration vers la France. Bien plus, assaillie par le flot de demandes dès l'indépendance du Maroc en 1956, l'administration française freinera de toutes ses forces la naturalisation des juifs du Maroc, considérée comme trop coûteuse et politiquement peu rentable (compte tenu du nombre important de rapatriés d'Algérie auxquels elle devait répondre et du contexte général hostile aux «pieds-noirs»). Exclus du pacte post-colonial passé entre la France et ses anciens ressortissants du Maghreb, les juifs du Maroc seront sensibles aux aides fournies par les grandes organisations sionistes (qui faciliteront la migration de 80% d'entre eux en Israël) et juives américaines et canadiennes (Jewish Immigrant Aid Services – JIAS) dans leur choix du pays d'immigration.

C'est dans ce contexte et alors qu'ils cherchent des pays d'accueil au cours des années 1960, que plusieurs milliers de juifs marocains immigrent au Québec choisissant cette Province en fonction de l'avantage qu'elle présente comme terre américaine francophone accueillante aux immigrants.[11] De fait, ils ne connaissent absolument pas le Québec, et en ont rarement entendu parler, mais réagissent comme cette famille Danan de Marrakech qu'Elias Canetti décrit si bien dans *Les voix de Marrakech*[12] et qui a embrassé le rêve américain comme si c'était une réalité concrète et tangible. Ils émigrent donc en Amérique française sur la foi du mythe américain et de ses promesses de liberté![13]

Où aller ? Des interprétations contrastées

Il faut d'emblée distinguer les migrations des juifs d'Algérie (qui avaient la nationalité française et bénéficiaient ainsi de certains droits) de celles des juifs de Tunisie et du Maroc dont les départs s'apparentent selon les cas et les périodes autant à un exode qu'à un départ volontaire, organisé et concerté.

Le «choix» des destinations et des périodes de migrations révèle également plusieurs indices : la France est la destination «naturelle» pour la grande majorité des Algériens un peu avant, mais surtout après la guerre d'Algérie ; pour 80% des Marocains, Israël le sera à sa création et en plusieurs autres vagues tout au long des années 1960 et 1970. Enfin, les quelques milliers de juifs du Maroc et de Tunisie qui n'étaient pas partis durant cette période rejoindront la France et le Canada dans une seconde vague d'immigration à la fin des années 1960 et durant les années 1970. Comment s'est opéré le choix d'émigrer du Maroc à Montréal ? Quelles étaient les conditions qui ont permis ces départs ?

On comprend qu'une telle histoire requiert une analyse différenciée suivant les pays d'origine (Maroc, Algérie, Tunisie), les pays d'arrivée (Israël, France, Canada en particulier) et les périodes où ces migrations ont eu lieu, même si elles sont souvent examinées dans le cadre des migrations post-coloniales. Selon les cas, leur migration est abordée soit comme un rapatriement qui a suivi une expulsion / exclusion (les Algériens), un déplacement plus ou moins volontaire (les Marocains), une migration volontaire (les Tunisiens), un exil etc.

Différents problèmes administratifs (visas, ouverture plus ou moins grande à la nationalité etc.) et politiques (affaires étrangères et diplomatiques) doivent être pris en compte pour analyser les moments de départ et les lieux de destination de ces personnes. Toutes ces questions, complexes, car étroitement enchevêtrées, sont difficiles à situer dans l'échelle des déterminations individuelles et collectives qui ont conduit des individus et leurs familles à prendre le chemin du départ, sans grand espoir de retour.

Ces migrations ont lieu dans un contexte international marqué par des bouleversements majeurs : certains gouvernements et organisations juives internationales veulent contribuer à peupler leurs pays (Israël et le Canada), d'autres ont des obligations à l'égard de leurs nationaux après la décolonisation (la France à l'égard de l'Algérie), d'autres encore essaient de tirer parti de la situation. C'est ainsi que ces individus et ces familles s'exilent pour un pays qu'ils ne connaissent pas, ou peu, à la recherche d'une plus grande sécurité, parce qu'ils obéissent à des impératifs économiques ou religieux, ou parce que la vie en Israël, qui fut la première destination pour un tiers de ceux qui arrivent à Montréal, ne leur convient pas. Cette « rediasporisation » révèle bien les difficultés qu'ils rencontrent dans leurs migrations, en même temps qu'elle indique les parcours complexes typiques des migrations post-coloniales.

L'arrivée à Montréal

Parmi les nouveaux immigrants juifs qui s'installent au Québec après 1960, les juifs originaires du Maroc constituent le groupe « national » le plus nombreux. Comptant 7995 personnes arrivées entre 1960 et 1991 (selon le recensement de 1991), ils représentent plus du double des juifs originaires de Pologne (4250), et sont bien plus nombreux que les juifs originaires de tous les autres pays (France, Israël etc.). Cette vague d'immigrants juifs venant du Maroc va ainsi contribuer à transformer la composition de l'importante communauté juive canadienne, à Montréal particulièrement où elle jouit d'une implantation solide et ancienne.[14] L'arrivée d'un tel groupe en moins de 20 ans, va changer l'équilibre entre les différentes composantes ethniques ou nationales de la communauté juive de Montréal, qui compte alors près de 90 000 personnes.

Plus encore, la présence de ces quelque 20 000 juifs francophones à Montréal va permettre à certains historiens du Québec d'avancer la possibilité d'une convergence entre minorités juives et québécoises (francophones), en faisant un élément paradigmatique de l'interculturalisme préconisé plus tard par la Commission Bouchard-Taylor.[15] Dans cette interprétation, Gérard Bouchard met sur le même plan le fait que juifs et Québécois soient minoritaires, pour établir une communauté de destin entre eux. Toutefois, les Québécois francophones ne sont pas une minorité au Québec mais bien la majorité et détenteurs des leviers du pouvoir politique. Les juifs pour leur part, qu'ils soient francophones ou anglophones, occupent la position de minorité religieuse et ne peuvent échapper à cette condition. L'arrivée des juifs francophones a permis de penser qu'ils pourraient mettre fin à la situation paradoxale dans laquelle se trouvait la communauté juive du Québec, forte et vivante, mais relativement repliée sur elle-même, et qui se caractérisait par la « mé-rencontre » entre les différentes solitudes.[16]

De fait, l'intégration économique et sociale des juifs du Maroc au Québec est remarquable. Facilitée par l'existence de structures communautaires fortes,[17] elle permet l'émergence d'une couche sociale aisée que l'on retrouve dans les beaux quartiers francophones.[18] Par bien des aspects, les juifs originaires du Maroc ont réussi à créer leurs propres références identitaires entre judéité, francophonie et appartenance à Sépharad.[19]

La référence identitaire majeure demeure la religion,[20] véhiculée par les synagogues, les familles et les écoles propres à la communauté ;[21] la langue jouant un rôle également déterminant dans leurs rapports avec la société québécoise, même si leur utilisation du français et de l'anglais[22] c'est-à-dire les deux langues présentes au Québec montre leur volonté de s'intégrer dans l'espace nord-américain autant que francophone, gommant leur relation ancienne avec l'arabité (utilisation du dialecte judéo-arabe par exemple). En ce sens, il faut noter le caractère aléatoire et paradoxal de l'identification de ce groupe tantôt au Maroc, tantôt à Israël, tantôt à la France. Le recours à une identité sépharade mythique et recomposée autour du fait francophone permet de rendre compte de leur volonté d'adaptation à la modernité occidentale en même temps que leur difficulté d'assumer l'entièreté de leurs traditions.

Ce sont ces paradoxes qui nous ont incités à approfondir la question de la conscience que ces migrants ont de leur histoire et en particulier de leur migration. Les liens avec leur passé, qui ont été coupés de façon radicale compte tenu des conditions de leurs départs et de leur arrivée, doivent être reconstitués par une analyse fine attentive à la mémoire qu'ils en ont gardée. Contrairement à l'émigration de la majorité d'entre eux en Israël, ceux qui décident de partir pour Montréal le font plus tardivement, pour certains à l'issue de périples infructueux ailleurs, suite à des réunifications familiales ou dans l'espoir de trouver leur place en Amérique.

Questions paradoxales que sont les perceptions des départs par les migrants. Dans ce non-dit (tû) et ce presque non-pensé (traumatique?) résideraient peut-être quelques éléments d'analyse des mémoires et récits de leur migration reconstitués par les personnes interrogées. Quelles perceptions ont-ils de leurs migrations ? Comment appréhendent-ils ces événements ? Quelle place le départ occupe-t-il dans leur mémoire ?

Une migration dans l'aire culturelle française :
Deux enquêtes d'histoire orale réalisées en 1985 et en 2010

Nostalgie de la vie rêvée au Maroc en 1985

Les récits de vie (N=34) réalisés lors d'une première enquête d'histoire orale entre 1984 et 1985 sont organisés autour d'un questionnement qui part de la vie au Maroc. Les enregistrements montrent une préoccupation commune de la part des interviewés et de l'interviewer (Marie Berdugo-Cohen) d'enregistrer des descriptions de la vie quotidienne. La confection des plats, tout ce qui entoure la vie dans l'espace domestique, le déroulement des fêtes racontent la vie rêvée au Maroc. On y retrouve une certaine tendance à « l'archéologie orale » essentialisant la vie au Maroc, des souvenirs familiaux encore vivants. Les enregistrements mentionnent en toute fin les départs. Toutefois, ni la JIAS, ni le voyage, ni les premiers moments de leur arrivée ne sont des épisodes clairement identifiés. Étonnamment, peu de propos sur les conditions de départ et d'arrivée figurent dans ces entretiens, alors qu'ils étaient au centre du questionnement de l'enquête. Soit l'enquêtrice, soit les enquêtés n'ont pu trouver matière à exposition ou discussion lors des entretiens.

La Guerre des Six jours est considérée par Marie Berdugo-Cohen comme le catalyseur des départs, or cette guerre ne semble pas avoir été véritablement perçue comme telle par les interviewés. Beaucoup expliquent leur départ comme une suite logique à une première émigration familiale : une sœur, un frère, un parent est parti au Canada et en a dit du bien. Ils ou elles se portent comme référents mais pas obligatoirement. On parle peu des événements ou de l'histoire politique du Maroc, pré et post indépendance. L'indépendance n'est pas un épisode directement mentionné. La question des papiers (français ou canadiens) n'est pas abordée. Amnésie (aujourd'hui nous parlerons plutôt de traumatisme) du passé, départ qui paraît évident et dont il ne peut être question, la mémoire qui en est restée nous parut si mince que nous nous en inquiétâmes. Nous avions alors dû renoncer à traiter de cette question et avons tout simplement publié neuf entrevues que nous considérions les plus significatives de l'état d'esprit de trois générations d'hommes et de femmes dans notre livre *Juifs marocains à Montréal*.[23]

L'analyse de ce corpus nous avait permis de distinguer trois types de représentation.[24] Les plus âgés nous ont presque tous parlé en judéo-arabe ou judéo-espagnol de leur vie au Maroc. Ils ont quitté leur pays de toujours et en gardent une mémoire emprunte de nostalgie.[25] Ce sont les baby-boomers (35–65 ans) qui les ont entraînés avec eux, ou qui ont eu la possibilité de réaliser le projet de départ de leurs parents (ce qui est souvent le cas dans les migrations familiales). Ces derniers ont souhaité s'installer au Canada, nous ont parlé en français et ne semblent pas avoir de regret d'être partis. Leur représentation du départ est plutôt associée à une certaine libération, surtout pour les jeunes femmes. Nous avions qualifié ces représentations de mimétiques car ces personnes cherchaient à s'identifier au plus vite à la société d'accueil, dont ils disaient partager la langue et la culture. Les plus jeunes, qui ont suivi leurs parents, ont quelques souvenirs précis de leur vie de famille au Maroc. Ils n'adhèrent pas vraiment à l'identité judéo-marocaine et n'ont qu'une mémoire floue des événements qui les ont conduits à partir. Grand point d'interrogation pour les plus jeunes, qui se retrouvent dans un nouveau pays sans repères et sans voix, sauf qu'ils se constitueront un peu plus tard autour de l'identité religieuse juive.[26]

Au total donc, chez les interviewés qui évoquent les départs, l'émigration apparaît comme une réponse à une inquiétude liée à la politique internationale (la Guerre des Six jours pour la première et dans le cas de la famille de la seconde) et à une peur liée aux relations intercommunautaires après l'indépendance du pays (la peur d'un mariage hors de la communauté en 1958 dans le dernier cas). Pour nombre d'entre eux, le processus migratoire est une affaire de famille (comme dans les migrations en général) : on part rejoindre des membres de la famille partis plus tôt.

L'enquête, établie sur des récits de vie de migrations récentes, me laissait une impression de grande incertitude : les questions personnelles et collectives sur l'histoire de cette émigration me semblaient encore plus énigmatiques à l'issue de l'enquête qu'à son origine. Aussi est-ce avec un certain scepticisme que j'acceptais de reformuler les questions qui nous préoccupaient déjà dans les années 1980, dans le cadre d'une enquête longitudinale, comparative et pluridisciplinaire visant à recueillir des récits de vie de Montréalais déplacés par les guerres, les génocides et toutes autres atteintes aux droits de la personne (CURA-Concordia, 2007–).

Dits et non-dits de la migration en 2010

Au moment de commencer cette enquête, je me suis remémorée les difficultés que nous avions eu à retracer les épisodes de départ durant les précédentes entrevues et me disais qu'avec le temps (vingt ans plus tard) et les événements, nous réussirions à retrouver une mémoire et une conscience sinon plus vive, du moins plus réfléchie de cette histoire. Les résultats préliminaires de cette nouvelle enquête, de personnes originaires de différents pays du Maghreb-Machrek permettent de mieux cerner la question des départs. Je retiendrai les récits de six personnes que nous avons interviewées en 2009 et 2010, qui sont nées au Maroc et sont arrivées à Montréal à différents moments de leur vie. Il s'agit de trois hommes et de trois femmes nés dans les années 1920, 1930 et 1940.[27] Dans ce projet, qui porte explicitement sur leurs déplacements, on peut voir une grande résistance de leur part à caractériser ainsi leurs départs. Le terme même de déplacement fait problème.[28] Nous adopterons ici le terme plus neutre de migration, leur laissant le soin de caractériser eux-mêmes la perception qu'ils en ont aujourd'hui. En déconstruisant chacune des étapes qui ont conduit à la migration, on va voir qu'il y a pourtant quelques constantes qui émergent de ce corpus et qui rejoignent les éléments d'analyse macro historiques, présentés dans la première partie de ce texte.

CHRONOLOGIE DES DÉPARTS DU MAROC : DEUX VAGUES DISTINCTES

La première vague de départ a lieu après la Seconde Guerre mondiale à destination d'Israël, avant ou au moment de la création de l'État d'Israël en 1948. Ainsi, Léon évoque le départ de ses parents pour Israël en 1946. Son père, ouvrier électricien et « vagabond dans l'âme », part avec sa femme et trois de ses enfants. Partir en Israël était pour lui « un rêve de libération », il « voulait se sentir juif au milieu d'autres juifs ». Léon rattache ce départ à une « question identitaire » qui rejoint par quelques aspects le sionisme, mais le mot n'est pas employé. Au contraire de la famille d'Henri, qui a vécu toute sa jeunesse dans l'idéal sioniste / religieux de son père. Enfants d'une famille nombreuse (dix enfants), plutôt aisée et qualifiée de « moderne », Henri et ses deux sœurs évoquent le départ de leur frère aîné en Israël en 1948. Celui-ci part avec sa famille (sa femme et ses huit enfants) ainsi qu'avec ses deux plus jeunes sœurs, orphelines. Henri et sa sœur Annette notent que leur père, très religieux, avait déjà le projet de partir en Israël depuis les années 1920, mais qu'il n'avait pas réussi à convaincre les autorités consulaires britanniques de leur donner le visa d'entrée en Palestine. Ce projet sera repris par le fils aîné, et revient également dans les projets des frères et sœurs qui ont tous à un moment ou à un autre fait le voyage de retour à Israël avant de repartir s'installer en France ou au Canada. Ainsi, en 1952, Henri accompagné de son épouse a vécu quelques années à Marseille en France dans un camp de transit pour Israël, mais sous la pression de la famille de sa femme qui était restée au Maroc, est finalement retourné s'installer au pays. Les récits témoignent d'une mobilité très grande de ces familles, qui sont prêtes à partir et s'installent dans plusieurs pays avant d'arriver à destination, parfois ensemble mais le plus souvent de façon séparée, chacune des migrations laissant une partie de la famille sur place. La dislocation de ces familles apparaît comme une des conséquences les plus manifestes de ces migrations successives. Elle n'est toutefois pas ressentie dans les récits comme un drame humain, mais plutôt comme une fatalité qui accompagne des bouleversements indépendants de la volonté des personnes.

La seconde vague de départs pour la France et le Canada s'échelonnent dans les décennies 1950, 1960 et 1970. Jacques évoque son départ au Canada en janvier 1957, accompagné de son père et de son frère. En 1955, suite à une petite annonce professionnelle dans un magazine, son père a fait des démarches auprès du Consulat d'Angleterre où il a obtenu un visa pour le Canada. Ce sont d'abord les hommes de la famille qui sont partis, les femmes (mère et filles), chargées de liquider les biens, les ont rejoints par la suite. Fréha est partie rejoindre son mari qui étudiait la médecine à Paris en 1961. Ses parents, partis en France d'abord avec quelques unes de ses sœurs, se sont installés à Montréal en 1964. Deux ans plus tard, après un retour au Maroc, décidé par son mari pour faire son internat et pour voir ses parents, Fréha est repartie à la naissance de son fils avec son mari à Paris. La famille est ensuite partie dans les années 1970 au Canada puis aux États-Unis où son mari voulait exercer la médecine. Après son divorce, GCS est revenue à Montréal où se trouvaient ses parents. En 1974, Henri et son épouse et trois de leurs enfants partent finalement du Maroc (où ils sont revenus en 1952 après quelques années en France) pour rejoindre la famille de sa femme qui s'était installée quelques années auparavant à Montréal. Lors de cette seconde vague de migrations, on note la succession de départs et de retours des individus, seuls ou avec leurs familles. Des considérations nombreuses sont alors prises en compte par les personnes qui racontent leur migration (se rapprocher de leurs familles, continuer des études, etc.), témoignant des choix qu'ils tentent de faire entre différentes destinations; ce qui n'était pas le cas lors de la première vague migratoire, où le départ est précipité et la destination imposée par la situation.

DES PARCOURS MIGRATOIRES MULTIPLES ET COMPLEXES

Les parcours migratoires des interviewés sont complexes : différents lieux de destinations (Israël, France, Canada, États-Unis), parfois dans un même parcours ; des arrêts de parcours prolongés (notamment à Marseille) ; des retours (possibles mais provisoires) au Maroc avant un départ définitif. Les familles sont souvent dispersées en raison de départs différés et de différents lieux de destination ; elles se réunissent parfois à un moment donné. Par exemple, dans la famille de Henri, parmi les dix enfants, certains sont partis en Israël, d'autres en France, certains sont restés au Maroc plus longtemps ; d'autres y sont revenus après un départ avorté en Israël (arrêt de parcours de quelques années à Marseille en France) et sont finalement partis au Canada. Léon évoque le parcours de ses parents partis du Maroc pour Israël en 1946 (après un arrêt de parcours de six mois en France à Marseille). Revenus en France dans les années 1950 après une expérience difficile en Israël en tant que juifs orientaux, ils y sont repartis en 1965 avec leurs plus jeunes enfants (car le père avait peur que ses filles épousent des non-juifs). Revenus finalement en France, Léon les a fait venir au Canada où il était installé depuis 1968.

Dans deux histoires familiales, on retrouve le rôle important du fils aîné dans l'émigration de la famille. Par exemple, dans la famille de Henri, le frère aîné, à la mort des parents, a pris en charge l'émigration en Israël de ses deux plus jeunes sœurs orphelines. Ce frère aîné avait loué une maison à Marseille pour faire transiter les membres de la famille qu'il voulait emmener en Israël. Autre exemple, Léon, fils aîné d'une famille de 9 enfants, s'est inquiété de l'éducation de ses jeunes frères qu'il a finalement fait venir au Canada. Il a ensuite contribué au regroupement de toute sa famille à Montréal.

DES DÉPARTS VÉCUS DANS LA CLANDESTINITÉ

Pour la plupart des interviewés, les départs évoqués ont lieu dans la clandestinité. Fréha se souvient de son père qui avait vendu la moitié de son immeuble avant de partir et qui ne pouvait pas sortir l'argent du pays. Il faisait transiter son argent par l'intermédiaire d'un colonel français (un ami d'amis). Elle se souvient aussi, lors son deuxième départ du Maroc vers la France, d'avoir caché de l'argent dans les langes de son bébé au moment de passer la frontière. Henri évoque un déménagement « non-officiel ». « On a laissé la maison toute rangée et on est partis comme si on partait en vacances » dit-il. Il a fait envoyer des affaires à Casablanca dans des containers d'Européens, ce qui comportait des risques. Il se souvient aussi du passage de la frontière et d'une remarque sur le fait que son fils ait son cartable, ce qui paraissait suspect pour un départ en vacances.

Dans la famille de Henri, la dispersion de la famille a pu créer des tensions entre les frères et sœurs car certains sont partis en Israël où la vie était difficile tandis que d'autres n'ont finalement pas suivi. Un frère y est allé mais n'y est pas resté. Son retour au Maroc a été vécu très tragiquement par ceux qui sont restés en Israël (pleurs, Annette évoque un « deuil »). Annette se souvient de la déception de son frère aîné qui n'a pas vu ses frères et sœurs suivre le « chemin qu'il avait préparé ». Mais les avis divergent : Henri dit que ses frères l'ont dissuadé de venir en Israël « ne vient pas, y'a que des bombes, y'a nulle part où habiter » lui auraient-ils dit tandis que AA dit que ce sont les frères restés au Maroc qui l'ont dissuadé d'y aller. Annette évoque que le fait d'être « loin les uns des autres » pendant plus de trente ans a été très difficile à vivre pour elle. Elle a l'impression d'avoir été « expédiée comme un colis » en Israël sans avoir pu donner son avis. Tandis que sa plus jeune sœur Marguerite ne l'a pas aussi mal vécu même si la séparation avec le Maroc qui suivait de peu de temps la mort de ses parents a été aussi difficile à vivre pour elle.

DES DÉPARTS CHOISIS MAIS CONTRAINTS : LE POIDS DES ÉVÉNEMENTS

Comment les juifs marocains interviewés interprètent-ils leur(s) départ(s) du Maroc ou celui/ceux des membres de leur famille ? S'agit-il de déplacements, de départs forcés ou librement choisis ? On peut d'abord constater une grande résistance de leur part à considérer leurs départs comme un « déplacement » (terme employé dans le projet). Pour la plupart d'entre eux, ils disent être partis volontairement du Maroc, en payant leur propre passage pour la France ou directement pour le Canada, ou avec l'aide ou non des organisations juives. Certes, leur départ était longuement prémédité mais organisé dans la hâte et dans la peur. Toutefois, ils ne sont pas prêts à assimiler leur déplacement à celui des populations auxquelles ils pensent. Ils ne se voient pas comme des personnes déplacées ou des réfugiés mais plutôt comme « des émigrants poussés au départ par la situation ». Les facteurs évoqués par les interviewés pour expliquer leur(s) départ(s) du Maroc ou celui / ceux des membres de leur famille ont contribué selon eux à la détérioration de « la situation ».

Plusieurs considérations reviennent dans les récits qui incluent leur rapport plus ou moins distancé à la situation internationale. Ainsi, l'idéal sioniste anime les premiers départs. Le frère d'Henri est animé d'une volonté farouche de partir au plus vite en Terre Sainte et il ne se demande pas longtemps ce qu'il doit faire de ses deux jeunes sœurs. Il les emmène avec le reste de sa famille en Israël en 1948, car la situation l'exigeait. Mises devant le fait accompli par leur frère aîné, elles se considèrent cinquante ans plus tard comme de véritables Israéliennes, même si cela a signifié leur séparation durable avec leurs autres frères et sœurs, restés au Maroc puis partis en France et au Canada, plutôt qu'en Israël. Les départs de cette première vague sont ainsi rattachés par les interviewés au sionisme qui animait certains juifs du Maroc (Léon, Henri et Annette). Léon évoque des « canaux existants » qui ont permis à ses parents de partir en 1946. Dans la famille de Henri, si le départ du frère aîné a été influencé par le sionisme, le départ n'a, semble-t-il, pas été financé par une organisation sioniste et est considéré comme un départ volontaire, autonome. Dans son entrevue, Jacques note que ce sont les juifs du mellah, assez pauvres, qui ont été sollicités par les organisations sionistes pour partir en Israël avec la promesse d'un avenir meilleur. Son oncle et ses tantes ont été ainsi sollicités et sont partis, contrairement à son père qui était « sorti du mellah » : de retour d'une formation de coiffeur à Paris, il s'est installé dans la ville nouvelle et a ouvert un salon de coiffure dans une rue centrale et commerçante. Jacques explique cette sortie du mellah par un changement de classe sociale. GCS se souvient que le premier grand mouvement d'émigration en Israël en 1948 concernait les plus pauvres, les moins éduqués. Cette idée du départ vers Israël semble avoir joué sur une mémoire et une transmission de « la volonté de partir ». Dans la famille de Henri, les enfants ont entendu leurs parents évoquer ce départ qui n'a pu être mis en œuvre, en raison des « papiers » (refus de visas de la part des autorités britanniques). Cette évocation d'un départ désiré semble les avoir marqués et la déception du père est évoquée à plusieurs reprises (Henri, Annette et Marguerite). Par contre ce que pensait la mère de ce départ est peu abordé (et questionné) : Henri dit que sa mère « suivait ». La question du rôle des mères de famille dans les projets d'émigration, en particulier le choix du lieu de destination, pourtant attesté dans d'autres études,[29] ne semble pas ici être pris en compte.

Outre le sionisme, reviennent souvent en filigrane ou explicitement les références à une configuration triangulaire complexe : les rapports entre les Français, les Arabes et les juifs pendant la colonisation du Maroc ont laissé des traces durables dans la mémoire des personnes qui nous ont livré leur récit. Concernant la vie quotidienne au Maroc et les rapports sociaux entre juifs, Français et Arabes abordés par les interviewers comme ayant pu inciter les Juifs à partir, les réponses sont assez contrastées. La convivialité de ces rapports est d'abord soulignée. L'amitié entre les juifs et les Arabes est souvent évoquée, en particulier dans les relations de travail. Henri note que le Français était « le dominateur », ce qui pourrait expliquer selon lui ce rapprochement entre les juifs et les Arabes. Fréha note que seuls les hommes sont impliqués dans ce type de relation, les femmes étant le plus souvent tenues à l'écart des Arabes, les familles redoutant des mariages de leurs filles avec des musulmans (les mariages avec des catholiques étant plus tolérés). Les parents de Fréha disent notamment être partis, car un Arabe poursuivait leur fille. Plusieurs interviewés évoquent la protection des juifs par le roi du Maroc sous le régime de Vichy. Cette protection pourrait expliquer une certaine reconnaissance envers le Maroc qui transparaît dans les entrevues. L'histoire de cette protection est notamment transmise entre les générations. Fréha se souvient : « mes grands-mères m'ont raconté que le roi protégeait les juifs ». Elle se rappelle aussi de l'antisémitisme des Français, au Maroc mais aussi en France. Henri lui évoque l'antisémitisme des Français au Maroc, notamment sous le gouvernement de Vichy : « il y avait un *numerus clausus* dans notre école, et ils choisissaient de renvoyer cinq personnes par classe. On ne savait pas qui c'était. Seulement, j'avais une amie qui avait été ainsi renvoyée de l'école sur le champ ». Jacques note que, pendant la Seconde Guerre mondiale, l'immeuble où il habitait avec sa famille (et où logeaient aussi d'autres familles juives) avait été marqué d'une croix en vue d'une rafle. Il se souvient aussi d'avoir subi lui-même la discrimination : « dans mon école, située dans la ville nouvelle (dans le quartier européen), on m'avait assis au fond de la classe parce que j'étais juif ». Contrairement à son frère, Jacques n'a jamais eu de problème particulier avec les Arabes. D'ailleurs c'est suite à une bagarre de son frère avec un Arabe que son père, qui avait déjà entrepris toutes les démarches d'émigration au Canada et dont le salon de coiffure périclitait, a décidé de partir, six mois après l'indépendance du Maroc. L'appartenance de classe a aussi joué dans les relations avec les autres groupes (Français et Arabes) mais aussi à l'intérieur de la communauté juive. Léon évoque les mauvais souvenirs que son père gardait du Maroc, notamment le fait d'être relégué, en raison de sa pauvreté, au fond de la synagogue par les juifs les plus riches. «Mon père aussi avait été maltraité par les Arabes, aussi il était assez content de la présence française».

Des «petits trucs», «petits événements» sont évoqués concernant les relations avec les Français et avec les Arabes dans le long terme. La comparaison est aussi souvent faite avec ce qui est arrivé aux autres juifs, ce qui amène les interviewés à minimiser ce qui leur est arrivé (jets de pierres, razzias dans le mellah). Alors certes, le souvenir des exactions subies, que ce soit les petites humiliations quotidiennes, rarement des grands événements publics, ces choses-là se trouvent reléguées dans une mémoire floue. Au détour d'une conversation, d'un souvenir d'école, ces souvenirs reviennent. Ainsi, Marguerite se souvient d'une attaque survenue le jour de Kippour à Meknès dans les années de l'immédiat après guerre. Elle s'apparente autant à une attaque anti-sémite contre les juifs du mellah (forcés de se retrancher sur leurs ter-rasses pour se protéger des projectiles), qu'à un coup de main d'une bande de voyous qui cherchaient à leur faire peur. La mémoire de cet événement semble marquer une étape dans le détachement qu'il lui a fallu faire par rapport aux voisins. L'indifférence et même la non inter-vention des Français lors de ces moments de tensions entre juifs et Arabes est aussi évoquée. Henri laisse entendre que cette attitude était voulue afin de «diviser pour mieux régner».

Toutefois, ces rapports changent avec l'indépendance du Maroc en 1956, puisque les Français n'ont plus de pouvoir direct sur les rapports inter-communautaires. Fréha dit que les juifs «avaient peur d'être entre les deux» (Français et Arabes) qu'«ils étaient au milieu» au moment de l'indépendance du pays. «Mon père, qui avait un commerce d'électro-ménager, a vu le nombre de clients chuter après l'indépendance», sa clientèle était en effet largement composée de Français. Elle ajoute: «on ne parlait jamais de politique» et elle évoque une «répression invi-sible». On peut voir qu'un changement politique peut conduire à un changement économique qui a joué en partie sur la décision du départ. Jacques considère que «suite à l'indépendance du Maroc, l'avenir de juifs paraissait sombre, notamment pour ceux qui n'avaient pas beau-coup d'argent. La lutte des Marocains pour l'indépendance m'a forte-ment marqué, surtout après les explosions de bombes à Casablanca. Ces évènements ont troublé ma vie 'relax' et m'ont poussé à partir».

Une rumeur l'a aussi conforté dans son désir de partir : en 1957, on disait que des juifs allaient être enrôlés dans l'armée marocaine et Jacques ne se voyait pas servir et a eu peur d'être envoyé combattre en Israël.

La conscience des tensions internationales résultant du conflit israélo-arabe met au jour les conflits potentiels entre voisins. Le conflit au Proche-Orient qui s'étale sur plusieurs décennies a ainsi joué un rôle important dans le changement des relations sociales entre les communautés arabe et juive au Maroc. Léon évoque un souvenir : « au milieu des années 1950, j'avais 13 ans, j'étais allé voir mon oncle à Marrakech et je suis allé me promener sur la place Jemaa El Fnaa. Aussitôt que mon oncle a su où j'étais, il est venu me chercher en catastrophe, de peur qu'il ne m'arrive quelque chose ». Léon rattache cette peur à des événements au Proche-Orient. Henri aussi pense que la la Guerre des Six jours en 1967 provoque des changements : « la Guerre des Six jours nous est tombée sur la tête du jour au lendemain. Mes relations de travail en ont pati ; mais en quelques mois ça s'est arrangé ». Henri ne dit pas si ce moment a provoqué sa décision de partir, mais avec sa femme et ses enfants, ils partiront sept ans plus tard. Il constate encore que depuis l'indépendance, des Arabes soupçonnaient les juifs d'entretenir, voire de financer Israël : « il y avait des tensions, une certaine surveillance, parfois des demandes de rançon et une « atmosphère lourde ».

Ces événements forment une trame de fond dans laquelle s'inscrit le facteur souvent évoqué comme déterminant dans le départ, soit que les parents voient peu d'avenir au Maroc pour leurs enfants. Même si Henri considère sa situation économique florissante, le choix de partir prend le dessus. Des enfants sont d'ailleurs partis faire leurs études à Paris (la fille aînée de Henri et le mari de Fréha) avant le départ des parents. On peut aussi remarquer, qu'au sein des familles, il y a un souci d'éducation pour les filles qui peuvent quitter le domicile familial (y compris changer de pays) pour cette raison.

Conclusion

À partir de ces quelques entrevues, nous pouvons tracer quelques pistes de réflexion pour mieux comprendre les processus qui ont conduit la communauté juive à quitter le Maroc par vagues successives à partir de la fin de la Seconde Guerre mondiale. Les différentes interprétations de ces départs sont le plus souvent le fait d'une analyse de niveau macro. L'approche par les parcours individuels et les interprétations données par les individus qui ont vécu ces départs permet un approfondissement de l'analyse et met en évidence la complexité du phénomène. Dans ces récits, on a pu identifier un enchevêtrement de différents niveaux dans l'expérience des interviewés : individuel, familial, social, national, international. À l'intérieur de ces différents niveaux, le vécu des individus est traversé par le genre, l'âge, la place dans la famille, la classe sociale, l'identité religieuse. L'histoire familiale transmise, son expérience migratoire ou les représentations de la migration en son sein semblent aussi avoir joué un rôle important dans les départs. La chronologie des départs devrait ainsi être analysée dans la longue durée, la volonté de partir s'inscrivant bien souvent dans une histoire familiale et dans les transformations majeures qu'a connues le Maroc post-colonial.

Émigration volontaire ou sous la contrainte ? À la lumière des récits, ces différentes interprétations ne paraissent pas s'opposer. Les choix individuels et familiaux sont traversés par l'histoire nationale et internationale mais la volonté et la spontanéité des départs ne paraissent pas s'opposer aux contraintes d'ordre social qui découlent bien souvent de conflits lointains. L'émigration ne peut se comprendre sans l'immigration et il faudra poursuivre par l'analyse des facteurs d'immigration et approfondir la question des chaînes migratoires et des promesses des lieux de destination choisis. En l'occurrence, la promesse d'émancipation offerte par la culture et la langue française entrevue au Maroc mais rapidement déçue par l'oppression coloniale semble renaître dans le projet d'émigration au Québec. Ainsi, la langue française apparaît rapidement à ces immigrants à Montréal comme leur offrant la possibilité de créer un nouveau creuset identitaire propice à leur épanouissement.

La maîtrise de la langue française occupe dans leur projet de départ, dans leur sélection par les administrations canadiennes et québécoises et dans les études qui leur sont consacrées une place déterminante. La plupart de ceux que nous avons interrogés sont des hommes et des femmes qui ont fait leurs études en français, soit dans les écoles de l'Alliance israélite universelle, soit dans des lycées et écoles de la mission française. Leurs parents parlent plutôt le judéo-arabe ou le judéo-espagnol, quelques fois le français mais pas toujours. Ils ont pu émigrer grâce aux politiques de regroupement familial alors pratiquées par le gouvernement canadien. De ce fait, l'attachement au français, langue commune de la colonisation mais aussi de leur émancipation, trouve certainement un écho au Québec où elle détermine largement l'identité québécoise alors en pleine affirmation. Et l'on voit bien aussi combien les études qui leur ont été consacrées ont aussi instrumentalisé l'arrivée de ces nouveaux venus, jetés d'emblée dans la bataille linguistique qui faisait rage alors.

Dans un contexte où le français est en train de s'imposer comme langue principale de la citoyenneté québécoise, le fait que ces nouveaux immigrants soient majoritairement francophones contribue à changer les termes de la relation entre juifs et non juifs, mais aussi leur rapport avec la majorité ashkénaze essentiellement anglophone. La cohésion linguistique des différents groupes juifs ashkénazes autour de l'anglais (le yiddish n'étant plus qu'une réminiscence) apparaît compromise. Ainsi l'arrivée des juifs du Maroc contribue à la renaissance d'une identité sépharade en pleine affirmation à Montréal et dans la diaspora. Même si elle renforce le caractère multinational et pluriel de la communauté juive de Montréal, en y ajoutant des caractéristiques linguistiques et culturelles totalement nouvelles, elle vise initialement à contester la discrimination dont les juifs marocains ont été victimes en Israël et ailleurs. En fait, elle aura aussi contribué à définir de nouveaux paramètres de la judaïté pour la seconde génération. Pour ceux qui émigrent à Montréal toutefois et dont on a présenté le parcours, la langue et l'origine ethnique, bien plus que leur pratique religieuse, vont devenir de puissants marqueurs de leur identité recomposée.[30]

Cette identité va ainsi se cristalliser autour d'une représentation particulière des Sépharades dans l'ensemble communautaire et plus largement dans la société québécoise. Des processus de reconstruction identitaire qui impliquent le retour à des référents anciens et parfois mythiques (l'âge d'or de *Sepharad*) s'agrègent alors autour d'une réinterprétation de leurs traditions à la lumière des nouveaux paramètres identitaires québécois, dont la langue est le principal vecteur. Une sorte d'équation se met alors en place entre sépharade et francophone.

La reconstruction d'une identité sépharade dans le contexte communautaire montréalais et québécois diffère de celle que l'on trouve en Israël et en France à la même époque. Au Québec et en France, ce mode d'identification passe par le partage du français comme langue commune avec la société d'accueil, par le rajeunissement d'une communauté juive vieillissante,[31] et par le renforcement du sentiment de cohésion communautaire.[32]

Ainsi ils contribueront à renouveler les structures communautaires avec la création de nouveaux ensembles institutionnels autour de l'identité sépharade (la CSQ qui est devenue la CSUQ, les écoles Maïmonides, la publication d'une revue *La voix sépharade*, etc.).[33] Cette identification complexe au sépharadisme a été somme toute salutaire pour les juifs du Maroc à Montréal. Car si elle gomme en partie le caractère post-colonial de cette immigration, et institue une confrontation pas toujours heureuse avec le monde juif ashkénaze surtout anglophone, elle permet aux juifs marocains qui s'en emparent de se constituer en groupe d'intérêt et en communauté culturelle. En ce sens, elle s'inscrit dans un paysage politique québécois qui favorise l'appartenance à l'aire culturelle francophone, en même temps qu'elle bénéficie des politiques (et subventions) favorisant l'éclosion du multiculturalisme canadien dans une ville cosmopolite comme Montréal.

NOTES

1   Je tiens à remercier Steve High et Frank Chalk qui ont permis à ce projet de prendre une ampleur tout à fait inattendue, grâce à leurs encouragements et à leur soutien moral et financier. Les six entretiens ont été réalisés au sein du projet *Histoires de vie des Montréalais déplacés par la guerre, le génocide et autres violations aux droits de la personne* par l'équipe que je dirige à l'UQAM. Je remercie Linda Guerry de son aide dans le recueil de ces récits ainsi que dans l'analyse des premiers résultats présentés dans ce texte.

2   En 1948, la population juive d'Afrique du Nord était composée d'environ 550 000 personnes. Dans les années 80, elle ne compte plus que 30 000 personnes; près de 20 000 Juifs nord-africains émigrent au Canada, 230 000 (120 000 d'origine d'Algérie, 60 000 de Tunisie, et 35 000 du Maroc) s'établissent en France et 300 000 en Israël. Jacques Taïeb, «Historique d'un exode: l'émigration des Juifs du Maghreb de la fin des années quarante à nos jours», *Yod* 10 (1979): 88–100.

3   Voir les ouvrages désormais classiques de Norman Stillman, *The Jews of Arab Lands In Modern Times* (Philadelphia: Jewish Publication Society, 1991); Michel Abitbol, *The Jews of North Africa during the Second World War* (Detroit: Wayne State University Press, 1989); Michael M. Laskier, *North African Jewry in the Twentieth Century, The Jews of Morocco, Tunisia and Algeria* (New York: New York University Press, 1994); Mohamed Kenbib, *Juifs et musulmans au Maroc (1859–1948): Contribution à l'histoire des relations inter-communautaires en terre d'Islam* (Rabat: Université Mohamed V, Publication de la Faculté des Lettres et des Sciences humaines, Série – Thèses et mémoires, no. 21, 1994). Voir aussi les études plus récentes publiées sous la direction de Shmuel Trigano, *La fin du judaïsme en terres d'Islam* (Paris: Denoël, 2009).

4 Sami S. Chétrit, *The Mizrahi Struggle in Israel : 1948–2003* (Tel-Aviv : Am-Oved, 2004) (en hébreu).

5 Yigal Bin-Nun, "Psychosis or an Ability to Foresee the Future ? The Contribution of the World Jewish Organizations to the Establishment of Rights for Jews in Independent Morocco, 1955–1961," *Revue Européenne d'Etudes Hébraïques* 10 (2004).

6 Nous avons pu nous en rendre compte lors du colloque international d'Essaouira *Migrations, Identité et Modernité au Maghreb* (17–20 mars 2010) qui rassemblait un grand nombre des chercheurs actifs dans ce domaine, et où les débats entre historiens marocains, juifs et musulmans, israéliens et du reste du monde témoignaient de l'intensité des enjeux : http:// mediamed.mmsh.univ-aix.fr/chaines/Migrations/Pages/default.aspx (page consultée le 15 novembre 2010).

7 Voir Jean- Luc Bédard, « Identité et transmission intergénérationnelle chez les Sépharades à Montréal » (PhD diss., Université Laval, 2005).

8 Notre enquête est intégrée au Groupe de travail sur la Shoah et les autres persécutions contre les Juifs. Ce projet, axé sur l'histoire orale, aborde l'expérience et le souvenir des violences de masse et des déplacements des Juifs dans le monde. Une équipe de chercheurs universitaires et communautaires travaillent ensemble à ce projet qui est basé au Centre d'histoire orale et de récits numérisés de l'Université Concordia à Montréal (2007–12).

9 C'est une histoire qui est aussi la mienne. Ayant quitté le Maroc en 1968 alors que j'avais 18 ans pour faire des études à Paris, j'ai ensuite suivi ma famille (parents et mes trois frères et sœur) à Montréal en 1976, deux ans après qu'ils soient eux-mêmes partis de Meknès pour Montréal, en 1974. J'en ai fait le récit lors de la conférence que j'ai prononcé à l'Institut Émilie du Châtelet à Paris, le 6 mars 2010 : http://www.institutemilieduchatelet. org/Conferences/conference-Cohen.html (page consultée le 15 novembre 2010). Voir aussi mon article, « De Meknès à Montréal », *Genre & Histoire* 6 (printemps 2010), http://genrehistoire.revues.org/index1021.html (page consultée le 25 mai 2013). Cette référence permet de replacer les interprétations que je ferai des migrations des juifs marocains à Montréal dans la subjectivité qui est la mienne.

10 Les migrations des juifs dans le bassin méditerranéen ont été nombreuses depuis l'Antiquité et la présence juive en Afrique du Nord a été renforcée par l'arrivée des juifs chassés de la péninsule ibérique par l'Inquisition catholique. L'arrivée des juifs en terre d'Islam leur permit d'échapper à l'anti-judaïsme chrétien.

11 Les différentes études démographiques consacrées à la population juive distinguent les Sépharades des Ashkénazes. Si l'on reprend les données du recensement de 2001, on constate que les juifs nés au Maroc constituent le groupe sépharade le plus important qui a immigré entre 1960 et 1980 au Québec : ils sont 220 a avoir immigré avant 1960, 2475 entre 1960 et 1969 (soit 66%), 2525 entre 1970 et 1979 (soit 69,9%), 1375 entre 1980 et 1989 (soit 53%) et 620 entre 1990 et 2001 (soit 43,2%). Les autres pays d'émigration des juifs sépharades, que l'on retrouve à partir de leurs lieux de naissance sont : l'Égypte, l'Algérie-Tunisie-Lybie, l'Irak, l'Iran, la Turquie, le Liban (Charles Shahar et Elisabeth Perez, *Analyse du recensement de 2001* (Montréal : Fédération CJA, octobre 2005 : 22).

12 Elias Canetti, *Les voix de Marrakech, journal d'un voyage* (Paris : Albin Michel, 1980).

13 Yolande Cohen et Joseph Lévy, « Élites et organisation communautaire chez les juifs marocains à Montréal : Du soleil à la liberté », *Annuaire de l'Émigration* (Rabat : Ministère des communautés marocaines vivant à l'étranger, 1995) : 320–7.

14 Le phénomène va aussi renforcer une distinction entre ces nouveaux venus, principalement des Sépharades, et les Ashkénazes, immigrants plus anciennement établis. L'histoire juive est marquée par de nombreuses ruptures religieuses et géographiques qui ont donné naissance à différents groupes juifs et à différentes diasporas que l'on regroupe en deux grands ensembles : les Ashkénazes (descendants des juifs installés dans l'Europe chrétienne médiévale, essentiellement, parlant aussi souvent le yiddish) et les Sépharades. Ces derniers, ont dû fuir la Péninsule Ibérique après l'Inquisition espagnole et se sont réfugiés en Afrique du Nord, dans les Balkans et ailleurs en Europe. Même s'ils partagent une même liturgie, leurs rituels religieux diffèrent de même que leur rapport à l'histoire (colonisation puis émigration pour les uns, émancipation occidentale et Shoah pour les autres).

15 Se penchant sur les causes de l'antisémitisme québécois, Bouchard ajoute à la thèse de Pierre Anctil (les juifs porteurs de la modernité menaçant les valeurs traditionnelles), celle du « développement collectif remarquable [de la communauté juive] alors que les Canadiens français empruntaient un cheminement plus incertain », ce qui aurait assuré aux juifs une mobilité sociale ascendante aux côtés des anglophones. Ainsi l'auteur émet l'hypothèse que les « expressions d'antisémitisme canadien-français visaient moins le juif lui-même que l'allié d'une classe dominante réprouvée … Le juif [serait] une sorte de Canadien français inversé qui aurait renoncé à une partie de son identité pour sortir de sa condition de défavorisé »,

dans Pierre Anctil, Ira Robinson et Gérard Bouchard, eds., *Juifs et Canadiens français dans la société québécoise* (Sillery : Septentrion, 2000), 27.

16 Reprenant le terme de Zygmunt Bauman, Ignaki Olazabal parvient aussi au constat d'une grande distance entre les trois grands groupes religieux : Ignaki Olazabal «Entre les processus de communalisation et d'*intersystème*; Juifs et Québécois francophones à Montréal à travers quatre générations» dans *Juifs et Canadiens Français dans la Société Québécoise*, Pierre Anctil, Ira Robinson, et Gérard Bouchard, eds (Sillery : Septentrion, 2000), 109.

17 Céline Brière, «Les Juifs sépharades à Montréal : traces passagères et marqueurs spatiaux d'une minorité dans une métropole nord-américaine» (Mémoire de Maîtrise, Géographie, Université d'Angers, 1990).

18 Maurice Légaré, «La population juive de Montréal est-elle victime d'une ségrégation qu'elle se serait elle-même imposée?» *Recherches sociographiques* vol. IV, 3 (septembre-décembre 1965) : 312.

19 Nicolas Sourisce, «La Communauté juive montréalaise : enracinement original. La presse des communautés culturelles : un nouvel outil de recherche» (Mémoire de Maîtrise, Géographie, Université d'Angers, 1996).

20 Betty Elkaïm, «Evaluations des séquelles psychologiques du deuil» (Mémoire de Maîtrise, Psychologie, Université de Montréal, 1981).

21 Paula Brami, «Identité ethnique et acculturation chez les étudiants juifs sépharades à Montréal» (Mémoire de Maîtrise, Psychologie, Université de Montréal, 1996).

22 Hakima Boussouga, «La Vitalité ethnolinguistique de la communauté juive marocaine de Montréal» (Mémoire de Maîtrise, Université du Québec à Montréal, 2003).

23 Marie Berdugo-Cohen, Yolande Cohen et Joseph Lévy, *Juifs marocains à Montréal : témoignages d'une immigration moderne* (Montréal : VLB, 1987).

24 La plupart de ceux et celles dont nous avons recueilli les témoignages sont arrivés à Montréal entre 1967 et 1973 ; quelques-uns sont arrivés après 1958 et décrivent leurs premiers pas dans un Montréal peu «sépharade».

25 André Elbaz en saisissant l'imaginaire des anciens, a montré que cette génération avait subi un traumatisme qu'ils essaient de cacher par une reconstruction et une mythification du présent : André Elbaz, «Ma mémoire sépharade» in *La Mémoire sépharade*, Trigano Shmuel et Trigano Hélène, éds. (Paris : In Press, 2000). Voir aussi André Elbaz, *Sépharadisme d'hier et de demain : trois autobiographies d'immigrants Juifs marocains* (Ottawa : Musée Canadien des civilisations, 1988).

26 L'accueil réservé par les instances communautaires à ces récits, publiés dans un ouvrage en 1987, fut réservé. L'historien Pierre Anctil en fit un compte-rendu très élogieux dans le quotidien *Le Devoir*, mais ce premier

ouvrage sur les juifs du Maroc à Montréal ne fit l'objet d'aucune discussion ou débat public au sein de la communauté. Nous avons alors pensé que les images que ces récits ou trajectoires renvoyaient des migrations juives marocaines ne convenaient tout simplement pas, ou qu'il était trop tôt pour en parler en public.

27   Henri (né en 1926), ses sœurs Annette (née en 1930) et Marguerite (née en 1934) ; Fréha (née en 1940) ; Léon (né en 1942) ; Jacques (né en 1937).

28   On trouve de semblables difficultés à caractériser les départs des juifs du Maroc dans d'autres études qui leur sont consacrées : Bédard parle de départ et d'arrivée de façon plus neutre (Bédard, *Identité et transmission*) ; Trigano parle d'exode pour les juifs marocains, d'expulsion pour les Algériens (Trigano, *La fin du judaïsme en terres d'Islam*.) ; Elbaz parle d'arrachement et de transplantation (Michael Elbaz, « Parias, parvenus et rebelles. Juifs marocains et Marocains juifs » in *L'insoumis. Juifs, Marocains et rebelles*, Abraham Serfaty et Michael Elbaz, ed. (Paris : Desclée de Brouwer, 2001), 23–65).

29   Berdugo-Cohen, Cohen, Lévy, *Juifs marocains à Montréal*.

30   Il est intéressant de constater qu'au sein de la République laïque française, ce furent les institutions consistoriales mises en place par Napoléon qui vont définir durablement le franco-judaïsme, marqué par la confessionnalisation d'un judaïsme acquis aux valeurs républicaines. On y distingue une diversité de croyances et de pratiques et un pluralisme religieux faisant du judaïsme consistorial ou traditionnaliste le centre d'une nébuleuse qui va de l'orthodoxie et néo-orthodoxie au libéralisme et au « reconstructionnisme massorti ». Joëlle Allouche-Benayoun, « Diversité et pluralisme religieux au sein du judaïsme » in *Connaissance du monde juif*, Evelyne Martini et Gérard Rabinovitch, ed. (Champigny-sur-Marne : SCÉRÉN-CRDP de Créteil, 2008), 73–84.

31   En France, on peut voir comme en Israël une inversion de la proportion de Sépharades dans la population juive, qui devient majoritaire avec 60% des 500 000 à 700 000 juifs vivant en France en 2007 (alors que la population ashkénaze est majoritaire mondialement avec 12 millions sur 16 millions de Juifs).

32   C'est à Montréal que l'on trouve le plus faible taux de mariages interreligieux (qui est passé de 5,9% en 1981 à 6,8% en 1991 dans la communauté, alors qu'il est respectivement de 9,7% et 13% au Canada).

33   Différents types d'intégration ont été étudiées : l'intégration économique réussie des Juifs du Maghreb a été attestée par l'économiste Naomi Moldofsky ("The Economic Adjustment of North African Jewish Immigrants in Montréal" [PhD diss., Economics and Political Science,

McGill University, 1969]) et par le psycho-sociologue Jean-Claude Lasry (Jean-Claude Lasry, Jean-Claude et Claude Tapia ed., *Les Juifs du Maghreb. Diasporas contemporaines*, Montréal/Paris: Presses de l'Université de Montréal/L'Harmattan, 1989) qui démontre que les membres de la communauté ont pour la plupart d'entre eux réussi à retrouver le niveau professionnel qu'ils avaient dans leur pays d'origine, d'autant que nombre d'entre eux se sont trouvé des emplois dans des entreprises dites ethniques, sépharades ou ashkénazes. Leur intégration géographique est aussi attestée par Céline Brière, (Brière, *Les Juifs Sépharades à Montréal*), puisqu'ils s'installent essentiellement dans les quartiers traditionnellement juifs (au centre-ville) et nouvellement juifs (Côte Saint-Luc) et créent leurs propres référents identitaires (entre judéité, francophonie et séphardité) voir Sourisce, *La communauté juive montréalaise.*

PART FIVE

Rwanda in the Aftermath of Genocide

15 Viols des femmes tutsi pendant le génocide: Témoignage de Mme Mukarwego

ATHANASIE MUKARWEGO[1]

C'est le matin que mon mari m'a dit que l'avion du président a été ... est tombé. Parce qu'il y avait l'information à la radio qui disait: «La population rwandaise doit rester chez elle pour que les forces de l'ordre puissent faire leur devoir». On est resté dans la maison ... on n'est pas sorti pour travailler, sauf que nous, les enseignants on était en vacances de Pâques ... Donc les massacres ont commencé ... toute la journée, progressivement, jusqu'à ce que le quartier là où j'habitais soit atteint. J'entendais «machetter» chez les voisins et puis, le huit (Ndlr: le 8 avril 1994), on est venu prendre mon mari, on l'a emmené à la barrière parce que les barrières étaient déjà installées dans chaque ... quartier; après 5 ou 6 maisons il y avait des barrières, qui étaient surveillées, contrôlées par des hommes hutus. Mais aussi on avait obligé les Tutsis à aller à la barrière. C'est comme ça qu'ils ont pris mon mari pour l'emmener à la barrière. Donc il était obligé; il est allé, il a ... il a dû vivre pendant huit jours, huit ... six jours parce qu'il a été tué le 15 avril ... On a commencé à le torturer la nuit du 14; il a été achevé le 15 avril (tôt) le matin; c'est là que la nouvelle m'est parvenue, par l'un de ses amis, hutu, un ami de la famille, qui s'appelait Kamanzi. Il est venu à trois heures, le matin. Il m'a dit: «Madame, je viens t'annoncer la mort de ton mari Canisius», et puis la chemise qu'il portait était tachée de sang, le sang vif. Les mains étaient aussi ... il avait du sang dans les paumes de ses mains. Il me le disait en pleurant; il m'a dit: «Malgré que ... moi aussi on m'a obligé de le tuer parce que j'étais son ami; je vais me charger de ses enfants. Donc, ses enfants, les enfants de Canisius ne mourront pas de faim tant que je pourrai les nourrir». Il est parti. Donc c'était le 15; le 16 à 19h il y a eu une sentinelle qui ... qui occupait la maison de ... d'un agent des affaires étrangères qui était déjà parti; il était originaire d'une autre province ; il avait quitté la ville pour aller dans sa province d'origine … en période de, de guerre. Donc la sentinelle est venue à 19 heures, il m'a dit : « Tu as beaucoup fait pour moi ; tu m'as rendu plusieurs services, je peux pas te cacher, je viens de la barrière ; on vient de dire que les femmes dont les maris sont déjà tués, les femmes tutsis, on va les tuer cette nuit. On a même prononcé ton nom. Donc je te dis ça pour que tu puisses prendre des précautions. Alors ce que je te conseille : viens passer la nuit chez moi, on ne saura pas, on ne viendra pas fouiller la maison de mon patron parce qu'on sait que mon patron est hutu ». Ma belle-mère était au courant. Elle m'a encouragée d'aller avec euh cet homme-là. Je suis partie dans la nuit du seize au dix-sept. Quand je suis entrée dans la maison, le temps de m'asseoir au salon il m'a dit : « Non, ne t'assois pas là ; viens je vais te montrer un endroit plus sécuritaire » (bas). Il m'a emmenée dans la chambre et quand je suis entrée dans la chambre j'ai vite vu, l'épée … qui était accrochée au mur, il avait, il l'avait sortie de l'étui ; et quand j'ai vu l'épée j'ai eu peur. Je commençais à perdre connaissance, donc je disais c'est avec cette épée-là qu'il va me tuer. Il a vite fermé la porte à clé et il m'a dit : « Sauve ta vie ! » C'est le dernier mot que j'ai entendu, j'étais vraiment … perdue. Il m'a déshabillée ; mais le temps de me déshabiller moi j'étais déjà partie ; j'étais comme morte. Donc il m'a violée. Je suis j'ai passé la nuit … là dans la chambre. Très tôt le matin, le monsieur qui m'avait promis qu'il va s'occuper de mes enfants, j'ai appris qu'il est … donc il était devant la maison, il m'attendait. Il disait : « Sors de cette maison, qu'est-ce que tu fais là ? » Je suis sortie, mais je me demandais si mes enfants n'ont pas été tués par ces gens qui sont venus la nuit me chercher. Quand je suis arrivée devant le monsieur, il m'a donné une gifle, je suis tombée ; je m'attendais pas à ça. Je suis rentrée chez moi, là c'était le 17. J'ai demandé à ma belle-mère s'il y a des gens qui sont venus me chercher la nuit. Ma belle-mère m'a dit « Il y a personne qui est venu sauf le monsieur là Kamanzi », celui qui venait de donner la gifle. Lui il est venu me chercher pour me violer, mais il m'a pas trouvée ; donc ma belle-mère lui a dit que j'étais dans la maison euh … à côté. Le 17 je suis restée là, mais je me demandais quelle sera la suite. Le jour suivant c'était le 19, le 18. À neuf heures, il y a eu un groupe de gens ; parmi ces gens il y avait des voisins que je connaissais, mais il y avait aussi des militaires qui sont venus, ils ont envahi la maison ; les voisins ont commencé à faire sortir les objets en se pressant : matelas et tout ce qui était dans la maison. Les militaires nous ont obligés de nous asseoir au salon, ma belle-mère, mes enfants et moi ; chaque personne avec un fusil dans la poitrine et puis ils m'ont fixée pendant une dizaine de minutes dans les yeux … (long silence). Et puis ils m'ont dit : « Viens donner l'argent que ton mari vous a, vous a laissé ». Moi j'avais peur ; lorsqu'ils ont commencé à me tirer, à me sortir du salon pour m'emmener dans la chambre … j'ai essayé de résister mais j'avais pas de forces à cause de la peur. Donc, ils m'ont enlevée de force du salon, et ils m'ont forcée d'entrer dans la chambre ; mais quand je suis arrivée à l'entrée de la chambre, il y a un qui m'a donné une gifle de ce côté-ci, il y a un autre qui m'a donné un coup de pied au coccyx, je sais pas un autre m'a donné un crosse de fusil à l'épaule droite, donc spontanément je suis tombée dans, à l'intérieur de la chambre, je suis tombée évanouie. Le matelas était déjà plié, donc ils m'ont couché sur le lit sans matelas. Là je venais de faire une fausse couche de cinq mois ; je je c'était à peine que je revenais de l'hôpital. Je sais pas le temps que ça a duré mais plus tard je j'ai retrouvé encore conscience et je me suis vue entourée des hommes, une dizaine d'hommes nus, tout nus, moi aussi j'étais nue, les jambes écartées sur le lit. Eux me regardaient d'un regard, sais pas, comment dirais-je ; et puis ils m'ont dit : « Écoute madame on ne va pas te violer … on ne va pas te tuer en utilisant une autre arme ; on va te violer jusqu'à ce que tu meures ». Je suis restée là mais je me disais. Ils m'ont demandé si je savais si le viol pouvait tuer, si on pouvait mourir par viol. J'ai pas répondu. Tous les jours, jour et nuit, ils venaient, en groupe, dix, quinze, une vingtaine – la chambre était … un peu spacieuse-. Ils occupaient toute la chambre parce qu'ils venaient par l'autobus qui assurait le transport en commun. Et puis, un jour je me suis sentie, dépassée, parce que au fur et à mesure que les jours passaient … ma vie était diminuée, j'avais commencé à avoir des problèmes gynécologiques, surtout à cause de, de ce, la fausse couche là que j'avais faite, j'étais encore, le corps était très sensible au choc. Je me suis dit : « Le temps d'attendre que ces gens reviennent encore, il faut que j'aille, mettre fin à ma vie », parce que j'étais dépassée. Je priais mais il n'y avait pas de changement. Je me dis … À côté de chez moi il y avait une, une une fosse commune, là où on jetait jour et nuit, les voisins, les gens qui essayaient de se réfugier ou de fuir en passant pas mon quartier. Et j'entendais leurs cris, le dernier cri parce qu'on les jetait à moitié vivants dans la fosse commune. Je me suis dit : C'est là où je vais me jeter et je vais pas laisser mes enfants parce que il n'y a personne qui va s'en occuper ». Mais le temps de penser par qui je vais commencer, comment je vais procéder pour faire sortir les enfants de la chambre et les emmener dans, vers la fosse commune, j'ai rédigé une petite prière. J'ai dit : « Seigneur, j'ai beau crier vers toi, j'ai demandé secours, t'as pas voulu m'écouter, t'as pas voulu venir à mon aide alors je vais, mettre fin à ma vie et à celle de mes enfants mais sois responsable de mon âme ». Je suis sortie. Quand je suis arrivée devant la porte de la chambre des enfants pour les, les faire sortir, j'ai entendu une voix qui me disait : « Patience, patience », deux fois et c'était une voix rassurante (applaudissements). Je me suis sentie retournée encore une fois vers ma chambre ; je me suis agenouillée, j'ai dit c'est quelqu'un, c'est la voix divine qui me dit de ne pas mettre fin à ma vie. Donc j'ai résisté. Mais au fur et à mesure que les jours passaient les viols ont continué, jusqu'à ce que ces gens m'ont emmenée à la fosse là où j'ai voulu m'emmener avec les enfants, c'était à deux heures du matin. Ils m'ont dit, ils étaient à quatre, quatre militaires, ils avaient confisqué ma carte d'identité. Ils m'ont dit : « On te donne, je te donne le temps de nous dire ton dernier mot. Je leur ai dit : « Est-ce que euh … parce que moi j'enseignais le cours d'éducation civique et là on disait que le Rwanda égale : donc les trois ethnies, les hutus, les twas et les tutsis. Et j'ai dit : « Vous venez d'exterminer une ; est-ce que le Rwanda va continuer d'être appelé Rwanda ou vous allez changer le nom du Rwanda ». Et puis ils venaient de me dire que c'est moi qui restait ; après moi il n'y avait plus d'autres tutsis, c'était moi qui était encore là, tous les autres étaient déjà exterminés. Je leur disais : « Ces gens qui sont morts, ça c'est pas une mort parce que nous nous, nous passons de la vie, de la mort à la vie, mais vous quand vous allez mourir c'est pour de bon parce que autant de fois que vous tuez des tutsis, c'est vous-mêmes, c'est votre vie que vous supprimez ». Tout ça c'était pour les conscientiser. Je suis restée là avec des problèmes gynécologiques très sérieux. J'avais la nausée. L'utérus avait gonflé, j'avais du mal à respirer ; la voie urinaire était bouchée, je pouvais pas uriner, je sais pas ce qui s'était passé et puis … je parvenais pas à savoir. Je parvenais plus à confondre, à … comment, à distinguer les odeurs, je sentais seulement l'odeur du sperme, odeur du sperme, odeur du sperme, rien que ça que je sentais. Le monsieur qui m'avait promis qu'il va s'occuper de mes enfants est revenu, c'était à midi parce qu'à midi les militaires allaient prendre leur repas de midi, je sais où. Il est revenu il m'a dit : moi aussi je suis, je vais te prouver que je suis un homme comme tous ces gens qui viennent te violer chaque jour. Puis je lui 'ai dit : « Qu'est-ce que tu veux dire. Il m'a dit : « Je vais te violer ». J'ai dit : « Je croyais que tu es … le seul hutu qui ne sera pas responsable de mon sang, mais comme tu … tu … comme tu es désigné à … à le faire … » moi j'étais déjà dépassée ; je cherchais à tout prix à mourir mais je pouvais pas. Il a fait tomber son pantalon ; le temps de monter au lit il y a eu euh une roquette qui est tombée dans le coin de la chambre, il y a un éclat qui est tombé, une partie, ça a détruit la tôle Ndlr : le toit) de la maison et puis le monsieur a eu peur ; il est sorti avec son pantalon mais il avait l'intention, il voulait me violer lui aussi. Je ne, … je ne l'ai plus revu. Alors c'était ça mais le temps que le génocide a pris fin moi j'étais vraiment à bout, j'étais, j'avais perdu conscience je savais plus, il n'y avait plus de lien entre mes enfants et moi, parce que je pouvais pas communiquer avec eux, malgré qu'on était dans la même maison. Et, quand j'avais encore un souffle je criais. Et quand je criais ça faisait pleurer les enfants. Ils ne me voyaient pas mais c'est comme s'ils vivaient le même problème que moi je vivais parce que quand je pleurais ils pleuraient, quand je criais, ils criaient. C'est grâce à l'armée du Front patriotique que j'ai pu sortir de la maison et revoir encore le jour (applaudissements).

NOTE

1 Athanasie Mukarwego est cette héroïne du documentaire réalisé par Léo Kalinda : « Mères Courage », une production de Daniel Bertolino

16 Les viols pendant le génocide des Tutsi : Un crime d'envie

EMMANUEL HABIMANA,[1] CAROLE VACHER,[2]
BERTHE KAYITESI,[3] ET CALLIXTE KABAYIZA[4]

Le génocide contre les Tutsi du Rwanda en 1994 a occasionné plus ou moins un million de morts. Cette tragédie qui a duré 100 jours, se caractérise par la proximité physique et sociale très étroite entre les victimes et les bourreaux et le recours aux armes blanches pour faire souffrir les victimes de façon sadique. Parmi celles-ci, plusieurs durent implorer, voire soudoyer les bourreaux au moyen d'importantes sommes d'argent pour être achevées au fusil plutôt que déchiquetées à la machette.[5] Par ailleurs, le génocide des Tutsi du Rwanda se caractérise aussi par l'ampleur des viols et par les mutilations nombreuses et divers rituels sadiques à caractère sexuel. À côté de ces actes d'une extrême cruauté, une indifférence quasi totale du reste de la population. Car la plupart des Hutu qui n'étaient pas impliqués dans les massacres continuèrent néanmoins à s'adonner à leurs activités routinières (travaux aux champs, assistance aux messes chrétiennes du dimanche, baptêmes, mariages).

Préludes au génocide

Le génocide de 1994 s'inscrit dans la continuité de violences, de marginalisation et de discrimination contre les Tutsi depuis 1959, peu avant l'indépendance du pays. Déjà à cette époque, les discours et la propagande du Parmehutu (le parti pour l'émancipation des Hutu) martelaient fort que les Tutsi étaient des envahisseurs : « iwanyu rwose ni muli Abisiniya » (« chez vous – en parlant des Tutsi – c'est l'Abyssinie », actuelle Éthiopie), tel était le leitmotiv d'une des chansons révolutionnaire hutu en 1960.

L'appel à la mobilisation hutu contre la menace tutsi se fit de façon systématique dès cette époque. D'abord les autorités politiques mirent l'accent sur le juste équilibre, qui consistait à renverser les privilèges anciennement détenus par une petite minorité de Tutsi et les attribuer aux Hutu. Discours, slogans et décrets présidentiels furent abondamment utilisés pour justifier et normaliser une sorte de discrimination positive. Mais celle-ci était accompagnée de discours culpabilisants et généralisants qui assimilaient tous les Tutsi (et non plus la petite minorité privilégiée) à des exploiteurs ignobles, arrogants et méprisants à l'endroit de tous les Hutu. Ce mouvement se poursuivit avec la redéfinition de l'histoire du pays qui reconsidérait le peuplement du pays. Les Tutsi furent assimilés à des envahisseurs, à des colonisateurs qu'il aurait convenu de chasser du pays au moment de l'indépendance. Cette propagande était facilitée par le bouillonnement et l'embrasement de tout le continent africain qui réclamait son indépendance à la fin des années 50 et au début des années 60. Mais, alors que dans le reste de l'Afrique les peuples voulaient leur autonomie en chassant les colons, au Rwanda, les Hutu firent alliance avec les colons Belges pour se débarrasser des Tutsi. Un peu partout on assista à des scènes de pillages, d'incendie, de viols, voire de meurtres.

Les Hutu, disaient les propagandistes, ont accueilli gentiment les Tutsi et en guise de gratitude ces derniers les ont méprisés et réduits à l'esclavage. Si les Hutu voulaient s'affranchir, ils n'avaient pas d'autre choix que d'éliminer les Tutsi. C'est en ce moment qu'est apparu le terme « travailler » c'est à dire attaquer et éliminer les Tutsi. L'appel à la mobilisation via les médias en utilisant un tel terme en apparence neutre, voire positif, avait entre autres la fonction d'endormir les étrangers qui ne pouvaient pas se douter que par « travail », on entendait des actions violentes et meurtrières. Les gens étaient appelés à « travailler », avec enthousiasme, avec entrain, et avec énergie, sans relâche. Durant le génocide, l'évocation de l'importance de « bien travailler », de se remettre au « travail » n'était une ambiguïté pour personne, que ce soient les victimes visées qu'étaient les Tutsi, ou pour les bourreaux potentiels qu'étaient les Hutu. Jean Hatzfeld, dans son livre « Une saison de machettes », explique comment le « travail » de tuer était perçu comme une simple banalité par les bourreaux. Ces derniers décrivent leur « travail » en des termes qui dérouter le profane : l'importance de bien apprendre le travail, comment s'exercer sur de jeunes enfants, quels conseils donner aux timides et aux maladroits, comment les encadrer, l'importance d'alterner brimades, compliments et récompenses, etc. Tuer était tellement associé au travail que certains « ouvriers » respectaient scrupuleusement les heures de travail et avaient hâte de rentrer chez eux savourer le repas préparé par leurs épouses et bénéficier d'un repos mérité.[6]

D'autres termes furent exploités avec un sens fabriqué pour la circonstance : « démocratie » par exemple. Comme le pays accédait au vote démocratique, le terme « démocratie » fut habilement falsifié et renversé pour désigner la confiscation des terres appartenant aux Tutsi. Sorte de réforme agraire à la rwandaise, les nouvelles terres servirent à des fins individuelles ou communautaires. Ainsi, même aujourd'hui, les « champs de la démocratie » sont des terrains qui peuvent être utilisés à des fins collectives comme la construction d'écoles, de dispensaires ou de parcelles servant à l'expérimentation de nouveaux produits vivriers, et ce sont généralement des propriétés ayant appartenu aux Tutsi massacrés ou exilés.

En perdant leurs terres qui furent ainsi « démocratisées », des centaines de milliers de Tutsi rescapés furent forcés à l'exil dans les pays limitrophes et des milliers d'autres furent poussés dans des régions jusque là inhospitalières où sévissait la malaria. À ce propos, le témoignage de Mukasonga contient des précieuses informations sur cette déportation intérieure et les persécutions que les Tutsis y ont subies. Née dans le Sud-Ouest du Rwanda, Mukansonga fut déportée encore sur le dos de sa mère dans le Bugesera. Elle décrit cette région ainsi :

> Je ne sais quand mes parents se sont rendus compte qu'on les avait déportés à Nyamata, au Bugesera. Le Bugesera ! Le nom avait quelque chose de sinistre pour tous les Rwandais. C'était une savane presque inhabitée, la demeure des grands animaux sauvages, infestée par la mouche tsé-tsé.[7]

En chassant les Tutsi, les Hutu extrémistes voulaient s'approprier leurs terres et tous leurs biens. Plusieurs auteurs ont élaboré des hypothèses pour expliquer cette tragédie rwandaise. Pour notre part, nous allons tenter de montrer que le génocide des Tutsi du Rwanda découle en grande partie de l'envie ressentie à divers niveaux par les Hutu envers les Tutsi.

Une société rongée par l'envie

Il y a des sociétés compétitives, individualistes et d'autres plus solidaires, des sociétés pieuses et d'autres fanatiques, des sociétés pacifiques ou belliqueuses. Comment peut-on décrire la société rwandaise ? Le premier auteur de cet article est Rwandais et décrit sa culture comme principalement envieuse. La plupart des personnes confondent envie et jalousie. Bien que connexes, ces affects sont différents. En effet, la jalousie est un affect que nous ressentons lorsque quelqu'un risque de nous prendre quelque chose qui nous appartient (par exemple dans la jalousie amoureuse où nous pouvons avoir peur de perdre notre bien-aimé lorsqu'une personne essaye de le séduire). Qu'en est-il de l'envie?

Dans «Envie et gratitude», Klein définit l'envie comme «le sentiment de colère ressenti parce qu'une autre personne possède ou jouit de quelque chose de désirable; la pulsion envieuse étant de prendre cette chose et à défaut de l'avoir de l'endommager».[8] Bien qu'il y ait plusieurs intensités d'envie: l'envie malicieuse, l'envie non malicieuse, l'envie comme source d'émulation,[9] la forme que nous allons développer et qui est répandue au Rwanda est l'envie malicieuse. Celle-ci se caractérise par la colère, la malveillance, la rage, la médisance et divers autres affects, attitudes et comportements négatifs à l'égard de la personne enviée. Dans les cas extrêmes, l'excès de rage pousse l'envieux à détruire l'objet envié. Nous sommes à l'occasion témoins de cas de vandalisme gratuits commis uniquement pour le plaisir de détruire. Les Rwandais ont de tout temps redouté d'être les victimes d'empoisonnement. Or, les empoisonneurs hypothétiques ne sont pas des étrangers mais des proches voisins, et de membres de la famille. Les guérisseurs rwandais mentionnent que la motivation première de ces empoisonneurs est l'envie.[10] En effet, selon les guérisseurs, lorsqu'un membre de la famille ou un voisin est prospère, lorsqu'il a de belles vaches ou des champs plus fertiles, faute de lui ravir ses biens, il faut le faire empoisonner afin qu'il ne puisse pas jouir de ce qu'il a plus que les autres. Il faut faire en sortes que ce voisin prospère qui attise l'envie, ne puisse jamais connaître le bonheur; lui, il faut s'arranger pour que son âme ne soit jamais en paix. Et lorsqu'on est voisin ou parent de cette personne que l'on envie, il faut être aux premières loges pour compatir à ses malheurs, afin qu'il ne vous soupçonne pas d'en être l'origine.

De plus en plus, la richesse première n'est plus le fait d'avoir des vaches mais des enfants intelligents car lorsque ceux-ci réussissent bien à l'école, ils sont promis à un avenir meilleur au point de s'élever au dessus de la masse paysanne, aussi bien eux-mêmes que toute leur famille. Par conséquent, l'empoisonnement des enfants est devenu la menace qui pèse le plus sur les familles. Pour Schoeck, l'envieux ne recherche pas toujours la possession des biens de la personne enviée. Ces biens peuvent ne pas lui être d'aucune utilité. Mais c'est de voir l'autre en tirer plaisir qui fait mal et déclenche le désir de détruire.[11]

En 1960, alors que les Hutu s'exercèrent à faire le «travail» sur les vaches des Tutsi, le désir n'était pas seulement de manger ces dernières, mais de les frapper, de leur donner des coups de machettes partout, puis de les achever pour enfin les manger. Beaucoup de Hutu pauvres auraient pu prendre ces vaches, les élever et avoir plus tard du lait et du fumier pour leurs terres. Mais maltraiter ces animaux donnait plus de jouissance que d'en tirer matériellement profit.

Comment naît l'envie ?

L'envie naît dans un contexte de comparaison sociale. On envie une personne à qui on peut se comparer : celui qui a partagé notre condition, qui nous était par ce fait égal, et qui pour une raison ou une autre nous dépasse aujourd'hui.[12] Il est plus facile d'envier une personne habitant son quartier ou sa colline qu'un étranger. La réussite de ce voisin nous submerge d'une gamme d'émotions : honte, humiliation, tristesse, dépression, colère, et une rage qui ne peut se calmer qu'à la destruction de l'autre. Greenleaf, Segal, et Smith, mentionnent que la personne envieuse considère la personne enviée comme étant responsable de cette rage, d'où la pulsion de la punir, de l'agresser sans la moindre culpabilité puisque l'envieux justifie sa colère comme légitime.[13] C'est donc la faute à la personne enviée, c'est elle qui n'est pas correcte, c'est elle qui déclenche cette animosité et en l'agressant, c'est comme si on posait un acte réparateur, une façon de rétablir la justice face à de telles humiliations.[14] Schoeck et Greenleaf notent que l'envie est plus complexe que d'autres états d'âme. Elle englobe une foule d'affects et d'attitudes ainsi que des réactions physiologiques telles que les palpitations cardiaques, la tension musculaire, la sécheresse de la bouche, des réactions gênées comme un silence soudain, un sourire forcé et une réaction qui trompe rarement : le grincement des dents.[15]

Les crimes de l'envie durant le génocide des Tutsi

Les Hutu avaient plein de choses à envier aux Tutsi : le fait d'avoir été privilégiés et adulés par les Blancs, le fait d'avoir des troupeaux de vaches, animaux qui remplacèrent les houes et les chèvres comme monnaie d'échange et en particulier la dot, le fait de détenir les postes de commandes et de posséder de larges propriétés. Certes la majorité de Tutsi croupissait dans la misère comme un grand nombre de Hutu, mais ce que les Tutsi avaient de plus que les Hutu, y compris les Tutsi pauvres, ce fut la beauté physique. La beauté des Tutsi était tout particulièrement représentée par l'élégance de leurs filles et par la noblesse de leurs traits, des traits fins comme ceux des Blancs avec un nez long, des lèvres minces, des mains fines et des belles jambes. Au contraire, le corps des Hutu était décrit comme grossier, trapu, ayant des traits né- groïdes : nez épaté et lèvres épaisses. À cela s'ajoutait l'intelligence et la ruse chez les premiers et la stupidité chez les seconds.

L'élite hutu s'est vite débarrassée du complexe d'intelligence, et n'avait plus à envier matériellement les Tutsi. Mais le complexe de lai- deur est resté et a été habilement exploité durant le génocide. Si le Hutu riche et instruit pouvait posséder une femme tutsi par le mariage ou le concubinage, le Hutu ordinaire était condamné à regarder avec une distance respectueuse cette belle Tutsi, mince, élégante, et raffinée. Ses fantasmes sexuels à l'égard de cette femme, n'avaient aucune pos- sibilité de se réaliser et restaient inassouvis. Durant le génocide, les autorités hutu allaient exploiter ces manques imaginaires en incitant les extrémistes hutu à posséder, humilier, violer et détruire cette femme tant convoitée, objet de désirs inassouvis, responsable de frustrations sexuelles refoulées. Beaucoup de femmes hutu, encouragèrent les mili- ciens à violer puis à tuer les femmes Tutsi. Landsman rapporte que de passage à Butare, au sud du pays, la célèbre ministre de la famille et des affaires sociales Pauline Nyiramasuhuko donna ordre aux mili- ciens de violer les femmes Tutsi avant de les tuer.[16] Mais certains mili- ciens déclarèrent plus tard qu'ils avaient tellement tué toute la journée qu'ils n'avaient plus l'énergie pour violer ces femmes et qu'ils se sont contentés de les brûler avec de l'essence fournie par la même ministre. Certaines femmes Hutu y compris Pauline Nyiramasuhuko, incitèrent même leurs propres fils à violer. Par ces viols, les femmes Hutu pou- vaient enfin avoir l'impression d'être supérieures à ces femmes Tutsi qui les avaient tant humiliées en prenant leurs frères, et parfois leurs fils. En effet, durant le génocide, tout a été appliqué pour réparer cette injustice de la nature. Il fallait détruire ce qui pouvait rappeler la supé- riorité basée sur la beauté : mutiler le nez parce que les Tutsi sont cen- sés avoir un plus beau nez que les Hutu, mutiler la bouche parce que les lèvres des Tutsi sont plus minces, couper à la machette les jambes des Tutsi afin de les réduire à la taille des courtes jambes des Hutu, couper les mains parce que les doigts des Tutsi sont plus longs, bref détruire totalement cette beauté tant enviée et à l'origine de l'humilia- tion des Hutu.

Les femmes hutu pouvaient se consoler par ce deuxième commande- ment du hutu qui stipule que : «Tout hutu doit savoir que nos filles Hutu sont plus dignes et plus consciencieuses dans leur rôle de femme, d'épouse et de mère de famille. Ne sont-elles pas jolies, bonnes secrétaires et plus honnêtes ? »

Ce deuxième commandement illustre à quel point les Hutu avaient intériorisé leur complexe laideur par rapport aux Tutsi. Chaque fois qu'un Hutu épousait une femme Tutsi, c'était une gifle pour les femmes Hutu. Surtout quand ce Hutu était scolarisé et donc promis à un bel avenir. On peut comprendre le cri de désespoir de ce troisième commandement du Hutu : « Femmes Hutu, soyez vigilantes et ramenez vos maris, vos frères et vos sœurs à la raison ».

Les mariages interethniques majoritairement à sens unique à savoir homme hutu- femme tutsi ont été les pires humiliations pour les femmes hutu, car ces unions renforçaient le stéréotype selon lequel les filles tutsi étaient plus belles que les hutu. C'est donc avec amertume et envie que nombre d'entre elles célébrèrent les noces de leurs frères hutu. Et quand l'heure de la vengeance sonna, certaines femmes n'ont pas hésité à prêter main forte aux miliciens. Ces femmes arrogantes et voleuses d'hommes allaient payer le prix de leur insolence, le prix de leur beauté tant enviée et qui symbolisait la honte et la rancoeur du Hutu.

Dans les premières heures du génocide, beaucoup de Hutu, principalement du sud et du centre du pays qui avaient épousé des femmes tutsi, furent massacrés pour avoir violé le premier commandement « femme tutsi tu n'épouseras ». Pauline Nyiramasuhuko, la ministre de la famille, sera la première femme à être accusée de crimes contre l'humanité pour son rôle dans les viols collectifs et les meurtres des femmes tutsi.[17]

La « libération » des femmes Tutsi ou les viols légalisés

Au début des années 1990, un autre terme, à savoir « libérer » avait comme double sens « reprendre, se réapproprier quelque chose qui a été indûment pris, reprendre ses droits ». L'astuce du double langage est de prendre un terme et de l'investir d'un sens contraire, de sorte que seuls les initiés comprennent ce nouveau sens. Tout comme travailler voulait dire dans les faits tuer, « libérer » voulait dire violer quand appliqué aux femmes, et piller quand appliqué aux choses. « Libérer » revenait à reprendre ses supposés droits, à posséder les femmes qui furent pendant des décennies inaccessibles à la masse hutu. Selon cette perception tordue, il ne s'agissait donc pas ni de viol, ni de vol ; mais plutôt prendre un bien injustement interdit. Bref, les femmes tutsi étaient, à travers ce terme, réduites à des objets à confisquer. Curieusement, après la victoire sur les extrémistes hutu, alors que les nouveaux conquérants se partageaient les maisons et les autres possessions des vaincus, la population généralisa le «kubohoza» (la libération) à la prise de possession des maisons et autres biens abandonnées par leurs propriétaires en fuite ou tués durant la guerre.

Ce détournement du sens des mots, cette perversion du discours, ces anti-phrases permettent de cacher aux étrangers la mise en place d'un plan d'extermination de l'ennemi. Comme le fait remarquer Lochak, une telle manœuvre permet de camoufler la dimension tragique et par conséquent de l'intégrer progressivement dans la vie ordinaire, autant des persécuteurs que des persécutés.[18] Effectivement, même aujourd'hui, lorsque les victimes parlent elles-mêmes de cette violence sexuelle subie, elles utilisent le terme «libération», «barambohoje».[19]

La beauté de la femme Tutsi était considérée comme l'arme secrète ayant permis aux Tutsi de dominer les Hutu durant des siècles.[20] Il fallait détruire cette arme ou voir les Hutu retomber dans la servitude.

> Tout Hutu doit savoir qu'une femme Tutsi, où qu'elle soit, travaille à la solde de son ethnie tutsi. Par conséquent est traître tout Hutu qui épouse une femme Tutsi, qui fait d'elle sa concubine, sa secrétaire ou sa protégée.[21]

C'est le premier des dix commandements des Hutu. Il cible directement l'alliance entre l'homme Hutu et la femme Tutsi! Au moment où les extrémistes Hutu commencèrent à dresser les listes des ennemis à abattre, et qu'ils passèrent à l'acte dans les minutes mêmes qui ont suivi l'écrasement de l'avion présidentiel, on peut imaginer la terreur qui secoua les milliers de Hutu qui avaient contracté des alliances matrimoniales avec les Tutsi, alliances connues de tout le monde dans ce pays densément peuplé où toutes les personnes de la colline ou du quartier se connaissent entre elles. Parmi les centaines des Hutu modérés haut-placés exécutés dans les heures et les jours qui suivirent, nombre d'entre eux avaient épousé des femmes Tutsi.

Face au drame rwandais, la question souvent posée est celle-ci: «comment se fait-il que des milliers de Hutu, toutes classes sociales confondues, aient massacré de sang froid leurs amis, voisins et parents Tutsi par alliance?» Est-ce la peur de représailles qui a poussé tant de monde à une collaboration aussi aveugle? Ou est ce dû à la perversité de la nature humaine?[22] On a un élément de réponse dans le commandement suivant.

Quatrième commandement: «... *est traître tout Hutu* qui fait alliance avec les Tutsi dans les affaires, qui investit son argent dans une entreprise d'un Tutsi, qui accorde aux Tutsi des faveurs dans les affaires (licence d'importation, prêts bancaires, parcelles de construction etc.). » Au déclenchement du génocide, des milliers de Hutu infidèles à la cause hutu étaient automatiquement désignés, car ils étaient connus pour brasser des affaires avec les Tutsi. Mais si la peur de représailles peut expliquer en partie le nombre excessivement important de collaborateurs, elle ne peut expliquer la violence, la cruauté et le sadisme des génocidaires à l'encontre de leurs victimes, dont l'une des manifestations est le viol des femmes Tutsi. Au même titre que le massacre des enfants, le viol des femmes constitue la destruction du présent et de l'avenir du groupe que vise un génocide.

Dans ce sens, Primo Levi, rescapé de l'Holocauste, décrit la violence génocidaire en ces termes : « Je crois que les années hitlériennes ont partagé leur violence avec beaucoup d'autres espaces temps historiques, mais qu'elles sont caractérisées par une inutile violence diffuse, devenue une fin en soi visant uniquement à créer de la douleur [...] ».[23] En poussant la violence à l'extrême, le persécuteur crée un gouffre, une distance infranchissable entre lui et sa victime. Cette mesure vise à effacer toute ressemblance entre lui et sa victime et rend le passage à la destruction physique plus facile. D'après Garapon « le crime contre l'humanité naît dans la perte de cette commune mesure des actions »,[24] où le bourreau tient la victime à son entière disposition, comme un objet, une quelconque chose, sans valeur. C'est avec cette même intention de rendre moins qu'humain, que peut être classé le viol des femmes mais aussi d'hommes et d'enfants, lors du génocide perpétré contre les Tutsis du Rwanda.

Le viol : Un acte entouré de silence

Selon plusieurs sources[25] au moins 250 000 femmes Tutsi auraient été violées durant le génocide. D'autres chercheurs estiment que 70% des femmes rescapées, que ce soit des fillettes de moins de 10 ans ou des femmes de plus de 60 ans, auraient été violées. On relate aussi le viol des hommes et des jeunes garçons mais leur estimation est incertaine. En réalité, l'ampleur des viols durant le génocide restera sans doute inconnue parce que pour plusieurs raisons, les victimes ne veulent pas en parler. Tout d'abord, la mentalité selon laquelle une femme violée est impure perdure, même si on reconnaît généralement qu'elle est victime d'une agression. Et comme le souligne Guenivet (2006), « Le corps, par les tabous qu'il incarne, est utilisé à des degrés différents par les forces gouvernementales et les groupes paramilitaires qui y voient un outil de répression et d'oppression politique». Cette stigmatisation pousse les victimes à taire leur drame, et la honte ressentie les amène à se percevoir comme des damnées.[26]

L'ampleur du viol des femmes Tutsi n'est pas seulement stupéfiante par le nombre de victimes, elle l'est aussi par les procédés auxquels eurent recours les tortionnaires:

> Le viol est précédé d'une phase de terreur, les miliciens forçaient les femmes à assister au massacre de leur famille. Puis d'une phase d'humiliation où parfois, un père, un frère où un fils était forcé de violer une de ses proches. Cet inceste «sous la menace» permettait de détruire tout lien filial et participait au processus de déshumanisation par l'élimination des garde-fous sociaux et religieux. Arrive le viol, instant ultime lors duquel s'expriment toutes les frustrations sociales à travers le vocable «vous les Tutsis, vous avez toujours été fiers, maintenant, nous allons savoir quel goût vous avez» et la volonté «à tout prix» de pénétrer «l'autre» avec son sexe ou tout autre objet phallique. Alors seulement vient la destruction des moyens de reproduction, l'ablation des signes ethniques distinctifs, la poitrine, le nez, les doigts (que l'on garde comme trophée) et la mort qui vient presque comme un cadeau que l'on fait à la victime, une délivrance comparée aux souffrances qu'elle a endurées. Une mort qui parfois s'achète: de l'argent contre une balle plutôt que la machette.[27]

Totten mentionne également des cas où les tortionnaires introduisaient divers objets dans les organes génitaux de leurs victimes, leur coupaient les seins, ou éventraient celles qui étaient enceintes en jetant les fœtus aux chiens.

Il eut des viols collectifs, des femmes furent forcées de marcher nues en plein jour, on accoupla les femmes à des personnes atteintes de sida pour les contaminer, et pour humilier encore ces femmes, on les fit violer par les Batwa.[28] Quiconque étranger à la culture rwandaise aurait des difficultés à saisir l'importance de ce fait et la profondeur de l'humiliation qui est cachée derrière. Mais pour une femme rwandaise, avoir des rapports sexuels avec un homme de l'ethnie «Twa» est la déchéance totale. En effet, l'ethnie Twa était objet de discrimination des deux groupes majoritaires et toute proximité physique était exclue, fussent les salutations par le toucher.

La femme violée n'est pas seulement agressée dans ce qu'elle a de plus intime, elle est condamnée à la honte d'elle-même, à la honte de son corps. C'est comme si le violeur habite son corps car elle ne peut plus se regarder, se toucher ou se laisser toucher sans penser à lui. Par ailleurs, le violeur garde une emprise sur elle en la réduisant au silence, car elle risque de revivre les détails les plus atroces du viol si elle décide de l'exposer au grand jour. Que ce soit au Rwanda ou ailleurs, la femme violée est souvent contrainte à choisir de taire le viol. Se taire parce que dévoiler revient à exposer sa pudeur et à raviver le traumatisme. Comment nommer une telle agression et la souffrance qu'elle engendre? Quels termes utiliser? Comment dénoncer un pareil crime tout en préservant ce qui reste du peu d'intimité lorsque le viol a été accompagné par des actes sadiques? Quels faits ou propos pris dans les nombreux souvenirs douloureux la femme peut-elle rapporter, en particulier si elle est face à son bourreau, qui, par sa présence, rappelle et reproduit la vivacité de l'horreur? Par ailleurs, comment se sentir épaulé face aux juges et aux avocats qui mènent l'instruction, enfermés dans la neutralité et les rituels exigés par leurs fonctions! En effet, ceux qui font l'instruction sur ces crimes posent des questions et veulent des détails précis. Or, l'éducation et les coutumes n'encouragent pas à nommer certains de ces détails, tels que les organes génitaux, et encore moins les objets qu'on y a introduits. Demander à une femme violée de donner des précisions sur son drame provoque la honte chez la victime, cela peut déclencher la reviviscence du viol. Dans plusieurs rapports sur le drame des femmes violées, celles-ci soulignent qu'elles ont peur de s'exposer au mépris, aux jugements, à la condescendance, voire à la crainte de ne pas trouver de conjoint. C'est donc un secret lourd à porter, un secret que l'on a même peur de partager avec le meilleur des confidents. Certaines femmes violées ne veulent pas retourner dans leur village parce que tout le monde sait qu'elles y ont été violées et elles ne veulent pas croiser le regard des anciens voisins. De là, le dilemme de témoigner, car le faire équivaut à se livrer, à dévoiler le secret tant gardé. À titre d'exemple, un rescapé témoin du viol d'une rescapée, confiait son impossibilité à révéler l'entièreté de son expérience, car il ne pouvait évoquer cet épisode qui impliquait l'autre personne, alors que cette dernière avait choisi le silence. Du coup, ce n'est plus seulement la victime du viol qui est enfermée mais aussi ceux avec qui elle partage ce lourd secret.

Certes la société rwandaise reconnaît l'importance d'aider les victimes, de les écouter, de les soutenir. Mais cela ne signifie pas pour autant que les hommes soient sensibilisés et préparés, à tendre les bras aux femmes violées et à les accepter. Dans la tradition rwandaise, vivre avec une conjointe violée est vécu comme humiliant notamment par peur des moqueries de la part des autres. De même, les enfants dont les mères ont été violées vivent dans la hantise que ce drame puisse être dévoilé, par crainte d'être l'objet d'insultes et de mépris de la part des autres. Toute la famille est donc condamnée à taire cet avilissement. Dans le cas d'une jeune femme, taire le viol lui donne l'espoir d'avoir des prétendants, s'ils sont tenus dans l'ignorance, non par désir délibéré de dissimuler un fait aussi important, mais par peur de blesser l'être aimé. Guenivet résume ainsi cette tragédie :

> ... quel avenir la paix offre-t-elle à ces femmes qui vivent cloîtrées dans un silence qu'on leur impose parce que rien ou presque n'est mis en place (...) au Rwanda ou ailleurs pour leur permettre de se reconstituer ? Aucune réponse à leur douleur, aucun suivi psychologique, aucune considération mais bien du mépris pour celles qui ont vécu « l'indicible ». Leurs bourreaux avaient raison de les laisser vivre en leur disant « tu es déjà morte ». Elles ne sont plus que des ombres d'elles-mêmes qui doivent se battre contre leurs fantômes, leurs peurs mais aussi la culpabilité inhérente à toutes les victimes de sévices sexuels. Quelles seront leurs chances d'accepter leurs enfants nés de ces viols, ces « enfants du mauvais souvenir » si elles n'ont pas la force de s'accepter elles- mêmes ? [29]

Certes, quelques thérapeutes et tout particulièrement l'AVEGA (association des veuves du génocide) font un travail remarquable pour aider quelques-unes de victimes, mais la majorité des femmes violées restent emmurées dans le silence. C'est donc un défi de taille auquel sont confrontés les intervenants car on ne peut atténuer une telle souffrance sans nommer le mal qui ronge, ce mal corrosif comme la rouille sur un métal enfoui dans le sol.

La femme Tutsi, une véritable obsession pour les Hutu durant le génocide

Depuis l'indépendance du pays en 1962, le mariage hutu-tutsi a donné lieu à un métissage ethnique, au point que 40 ans plus tard, il fut quasiment impossible de trouver une famille tutsi n'ayant pas donné en mariage au moins une de ses filles à une famille hutu. On peut présumer que plusieurs de ces mariages furent le résultat d'un véritable amour. Mais dans d'autres cas, il y a lieu de penser que de nombreux Hutu riches, puissants ou scolarisés pouvaient enfin réaliser le fantasme de posséder des femmes tutsi réputées plus belles que les femmes hutu. Du côté des Tutsi, le mariage ou le concubinage avec les Hutu au pouvoir leur permettait de sauver quelques membres de leurs familles de la discrimination et de l'exclusion sociale, en ayant accès à quelques places dans les écoles ou à la fonction publique pour contourner la politique de l'équilibre ethnique. L'armée rwandaise, qui était essentiellement hutu, était par contre strictement opposée au mariage mixte surtout lorsque celui-ci impliquait un officier hutu. Les mariages mixtes étaient également critiqués, aussi bien par les Hutu que par les Tutsi, ce qui ne favorisait pas l'harmonie au sein du couple. Très souvent, les belles-familles hutu acceptaient rarement les femmes tutsi, car perçues comme arrogantes ; et d'un autre coté la parenté tutsi exprimait un certain mépris à l'endroit des femmes qui étaient parties épouser des Hutu. Ces préjugés respectifs n'ont pas empêché la multiplication des mariages mixtes, d'autant plus que d'un groupe ethnique à l'autre, on faisait semblant qu'il n'y avait pas problème. Les Rwandais sont en général portés à taire des propos blessants, ce que certains qualifieraient de dissimulation. Mais c'est le prix à payer pour préserver un équilibre social dans un pays où les gens se côtoient quotidiennement et où le contexte social les force à se prêter une assistance mutuelle de façon régulière. En effet, même après le génocide, avec les horreurs qu'a connues le pays, beaucoup de gens continuent à faire comme s'ils ont toujours été de bons amis, voisins ou collègues. Aborder de front les conflits, reconnaître qu'il y a un malaise, évoquer des injustices, la discrimination ou le génocide, que ce soit à l'école ou au travail, demeure tabou.

Conclusion

Le viol des femmes tutsi au Rwanda fut caractérisé par une multitude d'horreurs. Il fut utilisé comme arme ultime pour exterminer les Tutsi. Des milliers de femmes furent violées mutilées et enterrées dans les fosses communes ou jetées dans les latrines. Les miliciens rivalisèrent d'imagination pour venger la honte associée à leur infériorité par rapport aux Tutsi. Dans l'histoire moderne, le génocide des Tutsi du Rwanda est le plus grand crime de l'envie. L'historiographie devrait retenir qu'on fit porter aux victimes la responsabilité de ce crime, que les victimes contaminées par le VIH moururent sans soins alors que leurs bourreaux, nourris et logés eurent droit aux traitements. Le viol des femmes a aussi donné lieu aux naissances de ce qu'on appelle les « enfants de la honte ». Ils sont par dizaines de milliers ostracisés par la société et sans véritable avenir. Si les signes de reconstruction physique sont bien palpables, voire impressionnants, la reconstruction psychologique des femmes violées et des enfants rescapés reste à faire.

NOTES

1 Professeur, Département de psychologie, Université du Québec à Trois-Rivières.
2 Université de Montréal, département de service social.
3 Université d'Ottawa, département d'éducation.
4 Centre Rebero de recherche et d'intervention en santé mentale.
5 S. Totten, "The Plight and Fate of Female during and following the 1994 Rwandan Genocide," in S. Totten, ed., *Plight and Fate of Women During and Following Genocide* (New Brunswick: Transaction, 2009).
6 Jean Hatzfeld, *Dans le nu de la vie. Récits des marais rwandais* (Paris: Seuil, 2000).
7 S. Mukasonga, *Inyenzi ou les Cafards* (Paris: Gallimard, 2006), 19.
8 Mélanie Klein, *Envie et gratitude et autres essais* (Paris: Gallimard, 1957).
9 Pour plus de détails voir Klein; Emmanuel Habimana et Line Massé, "Envy manifestations and personality disorders," *European Psychiatry* 15, no. 1 (2000): 15–21; Nicole Jeammet, *Le plaisir et le péché: Essai sur l'envie* (Paris: Desclée de Brouwer, 1998); Helmut Schoeck, *Envy: A Theory of Social Behaviour* (New York: Harcourt, Brace, and World, 1969).
10 Emmanuel Habimana, « Envie comme cause d'attribution des maladies mentales *ibitega* ». Thèse de doctorat en psychologie, Université du Québec à Montréal, 1989. Emmanuel Habimana et Michel Tousignant (2003). « Les pratiques de sorcellerie et les Ibitega au Rwanda: une étiologie de la psychose autour de l'envie », *Cahiers de psychologie clinique* 21, no. 2 (2003): 219–29.
11 Helmut Schoeck, *Envy: A Theory of Social Behaviour* (New York: Harcourt, Brace, and World, 1969).
12 Peter Salovey, "Social Comparison Processes in Envy and Jealousy," in J. Suls and T. A. Wills, eds., *Social Comparison: Contemporary Theory and Research* (Hillsdale, NJ: Lawrence Erlbaum Associates, 1991), 261–86.
13 Victoria C.G. Greenleaf, *Envy: A Survey of Its Psychology and History Fort Bragg* (California: Cypress House, 2009); Hanna Segal, *Introduction to*

the Work of Melanie Klein (New York: Basic Books, 1975); et Richard H. Smith, "Envy and the Sense of Injustice, " in P. Salovey, ed., *The Psychology of Jealousy and Envy* (New York: Guilford Press, 1991), 79–102.

14 Helmut Schoeck, *Envy: A Theory of Social Behaviour* (New York: Harcourt, Brace, and World, 1969).

15 Helmut Schoeck, *Envy: A Theory of Social Behaviour* (New York: Harcourt, Brace, and World, 1969); et Victoria C.G. Greenleaf, *Envy. A Survey of Its Psychology and History Fort Bragg* (California: Cypress House; Hanna Segal, 2009).

16 Peter Landesman, "A Woman's Work," *New York Times*, 15 September 2002.

17 African Rights, "Rwanda: Not So Innocent. When Women Become Killers" (1995), http://www.africanrights.org/publications/Innocent895.pdf.

18 D. Lochak, «La doctrine sous Vichy ou les mésaventures du positivisme», dans *Les usages sociaux du droit*, 251–85 (Paris: PUF, 1989).

19 D. Gishoma et Brackelaire. «Quand le corps abrite l'inconcevable. Comment dire le bouleversement dont témoignent les corps au Rwanda?» *Cahiers de psychologie clinique* 1, no. 30 (2008): 159–83.

20 Jean Pierre Chrétien, *Rwanda: Les medias du génocide* (Paris: Kathala, 1995); Karima Guenivet, «Femmes, les nouveaux champs de bataille», *Quasimodo* 9 (*Corps en guerre: Imaginaires, idéologies, destructions*, tome 2), Montpellier, 197–213.

21 Kangura, «Les dix commandements du Hutu», *Bimensuel indépendant* 6 (Déc. 1990): 6–8.

22 P. Zimbardo, *The Lucifer Effect: Understanding How Good People Turn Evil* (New York: Random House, 2008).

23 Primo Levi, *Les Naufragés et les rescapés: Quarente ans après Auschwitz* (Paris: Gallimard pour la traduction française, 1989), 104–5.

24 D'après A. Garapon, *Des crimes qu'on ne peut ni juger ni pardonner: Pour une justice internationale* (Paris: Odile Jacob, 2002), 128.

25 African Rights, Human Rights Watch, *Shattered Lives: Sexual Violence during the Rwandan Genocide and Its Aftermath* (New York: Human Rights Watch, 1996); Landesman, "A Woman's Work"; Françoise Nduwimana, *Le droit de survivre: Femmes, violence sexuelle et vih/sida* (Montréal: Droit et démocratie, 2004); UNIFEM, "A Life Free of Violence Is Our Right!" *The UN Trust Fund to End Violence against Women: 10 Years of Investment* (United Nations Development Fund for Women, 2007).

26 African Watch.

27 Guenivet, «Femmes, les nouveaux champs de bataille», 200.

28 African Watch; Nduwimana, *Le droit de survivre*, 2004.

29 Guenivet, "Femmes, les nouveaux champs de bataille," 211.

17 Hearing the Untold Story: Documenting LGBTI Lives in Rwanda

VALERIE LOVE

Archives have historically been spaces that reflect the histories and stories of those in power. The voices of the poor, the unwell, the persecuted, and the abused are seldom heard. It is rare for survivors of political violence or human rights abuses to have documentation of what they have endured. When war and catastrophe strike, people flee their homes and workplaces, leaving everything behind, sometimes never to return. Photographs and paper documentation, such as letters and diaries, are easily destroyed – assuming such documents even existed in the first place. Electronic records can be deleted and files can become corrupted in an instant. Hard drives and disks too are fragile and can fail. The destruction of cultural heritage is characteristic of many contemporary global conflicts and serves to further degrade and decimate communities. For communities and individuals literally struggling to survive, maintaining any sort of documentation may be impossible. Yet the absence of these histories of marginalized and persecuted communities or individuals can have serious political implications. The lesbian, gay, bisexual, transgender, and intersex (LGBTI)[1] community in post-genocide Rwanda has confronted this reality. This chapter explores my experiences as an American archivist working with this community during the summer of 2009, and offers a preliminary analysis from the documentation study I conducted with members of the LGBTI community in Kigali, Rwanda, and the impact of the greater visibility of the LGBTI community in Rwanda since then.

Since 1994, Rwanda, a small mountainous country in Central / East Africa, has become all but synonymous with genocide. For three months following the assassination of President Juvénal Habyarimana on 6 April 1994, Rwanda descended into a gruesome and highly orchestrated genocide in which between 800,000 and 1 million people, primarily from the Tutsi ethnic group, were killed.[2] Rwandans were killed at roadside checkpoints, in their homes, and in hospitals, schools, and churches where Tutsis gathered seeking shelter. While Rwanda's history and culture had been mostly ignored by Western scholars before the genocide, after 1994, literature on Rwanda and the genocide surged into appearance. While sexual orientation was not a factor in the genocide, contemporary Rwandan society is indeed shaped by the violence that occurred in 1994.[3] The post-genocide government of Rwanda drafted a new constitution in 2003, legally enshrining the concept of equality among all Rwandans. As article 11 of Rwanda's constitution states:

> All Rwandans are born and remain free and equal in rights and duties.
>   Discrimination of whatever kind based on, inter alia, ethnic origin, tribe, clan, colour, sex, region, social origin, religion or faith, opinion, economic status, culture, language, social status, physical or mental disability or any other form of discrimination is prohibited and punishable by law.[4]

Sexual orientation and gender identity and expression, however, are noticeably missing from this list. Although there are no laws in Rwanda explicitly criminalizing same-sex relations, the LGBTI community faces widespread invisibility and intolerance in Rwandese society. A 2010 article on Behind the Mask,[5] a now-defunct South African website that reported on LGBT issues in Africa between 2000 and 2012, offers a glimpse of the climate for LGBT Rwandans:

> Despite the emergence of movements that have began advocating for the rights of sexual minority groups, many people in Rwanda continue to deny the existence of homosexuality in the country … Dr. Raphael Gasinzigwa also told *Izuba Rirashe* (Rwandan newspaper) that homosexuality is "total deviation, sicknesses, and that such people are mentally disturbed and need treatment."[6]

The history regarding homosexuality and same-sex relationships in Rwanda, as in much of Africa, is a history marked by silence, and often one written by outsiders.[7] Colonial explorers and many early Western anthropologists denied that homosexuality existed in Africa, a view which is now held by many Africans themselves, who vehemently deny the existence of homosexuality in their own cultures.[8] As Cary

Alan Johnson, current executive director and former senior Africa specialist for the International Gay and Lesbian Human Rights Commission (IGLHRC), wrote in 1986 for an article on gay men in neighbouring Zaire (now the Democratic Republic of the Congo): "Homosexuality is a subject most Africans don't like to discuss. Many have accepted the myth that it doesn't exist in Africa, or if it does, that it was imported by Europeans."[9] Other researchers based their studies on the writings of European colonizers and perpetuated the fallacy that homosexuality does not traditionally occur in Africa. As Daniel B. Hrdy states,

> Nowhere in traditional African society is there the kind of sequential homosexual activity between men that is found in urban Western societies ... Most Africanists uniformly deny the presence of significant homosexual activity, as do Africans themselves. It is likely that, as elsewhere in the world, there are pockets of homosexuality in Africa, but homosexuality does not seem to be practiced as overtly and commonly as in other parts of the world. [10]

Historical evidence of male same-sex relationships in Rwanda and throughout African societies does, however, exist. Anthropologist Jacques Maquet briefly discusses same-sex relations among men in his 1961 book, *The Premise of Inequality in Ruanda: A Study of Political Relations in a Central African Kingdom*, stating that "homosexuality was widespread among Tutsi and Hutu young men,"[11] though he later clarifies that homosexuality "was almost exclusively ascribed to the lack of heterosexual contacts."[12] In his 2008 book *Heterosexual Africa?* Mark Epprecht states that "anthropologists, historians, and other social scientists were by [the 1960s and 1970s] revealing significant male-male sexual subcultures that existed side by side or were hidden within the heterosexual norms."[13] Heterosexist stereotypes about Africa cause much of this history to remain overlooked. Johnson, too, reminds us that "western images of gays and the self images of publicly known European homosexuals in Africa are incompatible with African gays, the vast majority of whom are married, affianced, have children, or are part of strong family units."[14]

This absence of a visible and known history creates significant challenges for the LGBTI community in Rwanda today. As Stephen Murray and Will Roscoe explain, "claims [that homosexuality is uncommon in Africa] are not merely a matter of scholarly interpretation. They have genuine social consequences because they stigmatize those who engage in homosexual behaviour and those who are grappling with gay identities."[15] In Rwanda, people I spoke with often insisted that same-sex relationships are "something new" and are antithetical to traditional east African culture,[16] a claim which I heard even among self-identified human rights activists in Rwanda. Because of the absence of a recognized history, LGBTI people in Rwanda are in the uneasy position of continually having their existence denied by the authorities and society as a whole, yet the fact that they face such widespread discrimination provides a perverse recognition of the existence of same-sex relationships in east Africa. *The Johannesburg Statement on Sexual Orientation, Gender Identity and Human Rights*, adopted in South Africa in 2004, elaborates on this phenomenon as well:

> Across Africa, we face human rights abuses which threaten our safety, our livelihoods, and our lives. That we are targets of such abuse proves that we exist – states do not persecute phantoms or ghosts. It also proves the necessity for action to safeguard our real situations and our basic rights.[17]

Scholarly literature regarding sexual orientation and gender identity expression in east and central Africa is still limited, particularly in comparison to Southern and even west African nations. A literature review conducted in May 2009 prior to my trip to Rwanda produced little information on sexual orientation in English-language scholarly journals.[18] Yet information on the subject from human rights organizations is growing. Non-government organizations have published reports on LGBTI issues throughout the region, and documents such as *The Johannesburg Statement* and Stephen Barris's report from the 2007 World Social Forum in Nairobi, Kenya, offer additional insights into the experiences of African LGBTI individuals.[19] In June 2009, the international non-governmental organization Human Rights Watch released a report titled *Together Apart: Organizing around Sexual Orientation and Gender Identity Worldwide*,[20] which documented the climate and difficulties for lesbian, gay, bisexual, and transgender (LGBT) individuals in fifty countries in the global south. The report provided an analysis of responses to a survey sent to LGBT organizations around the world. While they had received responses from activists in Uganda, Burundi, and other east African countries, there was no information in the report specifically regarding LGBT issues in Rwanda.[21] In advance of Rwanda's consideration before the United Nations Human Rights Committee's 95th session, from 16 March to 3 April 2009, the Coalition of African Lesbians (CAL), Global Rights, Horizon Community Association (HOCA), and IGLHRC partnered with the International Human Rights Clinic at the Harvard University Law School to release a shadow report assessing Rwanda's compliance with the International Covenant on Civil and Political Rights (ICCPR) in regard to the treatment of LGBT individuals in Rwanda.[22] While the shadow report lists incidents of harassment, discrimination, and violence at the hands of police and others in Rwandan society, it does not provide an account of daily life for LGBTI Rwandans. The first government-sanctioned study of men who have sex with men (MSM) – *Exploring HIV Risk among MSM in Kigali, Rwanda*, led by the National AIDS Control Commission (CNLS) of Rwanda – was released in July 2009, focusing on sexual health and HIV risk behaviours. It also provided a limited quantitative analysis of survey participants who reported experiencing discrimination, abuse, or stigma regarding their sexual orientation.[23]

Increasingly, organizations and LGBTI citizen journalists are sharing experiences and information on the Internet, both within Rwanda and with the transnational queer community. The digital divide in urban Rwanda is rapidly shrinking, and the use of social networking tools is increasing. At the time of my work in Rwanda in the summer of 2009, everyone I spoke with in the LGBTI community had an email address; however, only a few had a Facebook profile or a presence on other social websites, and those who did told me that they did not use Facebook regularly. In the time since then, a majority of people I interviewed have joined Facebook and now do use the Internet to share information and meet others in the global LGBTI community. The amount of online information on LGBTI issues in Rwanda is expanding as well. In addition to the aforementioned NGO reports, information on LGBTI life in Rwanda, as well as advocacy campaigns against proposed legislation criminalizing homosexuality in Rwanda and neighbouring countries, has begun appearing on websites and blogs as the east African LGBTI community becomes more outspoken.[24] Yet, despite the recent emergence of information online, virtually no documentation of LGBTI lives in Rwanda exists in archival repositories in Rwanda or outside the country. This is particularly problematic given the general instability of websites and their vulnerability to outages, broken links, corrupted files, or even cyberattack.[25]

Hearing the Unheard: Voices from the LGBTI
Community in Rwanda

Philosopher and theorist Jacques Derrida argues that archives go beyond providing a record of the past, that in fact they "should call into
question the coming of the future."[26] Documentation of marginalized
communities and human rights violations, in particular, may provide
the best evidence for this philosophy. By documenting past and contemporary conditions, human rights archival collections and oral histories
can have an added impact on the future, providing a contextualization
that may help more accurately interpret the past and present. Communities can employ oral history to document atrocities committed against
individuals and groups but also to preserve – and lend continuity to –
the struggles for social justice worldwide. Where traditional records are
lacking, oral histories can provide a historical understanding of the root
causes of contemporary conflict and social injustice, and offer legitimacy
and voice to groups and individuals who have been silenced or whose
histories have been denied. Mary Marshall Clark, director of the Oral
History Research Office at Columbia University and leader of the Telling
Lives September 11 Documentation Project in New York City, has written that oral history "investigate[s] the silences."[27] For LGBTI Rwandans,
the silences are all too common and all too real.

LGBTI activists in Rwanda who are working to increase recognition
and acceptance of gay men and lesbians in Rwandan society have begun speaking out about their experiences, providing first-hand, though
often anonymous, testimony about feeling same-sex attractions long
before they ever encountered Westerners or Western culture. During the
summer of 2009, I participated in a human rights delegation to Rwanda
sponsored by the American organization Global Youth Connect. As part
of the delegation, we participated in a seven-day cross-cultural human
rights workshop in Kigali with both American and Rwandese participants. An additional nine days of the delegation were devoted to engaging in service projects with Rwandese organizations working on a
variety of human rights issues including land rights, reproductive
health and sexuality, and youth empowerment through theatre and
the arts. Global Youth Connect assigned me to work with Horizon
Community Association (HOCA), a grassroots organization that advocates for the rights of Rwanda's LGBTI community. In their application
to participate in the Global Youth Connect human rights delegation,
HOCA described their mission and work as follows:

Lesbians and gays in Rwanda face discrimination and hardship on a daily basis, which has a profound impact on their quality of life. Though homosexuality is not against the law in Rwanda, many individuals find themselves harassed, threatened, imprisoned or abused because of their sexual orientation. Discrimination, and even physical violence, is a daily reality for many of those who are open about their sexual orientation, and as a result, many gays and lesbians live a secretive life, unable to tell their families or friends about their sexual orientation. There is a lack of social services targeting the gay and lesbian community, as Rwandan society and the Rwandan government prefers to deny or ignore the existence of a gay and lesbian community.[28]

Prior to the start of the volunteer placement, I met with the director of HOCA to discuss possible projects and collaborations. When I explained to her that I was an archivist and librarian in the United States, she asked me if I would be willing to conduct oral histories with HOCA members and create a documentation study in order to "help get the community's stories out there."[29] She also requested my help building a website for HOCA.[30] The goal of the project was both to create documentation that HOCA could use in advocacy campaigns in Rwanda, and to create a duplicate record of the stories and my experiences that I could make known and ensure were preserved in my institution's archives and special collections in the United States.

I initially expressed reservations about the project. I hadn't planned to conduct oral histories while in Rwanda and hadn't brought any equipment with me – no cassette or voice recorders, no microphone, no video camera. All I had were a laptop, a spiral notepad, and a five-year-old digital camera that could film only three minutes of video at a time. More importantly, I worried that my involvement in writing Web content and conducting an oral history project might, in fact, work against the goals of the organization. I wanted to be an ally to the Rwandese LGBTI community and to support HOCA's work, but I also worried that my presence as a white, lesbian-identified American might cause more harm than good to HOCA's advocacy efforts in a society where same-sex relationships are often considered antithetical to Rwandan culture and a result of external influences.[31] But the director assured me that she and HOCA wanted to work with me, and that HOCA had partnered with a number of international human rights organizations and activists in the past and felt that it was important to have an international coalition working on equality for LGBTI people in Rwanda.[32]

HOCA did the work of notifying its members of the project and gathering participants for me. At the time, HOCA had thirty-five members, and thirteen people participated in the project, all of whom identified themselves as gay, lesbian, bisexual, or transgender. The participants were all members of HOCA and all knew each other before gathering for the documentation study. One participant initially expressed reservations about speaking to an outsider after previously giving an interview for another project and then never hearing from the interviewer again.[33] But I soon discovered that most members of HOCA indeed wanted to share their stories with me and yearned for solidarity and connection beyond their small group. The lack of open dialogue about LGBTI issues in Rwanda resulted in a craving for conversation and a safe space to talk about their lives. I do not speak Kinyarwanda, and my French is rudimentary at best, but despite the language barrier, I often came back to the guesthouse where I was staying in Kigali to find people outside my room, waiting to talk to me with whatever English phrases they could. In order to conduct the oral histories, I needed an interpreter to translate between English and Kinyarwanda. For the safety and privacy of those I was interviewing, the translator was always a member of the group who also identified as LGBTI; however, this created logistical challenges. Initially, the head of the organization served as translator, but was only available for one day. As a result, we attempted to conduct all of the oral history interviews in a single session, though I was able to conduct a small number of follow-up questions with a second translator.

In effect, the project turned out to be more of a focus group interview than a traditional documentation project or oral history. The thirteen participants crammed into my dormitory-sized room at the guesthouse, crowded together on the squeaky metal twin bed or seated beside me on the concrete floor, where I had stretched out my yoga mat for cushioning. I asked a question, which was then be translated to Kinyarwanda, and we went around the room asking each person to answer, if they felt comfortable doing so. Four participants gave their answers in English, and the rest responded to the questions in Kinyarwanda, which was then translated to English for me.[34] Aside from one participant who was nineteen, the remaining participants were all in their twenties and thirties. In exchange for speaking with me, participants asked me to share my notes from the interviews with them, in order to have documentation of their own stories. I complied with the request, though for privacy and safety reasons, I did not include any names or contact information in the notes that I shared with the director of HOCA and with individual participants.[35]

Prior to the interviews, I met with the head of the organization to ensure that my questions were culturally appropriate and divided the questions into three sections: early life, coming out, and contemporary life. I began the oral histories with questions about childhood and education, first asking where the participants were born and raised, and what level of education they had reached. I specifically avoided asking questions that might trigger a discussion of the 1994 genocide, as the director of HOCA had asked me to focus on individuals' experiences as part of the Rwandese LGBTI community. Despite the seriousness of the issues discussed, there was also a feeling of levity and at times laughter, as participants shared their stories and were able to speak about their sexuality and experiences in a safe, LGBTI-friendly space. In response to my question, "When did you first know that you were LGBT?" a majority of participants explained that they had first felt same-sex attraction or transgenderism at a young age.[36]

"I knew that I was LGBT in Primary 6, and felt that I was a man, not a girl, at age 12."

"Age 10 – I was born like that. I felt like a man even though I had never heard anything about sexuality or transgender people. I felt that I had to fight it, and that I wasn't doing the right thing until I met others like me."

"I knew at age 14. I started dating women at Senior 2, started dating men at Senior 6, and got married. My husband and I had two children and were married for 5 years, but I became more interested in the same sex."

"I knew in high school, at boarding school. I was talking with my roommate – at the time I had a girlfriend, but I always had trouble with the girlfriend. So, I was talking with my roommate and I kissed him. I've never slept with a woman. I've always been gay since my childhood. I knew at 14; at 15 I began dating men."

"Ever since I was born, I felt I was a woman, despite having the biology of a man. People often think that I am a girl. I'm not known as a gay; people know me as a girl. Some people think I'm a boy, some people think I'm a girl, so they don't really know my sexuality."

All of the participants I spoke with stated that they had experienced discrimination and harassment at some point in their lives, and three said that they were currently dealing with harassment. Two reported that discrimination and harassment had prevented them from completing their education. Almost all participants reported harassment from their families. One woman reported that her traditional Muslim family forced her to marry at age thirteen. She had a child with her husband, but after one year of marriage, ran away. Others spoke of their experiences:

> "My family does not support me. They discovered documents and figured out about me, and they are on my case. I'm thinking of leaving home and staying alone."

> "Ever since I was born, I was a lesbian, but it's surprising to see that even at age 26, I am still not accepted in my family. But I will fight for my rights until I get them."

> "The country is very conservative. Most Rwandese people don't believe that it's normal. Explaining to our families is still a big struggle, but HOCA is working on it as a team, and we're still working on the process."

> "I don't discuss it with my family, but I demonstrate it by dressing like a man. Everyone knows about it, but we haven't had a lot of conversations."

> "I come from a family of more boys than girls, and my family discriminated against me, and rejected me in comparison to my brothers and sisters. My brothers tried to fight me and stop me from being a lesbian, but my mother has always been there for me."

Two individuals reported losing a job because of being gay, and a majority of the group stated that they had difficulty finding work as a result of their sexual orientation. The participants cited poverty and socio-economic disparities as a significant problem in post-genocide Rwanda. These social inequalities are not limited to the LGBTI community, but their difficulties are compounded by discrimination in the workplace and in schools. As one person stated, "There is an element of division. Some LGBT are known and are not abused because of their status within the country. Class and wealth divisions create protections and vulnerabilities. There are people in the government who are gay, but they are not open about it and will not admit it."

Participants also reported harassment in their communities and violence against them. A lesbian couple in the group reported that in April

2009, their names and address had been broadcast on a conservative radio station, which had outed them as lesbians. The radio broadcast described their appearances, and told listeners to be on the lookout for them.[37] They stated that people have reported them to the authorities for being two non-related women living together, and as a result they no longer felt safe or comfortable in their home and neighbourhood. The same couple described an attack at a bar / restaurant in late June 2009, where one woman was hit in the face while another attacker held her arms behind her so she couldn't fight back. The attackers also slammed her partner's hand in a door, and during the interview she held out her hand to show me her fingers, which were still visibly swollen and bruised. The attackers also told them that they know where they live and where they spend their time, and that they would continue to target them. Although the couple notified the police, they stated that the police did not investigate the case, and instead told the women to avoid their attackers in the future. I followed up with one of the women individually after the group conversation and tried to get more information about what had happened. I encouraged her to go to a human rights advocacy organization in Kigali that is supportive of LGBTI people to report the attack, but she stated that she was not comfortable doing so.

Interviewing individuals who are still in harmful situations is a challenge for oral historians. With this particular project, I worked closely with HOCA and other human rights organizations in Kigali, but I was unable to provide the assistance and support that the community truly needed. In the aftermath of the genocide, which devastated every fibre of Rwandan society, more banal violations such as discrimination or assault as a result of sexual orientation are simply not viewed as priorities among so many other social issues and abuses from the genocide that are still waiting to be addressed.[38]

Still, the issues LGBTI Rwandans face are directly tied to other rights issues in Rwandese society. When asked about the most pressing issues for LGBTI Rwandans, one participant responded, "We don't have any freedom at all – no free speech, no freedom of association, no freedom of assembly. We are not regarded as human beings." Another stated that employment is an issue and that discrimination often prevents them from getting and keeping jobs. As one member of the focus group stated, "We are already criminalized because of our culture, even though there is no official law which criminalizes homosexuality." The members of HOCA agreed that greater visibility of LGBTI people in Rwandan society was necessary in order to gain understanding and acceptance. The head of the Ligue Rwandaise pour la Promotion et la Défence des Droits de l'Homme, one of the larger human rights organizations in Kigali, confirmed this assertion, stating that the LGBTI community is considered a "new group" in Rwanda and that they are not a known community or considered part of the culture. She elaborated that LGBTI people often live in hiding because the culture doesn't accept them and that they face discrimination.[39]

At the time of my interviews, there was no mention of sexual orientation anywhere in the Rwandan constitution or legal code. However, those I interviewed spoke of a continuing fear that same-sex relations would be criminalized, particularly in light of recent legislation in neighbouring countries, including Burundi in April 2009, criminalizing homosexuality in that country for the first time,[40] and fierce anti-gay sentiment in Uganda, which later that year, proposed death as a punishment for the offence of "aggravated homosexuality."[41] Shortly after I returned to the United States in August 2009, legislation referred to as Article 217 was proposed in parliament to criminalize same-sex relations in Rwanda.

During the autumn of 2009, human rights organizations in Rwanda actively fought this legislation by publishing articles and on blogs, submitting letters to the editor in support of gay rights to Kigali's *New Times* newspaper, and giving news interviews to local radio stations and newspapers, all of which created a level of LGBTI visibility that was unprecedented in Rwanda.[42] In the space of a few months, the LGBTI community in Rwanda went from being invisible to making headlines, though the extreme anti-homosexuality legislation proposed in neighbouring Uganda around the same time attracted far more international media attention.[43] The International Gay and Lesbian Human Rights Commission (IGLHRC) and various other NGOs reported that a vote on Article 217 would take place on 16 December 2009; numerous media outlets and blogs also reported on the proposed legislation.[44] A group known as the Civil Society Coalition for the Protection of LGBTI Rights, which consisted of human rights, health, and faith-based non-governmental organizations operating in Rwanda, submitted a thirteen-page document to parliament in October 2009 opposing the anti-homosexuality legislation:

> The Rwanda Civil Society believes however that the article is contradictory to the Rwandan Constitution, a violation of human rights, a hindrance to the implementation of the Rwanda National Strategic Plan on HIV and

AIDS 2009–2011. Furthermore, article 217 is a betrayal of Rwanda's recent history and the political drive of national unity, tolerance, inclusiveness and dialogue among the Rwandan citizens and residents.[45]

As it turned out, the legislation was never actually voted on in the Rwandan parliament. Government officials stated that a vote was not scheduled, and that the story of the proposed legislation was a fabrication. The Rwandan minister of justice at the time, Tharcisse Karugarama, has condemned and refuted reports that the government intended to criminalize homosexual acts, stating in the Kigali-based *New Times* newspaper that sexual orientation is a private matter, not a state business.[46] An article in the *New Times* several days later reported that the Political Affairs Committee in the Lower Chamber of Parliament requested that its fellow lawmakers remove Article 217 from the proposed penal code following pressure from the United Nations AIDS Council.[47]

When I asked the members of HOCA in 2009 if they were concerned that increasing their visibility might create a backlash against them, they acknowledged the possibility. But they reiterated the importance of making the LGBTI community in Rwanda known so that it could be better understood, and stated that visibility was worth the risks. The necessary work of documenting human rights violations and "investigating the silences" calls on us to embody Howard Zinn's notion of being activist archivists and go beyond just serving as neutral gatekeepers of information.[48] At the 2008 Society of American Archivists Annual Meeting, outgoing SAA president Mark Greene proposed a set of ten values for the archival profession. "Activism" was listed at number three. As Greene reminds us,

we are not neutral or objective protectors and transmitters of primary sources, but shapers and interpreters of the sources as well. Archivists have to understand, accept, and work within the reality that we – through our selection, through our description, and even through our marketing – do as much to create the documentation of the past as the individuals and organizations that generated the records in the first place … I believe that as a profession – though not always as individual practitioners – we must embrace the importance of deliberately acting to identify (even create), acquire, preserve, and make accessible material documenting those whose voices in our institutions and in society are marginalized or overlooked.[49]

Indeed, in the years since then the Rwandese LGBTI community began filling those silences, Rwanda has become a leader in LGBTI rights in East Africa. In 2011, Rwanda was one of only five African countries to sign the United Nations Statement on Sexual Orientation and Gender Indentity.[50] Dr Aflodis Kagaba, executive director of Health Development Initiative Rwanda, discussed the progress made by the Rwandese LGBT community in an article in the *East African* newspaper in August 2011, stating:

> Around that time [2009] in the region, there was a drive to criminalise homosexuality – not only in Rwanda, but also in Uganda and Burundi … In the beginning, of course, it was very challenging. We were experiencing hate speech, people phoning in to radio programmes saying 'Kill them, take them back to the West — they're not part of us.' But the media themselves were fanatical at that time — so it required more of an individual engagement, talking to them and discussing the issues involved …
>
> But I think the main reason [Rwanda didn't criminalize homosexuality] is that Rwanda has a very strong historical memory of what discrimination can do to any particular group, which for me is why I think their response has been very positive, in contrast to the other countries in the region. The government has learned from its history that any discrimination against any particular group can cause more negative consequences, and I think that's why the leadership was very responsive on this issue.[51]

As archivists, we must scrutinize the traditional role of simply preserving and maintaining rather than analysing or helping to shape the historical record.[52] We must continue to draw attention to those experiences and voices that are all too often missing from the official historical records kept in archives. We must see these testimonies as a call to action, a call for recognition of suffering and of perseverance, and work together as archivists and educators to share these stories, where appropriate, and advocate for those who have had their rights denied.

NOTES

1 I use the term LGBTI (lesbian, gay, bisexual, transgender, intersex), to describe the sexual orientations and gender identity expression of the members of HOCA I spoke to. The founder of HOCA also used this term

to describe the organization's members and advocacy work, despite the Western origins of the acronym. There were individuals who self-identified or were identified by the founder as each of the five terms included in the umbrella label of LGBTI.

2 Alison Des Forges, *Leave None to Tell the Story: The Genocide in Rwanda* (New York: Human Rights Watch, 1999).

3 Romeo Dallaire, *Shake Hands with the Devil: The Failure of Humanity in Rwanda* (Toronto: Vintage Canada, 2004); my notes from interviews with LGBTI individuals conducted in Kigali, Rwanda, between June and July 2009.

4 The Constitution of the Republic of Rwanda, 26 May 2003.

5 Behind the Mask was a news website founded in May 2000 by Bart Luirink, a Dutch journalist living in South Africa. The online media NGO published news about lesbian, gay, bisexual, transgender, and intersex people's affairs in Africa. See Johnathan Alexander, "Behind the Mask: An African Gay Affirmative Website," *International Journal of Sexuality and Gender Studies* 7, nos. 2–3 (July 2002): 227–34. Some Behind the Mask content is available through the Internet Archive Wayback Machine, (http://archive.org/web/web.php) and I have included links to archived Behind the Mask website pages, where available as of June 2013.

6 "HOCA Opens Debate on Homosexuality in Rwanda," 15 April 2010. Behind the Mask website, http://www.mask.org.za/, http://web.archive.org/web/20120719201236/http://www.mask.org.za/workers-demonstrate-in-johannesburg-over-wage-payments/.

7 Stephen O. Murray and Will Roscoe, *Boy Wives and Female Husbands: Studies of African Homosexualities* (New York: St Martin's Press, 1998), 11.

8 Ibid., 9.

9 Cary Alan Johnson, "Inside Gay Africa," *New York Native*, 3 March 1986, 29.

10 Daniel B. Hrdy, "Cultural Practices Contributing to the Transmission of Human Immunodeficiency Virus in Africa," *Reviews of Infectious Diseases* 9, no. 6 (1987): 1113–14.

11 Jacques Maquet, *The Premise of Inequality in Ruanda: A Study of Political Relations in a Central African Kingdom* (London: Oxford University Press 1961), 77.

12 Ibid., 78.

13 Mark Epprecht, *Heterosexual Africa? The History of an Idea from the Age of Exploration to the Age of AIDS* (Athens: Ohio University Press, 2008), 120.

14 Johnson, "Inside Gay Africa," 29.

15 Stephen O. Murray and Will Roscoe, introduction to *Boy Wives and Female Husbands*, xiii and xvi.

16 My notes from interviews with LGBTI individuals conducted in Kigali, Rwanda, between June and July 2009.
17 *The Johannesburg Statement on Sexual Orientation, Gender Identity and Human Rights.* Signed 13 February 2004 in Johannesburg, South Africa, at a meeting of African lesbian, gay, bisexual, and transgender organizations, with fifty-five participants from twenty-two groups representing sixteen countries, including at least one representative from Rwanda.
18 In 2009, I found almost no English-language articles in scholarly or popular journals focusing specifically on social conditions for LGBT people in Rwanda or even east Africa. This is, perhaps, unsurprising, considering that the primary languages spoken in Rwanda are Kinyarwanda and French (though English is now an official language as well).
19 The International Lesbian, Gay, Bisexual, Trans and Intersex Association (ILGA) has materials on its website from the 2007 World Social Forum in Nairobi, including Stephen Barris's report from 26 February 2007, http://ilga.org/ilga/en/article/1020.
20 Human Rights Watch, *Together Apart: Organizing around Sexual Orientation and Gender Identity Worldwide* (New York: Human Rights Watch, 2009).
21 Ibid.
22 Sheila Myung et al., *The Violations of the Rights of Lesbian, Gay, Bisexual and Transgender Persons in RWANDA: A Shadow Report,* March 2009, http://www2.ohchr.org/english/bodies/hrc/docs/ngos/LGBT_HRC95_Rwanda.doc.
23 Agnes Binagwaho, et al., *Exploring HIV Risk among MSM in Kigali, Rwanda,* July 2010, 13–14, http://www.cpc.unc.edu/measure/publications/tr-09-72.
24 "HOCA Opens Debate on Homosexuality in Rwanda," 15 April 2010; Behind the Mask website, http://web.archive.org/web/20120719201236/, http://www.mask.org.za/workers-demonstrate-in-johannesburg-over-wage-payments/.
25 The issue of the long-term instability of websites is a serious one. Both the HOCA website, and the Behind the Mask website, the two African websites which contained the most information about HOCA and LGBT rights in Rwanda, are currently defunct as of June 2013. Some information from both sites is still visible by searching in the Internet Archive's Wayback Machine (http://archive.org/web/web.php). When I was in Rwanda, HOCA had an unfinished website (http://www.hoca4rwanda.9f.com/) and were interested in creating a new, improved site for the organization. The new website (http://www.hoca4rwanda.org/) was launched in November 2009 but has since expired. As of October 2011, the domain (http://www.hoca4rwanda.org/) was relaunched by an unknown individual as a blog, which no longer contained any content relating to HOCA

or Rwanda. As of June 2013, the domain (http://www.hoca4rwanda.org/) is no longer in use.

26 Jacques Derrida, *Archive Fever: A Freudian Impression* (Chicago: University of Chicago Press, 1996), 33–4.

27 Mary Marshall Clark, Gerry Albarelli, and Amy Starecheski, introduction to *The Telling Lives Oral History Curriculum Guide* (New York: Columbia University Oral History Research Office, 2005), 4.

28 Global Youth Connect Call for Applications, Summer Delegation 2009.

29 My notes, 9 July 2009, Kigali, Rwanda.

30 While I provided ideas and suggestions for content to be included on the new HOCA website, my recommendations were not used. The design and content of the website were created entirely by HOCA.

31 "HOCA Opens Debate on Homosexuality in Rwanda," 15 April 2010. Behind the Mask website, http://www.mask.org.za/, http://web.archive .org/web/20120719201236/, http://www.mask.org.za/workers-demonstrate-in-johannesburg-over-wage-payments/.

32 Indeed, there were previous interviews with the director of HOCA and anonymous statements by LGBTI people in Rwanda from 2005, 2008, and 2011 on the American website, Global Gayz, maintained by Richard Ammon of Laguna Beach, California and Westhampton, Massachusetts.

33 My notes, July 2009.

34 Admittedly, long responses in Kinyarwanda were often shortened by my translator to just a sentence or two in English, but additional participants who spoke some English confirmed that the essence of the translations was accurate.

35 As requested, I emailed the participants copies of my notes from the focus group after my return to the US in August 2009, and sent an additional copy to the director of HOCA in May 2010.

36 All quotations are taken from my notes of conversations translated to English from Kinyarwanda, from an LGBT focus group conducted in Kigali, Rwanda, on 7 July and 9 July 2009.

37 For additional documentation of radio outings of the LGBT community in Rwanda, see Sheila Myung et al., *Violations of the Rights*.

38 My notes from the Global Youth Connect Human Rights Delegation to Rwanda workshop discussions, July 2009.

39 My notes, translated from French to English, from a meeting with Nyampinga Gertrude at the office of the Ligue Rwandaise pour la Promotion et la Defense des Droits de l'Homme, in Kigali, Rwanda, on 16 July 2009.

40 Human Rights Watch, *Forbidden: Institutionalizing Discrimination against Gays and Lesbians in Burundi* (New York: Human Rights Watch, 2009).

41 Jeffrey Gettleman, "Gay in Uganda and Feeling Hunted," *New York Times*, 4 January 2010, http://www.nytimes.com/2010/01/04/world/africa/04gay.html?fta=y.

42 For example, see Sheila Karake and Philippe Rwigyema, "All Rwandans are Equal," *New Times*, 21 July 2009, http://www.newtimes.co.rw/news/index.php?a=17745&i=13963; Anonymous, "Being Rwandan and Gay," *New Times*, 5 September 2009, http://www.newtimes.co.rw/news/index.php?a=19586&i=14009; and Joseph Rwagatare, "Gay Rights: When Perversion turned to Orientation," *New Times*, 29 December 2009, http://www.newtimes.co.rw/news/index.php?a=24211&i=14124.

43 Numerous international media outlets, including *Sunday Times* (South Africa), *Guardian* (UK), *New York Times* (US), and American news commentator Rachel Maddow of *The Rachel Maddow Show* provided extensive coverage of the proposed Anti-Homosexuality Bill (2009) in Uganda.

44 International Gay and Lesbian Human Rights Commission, "Rwandan Parliament's Lower House to Vote on Criminalising Homosexuality," 15 December 2009, http://www.iglhrc.org/content/rwandan-parliaments-lower-house-vote-criminalizing-homosexuality.

45 Civil Society Coalition for the Protection of LGBTI Rights, "Safeguarding Rights of Minorities through a Protecting Penal Code: A Civil Society Position Paper on the Draft Penal Code. A Focus on the Rights of Lesbians, Gays, Bi-sexual, Trans-Gender and Intersexual (LGBTI)," http://www.rightsrwanda.org/docs/POSITION_PAPER%20_ON%20_LGBTS.doc.

46 Edwin Musoni, "Gov't Cannot Criminalise Homosexuality – Minister," *New Times*, 19 December 2009, http://www.newtimes.co.rw/news/index.php?a=23893&i=14114.

47 Nasra Bishumba, "Lawmakers Seek to Scrap Article on Homosexuality," *New Times*, 23 December 2009, http://www.newtimes.co.rw/news/index.php?a=24016&i=14118.

48 Howard Zinn, "Secrecy, Archives, and the Public Interest," *Midwestern Archivist* 2, no. 2 (1977): 20.

49 Mark Greene, "The Power of Archives: Archivists' Values and Value in the Post-Modern Age," paper presented at the annual meeting of the Society of American Archivists, San Francisco, California, 28 August 2008, http://www.archivists.org/governance/presidential/GreeneAddressAug08.pdf.

50 UN Human Rights Council, *Joint Statement on Ending Acts of Violence Related Human Rights Violations Based on Sexual Orientation and Gender Identity*, 22 March 2011, http://www.refworld.org/docid/4eb8f32e2.html.

51 "Rwanda Well Ahead of EA in Acceptance of Gays," *East African*, 7 August 2011, http://www.theeastafrican.co.ke/magazine/

Rwanda-well-ahead-in-EA-in--acceptance-of-gays/-/434746/1214748/-/ okdclg/-/index.html.

52 For examples, see Randall Jimerson, *Archives Power: Memory, Accountability and Social Justice* (Chicago: Society of American Archivists Press, 2009); Carolyn Hamilton et al., *Refiguring the Archive* (Cape Town: New Africa Books, 2002); Terry Cook and Joan M. Schwartz, "Archives, Records and Power: The Making of Modern Memory," *Archival Science* 2 (2002): 1–19; and Rodney G.S. Carter, "Of Things Said and Unsaid: Power, Archival Silences, and Power in Silence" *Archivaria* 61 (2006): 215–33.

Afterword

THI RY DUONG

The Montreal Life Stories project places a great deal of emphasis on the voice of community. At the same time, it enables a better understanding of the individual life stories of those displaced by mass violence and of the long-term impact of war, genocide, and other human rights violations on the individual and on the community. This "sharing authority" approach is at the heart of the project, whereby university researchers and community members join together in conversation. A true partnership between communities and universities exists when both parties share a common vision and when they have mutual understanding and respect. The Montreal Life Stories project has worked extremely hard to accomplish this over the past five years. Our communities are encouraged to be active members of the research project.

During my three-year involvement in the project, I came to realize that I am very fortunate to work with so many wonderful people from many different cultures. Everyone is invested in and motivated by the project, and the feeling is contagious. Each one of the seven working groups is unique and generates its own ideas, which promotes a stimulating exchange of knowledge. In this way, the participants have become more aware of each other's history and context. Montreal encompasses a large and diverse immigrant population. Consequently, we need to be aware of the violence that has marked so many of our lives. We all have a story to tell.

For many of us, these issues are intensely personal. I interviewed my father. At first, he was very reluctant to talk about his experience in Cambodia during the genocide; but in order to support his daughter in her cause and to set a good example for other community members, he agreed. People like my father are now leaving recorded life stories for their children and those of the younger generation so that they might avoid making the same mistakes. These interviews also promote greater awareness and interest in the wider public.

My father is a reserved and humble man who does not like to talk about himself. In part, this is who he is. But he also comes from a culture where talking about oneself is frowned upon, where there is always the fear that what you say will be judged and misinterpreted. Although my father acknowledges that his experience during the Cambodian genocide is important, he would not share everything with us. It is his way of protecting us. These are not pleasant memories.

I have great admiration for my father's resilience, sense of obligation, and hard work. At the age of fourteen, he apprenticed as a mechanic. Despite harsh treatment by older mechanics, he did not give up. In less than a year, he was promoted; customers – including some Cambodian movie stars – would request his services. My grandfather taught him the importance of self-sufficiency; he said, "You are young. You must acquire all the skills you can so that one day, you can become something of your own and will not need to depend on others. You will have in your possession all the tools you need and only then can you make a man out of yourself." My father still lives according to this advice in everything he does.

As a young boy, my father attended school for only a short period – at a temple in Khmer Krom (South Cambodia), today regarded as South Vietnam – before he had to flee to Phnom Penh (the capital city of Cambodia), taking only the clothes on his back. It had become unsafe for my grandfather, the village chief and a soldier, to remain in his homeland due to the escalating war between North and South Vietnam. Because his father was forced to leave using fraudulent papers, my father lacked the paper work proving his Khmer citizenship – and could not return to school.

In the years that followed, my father would often watch other children going to school and admire them during lunch hour. Whenever he had enough money, he liked to play a candy roulette game that was very popular among Cambodian children, in which he would spin a wheel to win audio cassettes of famous singers. He would listen to the songs over and over to teach himself how to speak proper Khmer. In this way – and combined with lessons from one of his close friends – my father managed to teach himself how to read and write.

Every evening, my father would sit down to read and practise his writing. My grandfather, who was a strong believer in education, was very proud to see his son taking an interest in school. He supported him by taking care of the chores, washing his dirty clothing by hand, cooking, and cleaning. This is why education has been so very important to us as a family: my father tried to do the same thing with his children, always making sure that we had enough time to do our homework. And this valuing of education is something I fully intend to pass on to my own children.

My father had a very difficult childhood. At age seventeen, he was separated from his family and lived on his own through the Khmer Rouge regime until he married. As the Khmer Rouge took power in Cambodia, a Vietnamese family friendly to my father claimed that he was their brother. But their act of kindness caused a huge problem, as he had to then prove he was Cambodian. He pleaded with the Khmer Rouge to spare his life: he could cook, clean, repair cars, and so on; he would be a valuable asset. They were unsure, and so placed unrealistic demands on him to prove himself. They ordered him to dig ditches, repair machinery, and cook for a group of twenty each day – and when he complied, they added new jobs. They were looking for an excuse to kill him. He was forced to raise the chickens and piglets, tasks that required constant attention. My father recalls how the piglets, too small to eat solid foods and separated from their mothers, could only survive on puréed rice sweetened with sugar cane juice. He had to wrap this in cloth and squeeze it out drop by drop, to feed the piglets as if from the mother pig. It worked and my father's life was spared. But he continued to live in fear that at night someone would steal one of the animals. People were starving.

Thankfully, one of the Khmer Rouge members in charge of my father's little group developed a liking for him. He would often set aside some food for my father and would come to his defence. My father worked hard to keep everyone happy and to appease them by cooking good meals. He says he always minded his own business. He didn't care for materials goods (jewellery, gold, etc.), which some people in the group kept hidden. He knew full well that these possessions created envy and would eventually be discovered. Friends and neighbours accused each other. My father quickly understood people's vulnerability, and kept to himself. In this way, my father lived through the Cambodian genocide.

My father met my mother in the Thai refugee camps. In 1979, my father and mother, struggling to earn a living in the refugee camps, illegally crossed the Thai border with a paid guide to buy and sell merchandise. My father shared the following incident with me: while relieving himself in a grassy wooded area known to be filled with landmines, my father, forgetting for a moment where he was, stepped on a landmine. He fell to the ground, covered in blood. To this day, he still carries the shrapnel in his chest. In the confusion, he was separated from his mother and siblings for some time. He did not think that he would ever see them again. After the war was over, he continued to search for them. Then one day, he spoke with a man who perfectly described his family: They did not make it. My father was devastated. It was not until later that he realized that his mother and siblings were still alive. But my grandfather and several other family members died in the war.

My father and mother started their own family before being sponsored to come to Canada. The challenge of being in a new country and starting over – living in someone else's home, not speaking the language, finding daycare, finding work, and the cold climate – made the first few years in Montreal very difficult ones.

My relationship with my father is very close. What I feel, he feels, and his pain is my pain. I can honestly say my father is my hero because he has taught me so much and has given me everything that I have today. I learned the importance of staying humble, the obligation to family, respect for others, and, most of all, to never give up in life. Through the worst of times, my parents remained positive, and today they live well. They may not be rich, but they made the best of their situation. Whenever I feel sad, I hear their voices. Because of them, I have developed a positive outlook on life. I used to be ashamed to tell people I am Khmer, as I didn't know many Khmer children when I went to school. Now though, I assume my identity with pride. I am comfortable with who I am. I am proud to be part of this research project. My involvement will forever stay with me, and it will be a guiding principle in my present and future interactions within my own community.

Bibliography

Abitbol, Michel. *The Jews of North Africa during the Second World War.* Detroit: Wayne State University Press, 1989.

Adelson, Alan, and Robert Lapides, eds. *Lodz Ghetto: Inside a Community under Siege.* New York: Penguin, 1989.

African Rights. "Rwanda: Not So Innocent. When Women Become Killers." 1995.

Agid, Shana. "Locked and Loaded." In *Through the Eye of Katrina*, edited by Kristin A. Bates and Richelle S. Swan, 55–69. Durham: Carolina Academic, 2007.

Allouche-Benayoun, Joëlle. "Diversité et pluralisme religieux au sein du judaïsme." Dans *Connaissance du monde juif*, Evelyne Martini et Gérard Rabinovitch, éds., 73–84. Champigny-sur-Marne: SCÉRÉN-CRDP de Créteil, 2008.

American Psychological Association. *Diagnostic and Statistical Manual of Mental Disorders,* 3rd ed. Washington, DC: APA, 1987.

Amery, Jean. *At the Mind's Limits: Contemplations by a Survivor of Auschwitz and Its Realities.* Bloomington: Indiana University Press, 1980.

Anctil, Pierre, Ira Robinson, et Gérard Bouchard, eds. *Juifs et canadiens Français dans la société québécoise.* Sillery: Septentrion, 2000.

Annan, Jeannie, Christopher Blattman, and Roger Horton. "The State of Youth and Youth Protection in Northern Uganda: Findings from the Survey of War Affected Youth." Kampala: UNICEF, 2006.

Archibald, Jo-ann/Q'um Q'um Xiiem. *Indigenous Storywork: Educating the Heart, Mind, Body, and Spirit.* Vancouver: UBC Press, 2008.

Bardzell, Jeffrey, Shaowen Bardzell, and Tyler Pace. "Emotion, Engagement and Internet Video." *One to One Interactive, New Media Research*, 2008. www.onetooneinteractive.com.

Bédard, Jean-Luc. "Identité et transmission intergénérationnelle chez les Sépharades à Montréal." PhD diss., Université Laval, 2005.

Belpotti, Marco, and Robert Gordon, eds. *The Voice of Memory: Interviews, 1961–1987*. New York: New Press, 2002.

Benjamin, Walter. "The Storyteller in Artisan Cultures" (1936). In *Critical Sociology*, edited by Paul Connerton. New York: Penguin, 1976.

Berdugo-Cohen, Marie, Yolande Cohen, et Joseph Lévy. *Juifs marocains à Montréal: témoignages d'une immigration moderne*. Montréal: VLB, 1987.

Bin-Nun, Yigal. "Psychosis or an Ability to Foresee the Future? The Contribution of the World Jewish Organizations to the Establishment of Rights for Jews in Independent Morocco, 1955–1961." *Revue Européenne d'Études Hébraïques* 10 (2004).

Blackman, Anna. *The PhotoVoice Manual*. London: K and N Press, 2007.

Boussouga, Hakima. "La vitalité ethnolinguistique de la communauté juive marocaine de Montréal." Mémoire de MA, Université du Québec à Montréal, 2003.

Brami, Paula. *Identité éthnique et acculturation chez les étudiants juifs sépharades à Montréal*. Mémoire de MA, Psychologie, Université de Montréal, 1996.

Brière, Céline. *Les Juifs Sépharades à Montréal: Traces passagères et marqueurs spatiaux d'une minorité dans une métropole nord-américaine*. Mémoire de MA, Géographie, Université d'Angers, 1990.

Brushwood Rose, Chloe. "The Migration between Selves and Worlds: On the Digital Autobiographies of Newcomer Women as Transnational and Transitional Spaces." Paper presented at the Canadian Society for the Study of Education Annual conference, Vancouver, BC, 2008.

Canetti, Elias. *Voix de Marrakech, journal d'un voyage*. Paris: Albin Michel, 1980.

Caruth, C. *Trauma: Explorations in Memory*. Baltimore: Johns Hopkins University Press, 1995.

Cecil, Katherine. "Race, Representation, and Recovery." Master's thesis, University of New Orleans, 2009.

Chamberlin, J. Edward. *If This Is Your Land, Where Are Your Stories?* Toronto: Alfred A. Knopf, 2003.

Chapman, Jane L. *Issues in Contemporary Documentary*. Cambridge, UK; Malden MA: Polity, 2009.

Chétrit, Sami S. *The Mizrahi Struggle in Israel: 1948–2003* (Hebrew). Tel-Aviv: Am-Oved, 2004.

Chrétien, Jean Pierre. *Rwanda: Les medias du génocide*. Paris: Kathala, 1995.

Cohen, Hart, Juan Francisco Salazar, and Iqbal Barkat. *Screen Media Arts: An Introduction to Concepts and Practices*. Oxford: Oxford University Press, 2009.

Cohen, Yolande. "De Meknès à Montréal," *Genre & Histoire*, no. 6 (printemps 2010). http://genrehistoire.revues.org/index1021.html.

Cohen, Yolande, et Joseph Lévy. "Élites et organisation communautaire chez les juifs marocains à Montréal: Du soleil à la liberté." *Annuaire de l'Émigration*. Rabat: Ministère des communautés marocaines vivant à l'étranger, 1995: 320–7.

Coleman, Stephan, and Karen Ross. *The Media and the Public: "Them" and "Us" in Media Discourse*. Malden, MA: Wiley-Blackwell, 2010.

Cruikshank, Julie. *The Social Life of Stories: Narrative and Knowledge in the Yukon Territory*. Lincoln: University of Nebraska Press, 1998.

Cruikshank, Julie, with A. Sidney, K. Smith, and A. Ned. *Life Lived Like a Story: Life Stories of Three Yukon Native Elders*. Vancouver: UBC Press, 1990.

Crump, Jeff. "Deconcentration by Demolition." *Environment and Planning: Society and Space* 20, no. 5 (2002): 581–96.

Dallaire, Romeo. *Shake Hands with the Devil: The Failure of Humanity in Rwanda*. Toronto: Vintage Canada, 2004.

Daniel, Pete. *Deep'n As It Come: The 1927 Mississippi River Flood*. New York: Oxford University, 1977.

Das, Veena. *Life and Words: Violence and the Descent into the Ordinary*. Berkeley: University of California Press, 2007.

Deleuze, Gilles, and Felix Guattari. *A Thousand Plateaus: Capitalism and Schizophrenia*. Minneapolis: University of Minnesota Press, 1987.

Derrida, Jacques. *Archive Fever: A Freudian Impression*. Chicago: University of Chicago Press, 1996.

Des Forges, Alison. *Leave None to Tell the Story: The Genocide in Rwanda*. New York: Human Rights Watch, 1999.

Downing, John. "Uncommunicative Partners: Social Movement Media Analysis and Radical Educators." Accessed from Media@McGill Website, http://media.mcgill.ca/en/john_downing_keynote.

DuBois, Lindsay. *The Politics of the Past in an Argentine Working Class Neighbourood*. Toronto: University of Toronto Press, 2005.

Duneier, Mitchell. *Slim's Table: Race, Respectability, and Masculinity*. Chicago: University of Chicago Press, 1992.

Eaton, Rebecca. "Escape Denied." *Texas Wesleyan Law Review* 13 (2006–7): 127–74.

Elbaz, André. "Ma mémoire sépharade." Dans *La Mémoire sépharade*, Trigano Shmuel et Hélène, éds. Paris, 2000.

Elbaz, André. *Sépharadisme d'hier et de demain: Trois autobiographies d'immigrants Juifs marocains*. Ottawa: Musée Canadien des civilisations, 1988.

Elbaz, Michael. "Parias, parvenus et rebelles. Juifs marocains et Marocains juifs." Dans *L'insoumis: Juifs, Marocains et rebelles*, Abraham Serfaty et Michael Elbaz, éds., 23–65. Paris: Desclée de Brouwer, 2001.

Elkaïm, Betty. "Evaluations des séquelles psychologiques du deuil." Mémoire de MA, Psychologie, Université de Montréal, 1981.

Epprecht, Mark. *Heterosexual Africa? The History of an Idea from the Age of Exploration to the Age of AIDS*. Athens: Ohio University Press, 2008.

Ermine, Willie, Raven Sinclair, and Bonnie Jeffery. *The Ethics of Research Involving Indigenous Peoples*. Saskatoon, SK: Indigenous Peoples' Health Research Centre, 2004.

Essley, Roger. *Visual Tools for Differentiating Reading and Writing Instruction*. New York: Scholastic Press, 2008.

Ewald, Wendy. *I Wanna Take Me a Picture*. Boston: Beacon Press, 2002.

Ewald, Wendy. *Towards a Promised Land*. London: Steidl/Artangel, 2006.

Fell, Lloyd, and David Russell. "The Dance of Understanding." In *Seized by Agreement, Swamped by Understanding*, edited by Lloyd Fell, David Russell, and Allan Stewart. 1994. http://www.pnc.com.au/~lfell/dance.pdf.

Fels, Lynn. "In the Wind, Clothes Dance on a Line." *JCT: Journal of Curriculum Theory* 14, no. 1 (1998): 27–36.

Fineman, Mia. "'Children of Bad Memories': Photographing a Generation Born of Rape during the Rwandan Genocide." Slate Website, 2009. http://www.slate.com/id/2219840/pagenum/all/(accessed 2010).

Finnegan, R. *Storying the Self: Personal Narratives and Identity*. In *Consumption and Everyday Life*, edited by H. McKay, 65–112. London: Sage, 1997.

Flaherty, Jordan. *Floodlines: Community and Resistance from Katrina to the Jena Six*. Chicago: Haymarket Books, 2010.

Fox, Jonathan. *Acts of Service: Spontaneity, Commitment, Tradition in the Nonscripted Theatre*. New Paltz: Tusitala Publishing, 1994.

Frisch, Michael. "Oral History and the Digital Revolution: Toward a Post-Documentary Sensibility." In *The Oral History Reader*, 2nd ed., edited by Robert Perks and Alistair Thomson, 102–14. London: Routledge, 2006.

Frisch, Michael. *A Shared Authority: Essays on the Craft and Meaning of Oral and Public History*. Albany: State University of New York Press, 1990.

Fullilove, Mindy Thompson. *Root Shock: How Tearing Up Cities Hurts America, and What We Can Do About It*. New York: One World/Ballantine Books, 2005.

Fussell, Elizabeth. "Constructing New Orleans, Constructing Race." *Journal of American History* 94 (2007): 846–55.

Gadamer, Hans-Georg. *Truth and Method*, 2nd rev. ed. Translated by Joel Weinsheimer and Donald G. Marshall. New York: Continuum, 1989.

Galeano, E. *Days and Nights of Love and War*. New York: Monthly Review Press, 2000.

Garapon, A. *Des crimes qu'on ne peut ni juger ni pardonner: Pour une justice internationale*. Paris: Odile Jacob, 2002.

Gaudet, Mary. "'We Are Going to Fight as Long as We Have Life': Histories and Politics of Argentine Activist Pensioners." Master's thesis, Dalhousie University, 2003.

Gellhorn, Martha. *Disbelief of Atrocities*. PBS, 2003. http://www.pbs.org/ perilousfight/psychology/disbelief_of_atrocities/letters/.

Germany, Kent. *New Orleans after the Promises: Poverty, Citizenship, and the Search for the Great Society*. Athens: University of Georgia Press, 2007.

Gishoma, D., et Brackelaire. "Quand le corps abrite l'inconcevable: Comment dire le bouleversement dont témoignent les corps au Rwanda?" *Cahiers de psychologie clinique* 1, no. 30 (2008): 159–83.

Grant, Bruce. *In the Soviet House of Culture: A Century of Peristroikas*. Princeton: Princeton University Press, 1995.

Greenspan, Henry. *On Listening to Holocaust Survivors: Beyond Testimony*. St Paul, MN: Paragon House, 2010.

Greenspan, Henry. "Sharing Authority in Interpreting Survivor Testimony: A Worthy and Realistic Goal? Part 1." CURA on CitizenShift, Life Stories Collection, 2009. http://citizenshift.org/henry-greenspan-sharing-authroity-interpreting-survivor-testimony-worthy-and-realistic-goal.

Greenspan, Henry. *Survivors: Recounting and Life History*. Westport, CT: Praeger, 1998.

Gregory, Sam. "Cameras Everywhere: Ubiquitous Video Documentation of Human Rights, New Forms of Video Advocacy, and Considerations of Safety, Security, Dignity and Consent. *Journal of Human Rights Practice* 2, no. 2 (2010): 191–207.

Grotowski, Jerzy. *Towards a Poor Theatre*. New York: Simon and Schuster, 1968.

Guenivet, Karima. "Femmes, les nouveaux champs de bataille." *Quasimodo*, no. 9 (*Corps en guerre. Imaginaires, idéologies, destructions*. Tome 2), Montpellier, 197–213.

Hansen, A.T., A.S. Owen, and M.P. Madden. *Parallels: The Soldier's Knowledge and the Oral History of Contemporary Warfare*. New York: Walter de Gruyter, 1992.

Hartman, Geoffrey. *The Longest Shadow*. New York: Palgrave Macmillan, 1996.

Hatzfeld, Jean. *Dans le nu de la vie: Récits des marais rwandais*. Paris: Seuil, 2000.

Hatzfeld, Jean. *Une saison de machette*. Paris: Seuil, 2003.

Hayner, Priscilla. *Unspeakable Truths: Confronting State Terror and Atrocity*. New York: Routledge, 2001.

Hedges, C. *War Is a Force That Gives Us Meaning*. New York: Anchor Press, 2003.

Herman, J. *Trauma and Recovery: The Aftermath of Violence from Domestic Abuse to Political Terror*. New York: Basic Books, 1997.

High, Steven. "Sharing Authority: An Introduction and Sharing Authority: Building Community University Research Alliances using Oral History, Digital Storytelling and Engaged Scholarship." *Journal of Canadian Studies* 43, no. 1 (2009): 12–34.

High, Steven, and David Sworn. "After the Interview: The Interpretive Challenges of Oral History Video Indexing." *Digital Studies/Le champ numérique* 1, no. 2 (2009), http://www.digitalstudies.org/ojs/index.php/digital_studies/article/view/173/215.

Hillman, James. "Anima Mundi: The Return of the Soul to the World." *Spring* (1982): 71–93.

Hirsch, Marianne. "Projected Memory: Holocaust Photographs in Personal and Public Fantasy." In *Acts of Memory: Cultural Recall in the Present*, edited by Mieke Bal, Jonathan Crewe, and Leo Spitzer. Hanover: University Press of New England, 1999.

Hirsch, Marianne. "Surviving Images: Holocaust Photographs and the Work of Postmemory." In *Visual Culture and the Holocaust*, edited by Barbie Zelizer, 215–46. New Brunswick, NJ: Rutgers University Press, 2001.

Histories de vie Montréal – Montreal Life Stories. "Ethics Guide Summary, CURA Research Protocol," 2008. http://www.lifestoriesmontreal.ca/en/ethics-guide-summary.

Holocaust—The Survivors Gather. PBS. 15–18 June 1981.

Howard, Peggy. "Interpreting the Evaluation Experience through Embodiment, Conversation and Anecdote." *Qualitative Studies in Education* 9, no. 2 (1996): 167–80.

Hrdy, Daniel B. "Cultural Practices Contributing to the Transmission of Human Immunodeficiency Virus in Africa." *Reviews of Infectious Diseases* 9, no. 6 (1987): 1113–14.

Human Rights Watch. *Forbidden: Institutionalizing Discrimination against Gays and Lesbians in Burundi*. New York: Human Rights Watch, 2009.

Human Rights Watch. *Shattered Lives: Sexual Violence during the Rwandan Genocide and Its Aftermath*. New York: Human Rights Watch, 1996.

Human Rights Watch. *Together Apart: Organizing around Sexual Orientation and Gender Identity Worldwide*. New York: Human Rights Watch, 2009.

Internal Displacement Monitoring Centre (IDMC). "Uganda: At a Glance." 2010. http://www.internal-displacement.org/8025708F004CE90B/(httpCountries)/04678346A648C087802570A7004B9719?opendocument.

International Center for Transitional Justice (ICTJ) "Memory, Memorials, and Museums: MMM Program." 2010. http://www.ictj.org/en/tj/785.html (accessed 2010).

James, Daniel. *Doña María's Story: Life History, Memory, and Political Identity*. Durham, NC: Duke University Press, 2000.

Jeammet, Nicole. *Le plaisir et le péché. Essai sur l'envie*. Paris: Desclée de Brouwer, 1998.

Johnson, David Read. "Developmental Transformations: Toward the Body as Presence." In *Current Approaches in Drama Therapy*, 2nd ed., edited by David R. Johnson and Renee Emunah, 89–116. Springfield, IL: Charles C. Thomas, 2009.

Johnson, David Read. "Performing Absence: The Limits of Testimony in the Recovery of a Combat Veteran." In *Healing Collective Trauma Using Sociodrama and Drama Therapy*, edited by Eva Leveton, 55–78. New York: Springer, 2010.

Johnson, Richard, G. McClennan, Bill Schwartz, and David Sutton, eds. *Making Histories: Studies in History Writing and Politics*. Minneapolis: University of Minnesota Press, 1982.

Juhasz, Alexandra. "Documentary on YouTube: The Failure of the Direct Cinema of the Slogan." In *Rethinking Documentary New Perspectives, New Practices*, edited by Thomas Austin and Wilma de Jong, 299–311. New York: McGraw-Hill/Open University Press, 2008.

Justice and Reconciliation Project. "Kill Every Living Thing: The Barlonyo Massacre." Field Note IX, February 2009.

Kabagwira, Sylvie. "Violences faites aux femmes Tutsi du Rwanda pendant le génocide de 1994." Allocution devant le Sénat Belge le 23 mars 2007.

Kambouri, Nelli, and Pavlos Hatzopoulos. "Making Violent Practices Public." In *The Video Vortex Reader: Responses to YouTube*, edited by Geert Lovink and Ned Rossiter, 125–31. Amsterdam: Institute of Network Cultures, 2008.

Kamler, B. *Relocating the Personal: A Critical Writing Pedagogy*. Albany: State University of New York Press, 2001.

Kangura. "Les dix commandements du Hutu." *Gisenyi* 6 (déc. 1990), 6–8.

Kenbib, Mohamed. *Juifs et musulmans au Maroc (1859–1948). Contribution à l'histoire des relations inter-communautaires en terre d'Islam*. Rabat: Université Mohamed V, Publication de la Faculté des Lettres et des Sciences humaines, Série – Thèses et mémoires, no. 21, 1994.

Kidd, Jenny. "Capture Wales Digital Storytelling: Community Media Meets the BBC." In *Making Our Media: Global Initiatives toward a Democratic Public Sphere*, edited by Laura Stein, Dorothy Kidd, and Clemencia Rodriguez, 293–308. Cresskill, NJ: Hampton Press, 2010.

King, Thomas. *The Truth about Stories: A Native Narrative.* Toronto: Anansi Press, 2003.

Kirshner, Mia. *I Live Here.* New York: Pantheon Books, 2008.

Kittle, Penny. *Write Beside Them: Risk, Voice and Clarity in High School Writing.* Portsmouth, NH: Heinemann, 2008.

Klein, Mélanie. *Envie et gratitude et autres essais.* Paris: Gallimard, 1957.

Kluger, Ruth. *Still Alive: A Holocaust Girlhood Remembered.* New York: Feminist Press, 2003.

Krippendorf, Klaus. "Major Metaphors of Communication and Some Constructivist Reflections on Their Use." *Cybernetics and Human Knowing* 2, no. 1 (1993): 3–25.

Lakoff, G., and M. Johnson, *Metaphors We Live By.* Chicago: University of Chicago Press, 1980.

Lambert, J. *Digital Storytelling: Capturing Lives, Creating Community.* Berkeley, CA: Digital Diner Press, 2002.

Lasry, Jean-Claude, et Claude Tapi, eds. *Les Juifs du Maghreb: Diasporas contemporaines.* Montréal/Paris: Presses de l'Université de Montréal/ L'Harmattan, 1989.

Laub, Dori. "From Speechlessness to Narrative." *Literature and Medicine* 24, no. 2 (2005): 253–65.

Lederach, John Paul. "Conflict Transformation." Beyond Intractability website. http://www.beyondintractability.org/essay/transformation/+related: www.berghof-handbook.net%2Fuploads%2Fdownload%2Fdialogue3_ warecon_intro.pdf (accessed 2010).

Légaré, Maurice. "La population juive de Montréal est-elle victime d'une ségrégation qu'elle se serait elle-même imposée?" *Recherches sociographiques* 4, no. 3 (1965): 312.

Levi, Primo. *Les Naufragés et les rescapés: Quarente ans après Auschwitz.* Paris: Gallimard (pour la traduction française), 1989.

Levi, Primo. *The Drowned and the Saved.* New York: Vintage, 1989.

Life in the Open Prison: Survival Stories from Two of the Millions. Cambodia 1975–1979, CitizenShift, http://citizenshift.org/life-open-prison-2.

Linds, Warren. "A Journey in Metaxis: Been, Being, Becoming, Imag(in)ing Drama Facilitation." PhD diss., University of British Columbia, 2002. https://circle.ubc.ca/bitstream/handle/2429/13085/ubc_2002-731952.pdf.

Little, Edward. "Editorial." *Alt.theatre: Cultural Diversity and the Stage* 7, no. 2 (2009): 6–9.

Liu, Shaw Pong. *Soldiers' Tales Untold: About.* http://www.soldierstalesuntold .org/.

Lloyd-Sherlock, Peter. *Old Age and Urban Poverty in the Developing World: The Shanty Towns of Buenos Aires*. New York: Macmillan, 1997.

Lochak, D. "La doctrine sous Vichy ou les mésaventures du positivisme." Dans *Les usages sociaux du droit*, 251–85. Paris: PUF, 1989.

Lovink, Geert. "The Art of Watching Databases: Introduction to the Video Vortex Reader." In *The Video Vortex Reader: Responses to YouTube*, edited by Geert Lovink and Ned Rossiter. Amsterdam: Institute of Network Cultures, 2008.

Macquet, J. *Pouvoir et société en Afrique*. Paris: Hachette, 1970.

Maquet, Jacques. *The Premise of Inequality in Ruanda: A Study of Political Relations in a Central African Kingdom*. London: Oxford University Press, 1961.

Margalit, Avishai. *The Ethics of Memory*. Cambridge, MA: Harvard University Press, 2002.

Marshall Clark, M, Gerry Albarelli, and Amy Starecheski. Introduction to *The Telling Lives Oral History Curriculum Guide*. New York: Columbia University Oral History Research Office, 2005.

Martin, Emily. "Review Essay: Violence, Language and Everyday Life." *American Ethnologist* 34, no. 4 (2007): 741–5.

Mason, Brian. "Towards Positions of Safe Uncertainty." *Human Systems: The Journal of Systemic Consultation & Management* 4 (1993): 189–200.

May, R. *The Cry for Myth*. New York: W.W. Norton, 1991.

McNiff, Sean. "Arts-Based Research." In *Handbook of the Arts in Qualitative Research*, edited by J. Gary Knowles and Ardra Cole, 29–40. Los Angeles: Sage, 2008.

Meyerowitz, Ruth, and Christine Zinni. "The Medium and the Message: Oral History, New Media, and a Grassroots History of Working Women." *Journal of Educational Technology Systems* 37, no. 3 (2009): 306–16.

Miall, Hugh. "Conflict Transformation: A Multi-Dimensional Task." In *Berghof Handbook of Conflict Transformation*. Berghof Research Center for Constructive Conflict Management, 2004.

Miller, Elizabeth. "Building Participation in the Outreach for the Documentary, *The Water Front*." *Journal of Canadian Studies* 43, no. 1 (2009): 59–86.

Minow, Martha. "Truth Commissions." In *Between Vengeance and Forgiveness: Facing History after Genocide and Mass Violence*. Boston: Beacon Press, 1998.

Moldofsky, Naomi. "The Economic Adjustment of North African Jewish Immigrants in Montréal." PhD diss., Economics and Political Science, McGill University, 1969.

Mollica, Richard. *Healing Invisible Wounds: Paths to Hope and Recovery in a Violent World*. Orlando: Houghton Mifflin Harcourt, 2006.

Mukasonga, S. *Inyenzi ou les Cafards*. Paris: Gallimard, 2006.

Mündel, Ingrid. "Radical Storytelling: Performing Processes in Canadian Popular Theatre." *Theatre Research in Canada* 24, nos. 1–2 (2003): 147–70.

Murray, Stephen O., and Will Roscoe. *Boy Wives and Female Husbands: Studies of African Homosexualities*. New York: St Martin's Press, 1998.

Nahimana, Ferdinand, et Édouard Karemera. *Le drame rwandais*. Lille: Éditions sources du Nil, 2006.

Nahimana, Ferdinand, et Édouard Karemera. *Rwanda. Les virages ratés*. Lille: Éditions Sources du Nil, 2007.

Nduwimana, Françoise. *Le droit de survivre: femmes, violence sexuelle et vih/sida*. Montréal: Droit et démocratie, 2004.

Olazabal, Ignaki. "Entre les processus de communalisation et d'*intersystème*; Juifs et Québécois francophones à Montréal à travers quatre générations." Dans *Juifs et Canadiens Français dans la Société Québécoise*, Anctil, Pierre, Ira Robinson, et Gérard Bouchard, éds., 107–126. Sillery: Septentrion, 2000.

O'Nell, T. "'Coming Home' among Northern Plains Vietnam Veterans: Psychological Transformations in Pragmatic Perspective." *Ethos* 27, no. 4 (1999): 441–65.

Pager, Devah. *Marked: Race, Crime, and Finding Work in an Era of Mass Incarceration*. Chicago: University of Chicago Press, 2007.

Palacios, L.B., Low, C. Brushwood Rose, and P. Salvio. "Framing the Scholarship on Participatory Video: From Celebration to Critical Engagement." Paper submitted to the Canadian Society for the Study of Education, Canada, May 2010.

Parr, Joy, Jessica Van Horssen, and Jon van der Veen. "The Practice of History Shared across Differences: Needs, Technologies and Ways of Knowing in the Megaprojects New Media Project." *Journal of Canadian Studies* 43, no. 1 (2009): 48–56.

Passerini, Luisa. *Fascism in Popular Memory: The Cultural Experience of the Turin Working Class*. New York: Cambridge University Press, 1987.

Passerini, Luisa, ed. *Memory and Totalitarianism*. Oxford: Oxford University Press. 1992.

Péan, Pierre. *Noires fureurs, blancs menteurs, Rwanda 1990–1994*. Paris: Éditions Mille et une nuits, 2005.

Penner, D'Ann. "Assault Rifles, Separated Families, and Murder in their Eyes: Unasked Questions after Hurricane Katrina," *Journal of American Studies* 44, no. 3 (2010): 580–3.

Penner, D'Ann. *Overcoming: The Hidden Fury of Hurricane Katrina's Aftermath and Implications for the Future of New Orleans*. Hooks Institute Working Paper Series. University of Memphis, 2010.

Phelan, Peggy. *Unmarked: The Politics of Performance*. New York: Routledge, 1993.

Philpot, Robin. *Ça ne s'est pas passé comme ça à Kigali*. Montréal: Les Éditions Les Intouchables, 2003.

Portelli. Allesandro. *The Death of Luigi Trastulli, and Other Stories: Form and Meaning in Oral History*. Albany: State University of New York Press, 1991.

Portelli. Allesandro. *The Order Has Been Carried Out: History, Memory and Meaning of a Nazi Massacre in Rome*. New York: Palgrave Macmillan, 2003.

Prentki, Tim, Jan Selman. *Popular Theatre in Political Culture: Britain and Canada in Focus*. Bristol: Intellect Press, 2000.

Pryluck, Calvin. "Ultimately We Are All Outsiders: The Ethics of Documentary Filming." In *New Challenges for Documentary*, 2nd ed., edited by Alan Rosenthal. Manchester: Manchester Univeristy Press, 2005.

Quigley, William P. "Thirteen Ways of Looking at Katrina." *Tulane Law Review* 81, no. 4 (2007): 955–1017.

Raczymow, Henri. "Memory Shot through with Holes." Translated by Alan Astro. *Yale French Studies* 85 (1994): 103.

Razack, Sherene H. *Race, Space, and the Law: Unmapping a White Settler Society*. Toronto: Between the Lines, 2002.

Rebel, Hermann. "Historical Anthropology as an Ethical Choice in the Age of Genocide," *Critique of Anthropology* 27, no. 4 (2007): 431–48.

Rebel, Hermann. "On Separating Memory from Historical Science: A Critique and Three Austrian Cases," *Focaal* 44 (2004): 119–37.

Reimann, Cordula. "Assessing the State of the Art in Conflict Transformation." In *Berghof Handbook for Conflict Transformation*. Berghof Center for Constructive Conflict Management, 2004.

Rheingold, Howard. "Using Participatory Media and Public Voice to Encourage Civic Engagement." In *Civic Life Online: Learning How Digital Media Can Engage Youth*, edited by W. Lance Bennett, 97–118. Cambridge, MA: MIT Press, 2008.

Ricoeur, Paul. "The Model of the Text: Meaningful Action considered as a Text." In *Hermeneutics and the Human Sciences*, edited by Paul Ricoeur and John B. Thompson, 197–221. Cambridge, UK: Cambridge University Press, 1981.

Rigney, Lester-Irabinna. "Internalization of an Indigenous Anticolonial Cultural Critique of Research Methodologies: A Guide to Indigenist Research Methodology and Its Principles." *Wicazo Sa Review* (Fall 1999): 109–21.

Ringer, Martin. "The Facile-itation of Facilitation? Searching for Competencies in Group Work Leadership." *Scisco Conscientia* 2, no. 1 (1999): 1–19. http://www.groupinstitute.com/site/gii/templates/pdfs/Facile_itationScisco%201.pdf.

Romero, Luís Alberto. *A History of Argentina in the Twentieth Century*. Translated by James P. Brennan. University Park: State University of Pennsylvania Press, 2002.

Roth, John. "Returning Home: Reflections on Post-Holocaust Ethics." In *Ethics after the Holocaust*, edited by John K. Roth, 280–95. St Paul, MN: Paragon House, 1999.

Rousso, Henri. *Le syndrome de Vichy*. Edition du Seuil, 1987.

Rowe, Nick. *Playing the Other: Dramatizing Personal Narratives in Playback Theatre*. London: Jessica Kingsley, 2007.

Rubin, Agi, and Henry Greenspan. *Reflections: Auschwitz, Memory and a Life Recreated*. St Paul, MN: Paragon House, 2006.

Russell, David, and Ray Ison. "Maturana's Intellectual Contribution as a Choreography of Conversation and Action." *Cybernetics and Human Knowing* 11, no. 2 (2004): 36–48.

Rutherford, Jonathan. "The Third Space: Interview with Homi K. Bhabha." In *Identity: Community, Culture, Difference*, edited by Jonathan Rutherford, 207–21. London: Lawrence and Wishart, 1990.

Salaam, Kalamu ya. "Pa Ferdinand." *Catalyst* (1989): 112.

Salaam, Kalamu ya. *What Is Life? Reclaiming the Black Blues Self*. Chicago: Third World Press, 1994.

Salas, Jo. *Improvising Real Life: Personal Story in Playback Theatre*. New Paltz, NY: Tusitala, 1993.

Salverson, Julie. "Change on Whose Terms? Testimony and an Erotics of Injury." *Theater* 31, no. 3 (2001): 119–25.

Salverson, Julie. "Clown, Opera, the Atomic Bomb and the Classroom." In *The Applied Theatre Reader*, edited by Tim Prentki and Sheila Preston, 33–40. London and New York: Routledge, 2009.

Salverson, Julie. "Performing Emergency: Witnessing, Popular Theatre, and the Lie of the Literal." *Theatre Topics* 6, no. 2 (1996): 181–91.

Salverson, Julie. "Taking Liberties: A Theatre Class of Foolish Witnesses." *Research in Drama Education* 13, no. 2 (2008): 245–55.

Salverson, Julie. "The Unimaginable Occurrence: Storytelling, Popular Theatre, and an Ethic of Risk." MA thesis, Ontario Institute for Studies in Education, University of Toronto, 1996.

Salverson, Julie. "Witnessing Subjects: A Fool's Help." In *A Boal Companion: Dialogues on Theatre and Cultural Politics*, edited by Jan Cohen-Cruz and Mady Schutzman, 146–57. New York and London: Routledge, 2006.

Sanders, E.R. "The Hamitic Hypothesis; Its Origin and Functions in Time Persepctive." *Journal of African History* 14 (1969): 521–32.

Sayer, Derek. "Everyday Forms of State Formation: Some Dissident Remarks on 'Hegemony.'" In *Everyday Forms of State Formation: Revolution and Negotiation of Rule in Modern Mexico*, edited by Gilbert M. Joseph and Daniel Nugent. Durham, NC: Duke University Press, 1994.

Scarry, E. *The Body in Pain: The Making and Unmaking of the World*. Oxford: Oxford University Press, 1987.

Scott, Rebecca. *Degrees of Freedom: Louisiana and Cuba after Slavery*. Cambridge, MA: Belknap Press of Harvard University Press, 2005.

Sennett, Richard. *The Fall of Public Man*. New York: Knopf, 1977.

Shahar, Charles, et Elisabeth Perez. *Analyse du recensement de 2001*. Montréal: Fédération CJA (octobre 2005): 22.

Shay, J. *Achilles in Vietnam: Combat Trauma and the Undoing of Character*. New York: Simon and Schuster, 1995.

Shay, J. *Odysseus in America: Combat Trauma and the Trials of Homecoming*. New York: Scribner, 2003.

Sheftel, Anna, and Stacey Zembrzycki. "Only Human: A Reflection on the Ethical and Methodological Challenges of Working with 'Difficult' Stories." *Oral History Review* 37 no. 2 (2010): 191–214.

Shirinian, Lorne. *History of Armenia and Other Fiction*. Kingston, ON: Blue Heron Press, 1999.

Shirinian, Lorne. *Rough Landing*. Kingston, ON: Blue Heron Press, 2000.

Simon, Roger. "Between Hope and Despair. The Pedagogical Encounter of Historical Remembrance." Introduction to *Between Hope and Despair: Pedagogy and the Remembrance of Historical Trauma*, edited by Roger Simon, Sharon Rosenberg, and Claudia Eppert. New York: Rowman and Littlefield, 2000.

Siniavskii, Andrei. *Soviet Civilization: A Cultural History*. Translated by Joanne Turnbull. New York: Arcade, 1990.

Smaill, Belinda. *The Documentary Politics, Emotion, Culture*. New York: Palgrave Macmillan, 2010.

Smith, P. *Le récit populaire au Rwanda*. Paris: Les Classiques Africains, 1975.

Soep, Elisabeth. "Beyond Literacy and Voice in Youth Media Production." *McGill Journal of Education* 41, no. 3 (2006): 197–214.

Solnit, Rebecca. *A Paradise Built in Hell: The Extraordinary Communities that Arise in Disaster*. New York: Viking, 2009.

Sonnenberg, S., A.M. Blank, and J.A. Talbot, eds. *The Trauma of War: Stress and Recovery in Vietnam Veterans*. Washington, DC: American Psychiatric Press, 1985.

Sourisce, Nicolas. "La Communauté juive montréalaise: enracinement original. La presse des communautés culturelles: Un nouvel outil de recherche." Mémoire de MA, Géographie, Université d'Angers, 1996.

Spolin, Viola. *Improvisation for the Theatre: A Handbook of Teaching and Directing Techniques*. Evanston, IL: Northwestern University Press, 1963.

Stephens, Kevin, et al. "Excess Mortality in the Aftermath of Hurricane Katrina." *Disaster Medicine and Public Health Preparedness* 1 (2007): 15–20.

Stillman, Norman. *The Jews of Arab Lands in Modern Times*. Philadelphia: Jewish Publication Society, 1991.

Sublette, Ned. *The World That Made New Orleans: From Spanish Silver to Congo Square*. Chicago: Lawrence Hill, 2008.

Taieb-Carlen, Sarah. "The North African Jews in Toronto Today: Assimilation or Survival." In *From Iberia to Diaspora: Studies in Sephardic Culture and History*, edited by Yedida K. Stillman and Norman A. Stillman, 151–67. Leiden: Brill, 1999.

Tan, Shaun. *The Arrival*. New York: Scholastic, 2007.

Taylor, Diana. *The Archive and the Repertoire: Performing Cultural Memory in the Americas*. London, Durham, NC: Duke University Press, 2003.

Thompson, James. *Performance Affects: Applied Theatre and the End of Effect*. New York: Palgrave MacMillan, 2009.

Thomson, Alistair. "Four Paradigm Transformations in Oral History." *Oral History Review* 34, no.1 (2007): 49–70.

Tomlinson, Carol Ann. *The Differentiated Classroom: Responding to the Needs of all Learners*. New York: Prentice Hall, 1999.

Tomlinson, Sherrie. "No New Orleanians Left Behind." *Connecticut Law Review* 38 (2005–6): 1153–88.

Tortti, María Cristina. *El "viejo" partido socialista y los orígenes de las "nueva" izquierda (1955–1965)*. Buenos Aires: Prometeo, 2009.

Totten, S. "The Plight and Fate of Female during and following the 1994 Rwandan Genocide." In *Plight and Fate of Women During and Following Genocide*, edited by S. Totten. New Brunswick, NJ: Transaction, 2009.

Trigano, Shmuel. *La fin du judaïsme en terres d'Islam*. Paris: Denoël, 2009.

Tuhiwai Smith, Linda. *Decolonizing Methodologies. Research and Indigenous Peoples*. London and New York: Zed Books, 1999.

Turnbull, David. "Reframing Science and Other Local Knowledge Traditions." *Futures* 29, no. 6 (1997): 551–62.

UNIFEM. "A Life Free of Violence Is Our Right!" *The UN Trust Fund to End Violence against Women: 10 Years of Investment*. United Nations Development Fund for Women, 2007.

van Alphen, Ernst. "Symptoms of Discursivity: Experience, Memory and Trauma." In *Acts of Memory: Cultural Recall in the Present*, edited by Mieke Bal, Jonathan Crewe, and Leo Spitzer. Hanover: University Press of New England, 1999.

van Cleave, Rachel. "Property Lessons in August Wilson's *The Piano Lesson* and the Wake of Hurricane Katrina." *California Western Law Review* 43 (2006–7): 97–129.

van der Kolk, B.A., A.C. McFarlane, and L. Weisaeth, eds. *Traumatic Stress: The Effects of Overwhelming Experience on Mind, Body and Society.* New York: Guilford Press, 1996.

Vidal-Naquet, Pierre. *Les assassins de la mémoire.* Paris: La Découverte, 1981.

Vilas, Carlos. "Neoliberal Meltdown and Social Protest: Argentina 2001–2002." *Critical Sociology* 32, no. 1 (2006): 163–86.

Vitaliev, Dmitri. "Digital Security and Privacy for Human Rights Defenders." *Frontline International Foundation for the Protection of Human Rights Defenders.* http://www.frontlinedefenders.org/esecman.

Wacquant, Loïc. "Urban Desolation and Symbolic Denigration in the Hyperghetto." *Social Psychology Quarterly* 73, no. 3 (2009–10): 1–5.

Wang, C. "Photovoice: A Participatory Action Research Strategy Applied to Women's Health." *Journal of Women's Health*, 8, no. 2 (1999): 185–92.

Wang, C., and M.A. Burns. "Photovoice: Concept, Methodology and Use for Participatory Needs Assessment." *Health and Behavior* 24, no. 3 (1977): 369–87.

Waugh, Thomas, Brendan Baker, and Ezra Winton, eds. *Challenge for Change – Activist Documentary at the National Film Board of Canada.* Montreal: McGill-Queen's University Press, 2010.

Weissman, Gary. *Fantasies of Witnessing: Postwar Efforts to Experience the Holocaust.* Ithaca, NY: Cornell University Press, 2004.

Welsh, Christine. *Keepers of the Fire.* National Film Board of Canada, 1994.

Wesch, Michael. "Anti-Teaching: Confronting the Crisis of Significance," *Education Canada* 48, no. 2 (2008): 4–7.

White, Shirley. *Participatory Video: Images that Transform and Empower.* New Delhi; Thousand Oaks, CA: Sage, 2003.

Wiesenthal, Simon. *Justice n'est pas vengeance.* Paris: Édition Robert Laffont, 1989.

Willett, John. *Brecht on Theatre: The Development of an Aesthetic.* New York: Hill and Wang, 1964.

Winton, Ezra. "Beyond the Textbook." *Point-of-View Magazine* 77 (Spring 2010): 14–17.

Zimbardo, P. *The Lucifer Effect: Understanding How Good People Turn Evil.* New York: Random House, 2008.

Contributors

Jessica Anderson is the co-founder of Collaborative Transitions Africa. She is currently a PhD student in political science at the George Washington University and a consultant in peacebuilding and humanitarian aid.

Hourig Attarian is a SSHRC Postdoctoral Fellow at the Centre for Oral History and Digital Storytelling. Her work focuses on storying memory and identity through visual and narrative explorations.

Rachel Bergenfield is the co-founder of Collaborative Transitions Africa. She is currently a master's candidate at the Jackson Institute for Global Affairs at Yale University.

Sandeep Bhagwati is a composer and theatre maker. As Canada Research Chair for Inter-X Arts, he directs the matralab, a centre for Research-Creation at Concordia University Montreal.

Robin Jarvis Brownlie teaches history at the University of Manitoba and recently co-edited (with Valerie Korinek) *Finding a Way to the Heart: Feminist Writings on Aboriginal and Women's History in Canada* (Winnipeg: University of Manitoba Press, 2012).

Yolande Cohen is full professor of modern European history at the Université du Québec à Montréal (UQAM). President of the Academy of Arts and Humanities of the Royal Society of Canada, she is also Chevalier de l'Ordre de la Légion d'honneur of France.

Roewan Crowe is an artist and associate professor at the University of Winnipeg, where she is also co-director of the Institute for Women's and Gender Studies.

Lindsay DuBois is a social anthropologist and associate professor at Dalhousie University. DuBois conducts ethnographic research on the relationship between culture, class, politics, and historical memory. Over the last two decades she has examined these questions in a variety of sites in urban Argentina.

Thi Ry Duong has a bachelor degree in social work and has worked as a community affiliate for the Canadian Cancer Society, an animator for the Montreal Alzheimer Society, and has volunteered as a coordinator of the Cambodian Working group for the Montreal Life Stories Project.

Noelia Gravotta was a high school student at St George's High School when she co-authored her chapter, a CEGEP (or junior college) student by the time it went through peer review, and a university student at Concordia University when it appeared in print. She is currently pondering the best avenues to address social and environmental justice by exploring history, politics, sociology, and even liberal arts.

Henry Greenspan is a psychologist and playwright at the University of Michigan, where he is also chair of the Program in Social Theory and Practice.

Jaswant Guzder (cover art) is an artist, book illustrator, associate professor of psychiatry at McGill University, and head of child psychiatry and director of Childhood Disorders Day Hospital at Montreal's Jewish General Hospital. Dr Guzder's art is intimately connected to her work with refugee and immigrant families – many of whom have experienced premigratory trauma. Her work has been exhibited in Canada, the United Kingdom, and India.

Emmanuel Habimana est directeur des études de premier cycle au département de psychologie, à l'Université du Québec à Trois-Rivières.

Steven High is co-director of the Centre for Oral History and Digital Storytelling and Principal Investigator of the Montreal Life Stories Project.

Callixte Kabayiza est psychologue et rescapé du génocide contre les Tutsi du Rwanda. Comme président de l'Association des parents et amis des victimes du génocide au Rwanda (Page-Rwanda), il a été coordonnateur du groupe de travail Rwanda dans le Projet Histoires de vie Montréal.

Berthe Kayitesi est doctorante à l'université d'Ottawa dans la faculté des sciences de l'éducation. Ses intérêts de recherche portent sur la résilience académique.

Michael Kilburn teaches politics and international studies at Endicott College in Beverly, MA. He is founding director of the Endicott Center for Oral History (ECOH) and co-chairs the OHA International Committee.

Reisa Levine has been working and playing in the realm of digital media since before the Web existed, and is currently the producer for CitizenShift, the National Film Board of Canada's former social media network.

Warren Linds is an associate professor in the Department of Applied Human Sciences of Concordia University and a member of the Living Histories Ensemble des Histoires Vivantes.

Edward (Ted) Little is a professor of theatre at Concordia University, Associate Artistic Director of Teesri Duniya Theatre, and past editor-in-chief of *alt.theatre: cultural diversity and the stage*. Ted led the Performance Working Group for the Montreal Life Stories Project.

Valerie Love is Research Librarian for Digital Materials at the Alexander Turnbull Library, National Library of New Zealand, Te Puna Matauranga o Aotearoa. Previously she worked as curator for Human Rights Collections at the Thomas J. Dodd Research Center, University of Connecticut.

Michele Luchs is director of English Language Arts programs for Quebec's Ministry of Education and co-coordinator of the Mapping Memories project.

Liz Miller is a documentary maker, community media artist, and professor in the Communication Studies program at Concordia University in Montreal. Her documentary films *Novela, Novela* and *The Water Front* have been exhibited and broadcast around the world and used to influence policy and educational initiatives. Miller has developed participatory media projects with women, youth, senior citizens, and a wide range of human rights organizations.

Athanasie Mukarwego est une rescapée et une veuve du génocide contre les Tutsi du Rwanda. Par différentes interventions, notamment dans un docu-mentaire intitulé *Mères Courage*, elle témoigne des sévices indescriptibles infligés aux filles et femmes tutsi par les bourreaux mais aussi de la nécessité d'aider les survivants à s'en sortir.

Lisa Ndejuru is a skilled practitioner of Playback Theatre and is a founding member of the Montreal-based Living Histories Ensemble. Motivated by her own family's story of trauma and displacement, her current PhD studies at

Concordia University are at the intersection of community engagement, clinical practice, and arts-based research.

D'Ann R. Penner is the former director of the Benjamin L. Hooks Institute for Social Change, where she was the principal investigator of The Saddest Days Oral History Project. Presently, she is scholar-in-residence for the Southern Institute for Education and Research at Tulane University and a law clerk for Judge Michael G. Bagneris at the Civil District Court, Parish of Orleans.

Nisha Sajnani is the director of the Drama Therapy/Psychodrama Program at Lesley University and the president of the North American Drama Therapy Association.

Lorne Shirinian is a writer, filmmaker, and professor emeritus of Comparative Literature at the Royal Military College of Canada in Kingston, Ontario.

Carole Vacher is a psychologist and interviewer for the Montreal Life Stories project within the Rwandan working group.

Rachael Van Fossen is an artist, educator, researcher, and arts consultant in areas of community collaboration and socially engaged performance.

Megan Webster, after teaching high school for twelve years, is now a full-time PhD student at the Faculty of Education at McGill. Her life's work is learning and teaching through social engagement and relationship.

Alan Wong recently completed a doctorate in the Special Individualized Program at Concordia University and teaches English literature and composition at Vanier College in Montreal.

Index

Aboriginal populations, displacement of, 87. *See also* Indigenous people

Aboriginal women. *See* Indigenous women

Aboriginal youth, 187; oral history project with, 203–17

Abu Ghraib, 143

Acadians, displacement of, 87

accountability, 229–30

acknowledgment, 72; social, 73

activism, 25; community, 25, 216; human rights, 300; LGBTI, 302; among pensioners in Argentina, 236–46; political, 204, 207, 238; as value for archivism, 309

Adorno, Theodor, 86

advocacy, 180, 191, 195–8, 307; against criminalization of homosexuality, 301, 303; digital media as tool for, 143; documentary as tool for, 173–4; testimony as, 11

Afghanistan, war in, 14, 64, 74

African Americans: deportation of, 228; displacement of, 225–9; human rights for, 219; intentional attempts to kill, 226; love of for New Orleans, 225; sacrifice of lives to protect white private property, 225; treatment of in post-Katrina New Orleans, 219–30

African Rights, 24

African Youth Initiative Network, 182n7

age, as factor among emigrant Moroccan Jews, 257, 266

Ahmad, Amena, 116, 124n3

Alcorn, Rev. Mildred, 219–20

Algeria: decolonization of, 254; emigration from, 250, 252, 253; Sephardic Jews from, 270n11

Allaire, Joliane, 91

alternative media, 230

alternative print, film, and analogue media practices, 134

Amery, Jean, 35, 43

Ammon, Richard, 313n32

amnesia, 256

anarchism, 240, 242

Anctil, Pierre, 270n15, 271n25

Anderson, Jessica, 20

Anderson, Kenneth, 223

Anishinabe beliefs and traditions, 205, 207